REVERBERATIONS

21 CLASSIC 1950s ROCK 'N' ROLL SONGS THAT STILL REVERBERATE

Ted Clark

Genius
Music Books

Milwaukee Wisconsin USA

For David Theodore Clark

May 12, 1964

June 27, 2024

Published by:
Genius Music Books, an Imprint of Genius Book Publishing
PO Box 250380
Milwaukee Wisconsin 53225 USA
GeniusMusicBooks.com

ISBN: 978-1-958727-50-8

241031 Letter

Contents

INTRODUCTION

I was fortunate to have been a participant in the emergence of Rock 'n' Roll in the mid-1950s. While I had all the 45s of the songs I have selected for this book, it wasn't until the 1960s that I began to realize what a tremendous impact these songs had on subsequent artists. It was The Beatles that really brought this fact home to me. Then, in the early 1970s, when I became a voracious record collector, I noticed how many other artists released 45s of these same songs.

At first, I kept 3"x 5" note cards for individual Rock 'n' Roll songs for which multiple 45 cover versions were issued. To the immediate left is a picture of the box in which I kept the index cards and the first of three cards for "Ain't That A Shame."

Then, when the home computer was introduced by IBM in 1981, I was among the first to purchase one. Although ostensibly for business purposes, it was, in truth, primarily to catalogue my burgeoning record collection and to render moot the 3" x 5" note cards.

CRITERIA FOR SELECTION

In selecting the featured artist for each of the songs highlighted in this book, I used the artist for whom the song is primarily associated. As a result, in several instances, I did not use the original artist. To perhaps the surprise of many, Bill Haley was not the original artist to record "Rock Around The Clock." Nor was Jerry Lee Lewis the first to record "Whole Lotta Shakin' Goin' On." Likewise, Big Mama Thornton—not Elvis—released the first version of "Hound Dog."

The following are the criteria I used to select the 21 1950s Rock 'n' Roll songs for inclusion in this book:

■ First, and foremost, it had to be a 1950s Rock 'n' Roll song that has been covered numerous times, and some of those releases had to be by artists that most music enthusiasts would recognize.

■ Second, the covers had to have been issued as 45s. If they were included on albums and CDs, it would have made the task virtually impossible. In a few instances, however, references have been made to particularly notable album/CD cover versions.

■ Third, I have primarily focused on U.S. and UK cover releases, the latter because the UK release of virtually all the 21 songs influenced the 1960's British Invasion and in many instances were covered by bands such as The Beatles and The Rolling Stones.

A quandary early on was how many releases should be listed for any one artist. I ultimately decided to limit the number of songs by any given artist to two. This meant that I had to choose among many titles for artists such as Elvis Presley, Chuck Berry, and Buddy Holly/The Crickets. Take Chuck Berry as an example. While I ended up choosing "Roll Over Beethoven" and "Johnny B. Goode," that meant that other Berry hits such as "Maybellene," "Rock and Roll Music," and "Memphis," among others, were not selected. Obviously, my selection process was subjective, although I did consider any number of objective facts, such as records sold, later covers by other artists, award recognition, use of the song in movies, etc. I fully recognize that other music fans may have made different selections.

In the same vein, I am sure any number of aficionados of 1950s Rock 'n' Roll will disagree with some of the songs that were not selected. Among the songs of which I collected covers and seriously considered but which did not make final cut are "Bony Moronie" by Larry Williams, "Bye Bye Love" by The Everly Brothers, "Get A Job" by the Silhouettes, "I Hear You Knocking" by Smiley Lewis, "I Got A Woman" by Ray Charles, "Lawdy Miss Clawdy" by Lloyd Price, "Let The Good Times Roll" by Shirley & Lee, "Little Bitty Pretty One" by Thurston Harris, "Love Is Strange" by Mickey and Sylvia, "Money Honey" by Clyde McPhatter and The Drifters, "Rockin' Robin" by Bobby Day, "Sea Cruise" by Frankie Ford, "Silhouettes" by The Rays, "Susie Q" by Dale Hawkins, and perhaps a dozen more. Admittedly, narrowing down the list to 21 songs was exceedingly difficult.

It is fair to say that each of the 21 songs selected for this book have achieved what very few songs have; that is, they are songs that defy age and continue to reverberate today.

SOURCES FOR FINDING 45 RPM COVER RECORDS

Early on, my sources for obtaining 45 rpm covers of these songs were many, ranging from record stores, of which there were numerous in the 1970s, flea markets, antique malls and stores, resale stores, thrift shops, yard sales, Salvation Army and Goodwill stores, rummage sales, and contributions from friends.

In the 1970s there were at least one or more record stores in every city of decent size, and even some in pretty small cities. Since I lived in the Chicago metropolitan area, I had many stores to visit from time to time. And, when business travel took me to other cities across the country, one of the first things I did was check out the classified section of the phone book to find record stores that carried used 45s. Now I use Google to locate record stores that still carry vinyl records, especially 45s.

Record conventions were also a major source for finding new records. Chicago had at least one each month, and I also went to record conventions in many other localities, including Milwaukee, Wisconsin; Orange County, California; and Allentown, Pennsylvania, the latter of which is an annual event in the spring. Early on I learned about the Austin [Texas] Record Convention, which is usually held in the spring and fall each year. I attended most of the Austin shows.

Another major source for finding covers was *Goldmine* magazine, as well as the record lists that I received from dozens of sellers around the United States and beyond. Then, in approximately 1996, I became aware of *eBay*, and that changed everything. While I still rely on all the foregoing sources to add to my record collection, my best source for adding new cover versions is *eBay*. The *Discogs* website has also been a good source. Instead of perusing multi-page lists looking for cover records, with the advent of *eBay* and *Discogs* all I have to do is type in the name of the song, and voila, up pops the 45s that are currently available for purchase or bid. I have added literally hundreds of 45 covers through *eBay* and *Discogs*.

FORMAT FOR EACH SONG SELECTED

A. Background Information on the Song, including the following:
- o   Record label information
- o   Writer or writers
- o   Date recorded
- o   Date of release
- o   The B-side
- o   The producer(s), if known
- o   *Billboard* chart information

B. Each Song's Story and its Subsequent Impact

This essential section discusses the circumstances surrounding the recording of each of the 21 songs, the *Billboard* and/or *Cash Box* reviews, and the chart activity for each. Also discussed are the contemporaneous and subsequent covers of the song, including whether any of the subsequent covers made the charts in either the U.S. and/or the UK. For many of the songs, a particular emphasis was to analyze the impact that a given song had on subsequent artists, such as The Beatles and The Rolling Stones, as well as an overall assessment of the impact of the song.

C. Contemporaneous Major Label Cover Versions

In the pre-rock and roll era, it was common practice for the major labels to issue contemporaneous versions of songs that showed any signs of becoming a hit. For songs like "Tennessee Waltz," for example, numerous cover versions were issued by different artists, with each trying to capture a share of the market. It was originally recorded by Cowboy Copas in 1947 and released in March 1948 on King 696-A, but it had been released earlier by Pee Wee King on RCA 20-2650 (78 rpm) on January 25, 1948, and subsequently issued as a 45 on RCA 48-0003 in 1949. A version by Roy Acuff and the Smokey Mountain Boys was released the following month on Columbia 20551 (78 rpm). It moved over to pop when Patti Page's version was issued in November 1949 on Mercury 5534-X45, followed in short order by versions by Les Paul and Mary Ford on Capitol F1316, Jo Stafford on Columbia 4-39065, the Fontaine Sisters on RCA 47-3979, and others. Altogether, *Billboard* in its 12/30/50 issue listed 18 different available versions of "Tennessee Waltz"!!! Even Petula Clark—yes, that Petula Clark—in January 1951, issued her 78 rpm version on Polygon P-1004 (England).

While many record collectors believe this was primarily an effort by white artists to cover versions of songs issued by black artists, the best example perhaps being Pat Boone's covers of Little Richard's "Tutti Frutti" and "Long Tall Sally," that was just one facet of the practice. Frequently, the record label that issued the original version of the record owned the publishing rights to the record and as the owner of the publishing rights, it made sense—and money—if other artists recorded the song.

Parenthetically, and surprisingly, cover records are a topic of academic study. Evidence of this is a collection of 25 articles written by a wide range of authors, almost all of whom have advanced academic degrees, compiled in *Play It Again Sam: Cover Songs in Popular Music* (edited by George Plasketes, Ashgate Publishing, 2010).

D. Contemporaneous Budget Label Cover Versions

There were numerous budget labels in the 1950s, such as Bell, Gilmar, Prom, and Tops, offering four to six songs per 45 EP (extended play) of the top hits of the day at cheap prices, typically from 39 cents to 59 cents. Most of the other songs listed for budget label EPs are by different artists/groups.

E. Subsequent Versions by the Artist Associated with the Song

For virtually any record that made the charts, and especially those that made the higher reaches of the charts, it was common practice to reissue the song as a "greatest hit," either on the same label and/or on reissue labels like Collectables, Oldies 45, Original Sound, Ripete, etc. In most instances the later releases were of the original version, but not always. Some artists like Bill Haley, Chuck Berry, and Little Richard signed with different labels than the labels on which the original versions of their hit songs were released. For example, Chuck Berry originally recorded for Chess, but he later signed with Mercury and re-recorded many of his Chess hits on Mercury. These are the same songs by the same artist, but they are re-recordings. *Caveat emptor* for collectors looking for the true original.

F. Subsequent Cover Versions

The definition used for subsequent cover versions is records that were released after the original version had its chart run. In some instances the subsequent cover version was issued within the same year as the original. The best example is Elvis Presley's version of "Blue Suede Shoes" that was released shortly after Carl Perkins' original version left the charts. This was intentional on Elvis's part as he did not want to steal the thunder from his close friend and fellow Sun artist.[1] Most of the subsequent covers, however, were issued at least one year to many, many years later.

---

1 The actual decision was made by the head of RCA's A&R, Steve Sholes, who presumably knew Presley's wishes.

G. In the Movies

Another consideration in judging the impact of a record is the frequency with which it has been used on movie soundtracks over the years. Prior to the advent of Rock 'n' Roll in the mid-50s, the use of popular records on movie soundtracks was not a common practice. Yes, movies had soundtracks, but the soundtracks were mostly instrumental in nature. The one major exception was musicals, such as *Singing in the Rain* or *Porgy and Bess*.

H. Documented Concert Performances

One of the ways in which songs retain continuing popularity is through their performance at concerts. As writer Paul Williams has noted, "… great songs are made to be sung again and again by succeeding generations of singers even though the 'perfect' recording of said song may already have been accomplished. Songs live in performance." *Setlist.fm* is an internet site that seeks to track the set lists for an amazing variety of artists and bands. Using this database, it is possible to get a handle on how frequently a given song has been played in concert. But this site is only as good as the information it can obtain about the set lists of artists, and it is constantly being updated. Generally, it is more complete for major artists and bands.

I. Honors and Accolades

Where known, the various honors and accolades presented to the selected song are listed under this heading. The following are the major organizations that have bestowed prestigious honors and accolades on individual songs:

- **The Grammy Hall of Fame**
  As described on its website (https://www.grammy.com/grammys/awards/hall-of-fame):
  > "The GRAMMY HALL OF FAME was established by the Recording Academy's National Trustees in 1973 to honor recordings of lasting qualitative or historical significance that are at least 25 years old. Inductees are selected annually by a special member committee of eminent and knowledgeable professionals from all branches of the recording arts."

- **The National Recording Registry of the Library of Congress**
  The NATIONAL RECORDING REGISTRY is a list of sound recordings that "are culturally, historically, or aesthetically important, and/or inform or reflect life in the United States." Selection for inclusion on the list is done annually by the National Recording Preservation Board, whose members are appointed by the Librarian of Congress. As of 2024, a total of 650 recordings have been selected for preservation in the Registry.

- **The National Endowment for the Arts (NEA) and the Record Industry Association of America (RIAA)**

  In 2001 the NEA/RIAA asked knowledgeable people to vote on the top 365 songs of the 20th century "from a master list of over 1,100 recordings of historical significance." The NEA/RIAA's press release noted that "[m]ore than 40 reference volumes, several popular music experts and award-winning lists from the RIAA, National Academy of Recording Arts and Sciences (NARAS), Broadcast Music, Inc. (BMI), the American Society of Composers, Authors and Publishers (ASCAP), National Association of Recording Merchandisers (NARM) and other organizations were used in the process."

  Among the other lists that were reviewed for honor/accolade information are the following:
  - The Rock & Roll Hall of Fame's list of the "500 Songs That Shaped Rock and Roll," an unranked list that includes songs from all eras
  - Joel Whitburn's "Honor Roll of Hits," a ranked list of 150 records based on the most accumulated awards using his "point system for each award"
  - *Rolling Stone's* 2004 list of "The 500 Greatest Songs of All Time"
  - National Public Radio's *NPR 100*, an unranked list of 100 records compiled by NPR's editors of the "most important musical works of the 20th century"
  - VH1's 2004 list of the "100 Greatest Rock Songs"

J. Also Worth Noting

Under this heading is a potpourri of facts and trivia about the song that might be of interest to readers.

INFORMATION SOURCES

A significant amount of the information for the records listed in each cover category comes from the records in my collection, including the title of the B-side and, where provided, the date of release, the geographical location of the label, etc. Other major sources include:

INTERNET SITES

- **45cat** (*45Cat.com*)—This website is "an online archive dedicated to the magic of the vinyl 7 seven-inch single (7" or 45)." It can be searched by artist, label, or song title. If known, for each 45, the composer(s) and producer(s) for each side are listed, along with the date of issue (if known), and the country of origin if it is other than the United States. For most of the records listed in *45cat* there is usually a picture of both sides of the label, which helped provide information for records that were not in my collection. Another useful feature is that users can leave comments about a given release. On occasion, these comments yielded useful information of which I had not been aware.

- **All Music** (*Allmusic.com*)—According to its website, "*AllMusic* provides comprehensive music info including reviews and biographies," as well as "recommendations for new music to listen to, stream or own." This website is useful in tracking down information on artists and writers. This was, for example, the website where I found the most useful information about Joe Lubin, the songwriter who further cleaned up the risqué lyrics for "Tutti Frutti" before Pat Boone recorded his cover version.

- **BMI** (*BMI.com*)—As its website notes, BMI "is the largest music rights organization in the U.S.," which "serves as an advocate for the value of music, representing over 17 million musical works created and owned by more than 1.1 million songwriters, composers and music publishers." Its website is where you can usually find out the current owners (i.e., usually, but not always, the composers) of any BMI listed music work.

- **Catalog of Copyright Entries** (*onlinebooks.library.upenn.edu/cce/*)—This multi-volume catalog published by the Library of Congress and accessible online provides a wealth of information on the dates that musical works were copyrighted, along with the writers and publishers. Although tedious to use, it is searchable by year and, with some perseverance, you can generally find what you are looking for.

- **Complete Recorded Music** (*Completerecordedmusic.com*)—This site offers subscription services for various genres of music and certain record labels, e.g., garage, hot rod, Meteor label, etc. But complete it is not. Nevertheless, it did alert me to some records, especially garage, of which I was not previously aware. At a monthly subscription charge of $9.95, it is not cheap.

- **Discogs** (*Discogs.com*)—Its self-described "mission [is] to build the biggest and most comprehensive international music database and marketplace." The large database can be searched in numerous ways, including by artist, label, or song title. If known, the following information is provided for each release: label, catalog number, date of release, song titles, composers, and country of origin, as well as the various known label variations. For most, there is a picture of the label.

- **Global Dog Productions** (*Globaldogproductions.com*)—This site provides extensive discographies for the releases on a multitude of record labels. As noted on its website, "While the bulk of the discographies on Global Dog are from the United States there are enough from Australia, Canada and the United Kingdom that we have added index pages for just those countries besides including them in the main indexes of all labels." The information provided includes the identification of the artist if there is one artist on one side and a different artist on the other side. Information is also provided as to whether the release was just on 78, both 45 and 78, or just 45, as well as the year of release.

- **IMDbPro** (*IMDbpro.com*)—*IMDbPro* is literally the "bible" for anything movie related. In addition to providing information about the cast, producers, and directors of each movie, it also lists whether the film was nominated for or received any awards (majors like Oscars or minors like film festival recognition). And, if you scroll down to details and then further down, you can see a list of all the songs heard for any given movie, and in most instances, but not all, the artist who performed the song. This was my primary source for the list of movies in which each of the 21 selected songs can be heard. Hint: If you are trying to see if a song has appeared in any movies, the best way to begin your search is to enter in the name of the song's composer.

- **MusicBrainz** (*Musicbrainz.com*)—This is a self-described "community-maintained open source encyclopedia of music information." This website is primarily focused on providing information about LPs and CDs. It would be an excellent source for information about the LPs and CDs that include the songs selected for this book, something that is beyond this book's scope. If you are looking for information on 45s, I recommend sites like *45cat.com* or *discogs.com*.

- **Music VF** (*musicvf.com*)—This website provides info on charted songs in both the U.S. and the UK, which is quite handy in comparing the chart positions of any given song in both the U.S. and UK, as well as the dates on which the song charted.

- **Official Charts Company** (*Officialcharts.com*)—As described in Wikipedia, the Official Charts Company "is a British inter-professional organisation that compiles various 'official' record charts in the United Kingdom, including the UK Singles Chart, the UK Albums Chart, the UK Singles Downloads Chart and the UK Album Downloads Chart, as well as genre-specific and music video charts…. Before the production of the 'official' charts, various less comprehensive charts were produced, most notably by the newspaper/magazine *New Musical Express* (*NME*) which began its chart in 1952; some of these older charts (including *NME*'s earliest singles charts) are now part of the official OCC canon."

- **Rockin' Country Style** (*RCS-discography.com*)—Compiled by Terry Gordon and described as "a discography of Country Rock & Roll and Related Records, 1951-64." Within the limits of its scope of coverage, a vast amount of information about releases is provided, which can be searched by artist, label, or song title. Included are, where known, the date of release, matrix numbers, label location, the date(s) of reviews in *Billboard* and/or *Cash Box*, and albums and/or CDs where the song has been comped. Label shots are provided where available and, in many instances, links to hear excerpts of the songs. All in all, this is a valuable research vehicle.

- **SecondHandSongs** (*Secondhandsongs.com*)—This website is devoted, in its own words, to "building the most comprehensive source of cover song information." While it lists numerous 45 rpm covers for each of the records selected for this book, it also includes covers issued on LPs and CDs, as well as documented "live" performances. As far as I know, it is not possible to narrow the search to just covers issued as 45s. And its information on 45 covers is not very comprehensive. While almost all the major-label cover records for a given song are included, many others such as garage covers on small labels are missing. In addition, the slew of budget-label covers is totally missing. That said, if you want to know which is the original version of a popular song, this is a good place to start.

- **Setlist** (*Setlist.fm*)—This website collects an amazingly detailed amount of information on the songs sung by artists at concerts around the world. While the information is astonishingly complete for the last five years or so, data on set lists going back decades is included to the extent known. And, it is constantly being updated with current set lists, as well as newly discovered lists from the past.

- **Song Facts** (*Songfacts.com*)—This website allows you to search by song title, artist, year, or genre, among other filters. For each song in the database, the write-up is relatively informative, but not exhaustive. It includes most of the basics, as well as interesting facts about each song.

- **Wikipedia**—Each of the 21 songs selected for this book has a dedicated page on Wikipedia. Some are chock full of useful information; others not so much. *Wikipedia* is an open source encyclopedia and, as such, its quality and accuracy can vary from entry to entry. It is, nevertheless, a helpful starting place for many inquiries.

- **Wirz's American Music** (*Wirz.de/music/america.htm*)—This website is the brainchild of Stefan Wirz, a German collector and American music enthusiast. His non-commercial and admittedly subjective discographies are, in his words, "… a wild mixture of black and white, acoustic and electric, rural and urban, silent and loud, female and male, guitar and piano oriented, conservative and progressive music, partially European, mostly of U.S. -American origin."

- **World Radio History** (previously known as **American Radio History**) (*Worldradiohistory. com*)—This website has the full-text weekly issues of *Billboard Magazine* from the 1950s through 2016. *Billboard* is a rich source for music charts, reviews of new releases, and record company ads. A new feature is the ability to search all issues from a given year or decade, or overall for information about a given song, artist, label, etc. This makes the task of looking for information about just one song a lot easier than having to peruse each issue from page to page to try to find what you are looking for. In addition, this site also has almost all issues of *Cash Box,* as well as many issues of the British music publications such as *New Music Express* (NME), but the full text issues of British publications are not nearly as comprehensive as they are for *Billboard* and *Cash Box.*

BOOKS AND ARTICLES

- Birnbaum, Larry, *Before Elvis: The Prehistory of Rock 'N' Roll* (Scarecrow Press, 2013). This book is encyclopedic in the breadth and depth of its coverage of the various genres, artists, and songs that led to the rise of Rock 'n' Roll in the 1950s.

- Busnar, Gene, *It's Only Rock 'n' Roll* (Wander Books, 1979). For anyone wishing to learn about the emergence of "Rock 'n' Roll in the 1950s and the artists and songs of that important era, as well as the context in which Rock 'n' Roll emerged as a cultural phenomenon," this short yet comprehensive book is well worth reading. For instance, for each year between 1954 and 1963, the author provides in condensed form the major events in Arts and Politics, In the News, The Arts, Television, Sports, Fads and Fashion, and the Top Rock 'n' Roll Records. This book also includes a lengthy excerpt of a recorded interview with Bobby Robinson, the legendary NYC record producer (e.g., he produced Wilbert Harrison's "Kansas City"), who provides a firsthand insight into Rock 'n' Roll and the music business in the 1950s.

■ Dawson, Jim, and Steve Propes, *What Was The First Rock 'N' Roll Record?* (30th Anniversary Edition, Updated and Revised, Genius Music Books, 2022). The authors do not definitively answer the perennial question, but they do posit 50 different candidates, ranging from 1944's "Blues, Part 2," by Jazz at the Philharmonic to 1956's "Heartbreak Hotel" by Elvis Presley. It is a well-written and researched book.

■ Gillette, Charlie, *Sound of the City: The Rise of Rock and Roll* (Pantheon, revised and expanded edition, 1983). Not unlike Frenchman De Tocqueville who in 1836 told Americans about *Democracy in America,* Englishman Charlie Gillette did the same for American Rock 'n' Roll music. As Jon Landau noted, "History has to start somewhere, and the history of rock 'n' roll began with this fine book."

■ Marcus, Greil, *The History of Rock 'N' Roll in Ten Songs* (Yale Press, 2014). Don't be fooled. This book is about much more than ten songs. For the past 40 years Greil Marcus has been one of the best critics of American music, especially roots music. His writing is both eclectic and evocative. Although only one of this book's 21 songs, "Money (That's What I Want)," made his top ten, he manages to weave in mentions or discussions of another 11 of this book's 21 songs: "Bo Diddley," "Heartbreak Hotel," "Hound Dog," "Johnny B. Goode," "Long Tall Sally," "Not Fade Away," "Shake, Rattle and Roll," "That'll Be The Day," "Tutti Frutti," "What'd I Say," and "Whole Lotta Shakin' Goin' On." In short, it is a *tour de force.*

■ Marsh, Dave, *The Heart of Rock and Soul: The 1001 Greatest Singles Ever Made* (New American Library, 1989). This is an opinionated list along with an essay—some lengthy, some truly short—for each of the 1001 songs. One glaring omission is Bill Haley's "Rock Around The Clock." This may be because Marsh was all of five years old when "Rock Around The Clock" became the first Rock 'n' Roll song to reach #1 on *Billboard's* "Honor Roll of Hits." This strengthens my firm belief that individuals such as Dave Marsh who did not experience the impact of "Rock Around The Clock" firsthand tend to be dismissive of its importance in the development of Rock 'n' Roll as mainstream music.

■ Miller, James, *Flowers in the Dust Bin: The Rise of Rock and Roll, 1947-1977* (Simon & Schuster, 1999). In this well documented book, Miller, a veteran music critic who wrote for such publications as *Rolling Stone* and *Newsweek,* gives his answer to the question he posed: "How did such a distinctively youthful form of music [i.e., Rock 'n' Roll] come to play a defining role in the global culture of the postwar period?" In doing so, he chronicles major events between 1947's "Good Rockin' Tonight" by Wynonie Harris and the death of Elvis in 1977, including his take on the impact of eight of the songs selected for this book: "Kansas City," "Rock Around The Clock," "Ain't It A Shame," "Tutti Frutti," "Why Do Fools Fall In Love," "Blue Suede Shoes," "Hound Dog," and "Heartbreak Hotel."

- Pelletier, Paul, *British London Label Complete Listing—Part Three* (Record Information Services, 1975). This UK publication covers records issued on the British *London* record label between 1949 and 1974. Since the releases are listed month by month, it is possible to pin down the month in which a given record was released in the UK, which in many instances was later—and sometimes much later—than when it was released in the United States.

- Propes, Stephen C., *Those Old School Records* (Genius Music Books, 2023). This book highlights 1,000 songs, primarily R&B, Rock 'n' Roll, and Soul, released as "free standing" singles from 1946 (Arthur Big Boy Crudup, "That's All Right") through 1987 (Los Lobos, "La Bamba"). The author discusses each of the songs, some at length and others more briefly, along with suggested pairings for most songs. This book is an essential resource for anyone interested in learning about the top singles released between 1946 and 1987. All but two of this book's 21 songs are included. Inexplicably, Jerry Lee Lewis's "Great Balls of Fire" is not included. Nor is Buddy Holly and The Crickets' "Not Fade Away," although The Rolling Stones' cover is included.

- *The R&B Indies.* Self-described as "An encyclopedic exploration of African-American Music and independent record labels from 1940 to 1980." Its four large volumes contain discographies for hundreds and hundreds of labels, big and small. The name of the artist, the titles of both sides, the year of release, and the matrix numbers are provided to the extent known.

- Shaw, Arnold, *Honkers and Shouters: The Golden Years of Rhythm & Blues* (Collier Books, 1978). B.B. King's blurb on the back cover accurately sums up this vital book: "*Honkers and Shouters* is the first book that presents Rhythm and Blues in all its variety and gives recognition to its true status as a unique black art form. It's a must for anyone who wants to understand where Rock and Roll came from."

- Whitburn, Joel, *Top Pop Singles, 1955-2018* (Record Research, 2019). For anything chart related in the United States, Whitburn's comprehensive volumes are essential. Also see:
  - Whitburn, Joel, *Top Country Singles, 1944-2017* (Record Research, 2018).
  - Whitburn, Joel, *Top R&B Singles, 1942-2016* (Record Research, 2017).

- Williams, Paul, *Rock and Roll: 100 Best Singles* (Carroll & Graf, 1993). The songs selected start with Robert Johnson's "Terraplane Blues" (1937) and end with Nirvana's "Smells Like Teen Spirit" (1991). Among the 100 songs are four selected for this book: "Tutti Frutti," "Heartbreak Hotel," "Whole Lotta Shakin' Goin' On," and "Johnny B. Goode."

Additional sources that are specific to a given song are listed at the end of each chapter.

NOTE ON COPYRIGHT ISSUES

Quotes and excerpts of *Billboard* and *Cash Box* reviews, articles, and record company ads are used pursuant to the "fair use" and "noncommercial use" doctrines. Unless otherwise specifically noted, all photos of record labels, picture sleeves, sheet music, and other music memorabilia have been taken from my personal record and music memorabilia collection. While some images and text used throughout this book may be protected by individual copyright holders, it is my belief that the use of such copyrighted material is pursuant to the "fair use" and "noncommercial use" doctrines. If any persons or entities believe that their work has been used in any way that constitutes copyright infringement, please contact the author (R. Theodore Clark, Jr., Clark Baird Smith LLP, 6133 N. River Road, Rosemont, IL 60018).

CHAPTER 1

"HOUND DOG"

WILLIE MAE "BIG MAMA" THORNTON (FEBRUARY 1953) AND ELVIS PRESLEY (JULY 1956)

Peacock 5-1612

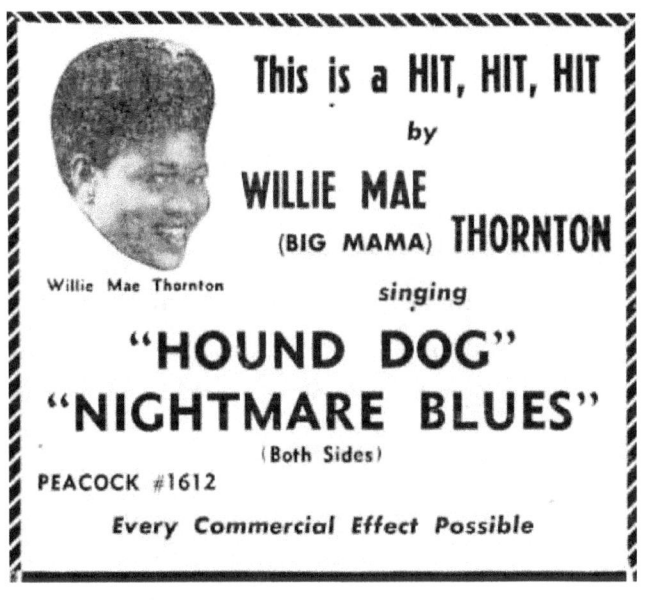

Billboard, March 7, 1953

"HOUND DOG" (WILLIE MAE THORNTON'S VERSION)— THE BASIC FACTS

Label: Peacock 5-1612 (45) and Peacock 1612 (78)

Writers: Jerry Leiber and Mike Stoller

Date recorded: August 13, 1952

Date released: February 1953

Producers: Jerry Leiber and Mike Stoller

B-side: "Night Mare" (the *Billboard* ad above incorrectly listed it as "Nightmare Blues")

Billboard chart:

R&B Chart

- Debut: 3/28/53
- Peak: #1 (7 weeks)
- Duration: 14 weeks

THE SONG BY BIG MAMA THORNTON AND ITS IMPACT

"Hound Dog" was the brainchild of Jerry Leiber and Mike Stoller who penned it while they were still teenagers. West Coast band leader Johnny Otis was looking for a song for Willie Mae "Big Mama" Thornton and invited Leiber and Stoller to hear her sing. Shortly thereafter, according to Stoller, they penned the song in about 15 minutes. When they returned and presented the song to Otis and Thornton, Thornton crooned the song as a ballad. Jerry Leiber, despite being intimidated by Big Mama's massive physical presence and demeanor, told Big Mama, "that ain't the way it goes." To show her what he intended, Jerry sang a few verses. As Mike Stoller later commented:

> Big Mama… heard the rough-and-tough of the song and, just as important, the implicit sexual humor. In short, she got it.

A day later on August 13, 1952, with Otis on drums, Pete Lewis on guitar, and Mario Delagarde on bass, with Leiber and Stoller at the controls, the song was perfected in just two takes. Jerry Leiber labeled it a "masterpiece," noting that "Big Mama didn't croon; she growled."

As originally released on Peacock 5-1612, in addition to Leiber and Stoller, Johnny Otis was also credited as one of the writers. However, the original copyright application filed with the Library of Congress in 1952 listed the composers as:

```
HOUND DOG; w & m Don Deadric Robey &
    Willie Mae Thornton © Lion Pub. Co.
    9Sep52 EU287247
```

Robey later amended the application to list Leiber, Stoller, and Otis, the latter being added based on Otis telling Robey that he along with Leiber and Stoller penned the song. Years later, following litigation, Otis's name was removed as a writer.

Although "Hound Dog" was recorded in mid-August 1952, it was not released until February 1953. *Billboard's* March 14, 1953, review commented: "This is a wild and exciting rhumba blues and the thrush sells it in a sock style, while the work comes thru with an infectious backing that rocks all the way." On the same day *Cash Box* listed "Hound Dog" as the R&B "Sleeper of the Week," observing that "the rhythmic handclapper has just enough of the spiritual feel to stir up the emotions and raise the blood pressure." Debuting on the March 28, 1953, *Billboard* R&B chart, it rose to #1 where it stayed for seven weeks.

There were two releases on Peacock of the song by her in 1953, both with the same catalog number: 5-1612. The B-side of the true first release was "Night Mare." The B-side of the second release issued a few months later was "Rock A Bye Baby,"[2] a song that was recorded at the same session as "Hound Dog."

---

2 The probable reason for the relatively quick release of "Hound Dog" with a different B-side is because Don Robey, the owner of Peacock and a co-author of the B-side, wanted to get a share of the writer's royalties for

Big Mama Thornton's growling vocal on "Hound Dog" had a major impact on Janis Joplin. In Holly George-Warren's 2019 biography *Janis*, she related:

> [Janis] became so enamored of "Hound Dog," she somehow tracked down the original version [by Willie Mae Thornton].

In many respects Joplin's growling/raspy singing style is similar to Willie Mae's. It is probably not a coincidence that one of the songs that initially brought Joplin to fame was her cover of Willie Mae's "Ball and Chain" when she was the lead singer for Big Brother and the Holding Company on the LP *Cheap Thrills* on Columbia KCS 9700 (1968).[3] Parenthetically, Big Mama Thornton's "Ball and Chain" is included on the Rock & Roll Hall of Fame list of the "500 Songs that Shaped Rock and Roll."

In evaluating Big Mama's masterpiece, author and music critic Maureen Mahon concluded:

> Thornton's "Hound Dog" differed from most of the rhythm and blues records of the era in its spare arrangement. There are none of the honking saxophone solos or pounding piano flourishes that marked the R&B sound. Instead, supported by guitar, bass and drums, her resonant vocals dominate the foreground, conveying her haughty relief at being through with a trifling man. Thornton maintains a confident attitude, bringing the blues tradition of outspoken women into the R&B context and helping to set the style for rock and roll by putting sexuality and play with gender expectations in the foreground.

As one *Discogs* commentator observed, "… this song makes a hell of a lot more sense being sung by a woman and the bluesy voice of Big Mama brings in the sexuality that is missing in the Presley version."

---

sales of "Hound Dog." The original B-side was penned by Jerry Leiber and Mike Stoller and pursuant to industry practice writer royalties for the sale of records are divided equally between the writer(s) of the A-side and the B-side, even if it is the A-side that drives sales. By issuing "Hound Dog" with a different B-side, Robey was, in effect, getting writer royalties for the B-side and limiting the royalties to be paid to Leiber/Stoller to just the A-side.

3 Thornton's original recording of "Ball and Chain," which she penned, was recorded on January 28, 1968, and was released shortly thereafter on Arhoolie 45-520. The Big Brother and The Holding Company LP that includes Joplin's cover of "Ball and Chain" was released on August 12, 1968. Joplin's cover of "Ball and Chain" was recorded live at Bill Graham's Fillmore Auditorium.

In an effort to capitalize on the popularity of "Hound Dog," Big Mama recorded another song written by Jerry Leiber and Mike Stoller, "I Smell A Rat," that was released in 1954 on Peacock 5-1632. Although it used essentially the same arrangement and vocal inflection, it did not chart.

Regrettably, but reflective of the realities of the music business in the 1950s, especially among many of the small independent record labels, neither Big Mama Thornton nor Leiber and Stoller profited from "Hound Dog," even though at least 500,000 copies were sold. Thornton is quoted as saying, "I got one check for $500 and never saw another." When Leiber and Stoller confronted Don Robey, the head of the Peacock label, he gave them a check for $1,200 as an advance, but, as Stoller later said, "the check bounced." Leiber and Stoller, however, did very well monetarily when Elvis subsequently covered "Hound Dog."

As documented in greater detail below, Thornton's original version of "Hound Dog" has garnered several prestigious honors, including being inducted into the Grammy Hall of Fame and selected for inclusion on the National Recording Registry of the Library of Congress by the National Recording Preservation Board, which annually selects songs that are "culturally, historically, or aesthetically significant."

"Hound Dog" Answer Records

In addition to the eight contemporaneous covers of "Hound Dog" detailed below, there were slew of answer records, the most notable being "(The Answer to 'Hound Dog') Bear Cat" penned by Sam Phillips and sung by Rufus "Hound Dog" Thomas. Released on Sun 181, *Billboard* listed it as a "new record to watch," observing that it was "[t]he fastest 'answer' record yet to hit the market." It did not take long for "Bear Cat" to hit the *Billboard* R&B chart and shortly thereafter rise to #3. It became Sun's first hit. While Phillips changed the lyrics to be from a male perspective, the melody and arrangement were copied virtually "lock, stock, and barrel" from Thornton's original. When Phillips and Sun failed to get a license for the song despite being requested to do so, Robey and Peacock sued for copyright infringement. Robey and Peacock prevailed, resulting in Sun having to pay two cents for every copy of "Bear Cat" sold, as well as court costs. Peter Guralnick, in his epic *Sam Phillips* biography (2015), reported that Phillips ended up writing a check to Roby's Lion Musical Publishing Company for $1,580.80. Peacock did agree to give Sun a license so that "Bear Cat" could continue to be sold, but with the phrase "The Answer to Hound Dog" removed. This result also largely ended the issuance of "answer records" that closely mimicked the original. As *Billboard* noted, "… since the Hound Dog decision few record firms have attempted to 'answer' smash hits by other companies by using the same tune with different lyrics."

In addition to "Bear Cat," "Hound Dog" also attracted several other "answer" records, including the following:

- "Rattlesnake" by John Brim on Checker 769, which was subsequently withdrawn when Peacock threatened to sue for copyright infringement
- "Mr. Hound Dog Is In Town" by Roy Brown on King 4627
- "(You Ain't Nothing But A Female) Hound Dog" by Charlie Gore and Louis Innis on King 1212
- "You Can Call Me A Hound Dog" by Eugene Jackson and Juanita Moore on Recorded in Hollywood 421
- "New Hound Dog" by Frank Motley on Big Town 116 (1954) (vocal by Curley Bridges); credited to Motley but close lyrically and musically to Big Mama's original; re-released in 1956 on Big Town 408 in an obvious effort to earn some coin based on Presley's version
- "Call Me A Hound Dog" by Jimmie Wilson on Big Town 103

Is Big Mama Thornton's "Hound Dog" An Answer Record?

Many of the articles about "Hound Dog" also list "Real Gone Hound Dog" by Chuck Higgins on Combo 25 as one of the many answer records to Big Mama's "Hound Dog." Thus, George Moonoogian in his excellent article on "Hound Dog" that was published in *Whiskey, Women and…*, Stephen Propes in his 2023 book *Those Old School Records*, and *Wikipedia* in its extensive writeup on "Hound Dog" all list "Real Gone Hound Dog" as one of those answer records, i.e., records that were issued *after* "Hound Dog" was issued in February 1953. However, a strong case can be made that Big Mama's "Hound Dog" was an answer record to Higgins' "Real Gone Hound Dog."

According to both *The Blues Discography—1943-1970* written by Les Fancourt & Bob McGrath and *Blues Records 1943 to 1970, Volume One*, written by Mike Leadbitter & Neil Slaven, "Real Gone Hound Dog" was recorded in Los Angeles on February 5, 1952. The *Global Dog* discography for the Combo label lists six 1952 releases before Higgins' release of the song on Combo 25 and nine 1952 releases thereafter. Assuming a relatively even distribution, that would put the release date for Combo 25 somewhere in the April to June 1952 time frame, i.e., *before* Leiber/Stoller penned and Thornton recorded "Hound Dog" on August 13, 1952, likewise in Los Angeles.[4] Since both Leiber and Stoller had immersed themselves in the lifestyles of the African-American and Chicano communities in L.A. and were well attuned to the R&B scene, it's not too much of a stretch of the imagination to assume that they had heard "Real Gone Hound Dog" and got the idea to pen "Hound Dog" as a female response.

Moreover, the following comparison of the lyrics of both songs would seem to confirm this conclusion:

EXCERPT OF "REAL GONE HOUND DOG" LYRICS AS RECORDED BY CHUCK HIGGINS	EXCERPT OF "HOUND DOG" LYRICS AS RECORDED BY BIG MAMA THORNTON
I know I'm a real cool lovin' hound dog… / All the women love me / I'm a gone hound dog.	Yes, you told me you was high-class / But I could see through that / And daddy, I know / You ain't no real cool cat

Thus, Big Mama's statement that "You ain't no real cool cat" can certainly be seen as a response to Higgins' boast that he was "a real cool lovin' hound dog."

CONTEMPORANEOUS 1953 COVER VERSIONS OF "HOUND DOG"

There were at least eight 1953 contemporaneous cover versions of Big Mama Thornton's "Hound Dog," including three on the Intro label, a subsidiary of Aladdin Records:

ARTIST	LABEL	COMMENTS
Tommy Duncan and The Miller Brothers	Intro 6071	B/w "I Guess You Were Right"; Duncan was a longtime member of Bob Wills' Texas Playboys
Betsy Gay	Intro 6070	B/w "This Is My Last Night In Town"
Charlie Gore and Louis Innes	King 1212	B/w "Mexican Joe"; BB review noted that "No country version yet stacks up to the r.&b. original"

---

4 Both the Fancourt/McGrath and Leadbitter/Slaven discographies list August 13, 1952, as the date for Big Mama Thornton's recording of "Hound Dog."

Eddie Hazelwood	Intro 6069	Country version; b/w "Last Minute Shopping"
Cleve Jackson and His Hound Dogs	Herald 6000	AKA Jack/Jackson Toombs; b/w "Has A Chicken Got A Leg"
Little Esther	Federal 45-12126	R&B version; like Thornton's original, interestingly, she was accompanied by Johnny Otis' band; b/w "Sweet Lips"
Billy Starr	Imperial 8186	Music critic Bill Dahl said that this cover "was a juke joint-honed blend of country and pre-rockabilly raunch"; b/w "Borrowed Heart"
Jack Turner and His Granger County Gang	RCA 47-5267	Country version; b/w "I Couldn't Keep From Sleeping"

Billboard ad, March 28, 1953

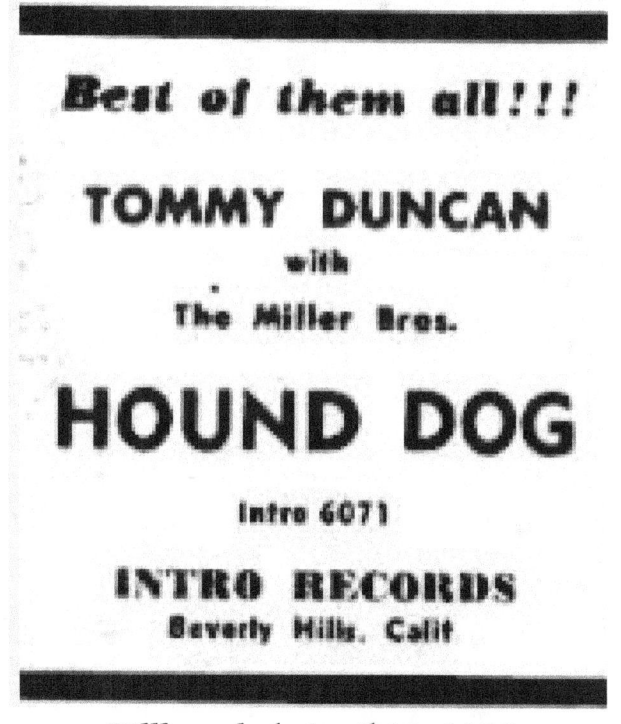

Billboard ad, April 11, 1953

Cleve Jackson on Herald 6000

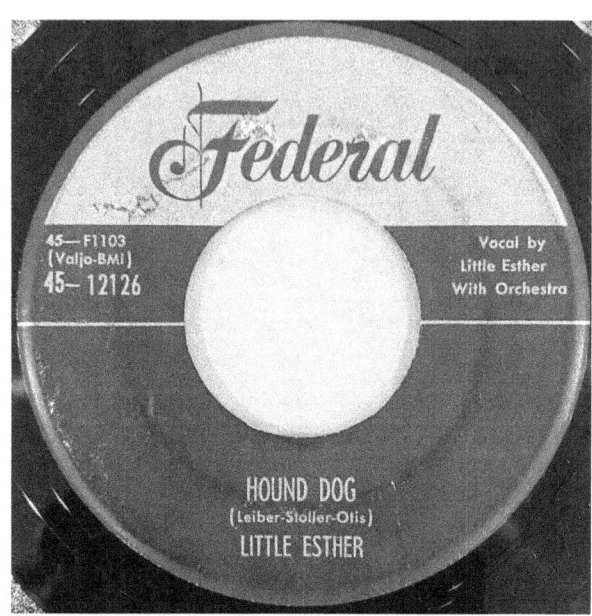

Little Esther on Federal 12126

CONTEMPORANEOUS 1953 BUDGET LABEL COVERS OF "HOUND DOG"

None of the mainstream budget labels (e.g., Tops, Promenade, Big 4 Hits, Gateway, etc.,) issued a cover of Big Mama's R&B hit, but the R&B budget label Tivoli did issue a cover:

ARTIST	LABEL	COMMENTS
Naomi Lewis	Tivoli EP 1041	B/w "I Cross My Heart"/"My Kind Of Woman"/"Mama"/"I Don't Know"

LATER RELEASES OF "HOUND DOG" BY BIG MAMA THORNTON

LABEL	YEAR	COMMENTS
Peacock 5-1612	1956	White label reissue to try to cash in on the success of Presley's version; b/w "Rock A Bye Baby," a reissue of the A-side of Peacock 5-1647 that was released a year earlier
Prestige PSP-1004 (Australia)	1957	B/w "Rock A Bye Baby"
Mercury 72981	1969	A re-recording; b/w "Let's Go Get Stoned"

Peacock 1612	c. late 1960s	B/w "Rock A Bye Baby"; note that the catalog number is just 1612, not 5-1612 that was used for the original, which at the time denoted that it was a 45
Goldies 45 D-1495	1973	Distributed by ABC/Dunhill; b/w "I Smell A Rat"
Angel 1	1980s???	B/w "She Belongs To Me," by Paul and Dale; presumably, a Mercury re-recording since the B-side is a song recorded on Mercury by Paul and Dale
American Pie 9133	Early 1990s	From the original Peacock release; b/w "Sweet Home Chicago" by Little Junior Parker; manufactured by MCA
Collectables COL 90056	c. 2000?	B/w "Sweet Home Chicago" by Little Junior Parker; manufactured by MCA

HONORS AND ACCOLADES — BIG MAMA THORNTON'S VERSION

- Inducted in 2013 into The Grammy Hall of Fame
- Selected in 2015 for inclusion on the National Recording Registry of the Library of Congress by the National Recording Preservation Board, which annually selects songs that are "culturally, historically, or aesthetically significant."
- Chosen by the Rock & Roll Hall of Fame as one of "The 500 Songs That Shaped Rock and Roll"
- Ranked #18 on the 1984 *Rolling Stone* list of "Women Who Rock—The Top 25 Girl-Power Anthems"
- *Cash Box* named "Hound Dog" as the "Best R & B Song of 1953"

ALSO WORTH NOTING . . .

- Peter Stoller, Mike Stoller's son, has said that "if you were to have asked Jerry Leiber or Mike Stoller on any day if they had ever made a perfect record, Thornton's recording of 'Hound Dog' would have been one of the few candidates. On some days, it would have been the only one."
- Doja Cat's song "Vegas," which is on the soundtrack to the 2022 biopic *Elvis,* was composed around samples from Thornton's "Hound Dog."

ELVIS PRESLEY'S COVER VERSION OF "HOUND DOG"

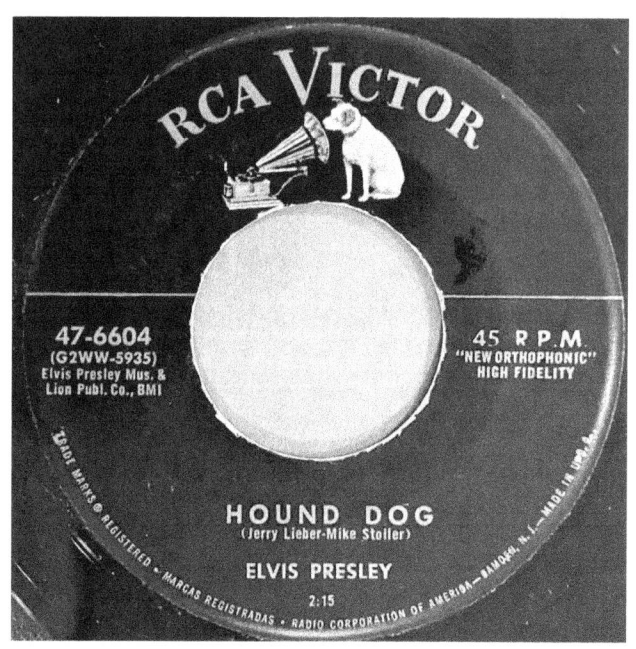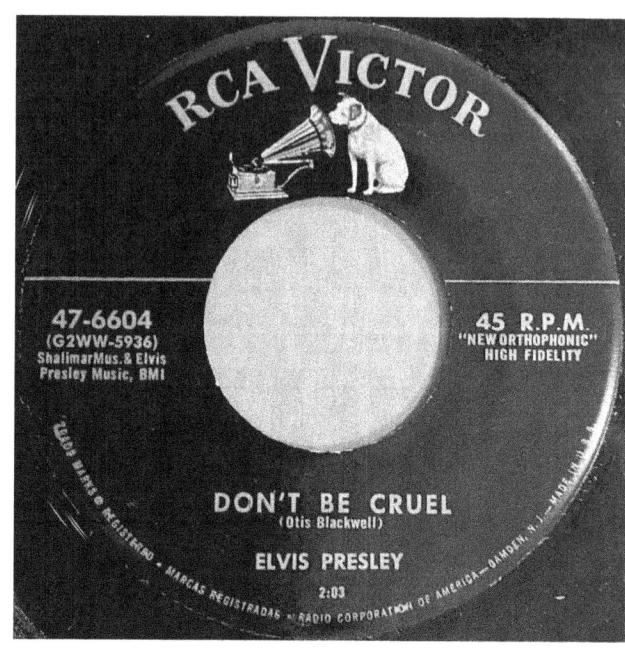

"HOUND DOG" (ELVIS PRESLEY VERSION) — THE BASIC FACTS

Label: RCA 47-6604 (45) and RCA 20-6604 (78)

Writers: Jerry Leiber and Mike Stoller

Date recorded: July 2, 1956

Date released: July 13, 1956

B-side: "Don't Be Cruel" (penned by Otis Blackwell)

Producer: Steve Sholes

Billboard charts:

Pop Chart
- Debut: 8/04/56
- Peak: #1 (10 weeks)
- Duration: 27 weeks

R&B Chart
- Debut: 8/11/56
- Peak: #1 (6 weeks)
- Duration: 14 weeks

Country Chart
- Debut: 8/04/56
- Peak: #1 (10 weeks)
- Duration: 28 weeks

THE SONG BY ELVIS PRESLEY AND ITS IMPACT

Although Elvis was undoubtedly aware of Thornton's original version that had topped the *Billboard's* R&B chart for seven weeks in 1953, it was the rendition of "Hound Dog" by Freddie Bell and the Bellboys that he heard while on tour in Las Vegas in early 1956 that caught his attention. This version had been issued a year earlier in 1955 on the Teen label. Although Leiber and Stoller continued to be credited as the writers, Bell's lyrics differed significantly from Thornton's original lyrics. While Big Mama's original was full of sexual innuendos (e.g., "You wag your tail/But I ain't gonna feed you no more"), Freddie Bell's revised lyrics removed those innuendos and changed the song to be specifically about a hound dog (e.g., "Well, you ain't never caught a rabbit/And you ain't no friend of mine"). And the musical genres were different. Big Mama's version was R&B; Freddie Bell's was Rock 'n' Roll. Thus, when Elvis sang "Hound Dog," he used the Freddie Bell lyrics. As Jerry Leiber aptly commented, "Elvis was really covering a cover."

When Presley's version hit the market, Leiber and Stoller were puzzled and more than a little perplexed by the altered lyrics:

- Mike Stoller: "I heard the record and I was disappointed. It just sounded terribly nervous, too fast, too white. But you know, after it sold seven or eight million records it started to sound better."

- Jerry Leiber: "[W]hen I heard Elvis's version, I had a bad feeling. I didn't like the way he did it. Somebody changed the lyrics…. To this day I have no idea what that rabbit business is all about. The song is not about a dog; it's about a man, a freeloading gigolo…. Of course, the fact that it sold about seven million copies took the sting out of what seemed a capricious change of lyrics. But, lick for lick, there's no comparison between the Presley version and the Big Mama original. Elvis played with the song; Big Mama nailed it."

After hearing the Freddie Bell version, Presley started including "Hound Dog" in his stage appearances. He then premiered "Hound Dog" on the nationally televised *Milton Berle Show* on June 5, 1956, with lots of gyrations, which the media widely criticized. To respond to this criticism, Steve Allen, who had booked him for his show on July 1, had Elvis dressed in a white tie and tails, as shown below, and had him croon to a basset hound with no wild gyrations.

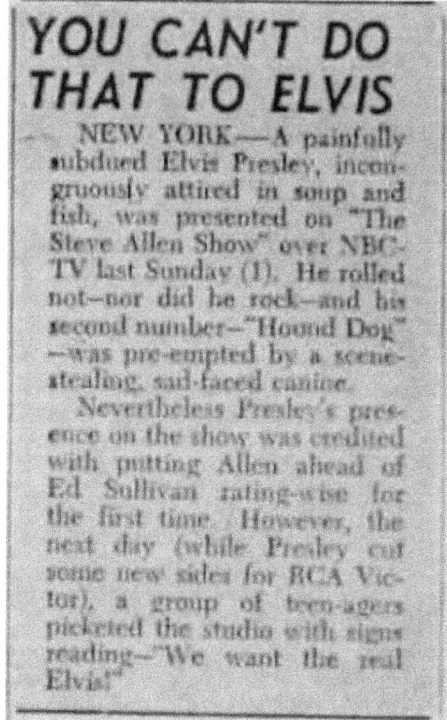

YOU CAN'T DO THAT TO ELVIS

NEW YORK—A painfully subdued Elvis Presley, incongruously attired in soup and fish, was presented on "The Steve Allen Show" over NBC-TV last Sunday (1). He rolled not—nor did he rock—and his second number—"Hound Dog" —was pre-empted by a scene-stealing, sad-faced canine.

Nevertheless Presley's presence on the show was credited with putting Allen ahead of Ed Sullivan rating-wise for the first time. However, the next day (while Presley cut some new sides for RCA Victor), a group of teen-agers picketed the studio with signs reading—"We want the real Elvis!"

Billboard, July 14, 1956

The very next day Presley went into RCA's New York studios to record it. Perfected over 31 different takes, it was released as the A-side of RCA 47-6604 on July 13, 1956, with "Don't Be Cruel," an Otis Blackwell penned song that was designated as the B-side. As *Rolling Stone* observed in ranking "Hound Dog" as the 19th Greatest Rock Song in 2004:

> With snarling vocal authority, D.J. Fontana's tommy-gun drumrolls and slashing guitar by Scotty Moore, Presley transformed the song's blues changes and put-down rhymes into a declaration of independence from his generation's cold, rigid elders.

Billboard's July 21, 1956 "Review Spotlight" noted that "Hound Dog" is "a highly charged rhythm opus in Presley's characteristic style and should enjoy heavy commercial acceptance." On the other hand, its review of "Don't Be Cruel" was less than enthusiastic, commenting that it "is in a more subdued, frankly popish vein, and demonstrates that the singer is a versatile stylist."

On July 28, 1956, *Billboard* listed "Hound Dog" as a "Best Buy," and presciently noted that "Don't Be Cruel" "may also develop after the excitement over 'Hound Dog' dies down a bit." The following week on August 4 "Hound Dog" entered *Billboard's* "Honor Roll of Hits" at #20. On August 11 it moved up to #10 and "Don't Be Cruel" first entered the chart at #25. By September 15, 1956, "Don't Be Cruel" held a higher chart position than "Hound Dog." The coupling of "Hound Dog" and "Don't Be Cruel" rose to #1 on the *Billboard* pop chart and spent 11 weeks at #1.[5] "Hound

---

5 "Don't Be Cruel" ended up being the biggest selling record of Elvis Presley's phenomenal career. Not too bad for a song

Dog" was the first record to top all three *Billboard* charts. It was #1 on the country and R&B charts for 10 weeks and six weeks, respectively.

In the UK, Elvis's cover of "Hound Dog" was released in early September 1956 on His Master's Voice 45-POP-249. It entered the UK charts shortly thereafter on September 27, 1957. It peaked for three weeks at #2 during its 23 weeks on the UK charts, including 17 weeks in the top 10. It subsequently reentered the UK charts twice, first in 1971 on RCA 2104 (peaking at #10), and then in 2007 on RCA 8869712240 (peaking at #14).

Of the 21 songs selected for this book, Elvis's mega twin hit was the only record to receive major honors for both sides. For example, it is the only 45 to be separately inducted into the Grammy Hall of Fame for each side, "Hound Dog" in 1998 and "Don't Be Cruel" in 2002. Similarly, the NEA/RIAA ranked "Don't Be Cruel/Hound Dog" at #68 on its list of the top 365 songs of the 20th century. Finally, both sides made the *Rolling Stone's* list of "The 500 Greatest Songs of All Time." Parenthetically, both sides of two songs—"What'd I Say" and the instrumental "Honky Tonk"—have received similar honors, but each had Part I on one side and Part II on the other. As a result, both parts were considered as one record for award purposes.

As can be seen on the RCA label for "Hound Dog," in addition to "Lion Publ. Co.," "Elvis Presley Mus." is listed as one of the publishers. One can sense the fine hand of Col. Parker at work here. Since his deal called for a 50/50 split with Elvis, it is not too hard to imagine the Colonel telling Don Robey, "If you want my boy Elvis to sing your song, we need a part of the action." In any event, according to Galen Gart & Roy C. Ames in their book *Duke/Peacock Records* (1990), "Robey's Houston lawyer disclosed mechanical royalties being divided three ways, with Leiber and Stoller receiving 46.25%, Robey getting 28.75% and Elvis Presley Music being assigned the remaining 25%."

CONTEMPORANEOUS 1956 COVER VERSIONS OF "HOUND DOG"

Although *Billboard* and some other sources listed Freddie Bell and the Bellboys as having an available cover of "Hound Dog" on Mercury 70919, that record does not exist. Mercury did issue a Freddie Bell and Bellboys record on Mercury 70919,[6] but the titles were "Stay Loose, Mother Goose" and "All Right, Ok, You Win." The following were the contemporaneous covers:

---

that started out on the B-side! In addition to the other honors it received, it was selected by music preservationist Roger Lee Hall as one the "100 Essential Songs of the 20th Century."

6 In 1957 Mercury did release an LP titled *Rock & Roll... All Flavors* on Mercury MG 20289 that included "Hound Dog," but it was re-recorded, i.e., it was not taken from the Teen 101 release.

ARTIST	LABEL	COMMENTS
Freddie Bell & The Bell Boys	Teen 101	Issued in 1955; b/w "Move Me Baby"
Big Mama Thornton	Peacock 5-1612	Re-issued by Peacock in the wake to Presley's version but with the same B-side as the second 1953 pressing, i.e., "Rock A Bye Baby"; this later release can be distinguished from the original 1953 pressing by its white label as shown below
Homer & Jethro	RCA 47-6706	Parody version; b/w "Screen Door," a parody of "Green Door"
Mickey Katz	Capitol F3607	Parody version titled "You're A Doity Dog (Hound Dog)"; b/w "The Litvak Square Dance"

WILLIE MAE THORNTON
Hound Dog 74
PEACOCK 1612—A re-issue of Miss Thornton's big hit, now enjoying new popularity in Elvis Presley's record. The Peacock disk will see a new round of activity, as a result. (Lion, BMI)
Rock-a-Bye, Baby....73
A new coupling for "Hound Dog," this side is a swinging blues lullaby, not calculated to induce sleep. It's a good commercial performance worth juke attention. (Lion, BMI)

Billboard **review, August 18, 1956**

Re-release of Peacock 5-1612

CONTEMPORANEOUS 1956 BUDGET COVERS OF "HOUND DOG"

ARTIST	LABEL	COMMENTS
"Scat Man" Crothers	Tops R290-49	B/w "My Prayer"/"Song for a Summer Night"/ "Canadian Sunset"
"Scat Man" Crothers	Tops RX301	EP with "Tonight You Belong To Me"/"Honky Tonk"/"Canadian Sunset"/"Whatever Will Be, Will Be"/"My Prayer"
Marv Lockard	Gateway Parade of Hits 1184	B/w "Canadian Sunset"
Marv Lockard	Big 4 Hits 197	EP with "Canadian Sunset"/"Somebody Up There Likes Me"/"My Prayer"
Marv Lockard	Big 4 Hits 204	EP with "Love Me Tender"/"Don't Be Cruel"/ "Singing The Blues"
Buddy Lucas	Bell 3	B/w "When My Dreamboat Comes Home"
None listed	Prom 720; Promenade RR-1	EP with "When My Dream Boat Comes Home"/"My Prayer"/"Whatever Will Be Will Be (Que Sera Sera)"
None listed	Value 127	EP with "When My Dream Boat Comes Home"/"My Prayer"/"Rip It Up"
None listed	Variety EPV-1801	Part of three EP box set entitled "18 Big Rock 'N Roll Hits"
None listed	Western HB-34	EP with "Don't Be Cruel"/"Singing the Blues"/ "I'm a One-Woman Man"/"Teen-Age Boogie"/"Mother Of A Honky Tonk Girl"

Buddy Lucas budget cover of "Hound Dog"

Bell picture sleeve for "Hound Dog"

LATER RELEASES OF "HOUND DOG" BY ELVIS PRESLEY

LABEL	YEAR	COMMENTS
RCA EPA-940	1956	Issued on August 17, 1956; EP with "Don't Be Cruel"/"My Baby Left Me"/"I Want You, I Need You, I Love You"
RCA 1095 (UK)	1958	B/w "Blue Suede Shoes"
RCA EPA-5120	1959	EP with "Don't Be Cruel"/"I Want You, I Need You, I Love You"/"My Baby Left Me"
RCA 447-0608	1959	B/w "Don't Be Cruel"; "Gold Standard Series"
RCA 2104 (UK)	1971	B/w "Heartbreak Hotel" and "Don't Be Cruel"; "Maxi-Million" Series
RCA PB-11099	1977	B/w "Don't Be Cruel"; RCA "Collectors' Series"
RCA PB-9265 (UK)	1978	B/w "Don't Be Cruel"

RCA PB-13351	1982	Titled "The Elvis Medley," which also includes "Don't Be Cruel"/"Teddy Bear"/"Burning Love"/"Jailhouse Rock"; b/w "Always On My Mind"
RCA-RCX 7190 (UK)	1982	EP with "Don't Be Cruel"/"I Want You, I Need You, I Love You"/"My Baby Left Me"
RCA PB-13875	1984	B/w "Baby Let's Play House"; recorded live on September 26, 1956, in Tupelo, MS, Presley's hometown
RCA PB-13886	1984	"Elvis 50th Anniversary" release; b/w "Don't Be Cruel"
Old Gold OG 8700 (UK)	1987	B/w "Don't Be Cruel"
RCA 07863-62449-7	1992	B/w "Heartbreak Hotel"; critically acclaimed remastered version
RCA 47-6604	2001	B/w "Don't Be Cruel"; red vinyl reissue; part of "Elvis #1 Hit Singles Collection"
Sun 224	???	With Scotty and Bill; b/w "I Want You, I Need You, I Love You"; unofficial bootleg

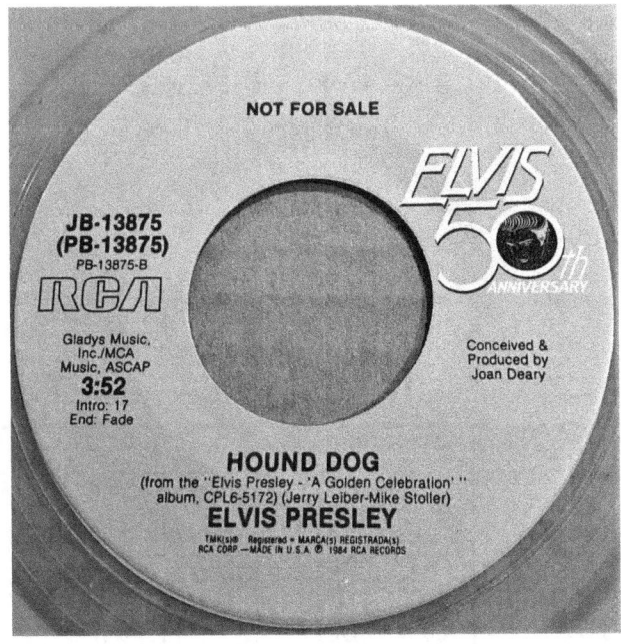

1984 release of live September 26, 1956, Tupelo, Mississippi, concert

1992 remastered reissue of 1956 original RCA release

HONORS AND ACCOLADES — ELVIS PRESLEY'S VERSION

- Inducted into The Grammy Hall of Fame in 1998; "Don't Be Cruel" was inducted in 2002
- Ranked #68, along with "Don't Be Cruel," on the National Endowment for the Arts (NEA) and the Recording Industry Association of America (RIAA) list of the top 365 songs of the 20ᵗʰ century
- Included, along with "Don't Be Cruel," on National Public Radio's list of the 20ᵗʰ century's 100 most important musical works, noting that "Elvis Presley's two hit singles fostered the birth of rock and roll"
- Ranked #19 on the *Rolling Stone's* 2004 list of "The 500 Greatest Songs of All Time"; "Don't Be Cruel" ranked #197
- Ranked #31 on Joel Whitburn's *Honor Roll of Hits;* "Don't Be Cruel" ranked #45
- Ranked #31 on the VH1 2004 list of the "100 Greatest Rock Songs"
- Ranked #19 on the BBC's list of the "100 Favourite Songs of the 20ᵗʰ Century"
- Ranked #966 in Dave Marsh's 1989 book, *The Heart of Rock & Soul: The 1001 Greatest Singles Ever Made*

SUBSEQUENT POST 1956 COVER VERSIONS OF "HOUND DOG"

ARTIST	LABEL	YEAR	COMMENTS
Ruby Andrews	Zodiac Z-1022	1971	Soul/funk, based on Thornton's original lyrics; b/w "Away From The Crowd"
The Attitude	Siamese PM 004	1980	B/w "Condo Bondage"; described as Southern California punk
Big Wheelie and the Hub Caps	Scepter 12375	1973	Medley with "All Shook Up" and "Jailhouse Rock"; b/w Chuck Berry Medley ("Johnny B. Goode" and "Sweet Little Sixteen")
The Beastles	Berandol BER 10013 (Canada)	1983	Medley with "Don't Be Cruel"; b/w "Jingle Bells"
Patsy Brewer	Pilot Master 8061-37	1978	B/w "Your Cheatin' Heart," a cover of Hank Williams

The Buff Medways	Transcopic TRAN 012 (UK)	2001	B/w "A Strange Kind Of Happyness [*sic*]"
Al Caiola	UA 787	1964	Instrumental version; b/w "Tuff Guitar," likewise an instrumental
Catfish	Epic 5-10496	1969	B/w "2120 South Michigan Avenue," the Chicago address of Chess/Checker records; Catfish was a Detroit blues boogie band
Eric Clapton	Duck EC 5 (UK)	1989	B/w "Not So Far"; "For Promo Use Only"
Eric Clapton	Duck/Reprise 5439-19719-7 (Germany)	1989	B/w "Running On Faith [radio edit]"
Dirty Blues Band	BluesWay 45-61016	1968	Harmonic electric blues version; b/w "New Orleans Woman"
The Distortions	Sea 100	1965	Garage; b/w "Can You Tell"; Birmingham, AL, label
Duffy's Nucleus	Decca F.22547	1967	B/w "Mary Open The Door"; Duffy Power does the vocals
The Everly Brothers	Warner Brothers WEP-609 (UK)	1964	EP with "Kansas City"/"I'm Gonna Move To The Outskirts Of Town"/"Lonely Weekends"
Chris Farlow and The Thunderbirds	Columbia DB 7379 (UK)	1964	B/w "Hey Hey, Hey Hey"
Fuse	Epic 5-10514	1969	B/w "Cruisin' For Burgers"; group later became Cheap Trick
Gene and the Gents	Pye 7N 17532 (UK)	1968	B/w "C'mon Everybody," an Eddie Cochran cover

Grim Reapers	Smack 15A5	1969	Garage; b/w "Cruisin' For Burgers"; pre-Fuse and Cheap Trick; re-released upon being signed by Epic (see above)
The Heartbreakers	Deuce 52187	c. 1960s	Titled "Houndog" [*sic*]; b/w "Donna," a cover of Ritchie Valens; Chicago, IL, label; long guitar break; other than info from *YouTube*, no other internet trace of this garage band could be found
Chuck Jackson	Wand 1159	1967	Soul; b/w "Love Me Tender"
Marian James	J and J 300	1967	Soul/funk; b/w "Don't Come Around"
Johnny J & The Hit Men	Roman 1000	c. 1980s	Neo-rockabilly; b/w "Lookin"
The Candy Johnson Show	Canjo 102	1964	Vocal by Don Hargrave and Jack Merrill; b/w "Baby What You Want Me To Do"
Bryan Keith	Dot 16532	1963	B/w "Cute Little Frown"
Terry Lee and The Poor Boys	Norton EP-064	1997	Taken from a 1958 unreleased acetate demo; EP with "Whole Lotta Shakin' Goin' On," likewise taken from the demo; b/w "My Little Sue" and "Driftin'," which were originally released on Soma 1116
John Lennon with Elephant's Memory	Heavy HVY-101 (unknown country)	1973?	Bootleg/repro; b/w "Long Tall Sally" by Paul McCartney and Wings; date below song title is 8/30/72
Little Richard	Oldies 45 OL-188	1964	B/w "Good Golly Miss Molly"

Little Richard	Goldies 45 D-2532	1973	B/w "Good Golly Miss Molly"
Lalo "Pancho Lopez" Guerrero	L & M 1000	1956	Titled "Pound Dog" and based on "Hound Dog" but with the lyrics revised by Guerrero; credited to Leiber-Stoller-Guerrero; b/w "Pancho Claus"
Danny Mirror & The Jordanaires	A&R MIR 124 (UK)	1981	Medley with four other Presley songs; b/w a medley of another five Presley songs
New Moan Hey	Foggy Mountain FM 1955	1970	Psych blues rock; b/w "Dust My Blues," a cover of Elmore James
Plastic Penny	Page One POF 107 (UK)	1968	Hard blues rock version; b/w "Currency"
Rock Bottom	J.A.R. 42172	c. 1973	B/w "Southward Bound (To Mississippi)"; Gulf Coast Recording Studio
Seeburg Spotlight Band	Seeburg 5005	1965	"Rhythm Series"; b/w "Blues For A Fantasy Train"
Seeburg Spotlight Band	Seeburg 1004	c. 1965	"Discotheque Series"; b/w "Saddle Soap"
Anne Shelvin	Columbia DB 9111 (UK)	1985	B/w "Right On The Edge"
Warren Smith	Bear Family BLE 010 (Germany)	2014	B/w "Black Jack David"; recorded live at the Big D Jamboree in the late 50s or early 60s
Spector Inc	Gree Jack 1001	1969	B/w "She Caught The Katy"
Walter Speding	Red Star RSS-2	1979	B/w "Get Ready"; NYC label; small hole 45

Bob Starr and His All-Star Band	Fable 712	c. 1959	Titled "Houndog" [*sic*]; b/w "Keep Her Satisfied"
Tages	Platina PA 104 (Sweden)	1965	Swedish band; b/w "Don't Turn Your Back"
Lee Tully	Flair-X 3007	1956	Titled "Around The World With Elwood Pretzel," a comedy/parody version with samplings of DJ introductions to "Hound Dog" in the U.S. , Russia, Japan, and England, with Elwood (AKA Lee Tully) mimicking Elvis
Vanilla Fudge	Atco EP-C-4260 (promo only)	1968	Medley with seven other songs including four Beatle songs; b/w "Fur Elise" and "Moonlight Sonata"
Gene Vincent	Norton 45-114	2004	Recorded live on the *Alan Freed Show*, August 1956; b/w "Be-Bop-A-Lula"
Geraint Watkins	BEEB 028 (UK)	1981	B/w "I'm A Fool To Care" and "Roberta"
White Cloud	Good Medicine 17000	1972	B/w "Collection Box"
Jeanette Williams	Back Beat 609	1969	Soul/funk; b/w "I Can Feel A Heartbreak," which made the lower reaches of the *Billboard* R&B chart; produced by Andre Williams
Jeanette Williams	Action ACT-4557 (UK)	1970	Soul/funk; b/w "I Can Feel A Heartbreak"
Buddy Wright	Jemal 556	1965	Soul/funk; b/w "Save Your Love For Me"

None Listed	Seeburg Discoteen DN-301 B	c. mid-60s	7 inch 33 1/3; b/w "Heat Wave"/"Mojo Workout"/"Johnny B. Goode"/"I Feel Fine"/"Get Back"

The Grim Reapers on Smack

Fuse on Epic

There were any number of records that played off the "Hound Dog" theme beyond the answer records discussed above, including:

- "Watch Dog" by Lulu Reed on King 4688 (1953), complete with a reference to "You're just like a hound dog watching a bone"
- "Hound Dog Special" by Cozy Cole and His All Stars on MGM K-11794 (1954)
- "Hound Dog & Alley Cat" by Vernon Anders on Money 221 (1956)
- "Go 'Way Hound Dog" by Cliff Johnson on Columbia 4-40865 (1957); song also released in the UK by Rock Island Line on RCA PB 5283 (1980)
- "Hound Dog Man (Play It Again)" by Lenny Le Blanc on Big Tree 16062 (1976); released in May 1976 before the death of Elvis, but after his death in August 1977 it charted as an Elvis tribute record
- "Hound Dog's Man Gone Home" by Arthur Alexander on Music Mill 1012 (1976), an Elvis tribute record released a month after Presley's death in August 1976

"HOUND DOG" IN THE MOVIES

In addition to being used as the title of the movie "Hounddog" [*sic*], "Hound Dog" can be heard on the soundtracks of the following movies:

MOVIE TITLE	YEAR	COMMENTS
Gunsmoke Blues	1971	Performed by Big Mama Thornton; during a production break, the TV crew from *Gunsmoke* filmed live performances of Muddy Waters, Big Mama Thornton, Big Joe Turner, and George "Harmonica" Smith, as well as some of their repartee while on their tour bus; well worth checking out on *YouTube*
The London Rock and Roll Concert	1973	Filmed on location at London's Wembley Stadium on August 5, 1972; Jerry Lee Lewis performs it as part of a medley of 1950s rock 'n' roll hits
Grease	1978	Performed by Sha Na Na; romantic musical starring John Travolta and Olivia Newton-John
Heartbreak Hotel	1988	Performed by The Bavarian Village Band; David Keith portrays Elvis in this movie
Jerry Lee Lewis: The Story of Rock 'n Roll	1991	Performed by Jerry Lee Lewis; biopic about the Killer's career
A Few Good Men	1992	Performed by Big Mama Thornton; military drama starring Tom Cruise, Jack Nicholson, and Demi Moore

Honeymoon in Vegas	1992	Performed by Jeff Beck and Jed Leiber; Jed is the son of Jerry Leiber; romantic comedy starring Nicolas Cage, James Caan, and Sarah Jessica Parker that features numerous Elvis songs sung by Elvis and others
Look Who's Talking Now	1993	Performed by Elvis Presley; romantic family comedy starring John Travolta and Kirstie Alley
Forrest Gump	1994	Performed by Elvis Presley; this film, starring Tom Hanks, won six Oscars, including "Best Picture"
Chocolat	2000	*IMDbPro* does not identify who performed the song; movie is a romantic drama set in France
Lilo & Stitch	2006	Performed by Elvis Presley; a Disney animated adventure comedy
Hounddog	2007	Performed separately by Elvis Presley, Jill Scott, and Dakota Fanning, the young girl who fantasies Elvis; includes a fantasied rape scene that was not well received by critics
Indiana Jones and the Kingdom of the Crystal Skull	2008	Performed by Elvis Presley; a Steven Spielberg adventure movie starring Harrison Ford and Kate Blanchett
The Express	2008	*IMDbPro* does not identify who performed the song; story is about Syracuse University football player Ernie Davis, the first African American to win the Heisman Trophy
Nowhere Boy (UK)	2009	Performed by Big Mama Thornton; story of the childhood and teenage years of John Lennon (1944-1960)
Zombieland: Double Tap	2019	*IMDbPro* does not identify who the performed the song; horror flick starring Woody Harrelson
Elvis	2022	Biopic about Elvis Presley starring Austin Butler as Elvis and Tom Hanks as Colonel Parker; "Hound Dog" sung twice, once by Butler portraying Elvis and once by Shonka Dukureh portraying Big Mama Thornton

DOCUMENTED CONCERT PERFORMANCES OF "HOUND DOG"

As of May 1, 2024, *Setlist.fm* documented that "Hound Dog" had been performed in concert 1,438 times by 220 different artists. In addition to Elvis Presley and Big Mama Thornton, who sang it in concert 742 and 15 times, respectively, artists who performed it more than 20 times in concert include James Taylor (25) and Jerry Lee Lewis (23). Other artists as varied as Tracy Chapman, Bryan Adams, Cyndi Lauper, Van Morrison, Scorpions, Limp Bizkit, and The Residents have played "Hound Dog" eight or more times in concert.

ALSO WORTH NOTING . . .

- According to *Setlist.fm* as of May 1, 2024, Elvis Presley performed "Hound Dog" in concert 742 times, more than any other song with exception of "Can't Help Falling in Love," which he sang in concert 769 times.
- In 1958, the "Hound Dog"/"Don't Be Cruel" two-sided hit became only the third record to sell three million copies, matching Bing Crosby's "White Christmas" and Gene Autry's "Rudolph The Red-Nosed Reindeer."
- Presley's success with "Hound Dog" resulted in Jerry Leiber and Mike Stoller being hired to write other songs for him, including "Don't," "King Creole," and "Jailhouse Rock."

ADDITIONAL SOURCES

Gart, Galen & Roy C. Ames, *Duke/Peacock Records: An Illustrated History with Discography* (Big Nickel, 1990)

Leiber, Jerry & Mike Stoller, *Hound Dog: The Leiber & Stoller Autobiography* (Simon & Schuster, 2009)

Moonoogian, George, "'Hound Dog': An R & B Classic," *Whiskey, Women, and . . .*, No. 14 (June 1984)

CHAPTER 2

"SHAKE, RATTLE AND ROLL"

BIG JOE TURNER (APRIL 1954) AND BILL HALEY (JULY 1954)

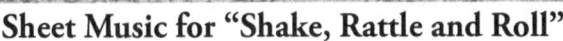

Sheet Music for "Shake, Rattle and Roll"

Turner's original release on Atlantic

"SHAKE, RATTLE AND ROLL" (JOE TURNER'S VERSION) — THE BASIC FACTS

Label: Atlantic 1026 (both 45 and 78)

Writer: Jesse Stone (as Charles E. Calhoun)

Date recorded: February 15, 1954

Date released: April 1954

B-side: "You Know I Love You"

Producers: Ahmet Ertegun and Jerry Wexler

Billboard charts:
<u>Pop Chart</u>
- Debut: 8/14/54
- Peak: #22
- Duration: 2 weeks

<u>R&B Chart</u>
- Debut: 5/08/54
- Peak: #1 (3 weeks)
- Duration: 32 weeks

THE SONG BY JOE TURNER AND ITS IMPACT

"Shake, Rattle and Roll" was penned by Jesse Stone, a veteran R&B band leader who issued many records on RCA, Atlantic, and other labels under his own name. The writer's credit on the label and sheet music was listed as Charles E. Calhoun, a pseudonym that Stone used when he penned R&B songs published by BMI as opposed to using his real name when he penned songs under the ASCAP banner. The song was copyrighted on April 19, 1954.

Downloaded from the Library of Congress 1954 List of Copyright Entries

Taking a phrase he used at his weekly poker games, Stone composed "Shake, Rattle and Roll" specifically for Big Joe Turner, a well-known blues shouter.[7] The "one-eyed cat" lyric, however, has been attributed to Baby Lovett, an Atlantic session drummer. It was recorded on February 15, 1954. Backing Big Joe's vocal was a chorus that consisted of Stone; Ahmet Ertegun, Atlantic's founder; and Jerry Wexler, the label's head of A & R. The studio musicians included Mickey Baker (the Mickey of Mickey and Sylvia's "Love is Strange" fame) on guitar and Sam "The Man" Taylor on the saxophone solo. Turner later explained, "Everybody was singing slow blues when I was young, and I thought I'd put a beat to it and sing it up-tempo."

Released in April 1955, on April 10, 1954, *Billboard* made it a "Review Spotlight" pick, raving that it is "a smash hit" and commented, "It's a wild blues and it receives a sock performance from the warbler, who makes it one of his best vocal jobs ever." As can be seen immediately below, on April 17, 1954, *Cash Box* joined *Billboard* in lauding Turner's "Shake, Rattle and Roll":

---

7 In 1919 vaudeville singer Al Bernard recorded a song titled "Shake, Rattle and Roll," which was about dice; it is definitely not the same song.

THE CASH BOX
★ AWARD O' THE WEEK ★

"SHAKE, RATTLE AND ROLL" (2:57)
[Progressive BMI—Calhoun]
"YOU KNOW I LOVE YOU" (3:08) [Lou Willie Turner]

JOE TURNER
Atlantic 1026

JOE TURNER

● Joe Turner is really loaded with this one. "Shake, Rattle and Roll" has everything. Great beat, simple tune, Turner vocal, and a sockful of punchy phrases that combine to make up a terrific lyric. Add this to the fact that Turner is currently one of the hottest record salesmen in the business and you have a mighty potent piece of wax. The under lid, "You Know I Love You," is a slow romantic blues, well done, but destined to be lost in view of the upper deck.

Not surprisingly, it didn't take long for "Shake, Rattle and Roll" to make the *Billboard* and *Cash Box* R&B charts. It debuted on *Cash Box's* R&B chart at #15 on May 1, 1954, and on *Billboard's* R&B chart on May 8, 1954. Eventually, it topped *Billboard's* R&B chart for three weeks and was on that chart for 32 weeks. It also crossed over to the *Billboard* pop chart for two weeks.

One of Turner's follow up songs was "Flip, Flop and Fly," which was recorded in early February 1955, and released on Atlantic 1053. It was penned by Jesse Stone and Turner (as Lou Willie Turner). Musically, it is quite like "Shake, Rattle and Roll." It made both the *Billboard* R&B and pop charts, peaking at #2 and #21, respectively.

With lyrics that include "You've got the nerve to tell me, tell me, to rattle those pots and pans," The Platters' "Bark, Battle and Ball" is an answer to "Shake, Rattle and Roll."[8] Released on Mercury 70633 in June 1955, it was the B-Side to "Only You (And You Alone)," The Platters' first top ten hit, peaking at #5 on *Billboard's* pop chart and at #1 on its R&B chart.

CONTEMPORANEOUS COVER VERSIONS OF "SHAKE, RATTLE AND ROLL"

The only contemporaneous cover version was by Bill Haley and His Comets, which is discussed in detail below.

LATER RELEASES OF "SHAKE, RATTLE AND ROLL" BY JOE TURNER

LABEL	YEAR	COMMENTS
Atlantic EP 565	1956	EP with "Flip Flop And Fly"/"In The Evening When The Sun Goes Down"
Coral 62429	1964	Re-recording; not taken from his Atlantic release; b/w "There'll Be Some Tears Fallin'"

---

8 "Bark, Battle and Ball" was not released in the UK as a 45 until 1984, when it was released on Pinner PRM 804 as the B-Side to the Gaylords' "Ma Ma Marie."

BluesTime 45001	1969	Re-recorded version produced by Bob Thiele; improperly credited to Carl Butler, who did pen a 1951 country song about a train that was titled "Shake, Rattle and Roll"; b/w "Two Loves Have I"
Blues Spectrum BS-14	1974	B/w "Honey Hush"; 1970s re-recordings
Atlantic 1026	1975 or later	Reissue of original on the "fan" Atlantic label; b/w "You Know I Love You"
Pablo 2310S791	c. 1978	With Pee Wee Crayton and Sonny Stitt; b/w "Every Day I Have The Blues"; Pablo was a Norman Grantz jazz label
Atlantic GS 45814 (Canada)	1980s	B/w "Corrine Corrina"; "Gold Standard Series"

HONORS AND ACCOLADES -- BIG JOE TURNER'S VERSION

- Inducted into the Grammy Hall of Fame in 1998
- Ranked #99 by the National Endowment for the Arts (NEA) and the Recording Industry Association of America (RIAA) on its list of the top 365 songs of the 20th century
- Inducted into the Blues Hall of Fame in 2001
- Ranked #127 on the *Rolling Stone*'s 2004 list of "The 500 Greatest Songs of All Time"
- Chosen by the Rock & Roll Hall of Fame as one of the "500 Songs That Shaped Rock and Roll"
- Ranked #12 on Joel Whitburn's "Non-Pop & Hot 100 Chart Honorees"
- Ranked #13 in Dave Marsh's 1989 book, *The Heart of Rock Soul: The 1,001 Greatest Singles Ever Made*

BILL HALEY'S COVER VERSION OF "SHAKE, RATTLE AND ROLL" (JULY 1954)

Bill Haley 1954 Original Decca "Lines" label

Haley 1954 Decca EP ED-2168

"SHAKE, RATTLE AND ROLL" (BILL HALEY'S COVER VERSION) — THE BASIC FACTS

Label: Decca 7- 29204 (45) and Decca 29204 (78)

Writer: Jesse Stone (as Charles E. Calhoun)

Date recorded: June 7, 1954

Date released: July 12, 1954

B-Side: "A.B.C. Boogie"

Producer: Milt Gabler

Billboard Chart:

> Pop Chart
> - Debut: 10/4/54
> - Peak: #7
> - Duration: 27 weeks

THE SONG BY BILL HALEY AND ITS IMPACT

On June 7, 1954, one month after Big Joe Turner's original version hit the *Billboard's* R&B chart, Bill Haley and His Comets recorded their cover version. But as the following comparison of Turner's lyrics with Haley's demonstrates, Haley's version was cleaned up to remove sexual verbiage to make it more palatable for radio station programmers:

BIG JOE TURNER LYRICS	BILL HALEY LYRICS
Way you wear those dresses, the sun comes shinin' through / Way you wear those dresses, the sun comes shinin' through / I can't believe my eyes, all that mess belongs to you	Wearin' those dresses, your hair done up so nice / Wearin' those dresses, your hair done up so nice / You look so warm, but your heart is cold as ice
I believe to my soul you're the devil in nylon hose / I believe to my soul you're the devil in nylon hose / Well, the more I work, the faster my money goes	I believe you're doin' me wrong and now I know / I believe you're doin' me wrong and now I know / The more I work, the faster my money goes
I'm like a one-eyed cat, peepin' in a seafood store / I'm like a one-eyed cat, peepin' in a seafood store / Well, I can look at you, tell you ain't no child no more	I'm like a one-eyed cat, peepin' in a seafood store / I'm like a one- eyed cat, peepin' in a seafood store / I can look at you, tell you don't love me no more

As noted above, Haley's lyrics retained the *double entendre* lines about a "a one-eyed cat, peepin' in a seafood store," which was arguably more sexually charged than the lyrics that were changed. In his Haley biography, John Svenson suggested that Haley kept that line because Haley was blind in one eye. In any event, those lyrics went over the heads of most Americans in the 1950s.

In 1987 when Bill Haley was inducted posthumously into the Rock & Roll Hall of Fame, an essay on Haley in the ceremony's program penned by William Hill included the following:

> "We steer clear of anything suggestive," Bill Haley declared as the battle raged over the lyrics of those newfangled rhythm-and-blues-based pop hits. Haley's version of "Shake, Rattle and Roll" was one of the tunes in question, since it happened to be sweeping the nation.

When Haley's version was released on July 12, 1954, Big Joe Turner's version was at #3 on *Billboard's* R&B chart. On July 10, 1954, *Billboard's* "Review Spotlight" gave Haley's version a strong plug. It eventually debuted on *Billboard's* pop chart on October 4, 1954, on its way to #7, becoming the first Rock 'n' Roll record to break into *Billboard's* top 10. It topped *Billboard's* Baltimore, MD, regional chart. It remained on *Billboard's* pop chart for 27 consecutive weeks.

Surprisingly, Big Joe Turner's original version was not released in the UK. However, Haley's version was released on Brunswick 05338 in October 1954, and it was on the UK charts for 14 weeks, topping out at #4. This was Haley's first charted record in the UK, and it marked the beginning of the

UK's enthusiastic embrace of his music. Between 1955 and 1981 Bill Haley had eight top 10 hits in the UK versus only four in the U.S.

Another Jesse Stone co-penned song that played off the "Shake, Rattle and Roll" motif is "Rattle My Bones," recorded by The Jodimars, a group made up of former Haley Comets, which was released in 1956 on Capitol F3436. It has a similar verse structure and includes the lyrics, "Gonna rattle, gonna shake, gonna rattle, gonna shake…"

Subsequent releases of "Shake, Rattle and Roll" include, notably, Presley's version that was recorded on February 3, 1956, and released on August 31, 1956, on RCA 47-6642, backed with "Lawdy, Miss Clawdy." He performed it live on December 18, 1955, on the Louisiana Hayride, and again on January 28, 1956, on the *Dorsey Brothers Stage Show*, his first appearance on national TV. Only one subsequent cover, however, dented the *Billboard* pop chart, namely Arthur Conley's 1967 cover on Atco 6494 that topped out at #31.

Referring to the subsequent covers by Bill Haley and Elvis Presley, NPR's Ed Ward in 2012 stated: "Although they didn't use some of his [Turner's] more colorful verses, their recordings ensured that 'Shake, Rattle and Roll' became one of the first rock 'n' roll standards."

Importantly, an internet article reports the following relevant information about the relationship between Big Joe Turner and Bill Haley[9]:

> Although musical revisionists and American media tried to paint Turner as a victim of the music industry due to Haley's covering of the song, in fact Haley's success helped Turner immensely although Turner was a well-established performer long before "Shake, Rattle and Roll." Listeners who hear Haley's version sought out Turner's. The two men became close friends, and performed on tour together in Australia in 1957. In 1966, at a time when Turner's career was at a low ebb, Haley arranged for his Comets to back the elder musician for a series of recordings in Mexico.

Although The Beatles did not release "Shake, Rattle and Roll" on a vinyl 45, they did include it in a medley with "Rip It Up" and "Blue Suede Shoes" that appeared on the Anthology 3 LP and CD that was released in 1995. It was recorded during the January 1969 *Get Back/Let It Be* sessions at Abbey Road Studios. The Beatles were obviously playing around in the studio since the resulting medley is ragged at best. The three songs were, in all likelihood, among the songs they sang during their apprenticeship at Hamburg, Germany's Star Club, and elsewhere in the early 1960s.

Special mention should also be made to 1989's "Swing The Mood" by Jive Bunny and The Mastermixers on Mastermix 7-99140, a mashup of many 1950s Rock 'n' Roll songs, including three Haley songs, "Shake, Rattle And Roll," "Rock Around The Clock," and "R-O-C-K Rock." This record from the other side of the pond topped the UK charts and rose to #11 on the *Billboard* "Hot 100" chart. Altogether, Jive Bunny had five top ten UK chart hits, including three chart toppers.

---

9 "Shake, Rattle and Roll - Comparison of The Joe Turner and Bill Haley Versions," at http://www.liquisearch.com/ shake_rattle_and_roll/comparison_of_the_joe_turner_and_bill_haley_versions.

CONTEMPORANEOUS BUDGET LABEL COVERS OF
"SHAKE, RATTLE AND ROLL"

ARTIST	LABEL	COMMENTS
Jim Brown and The Four Bells	Bell 1069	B / w "Mambo Baby"
Jim Brown and The Four Bells	Festival-Bell EX45-614 (Australia)	EP with "Mambo Baby" / "Susan Slept Here" / "Hold My Hand"
Patty Kay	Promenade NRR 3	EP with "Ka Ding Dong" / "Honky Tonk" / "Rock-A-Beatin' Boogie"
Gayle Larson and The Toppers	Tops R242X45-49	EP with "Skokiaan" / "This Ole House" / "If I Give My Heart To You"
Artie Malvin	Waldorf Music Hall 4511	EP with "Mr. Sandman" / "Runaround" / "Smile"
Artie Malvin	Waldorf Music Hall 45-181	EP with "Rock Around The Clock" / "Dim Dim The Lights" / "See You Later Alligator"
Artie Malvin	Waldorf T8-X45	EP with "Heartbreak Hotel" / "Ready Teddy" / "Fever" / "I Want You, I Need You, I Love You" / "My Baby Left Me"
Artie Malvin	18 Top Hits SP 4	Haley lyrics; b/w "Ling Ting Tong" / "Count Your Blessings" / "That's What I Like" / "Malaguena" / "Silk Stockings"
Artie Malvin	18 Top Hits 135	EP with "Teach Me Tonight" / "Run Around" / "Mambo Italiano" / "The Things I Didn't Do" / "Mister Sandman"
Bill St. Claire	Big 4 Hits 102	EP with "Sway" / "They Were Doing The Mambo" / "Cinnamon Sinner"
The Tomcats	Favorite 21004X	Haley lyrics; b/w "Mambo Baby" by Edna McGriff and the Tomcats

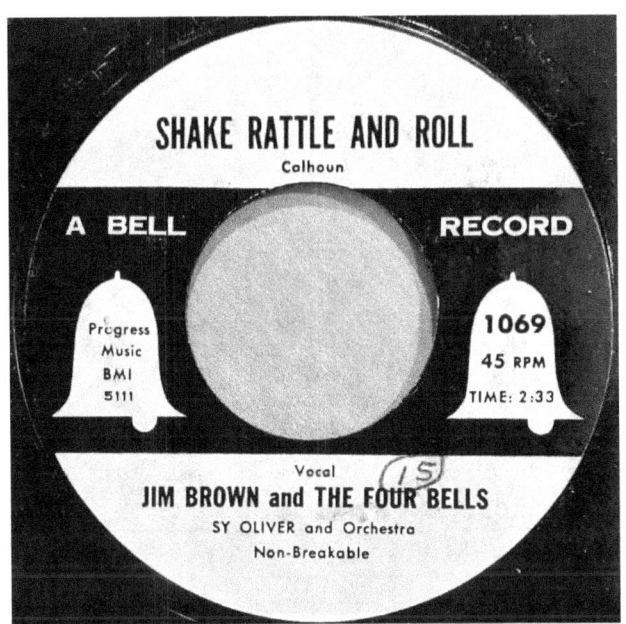 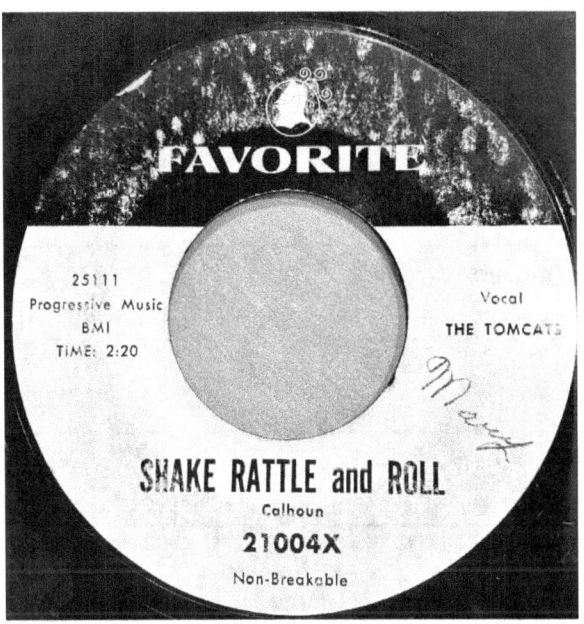

Budget label covers by Jim Brown and the Four Bells and The Tomcats

LATER RELEASES OF "SHAKE, RATTLE AND ROLL" BY BILL HALEY

LABEL	YEAR	COMMENTS
Decca ED-2168	1954	EP with "Rock Around The Clock"/"A.B.C. Boogie"/ "Thirteen Women"
Brunswick OE 9129 (UK)	1955	EP with "Dim, Dim the Lights"/ "A.B.C. Boogie"/"Happy Baby"
Brunswick OE 9431 (UK)	1958	EP with "Rock Around The Clock," and two songs by the Four Aces, "Stranger In Paradise" and "Three Coins In The Fountain"
WB 133	1964	Re-recorded; b/w "Love Letters In The Sand"
WB WEP 6136 (UK)	1964	Re-recorded; EP with "Rock Around The Clock"/"Love Letters In The Sand"/"Kansas City"
Decca G-21017 (Canada)	1965	B/w "(We Gonna) Rock Around The Clock"
WB 7124	1968	B/w "Rock Around The Clock"; "Back to Back Hits"; re-recorded, not the original Decca masters
MCA MU 1013 (UK)	1968	B/w "Rock Around The Clock"; from the Decca masters
Radio Active Gold RD 46	1972	B/w "Rock-a-Beatin' Boogie"; 1969 live recordings at NYC's Bitter End
MCA 60067	1973	B/w "See You Later Alligator"; from the original Decca releases

Forever Oldies SWF-21089	Mid-70s	B/w "Rock Around The Clock"
MCA 694 (UK)	1981	Titled "Haley's Golden Medley," with "Rock Around The Clock," "Rock-A-Beatin' Boogie," "Shake, Rattle And Roll," and "Choo Choo Ch' Boogie"; b/w "A.B.C. Boogie"
Collectables COL 90094	???	B/w "See You Later Alligator"; from the original Decca versions; "Back to Back Hit Series"
Old Gold OG 9221 (UK)	1982	B/w "See You Later Alligator"; from the Decca original masters
Buddah BG 8	1984	B/w "Rock Around The Clock"; Richard Nadler, Executive Producer; live versions
Maybelline 85 (E.E.C.)	1987	Picture disc with "See You Later Alligator"
Demon 45001/1 (UK)	2016	B/w "Rock Around The Clock"; from the Decca originals

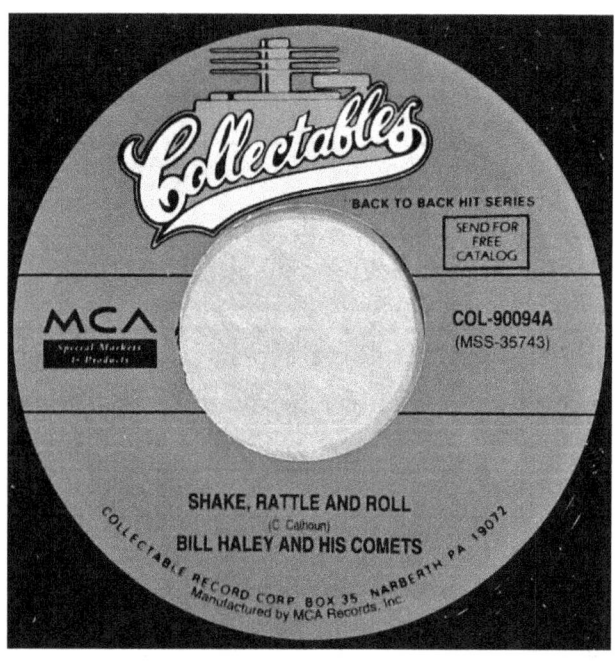

HONORS AND ACCOLADES -- BILL HALEY'S VERSION

- First Rock 'n' Roll song to make the top ten on *Billboard's* "Honor Roll of Hits," peaking at #7, despite being described by Decca on the label as a "Fox Trot"
- Voted #1 on *Billboard's* 1954 poll of DJs of their favorite R&B song; Big Joe Turner's version was voted #5

Rhythm & Blues

Based on actual vote of disk jockeys covering period of January
1, 1954, thru October 9, 1954.

**Which single record in the Rhythm & Blues category did you like
most during the past 12 months?**

PLACE	WINNER	LABEL

1. SHAKE, RATTLE AND ROLL, Bill Haley.....Decca

2. SH-BOOM, Crew Cuts ....Mercury

3. SH-BOOM, Chords ....Cat

4. HONEY LOVE, Drifters ....Atlantic

5. SHAKE, RATTLE AND ROLL, Joe Turner....Atlantic

SUBSEQUENT COVER VERSIONS OF "SHAKE, RATTLE AND ROLL"

ARTIST	LABEL	YEAR	COMMENTS
Winifred Atwell and Her Other Piano	Decca 45-F-10852 (UK)	1957	Two medleys titled "Let's Rock 'n Roll"; Side 1 also includes "Rock Around The Clock" and "Razzle Dazzle"; Side 2 with "Singing The Blues," "The Green Door," and "See You Later, Alligator"; made the UK charts
Winifred Atwell and Her Other Piano	London 45-1739	1957	Same songs as set forth immediately above
Arthur Murray (Big Dave and His Orchestra)	Capitol EAP 2-640	1955	EP with "Tweedlee Dee" / "Smilin' Al" / "Gibraltar Rock"
Count Basie & Joe Williams	Roulette 4203	1959	Vocal by Joe Williams; b/w "Ain't No Use"
Rod Bernard and Clifton Chenier	Jin 362	1976	B/w "Rockin' Pneumonia And The Boogie Woogie Flu"

Chuck Berry	Chess 2169	1975	B/w "Baby What You Want Me To Do"
Chuck Berry	Chess 6145 038 (UK)	1975	B/w "I'm Just A Name"
Big Ben Accordion Band	Columbia DB 3856 (UK)	1957	Medley with "Giddy Up Ding Dong" and "Razzle Dazzle"; b/w medley of "Rockin' Through The Rye," "Hound Dog," and "R.O.C.K."
The Blue Moon Boys (AKA Elvis Presley with Scotty Moore and Bill Black)	White Knight SP1-28 (unauthorized)	1975	Medley with "Flip, Flop And Fly"; recorded live on the *Dorsey Brothers Stage Show* on January 28, 1956; mostly Joe Turner's lyrics; b/w "I Got A Woman"; bootleg with picture sleeve
Arthur Conley	Atco 6494	1967	B/w "You Don't Have To See Me"; both sides produced by Otis Redding
Arthur Conley	Atlantic 2091-106 (UK)	1971	B/w "Sweet Soul Music"
Sam Cooke	RCA 1367 (England)	1963	B/w "Little Red Rooster," a Willie Dixon penned song
The Deep River Boys	His Master's Voice 7M 280 (UK)	1954	B/w "St. Louis Blues"
The Embers	EEE 7-8069	1967	B/w "Walk On By"; northern soul group
The Front Porch	Jubilee 5700	1967	Turner's lyrics; b/w "Song To St. Agnes"
Harry Hepcat	Rebop EP-RB965	1976	Turner's lyrics; b/w "Boogie Children" / "Go Cat, Go" / "Good Rockin' Tonight"; Cincinnati, OH, label
Buddy Holly	Coral FEP-2069 (UK)	1964	EP with "Blue Suede Shoes" / "Come Back Baby" / "Love's Made A Fool Of You"

Jive Bunny and The Mixmasters	Mastermix 7-99140	1989	Titled "Swing The Mood," a mash-up of ten songs; in addition to "Shake, Rattle And Roll," the others are "Rock Around The Clock," "Tutti Frutti," "R-O-C-K Rock," "Wake Up Little Susie," "Jailhouse Rock," "At The Hop," "Hound Dog," "All Shook Up," and "In The Mood"; hit # 11 on the *Billboard* pop chart, but it was # 1 on the UK charts; b/w "Glenn Miller Medley"
The Kraze	Theme TR-107	1982-83	B/w "Train Kept A Rollin'"; Coraopolis, PA, label
Larry Lynch	Starfire SF-501	1983	Rockabilly version ; b/w "Too Bad!"; produced by Rip Lay
Bob McFadden	Brunswick 9-55156	1959	Novelty—title includes "Sing Along With Mummy"; same song; b/w "Bingo"
Billy Lee Michaels	Extra Terrestrial E-T-101/E-T-102	1982	Weird parody with most of the same lyrics but titled "E.T. Rock—E.T. Roll"; not credited to anyone; b/w "Twas The Light Year Before X-mas"; produced by Freddie Cannon
Moose & Da Sharks	Butterscotch 7272	1974???	B/w "Barefootin'," Butterscotch 7171; Detroit, MI, area label
Mud	RAK 213	1974	Turner lyrics; medley with "See You Later Alligator"; b/w "One Night," a cover of Elvis Presley's cleaned up lyrics of the Smiley Lewis original version
Jack Parnell	Parlophone GEP 8532 (UK)	1955	EP with "Fanfare Boogie" / "The Fish"/ "Ting A Ling"
Elvis Presley	RCA 47-6642	1956	B/w "Lawdy, Miss Clawdy"

Elvis Presley	RCA EPA-830	1956	EP with "Lawdy, Miss Clawdy" / "Blue Moon" / "I Love You Because"
Elvis Presley	RCA 447-0615	1959	B/w "Lawdy, Miss Clawdy"; "Gold Standard Series"
Elvis Presley	Sun 227	1970s???	With the Jordanaires; unofficial bootleg release; b/w "Heartbreak Hotel"
Elvis Presley	RCA A72V 0074 (UK)	2001	EP with "One Sided Love Affair"/ "Money Honey" / "Lawdy, Miss Clawdy"
Paul Revere & The Raiders	Jerden JRLS-7000	1966	Haley lyrics; 7" 33 1/3 EP with "Work With Me Annie" / "So Fine" / "Mojo Workout" / "Blues Stay Away"/ "Irresistible You"
Ricky & The Red Streaks	Train 111-91	???	Garage/punk version with Turner lyrics; b/w "Calendar Girl," a Neil Sedaka cover; Sacramento, CA, label; longtime country and rodeo band
Jake Russell and The Counts	Count 800	1960s???	Instrumental version; b/w "When The Saints Go Marching In"; no internet info on this artist/band
Soul Patrol	Ripete R45-4005	1992	B/w "Release This Love" by Edwin Starr
Billy Swan	Columbia 3-10443	1976	Turner lyrics; b/w "I Got It For You"; on the *Billboard* country chart for two weeks, peaking at #95
Billy Swan	Monument S MNT 4836 (UK)	1976	Turner lyrics; b/w "I Got It For You"
Swinging Blue Jeans	Imperial 66049	1964	British group; b/w "You're No Good"

Swinging Blue Jeans	HMV 7EG.8850 (UK)	1964	EP with "Hippy Hippy Shake" / "Shakin' All Over" / "Shaking Feeling"
Hayden Thompson	Collector Item CI 001 (Sweden)	1984	EP with "Be-Bop-A-Lula" / "Good Rockin' Tonight" / "My Baby Left Me"
The Thundermen	Thundermen 612016	1986	Medley with "Be-Bop-A-Lula," "Peppermint Twist," "Party Doll," and "Claudette"; b/w "Mule Skinner Blues"; Eau Claire, WI, label
Dale Ward	Boyd 150	1965	B/w "You Gotta Let Me Know"; CB rev. 3/27/65: "Moving revival of the way back smash"
Bert Weedon	Polydor 2058 832 (UK)	1977	Medley titled "Rocking Guitar," which also includes "Guitar Boogie Shuffle," "What'd I Say," "See You Later Alligator," "Blue Suede Shoes," and "Rock Around The Clock"; b/w "Bella Ciao"
Link Wray	Line LS 1039 (Germany)	1980	B/w "Young Love," penned by Link and not a cover of the Tab Hunter/Sonny James hit versions

Later 1967 releases by Arthur Conley on Atco and The Embers on EEE

"SHAKE, RATTLE AND ROLL" IN THE MOVIES

In addition to lending its name as the title to a TV mini-series, "Shake, Rattle and Roll" can be heard in the following movies:

MOVIE TITLE	YEAR	COMMENTS
"Let The Good Times Roll"	1973	Performed by Bill Haley and His Comets; recorded live at a Richard Nader concert
The London Rock and Roll Concert	1973	Filmed on location at London's Wembley Stadium on August 5, 1972; performed by Bill Haley; also features Chuck Berry, Bo Diddley, Jerry Lee Lewis, Little Richard, among others

Blue Suede Shoes	1980	Documentary about the British Rock 'n' Roll revival in the late 1970s; performed by Bill Haley and His Comets
Clue	1985	Performed by Bill Haley and His Comets; criminal mystery comedy based on the Parker Brothers' board game of the same name
The Big Town	1987	Performed by Big Joe Turner; crime drama set in Chicago starring Matt Dillon, Diane Lane, and Tommy Lee Jones
Short Circuit 2	1988	Performed by Big Joe Turner; dramatic comedy
Bluesland: A Portrait in American Music	1993	Performed by Big Joe Turner; documentary about pre- and post-war American blues artists
Lone Star	1996	Performed by Big Joe Turner; mystery drama set in a Texas border town; #4 on Roger Ebert's best films of 1996; both Kris Kristofferson and Matthew McConaughey were in the cast
Shake, Rattle and Roll: An American Love Story (TV mini-series)	1999	Performed by Dicky Barrett with Dan Wilson; won Golden Reel Award for best sound editing for TV movies
Liberty Heights	1999	Performed by both Bill Haley and Big Joe Turner; coming of age movie set in Baltimore in 1954-55 involving high school integration following the Supreme Court's 1954 *Brown v. Board of Education* decision
Gunsmoke Blues	2004	Performed by Big Joe Turner; during a 1971 production break, the TV crew from Gunsmoke filmed live performances of Muddy Waters, Big Mama Thronton, Big Joe Turner, and George "Harmonica" Smith, as well as some of their repartee while on their tour bus; well worth checking out on *YouTube*

The Express	2008	Performed by Big Joe Turner; story about the Syracuse University running back, Ernie Davis, the first Black Heisman Trophy winner
Indiana Jones and the Kingdom of the Crystal Skull	2008	Performed by Bill Haley and His Comets; a Steven Spielberg adventure movie starring Harrison Ford and Kate Blanchett
Nowhere Boy (UK)	2009	Story of the childhood and teenage years of John Lennon (1944-1960); performed by Elvis Presley

DOCUMENTED CONCERT PERFORMANCES OF "SHAKE, RATTLE AND ROLL"

As of May 1, 2024, *Setlist.fm* documented that "Shake, Rattle and Roll" has been performed in concert 847 times by 135 artists. Among the artists who have included it on their set lists on more than ten occasions include Chris Robinson Brotherhood (78), Queen (53), Cliff Richard (43), Kid Rock (35), Van Morrison (27), Fats Domino (24), Elvis Presley (23), AC/DC (21), Huey Lewis and the News (19), and Eric Clapton (11). As recently as 2017 it was on 92 set lists, the most of any year in *Setlist.fm's* database.

ALSO WORTH NOTING . . .

- Referring to both Jerry Lee Lewis' "Whole Lotta Shakin' Goin' On" and Turner's version of "Shake, Rattle and Roll," rock critic Dave Marsh observed: "If there's a way to impute more pure, dripping lust into the word 'shake,' no one has ever found it, even though Lewis and Turner doubtless inspired many a search."
- "Shake, Rattle and Roll" was performed by Bruce Springsteen and the E Street Band at the Rock & Roll Hall of Fame concert held in Cleveland, OH, on September 2, 1995.
- It is believed that among the many recording masters destroyed in the 2008 Universal Music fire were Bill Haley's Decca masters.
- *Shake, Rattle and Roll* is, as its website in 2021 states, "A dazzling tribute to the music of the 50's & 60's in a spectacular fully choreographed stage production featuring an all-Australian cast of performers."
- "Shake, Rattle and Roll" is the name of a ride at theme parks such as Kings Island in Ohio.
- *Shake, Rattle and Roll* is the title of the Philippines' longest running horror movie franchise, which was first directed by famed director Peque Gallaga.

ADDITIONAL SOURCE

Cotton, Lee, *Shake Rattle & Roll: The Golden Age of American Rock 'n' Roll, Volume 1: 1952-1955* (Pierian Press, 1989)

CHAPTER 3

"ROCK AROUND THE CLOCK"

BILL HALEY AND HIS COMETS (MAY 1954)

Original release on the "old-style"
Decca lines label

Original UK release on the Brunswick
gold and black label

Decca "Personality Series" label

Later Decca "Star" label

"ROCK AROUND THE CLOCK" — THE BASIC FACTS

Label: Decca 9-29124 (45); Decca 29124 (78)

Writers: Jimmy E. Myers (as Jimmy De Knight) and Max D. Freedman

Date recorded: April 12, 1954

Date released: May 10, 1954

B-side: "Thirteen Women (and Only One Man in Town)"

Producer: Milt Gabler

Billboard charts:

    1954 Pop Chart[10]
- Debut: 5/29/54
- Peak: #23
- Duration: 1 week

    1955 Pop Chart
- Debut: 5/14/55
- Peak: #1 (8 weeks)
- Duration: 23 weeks

    1955 R&B Chart
- Debut: 6/11/55
- Peak: #3
- Duration: 14 weeks

    1974 Pop Chart
- Debut: 3/16/74
- Peak: #39
- Duration: 14 weeks

THE SONG AND ITS IMPACT

"Rock Around The Clock" is the world's best-selling Rock & Roll 45 rpm record, with sales of at least 25 million copies. Its impact on music and artists worldwide cannot be over-emphasized. But "Rock Around The Clock" had at best a lackluster start for a record that has accomplished so much. The tale of this amazing Phoenix-like comeback is set forth below.

"(We're Gonna) Rock Around The Clock" was written in 1952-53 by James E. Myers (under the pen name of Jimmy De Knight) and Max C. Freedman, and copyrighted on March 31, 1953.[11] It was first recorded by Sonny Dae and His Knights on Arcade 123, a small Philadelphia label in which,

---

10 The 1954 *Billboard* information is taken from Joel Whitburn's *Pop Memories 1890-1954* (Record Research, 1986). It should be noted that the 5/29/54 issue of *Billboard* does not confirm that "Rock Around The Clock" made any of the *Billboard* charts on that date.

11 The official title of the song is "(We're Gonna) Rock Around The Clock." In the interest of brevity, the phrase "We're Gonna" in parenthesis has been dropped in the remainder of this Chapter.

according to the Haley biography co-written by his son, "[Haley was] a silent but controlling partner." Sonny Dae's real name was Paschal Vennitti, an Italian American from Philadelphia and a friend of Bill Haley's. *Billboard* reviewed Arcade 123 as an R&B record. Its March 20, 1954, review of the song was less than enthusiastic:

"Effort has an insistent beat as the group chants of an upcoming night of pleasure. Could attract some juke coin."

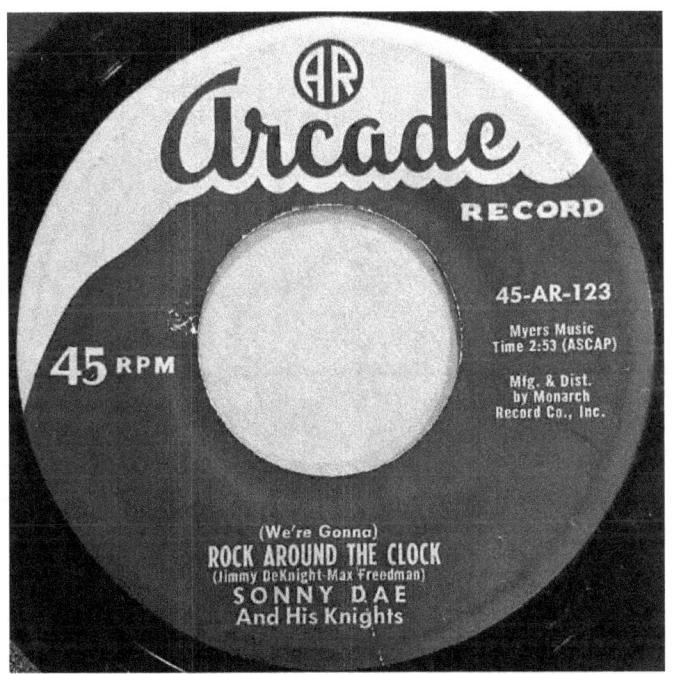

While interesting to listen to, it is nothing like Bill Haley's later version. In the first place, there is a 15-second instrumental interlude before the vocal begins. The vocal is up-tempo, but it is nothing that could be remotely called Rock 'n' Roll nor is there a memorable guitar break like Danny Cedrone's on Haley's later release. It's more in the vein of what you would expect to hear from Lawrence Welk's band trying to play a Rock 'n' Roll song.

Although he was not the first to record it, "Rock Around The Clock" was in Haley's repertoire no later than the summer of 1953, i.e., before Sonny Dae's version was released. Ralph Jones, a drummer in Haley's Comets, recalled that it was a big hit that summer in Wildwood, New Jersey. At that time, Haley was under contract to Essex Records, a Philadelphia label run by Dave Miller. Haley recorded a number of records for Essex between 1952 and 1954, including "Crazy Man Crazy" (Essex 327), the first Rock 'n' Roll record to crack the top 20 on *Billboard's* Honor Roll of Hits, and along the way, changed his group's name from the "Saddlemen" to the "Comets." Haley wanted to record the song, but Miller flatly refused. Various sources, including Bill Haley, agreed that there was bad blood between Miller and Myers, the latter being a co-penner of "Rock Around The Clock." Since Haley's contract at Essex was about to expire, Myers convinced Haley to let him contact Milt Gabler, the head of A&R at Decca, among others, in New York. Gabler, who had recorded greats like Louis Armstrong and Louis Jordan, jumped at the opportunity to sign Haley. And, as they say, the rest is history.

Haley's first Decca recording session, with Milt Gabler at the helm, was at New York City's famed Pythian Temple on April 12, 1954, just days after his Essex contract expired. As recounted by Marshall Lytle, who played bass on the record, the A-side was "Thirteen Women (and Only One Man in Town)," which was a cover of Dickie Thompson's earlier release on Herald 424. Out of their allotted three hours studio time, Lytle said that 2 ½ hours was devoted to the A-side, a song that Gabler is said to have had a financial interest. As for the remaining half-hour, Lytle recalled that Gabler "said we could do that 'rock' thing if we wanted." The take included an inspired guitar break by Danny Cedrone, which is essentially the same guitar break that he did on Haley's earlier "Rock The Joint" on Essex 303.[12] So, in the space of about 30 minutes, one of the greatest records in the history of Rock 'n' Roll was recorded. As Joey Ambrose, the man behind the tenor sax, later commented, "Fortunately, we'd rehearsed 'Rock Around The Clock' the night before at Bill's house."

The reviews for his first release on Decca were good but not outstanding:

BILL HALEY ORK
Thirteen Women .74
    DECCA 29124—Ops could make good use of a rhythm and blues-ish item about a guy in a town where he's the only man. The beat is strong and Haley sells the lyrics smartly. (Danby, BMI)
Rock Around the Clock....74
    Big beat and repetitious blues lyric makes this a good attempt at "cat music" and one which should grab coin in the right locations. (Myers, ASCAP)

Billboard, May 14, 1954

BILL HALEY & COMETS
(Decca 29124: 9-29124)
(B+) "THIRTEEN WOMEN" (2:50) [Danby BMI—Dickie Thompson] The "Crazy Man Crazy" boys team up on a socko rhythm jumper that's making big noise in the blues field. Bill and the Comets turn in a great reading. Could hit big!
(B) "ROCK AROUND THE CLOCK" (2:08) [Myers ASCAP—Knight, Freedman] The boys dish up another solid rhythm rocker that really hops. Terrific instrumental job that makes your feet fly.

Cash Box, May 15, 1954

And, as indicated in the above *Billboard* and *Cash Box* reviews, as well as on the *Cash Box* ad on May 14, 1954 (shown to the left), "Thirteen Women" was the designated A-side. But the Decca *Billboard* ad two weeks later on May 29, 1954, put "Rock Around The Clock" as the A-side:

BILL HALEY And His Comets

(WE'RE GONNA)

ROCK AROUND THE CLOCK

THIRTEEN WOMEN

29124

---

12 "Rock The Joint" is considered by many to be among the first rock and roll records. Tragically, Cedrone died from a fall in the summer of 1954 without knowing how his guitar work on "Rock Around The Clock" would influence countless thousands of future Rock 'n' Roll guitarists.

Although *Billboard*, on May 29, 1954, included "Rock Around The Clock" as one of the week's "best buys" and noted that the record was doing well in many markets, it only made the *Billboard* pop chart for one week in 1954. It reportedly only sold about 75,000 copies the first time around. In the meantime, Bill Haley's cover version of Big Joe Turner's "Shake, Rattle and Roll" became a major hit and, in the process, became the first Rock 'n' Roll record to dent the top 10 of *Billboard's* "Honor Roll of Hits." *See* Chapter 2 , which is devoted to "Shake, Rattle and Roll."

Interestingly, two other records with a song titled "Rock Around The Clock" had been released on major labels in the previous four years. The first was in 1950 by Hal "Cornbread" Singer on Mercury 8196 [Image: *Discogs*], with the vocal credited to Spo-Dee-Odee. The second was in 1952 by Wally Mercer on Dot 1099. While both songs are uptempo, neither are lyrically and melodically the same song.

Hal Singer on Mercury 8196 (1950)

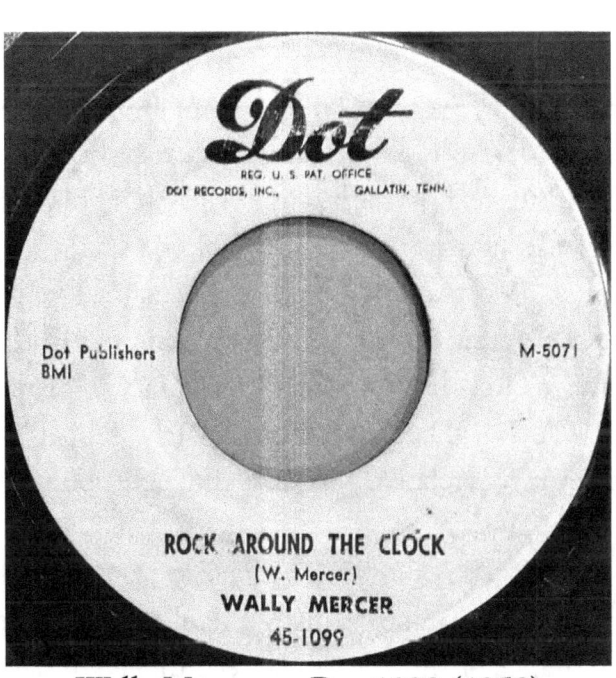

Wally Mercer on Dot 1099 (1952)

Blackboard Jungle to the Rescue

While apparently destined to a life of obscurity, "Rock Around The Clock" was given a second life when Richard Brooks decided to use it in *Blackboard Jungle,* a film he was directing starring Glenn Ford, Sidney Poitier, and Anne Francis.[13] Brooks had first heard the song being played loudly by Glenn Ford's son while on a visit to the Ford house. He liked it so much that he licensed it for use three times in the movie.

And use it he did, both loudly blaring over the opening scene showing teenage delinquents dancing in an inner-city schoolyard, and over the closing credits. The movie premiered in New York City on March 19, 1955, and nationwide one week later. It didn't take long for the predominantly

---

13 The film marked the acting debut of Jamie Farr who would later gain fame portraying Maxwell Q. Klinger in the TV sitcom *M*A*S*H*.

teenage record-buying public to buy it and play it on jukeboxes. It debuted again on the *Billboard* pop chart on May 14, 1955, and it hit #1 on July 9, where it stayed for eight weeks, becoming the first Rock 'n' Roll record to achieve that feat. It also made *Billboard's* R&B chart for 14 weeks, peaking at #3. The film and "Rock Around The Clock" played off each other and helped establish a teen identity. Or, as a writer for *The Wall Street Journal* observed in 2014, "the film forever fused rock 'n' roll with teenage rebellion."

Knocked from #1 on July 9, 1955, was Perez Prado's "Cherry Pink and Apple Blossom White" (RCA 47-5965). Symbolically, this changing of the guard was perfect. It demonstrated the sharp difference between the pop-dominated first half of the '50s (e.g., "Cherry Pink And Apple Blossom White") and the Rock 'n' Roll-dominated second half (e.g., "Rock Around The Clock").

"Rock Around The Clock" remained on the *Billboard* "Honor Roll of Hits" for 23 consecutive weeks. During its run, it helped ignite the Rock 'n' Roll revolution. As a result of Haley's string of Rock 'n' Roll hits—"Crazy Man Crazy," "Shake, Rattle and Roll" and, especially, "Rock Around The Clock"—Haley was appropriately dubbed the "King of Rock and Roll." His tenure as "King," however, was relatively brief, lasting only about a year until Elvis Presley arrived on the national scene in early 1956.

"Rock Around The Clock" once again entered the U.S. charts in 1974, some 20 years after its initial appearance. This is one of the longest periods of time between the first and the last chart appearance of the exact same recording![14] Its 1974 chart success was due to the convergence of two closely related events:

- The inclusion of "Rock Around The Clock" in *American Graffiti*, a highly successful film featuring a '50s soundtrack that was released in August 1973
- The blasting of "Rock Around The Clock" from a classic 1950s Seeburg jukebox over the opening credits for *Happy Days*, the very successful TV sitcom that debuted in 1974

---

14 Bing Crosby's perennial seasonal favorite, "White Christmas," takes top honors in this category. According to Joel Whitburn's research of the *Billboard* charts, Crosby's version of "White Christmas" first made the charts on October 3, 1942, and it last made the charts on December 29, 1962.

The Immense Impact of "Rock Around The Clock" in the UK

New Music Express, 2/1/1957

Upon hearing "Rock Around The Clock" in faraway Liverpool, Paul McCartney later recalled, "For the first time ever I got this electric tingle. That's for me." In his last interview, John Lennon told a *Playboy* writer that "Rock Around The Clock" inspired his pursuit of a musical career. While The Beatles never recorded "Rock Around The Clock," John Lennon did produce Harry Nilsson's 1974 LP, *Pussy Cats* (RCA CPL 1-0570), which included his take on "Rock Around The Clock." Keith Moon, Ringo Starr, and Jim Keltner were among the artists who played on this recording.

From where I sit on this side of the pond, Bill Haley and His Comets had a much bigger impact in England than they did in the States. Ian Whitcomb, the British recording artist and writer, observed:

For my money, the first rock 'n' record was "Rock Around The Clock" by Bill Haley and His Comets on the British Brunswick label in 1955. Millions of British would heartily agree with me.

And David Gilmore, guitarist and vocalist with Pink Floyd, told Matt Everitt of UK's BBC 6 Music:

The first record I bought and which turned me around a bit was "Rock Around The Clock" by Bill Haley, when I was ten. That was the first moment when I thought "this is something new and original."

While "Rock Around The Clock" only charted for one week when it was first released in the United States, it charted for two weeks in the UK, reaching #17 in January 1955, well before the opening of *Blackboard Jungle* in March of that year. "Rock Around The Clock" resonated longer in the British music conscience than it did in the United States. That can be measured in part by looking at the artists who have released covers of it that charted in the UK. Both Telex and the Sex Pistols released covers of "Rock Around The Clock" that charted in the UK.

Moreover, the chart life of "Rock Around The Clock" in the UK spanned a longer timeline than in the United States. It was on the UK charts between 1955 and 1957 for 36 weeks. Then, it was again on the UK charts in both 1968 (peaking at #20) and 1974 (peaking at #12), for another 21 weeks. And, in 1981, "Haley's Golden Medley," which included "Rock Around The Clock," made the UK charts for five weeks. In all, "Rock Around The Clock" appeared on the UK charts for 62 weeks, compared to only 39 weeks on the U.S. charts. Not surprisingly, "Rock Around The Clock" was the first record to sell over a million copies in the UK.

Also worthy of note is that an excerpt of "Rock Around The Clock" was included on Jive Bunny's 1989 "Swing The Mood," which spent five weeks at #1 on the UK charts during its 20-week stay.[15] Thus, in the UK, Bill Haley's monster hit, in one form or another, was on the charts in four different decades!!!

A further indication of Bill Haley's impact on the record-buying public in the UK is that while "Rock Around The Clock" topped the charts in both the U.S. and the UK, there were significant differences in the chart positions for the following 10 Bill Haley records in the U.S. and the UK:

Song Title	Top U.S. Chart Position	Top UK Chart Position
"Shake, Rattle and Roll"	7	4
"Mambo Rock"	18	14
"Razzle-Dazzle"	15	13
"Rock-A-Beatin' Boogie"	23	4
"The Saints Rock 'n' Roll"	18	5
"Rockin' Through The Rye"	78	3
"Rip It Up"	25	4
"Rudy's Rock"	34	26
"Rock The Joint"	Did not chart	20
"Don't Knock The Rock"	Did not chart	7

In total, Bill Haley had eight different top 10 songs in the UK versus only four in the U.S.

"Rock Around The Clock" — An Overall Assessment of Its Achievements

Despite the arrival of Elvis, Chuck Berry, Fats Domino, Jerry Lee Lewis, and Buddy Holly, among others, the impact that Bill Haley and "Rock Around The Clock" had was enormous worldwide. But unless you lived through this event firsthand, it is difficult to fully appreciate the tremendous impact it had on a whole generation of teenagers, an observation I have heard repeatedly over the years. All that those of us who did can try to do is pass along the sense—or in Paul McCartney's words the "electric tingle"—of what it was like back then and how it changed our lives forever. Along the way, "Rock Around The Clock" accomplished the following:

---

15 In the U.S., it also made the *Billboard* pop chart in 1989, peaking at #11.

- The first Rock 'n' Roll song to hit #1 on the *Billboard* "Honor Roll of Hits"
- The first Rock 'n' Roll song to be on the soundtrack of a movie (*Blackboard Jungle*), although no soundtrack album was ever issued
- The first record regardless of genre to sell one million records in the UK
- The first Rock 'n' Roll song to lend its name to a full-length movie (*Rock Around The Clock*), starring Bill Haley and Alan Freed, among others
- The largest-selling Rock 'n' Roll 45 rpm record of all time according to *Guinness World Records 2005*, with most accounts placing its worldwide sales at more than 25 million

Overall, the number of teenagers and beyond who got an "electric tingle" from this record must have been in the tens of millions. As John McDonough noted in a 2004 *Wall Street Journal* article, "Few pop recordings of the past century could be said to have had a more primal impact on the course of American music than 'Rock Around The Clock.'" Its impact beyond the U.S. was also immense, especially in the UK, Europe, and Australia.

CONTEMPORANEOUS COVER VERSIONS OF "ROCK AROUND THE CLOCK"

ARTIST	LABEL	YEAR	COMMENTS
MGM Studio Orchestra conducted by Charles Wolcott	MGM K12028	1955	"Recorded directly from the soundtrack of the M-G-M film, 'Blackboard Jungle'"; b/w "Love Theme From 'Blackboard Jungle'"; instrumentals
Sonny Dae and His Knights	Arcade 123	1954	Not a cover version since it was the original, but it was listed by *Billboard* as an available version when Haley's version made the *Billboard* "Honor Roll of Hits"

Soundtrack version of RATC

Love Theme From "Blackboard Jungle"

CONTEMPORANEOUS BUDGET LABEL COVERS OF "ROCK AROUND THE CLOCK"

ARTIST	LABEL(S)	COMMENTS
Gabe Drake	Prom 1118; Promenade NRR 1	B/w "Chee Chee-oo Chee" by Gabe Drake and Laura Leslie
The Four Bells	Bell 1098	Label notes that it is from the MGM picture "Blackboard Jungle"; b/w "Happy Holiday" by Jimmy Carroll and Orchestra
Fred Gibson	Tops R258-49; Tops RX-114; Gilmar RX-109; and Gilmar RX-114	Budget labels were notorious for issuing the same song on different company-owned labels, as well as issuing the same song on subsequent releases with a different lineup of songs, i.e., keeping some, adding some, and deleting some as the popularity of the songs increased or decreased

Artie Malvin	18 Top Hits 155; 18 Top Hits 160; Waldorf CA3; Waldorf Music Hall 181; and Rockin n' Roll T9A-X45	See the comments immediately above
Artie Malvin	Rock 'N Roll Jamboree 3	One of 12 shortened versions of 1950s songs
Dick Warren with The Glenn Horne Sextet	Gateway 1124	B/w "Learning the Blues"
None Listed	Variety 1812; and Variety EPV 6025	B/w "Blue Suede Shoes"/"Long Tall Sally"/"Ain't That A Shame"/"Hound Dog"/"See You Later, Alligator"
None Listed	Popular 8	B/w "Ain't That A Shame"/"Tina Marie"/ "The House Of Blue Lights"/"The Longest Walk"/"Want You To Be My Baby"

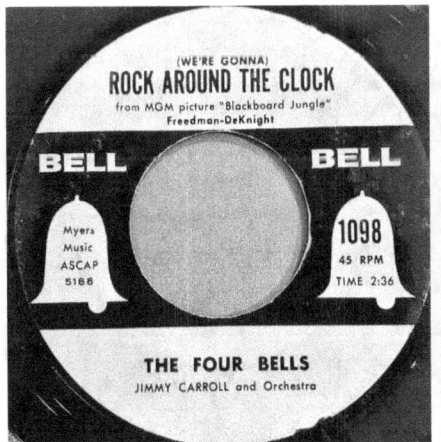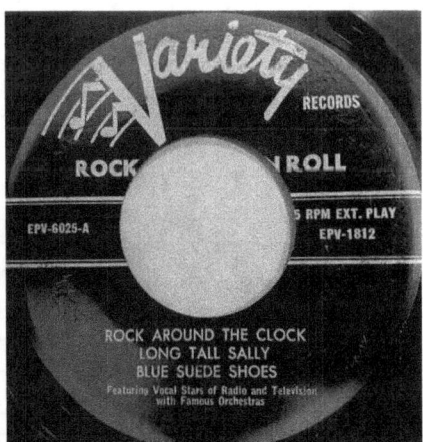

Budget label covers of "Rock Around The Clock" on Bell, Gateway, and Variety

LATER RELEASES OF "ROCK AROUND THE CLOCK" BY BILL HALEY

LABEL	YEAR	COMMENTS
Decca ED 2168	1954	EP with" Shake, Rattle and Roll"/"Thirteen Women"/"A.B.C. Boogie"
Festival SP45-679 (Australia)	1955	Released in July 1955; b/w "Thirteen Women"; made in Australia using the original Decca versions
Decca 45BM-05317 (UK Export Issue)	1955	B/w "Thirteen Women"; the Decca label was used for export to countries where the Brunswick name had already been taken
Brunswick OE 9250 (UK)	1956	EP with "Mambo Rock"/"R-O-C-K"/"See You Later, Alligator"
Brunswick OE 9431 (UK)	1958	EP with "Shake, Rattle & Roll" on one side and two songs by The Four Aces, "Stranger In Paradise" and "Three Coins In A Fountain," on the flip
Warner Bros. WB 133 (UK)	1964	Re-recorded, not the original Decca release; b/w "Love Letters In The Sand"
Warner Bros. WEP 6136	1964	EP with "Kansas City"/"Love Letters In The Sand"/"Shake, Rattle And Roll"; 1960 remakes
MCA MU 1013 (UK)	1968	B/w "Shake, Rattle and Roll"
Warner Brothers 7124	1968	B/w "Shake, Rattle And Roll"; 1960 remakes, not the Decca originals
Festival DK-2358 (Australia)	1968	B/w "Shake, Rattle And Roll"
Essex 102	Late 1960's?	An unauthorized, bootleg release, taken from the original Decca track; rumors that Haley recorded this as a demo while he was under contract at Essex have been debunked by various members of his Comets; b/w "Crazy Man Crazy"

Kama Sutra 508	1970	Taken from Kama Sutra LP *Bill Haley's Scrapbook*; b/w "Framed"; "live" versions of both songs
Kama Sutra 70X (Canada)	1970	"Golden Treasures" series; b/w "Shake, Rattle And Roll"; taken from Kama Sutra album *Bill Haley's Scrapbook*; "live" versions of both songs
Radio Active Gold RD-45	1970	B/w "Rock This Joint Tonight"; "live" recordings from his 1969 gig at NYC's Bitter End
MCA 60025	1973	B/w "Thirteen Women (And Only One Man In Town)"; both sides taken from the Decca masters
MCA 128 (UK)	1974	Three song 45 with "Shake, Rattle And Roll" and "Rip It Up" on the B-side; marketed as a single rather than an EP
Forever Oldies SWF-21089	c. mid-70s ???	"A product of Springboard International Records"; b/w "Shake, Rattle And Roll"; from the original Decca masters
Pushbike PBF 004 (UK)	1981	Single-sided flexi-disc advertising 7-Up
MCA 694 (UK)	1981	Titled "Haley's Golden Medley" with "Shake, Rattle And Roll," "Rock-A-Beatin' Boogie," "Choo Choo Ch' Boogie," and "See You Later, Alligator"; b/w "A.B.C. Boogie"
Old Gold OG 9220 (UK)	1982	B/w "Shake, Rattle and Roll"
Scoop 33 7SR (UK)	1983	33 1/3 7-inch EP with "Kansas City"/"Rip It Up"/"Me And Bobby McGee"/"Whole Lotta Shakin' Goin' On"/"Shake, Rattle And Roll"; taken from Haley's Sonnet recordings
Buddah BG 8	1984	B/w "Shake, Rattle And Roll"; Richard Nadler, Executive Producer; "live" versions
K-TEL 7913 (UK)	1981	EP titled "Class of '55" with "Tutti Frutti" by Little Richard," "Earth Angel" by The Crew Cuts," and "Blue Suede Shoes" by Carl Perkins

Maybelline 15 (E.E.U.)	1987	B/w "Rock"; 7" small hole 45; "Special Collectors 7"-PD Series"; limited edition picture disc
Collectables 90029	1990s?	From the Decca masters with spoken intro; mfg. by MCA Records; "Back to Back Hit Series"; b/w "Thirteen Women (And Only One Man In Town)"
Demon 45001/1 (UK)	2016	B/w "Shake, Rattle & Roll"; from the Decca originals

SUBSEQUENT COVER VERSIONS OF "ROCK AROUND THE CLOCK"

ARTIST	LABEL	YEAR	COMMENTS
D. Lynn Bingham	Hilltop HTS-136	1979	B/w "You Just Got The Loving Of Your Life"; Nashville, TN, label
The Bogmen	SRA BOG 1 (Ireland)	c. 1985	Incorrectly credited to Bee; medley with "The Twist"; b/w "Galway Bay"; Irish band known for terrible covers
Pat Boone	Dot RE-D 1132 (UK)	1958	EP with "Shot-Gun Boogie," "Please Send Me Someone To Love," and "Money Honey"
Fanny Boye	Gone 5095	1960	B/w "I Know That We're In Love"; both sides produced by Myers Music
The Willie Burgundy Five	MGM 14761	1974	B/w "Willie's Girl"
Freddie Cannon	We Make Rock 'N Roll Records 1601	1968	"Bubbled Under" at #121; b/w "Sock It To The Judge"
Chris & Gene	Scotty 651	1964	B/w "Lover Please"; from Wheeling, WV; manufactured by Gateway Recordings, Pittsburgh, PA

Sonny Dae and His Knights	Mayberry FIFE 001 (UK)	1980's??	Re-release of the original version on Arcade 123 that was released on March 20, 1954; b/w "Faithfully You" and "Raindrops" by Cadillac '59
The Deep River Boys	HMV POP.113 (UK)	1955	B/w "Adam Never Had No Mammy"; apparently never released as a 45 since the only confirmed release is as a 78
Jimmy DeKnight and His Knights of Rhythm	Peak 105	1959	AKA James E. Myers; BB review: "A solid, hard-hitting, rocking blues version of the old Bill Haley hit"; b/w "Rock Around The Clock Cha Cha"; Peak assigned the disc to ABC-Paramount shortly after its release on Peak; instrumentals.
Jimmy DeKnight and His Knights of Rhythm	Apt 25034	1959	AKA James E. Myers; b/w "Rock Around The Clock Cha Cha"; re-released on Apt after Peak assigned the disk to ABC-Paramount in early May 1959
Jimmy DeKnight and His Knights of Rhythm	President PT 476 (UK)	1979	AKA James E. Myers; b/w "Rock Around The Clock Cha Cha"; same recordings as the Peak and Apt releases; see above
The Evans Sisters	Black Gold BG-45-7461	1974	Minneapolis, MN, label; b/w "Mule Skinner Blues"; The Evans Sisters are from Manitoba, Canada
The Fabulous Mad Lads	Raynard 10020	1964	Fast garage version; b/w "Walkin' With My Angel," a Goffin-King composition; Milwaukee, WI, label

Marthe Fleurant	Vedettes 3070 (Canada)	1968	Partially sung in French; b/w "La Bolduc '68"
Phil Flowers	Kasey 706	1964	B/w "Razzle Dazzle" by Bill Haley, which is a re-recorded version
Gary's Gang	CBS 8267 (Mexico)	1979	B/w "The Little Rock Dancer From Dallas"; Bill Haley toured extensively in Mexico and issued numerous releases on the Mexican Orfeon label
Junie Lou	Country Star 1044	1982	Country version; b/w "Hand Him Down To Me"; Madison, TN, label
Mickey Katz	Capitol F3851	1957	Titled "K'nock Around The Clock," a novelty version as only Katz could do; lyrics were somewhat changed but still credited to Freedman/DeKnight; b/w "Kudnick, The Flying Schissel"
Mickey Katz	Capitol 4712	1962	Titled "Knock Around The Clock Twist," an updated novelty version to cash in on the "twist" craze; still credited to Freedman/DeKnight; b/w "Kudnick, The Flying Schissel"
Jonathan King	Decca 6103 047 (Holland)	1972	A slow and mellow version; b/w "Bubblerock Is Here To Stay"
Buddy Knox	Roulette EPR-1-301	1957	EP with "Party Doll"/"Rock Your Baby To Sleep"/"Hula Love"

The Mark Four	Mercury MF 815 (UK)	1964	Fast version, which has been referred to as "beat rock"; most members of the Mark Four later became The Creation; b/w "Slow Down"
Don May and The 4 Gigolos	Band Box 296	1962	Same song but titled "Twist Around The Clock" to cater to the "twist" craze; b/w "Don't Let The Sun Catch You Crying"
James E. Myers	Arzee 130	1979	AKA Jimmy DeKnight; b/w "Rock Around The Clock Cha Cha"; instrumentals
Rocking Ghosts	CBS 3322 (Denmark)	1968	Danish band; b/w "My Heart Still Sings"
Jack Scott	Underground 1022 (Canada)	c. 1979	"Recorded live April 3, 1979"; b/w "Hurt"
Seven well-known Australian rock artists	Festival SMX 46633 & SMX 46634	1977	Titled "21 Years Of Rock 'N' Roll"; limited edition Australian 45; b/w a spoken "Tribute To 'Rock Around The Clock'"
Sex Pistols	Virgin VS 290 (UK)	1979	Vocal by Ten Pole Tudor; b/w "The Great Rock 'n' Roll Swindle"; English punk band
Jumpin' Gene Simmons	Hi EP SBG 29	1964	EP with "Haunted House"/"Slippin' and Slidin'"/"Bony Moronie"
Telex	Sire 49170 (UK)	1979	An ultra-slow version by a Belgian synth-pop band; b/w "Moskow Diskow"
Ten Pole Tudor	Virgin VS 443 (UK)	1981	With the Sex Pistols; b/w "Who Killed Bambi"

Truth	Honest 001	c. mid-late 60s	Garage version from Detroit, MI; very rare; b/w "Being Bad"
Hedley Ward Trio	Melodisc 1344 (UK)	1955	B/w "Who Dat Up Dere"
Bert Weedon	Polydor 2058 832 (UK)	1977	Medley titled "Rocking Guitar," which also includes "Guitar Boogie Shuffle"/"What'd I Say"/"See You Later Alligator"/"Blue Suede Shoes"/"Shake, Rattle And Roll"; b/w "Bella Ciao"
Joey Welz	Palmer 5032	1970	Medley titled "The Mini Rock N' Revival," with "Rip It Up," "Rumble," and "Great Balls Of Fire"; co-produced by Ray Vernon, Link Wray's brother; b/w "A Rose And A Baby Ruth"
Joey Welz	Caprice 2344	1986	Lancaster, PA, label; Welz played keyboards for Bill Haley & the Comets from 1963 to 1966; b/w "Top Forty Radio (The History Of Rock)"
Joey Welz	Fraternity 3475	1982	B/w "Remember Rock And Roll"
Joey Welz	Trend 5393	c. 1995	40th anniversary collector's edition; b/w "Rock-A-Billy Son"

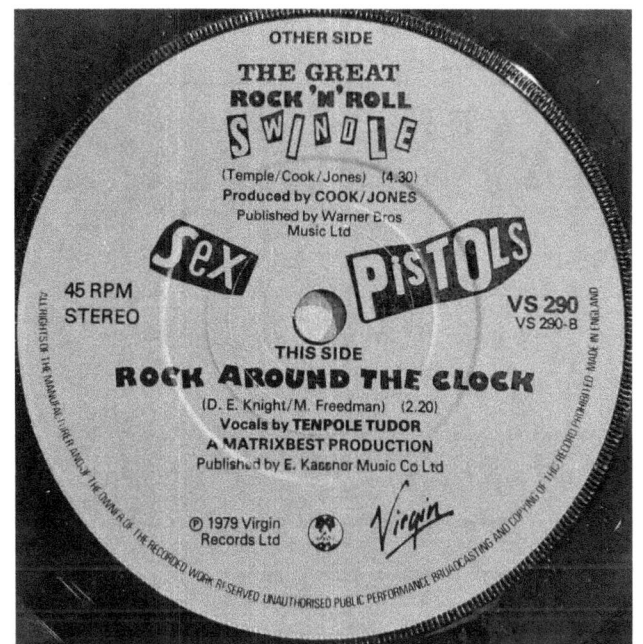

Sex Pistols 1979 cover (UK)

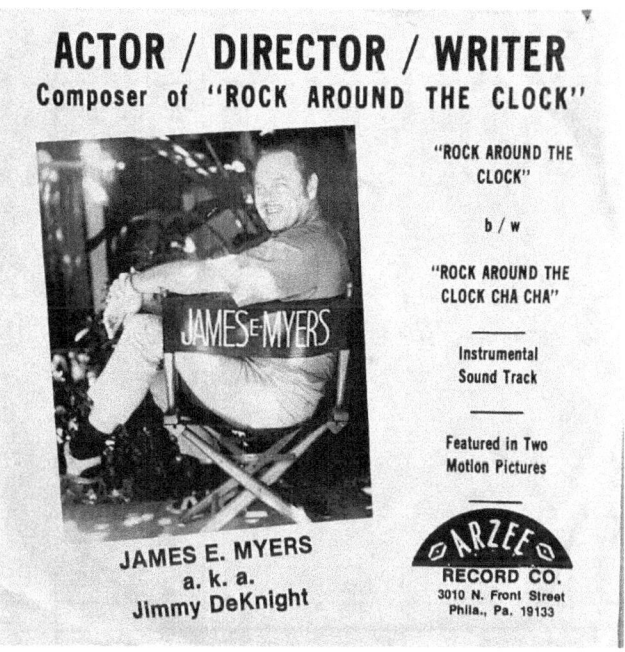

James E. Myers 1979 cover

"ROCK AROUND THE CLOCK" IN THE MOVIES

As already noted, the reason why "Rock Around The Clock" emerged from semi-obscurity in 1955 was its prominent placement in the movie "Blackboard Jungle." It was the first Rock 'n' Roll song used in a movie. Although there was no soundtrack album, MGM did release a 45 with an instrumental version of "Rock Around The Clock" backed with the "Love Theme from *Blackboard Jungle,*" both by the MGM Studio Orchestra conducted by Glen Wolcott (see photos above). In addition to *Blackboard Jungle*, "Rock Around The Clock" can be heard in the following movies:

MOVIE TITLE	YEAR	COMMENTS
Blackboard Jungle	1955	According to *IMDbPro*, *Blackboard Jungle* premiered in New York City on March 19, 1955, and was released to the rest of the nation on March 26, 1955.
Rock Around The Clock	1956	The first rock and roll song to lend its name to a full-length movie (*Rock Around The Clock*), starring Bill Haley and Alan Freed, among others; shown at Buckingham Place at the request of Queen Elizabeth, reportedly one of the first times this was done with a major motion picture
Rumble on the Docks	1956	Performed by Bill Haley and The Comets; released in December 1956 with James Darren in the lead role and included Freddie Bell and His Bellboys in the cast
Let the Good Times Roll	1973	Bill Haley and The Comets were recorded "live"; shot over three days at Richard Nader's Rock Revival concerts; released on May 25, 1973, in the U.S. and on August 2, 1973, in the U.K.
The London Rock and Roll Show (UK)	1973	Documentary film about the Rock 'n' Roll festival held in London's Wembley Stadium in August 1972; with Bill Haley, Chuck Berry, Little Richard, Jerry Lee Lewis, and Bo Diddley, among others
American Graffiti	1974	Haley's version used; produced by Francis Ford Coppola and directed by George Lucas; although the budget was only $777,000, it grossed over $115 million, making it one of the most profitable movies ever.
Superman	1978	Haley's version used; although used in the movie, it did not make the released soundtrack album for *Superman*; action/adventure pic

Blue Suede Shoes (UK)	1980	Documentary about the British Rock 'n' Roll revival in the late 1970's; performed by Bill Haley and the Comets; also includes performances by Eddie Cochran, Carl Perkins, Gene Vincent, and others
The Karate Kid, Part II	1986	The soundtrack version of "Rock Around The Clock" was performed by Paul Rogers; family/sport action film
Bull Durham	1988	Haley's version used; romantic baseball pic
Born on the Fourth of July	1989	Performed by Rodney Lay and Wild West; starring Tom Cruise and directed by Oliver Stone; biopic of a paralyzed Vietnam War vet who became an anti-war/pro human rights activist
Heavy Petting	1989	Performed by New Jersey Teenagers; documentary in which celebrities discuss their first sex experiences, some via archival footage
School Ties	1992	*IMDbPro* does not list who performed the song; star quarterback portrayed by Matt Damon gets opportunity to go to an elite prep school provided he hides that he is Jewish; other cast members included Ben Affleck, Brendan Fraser, and Chris O'Donnell
Rogue	2007	Performed by Bill Haley; action/drama/horror movie set in the Australian outback involving a man-eating crocodile
Finding Your Feet (UK)	2017	Performed by Bill Haley and His Comets; family comedy, drama
Cold War	2018	Performed by Bill Haley; romantic drama set against the cold war of the 1950s in Europe

1956 film "Rock Around The Clock"　　**1973 London Wembley concert film**

"ROCK AROUND THE CLOCK" ON TELEVISION

The most noteworthy use of "Rock Around The Clock" on television was its prime placement over the opening credits in the first two seasons of "Happy Days" blaring from a classic Seeburg 1950s jukebox. The version used on "Happy Days," however, was not the original Decca version, but rather a version that Bill Haley and His Comets specifically recorded for the show in 1973 because the producers did not want to pay Decca royalties for the use of the original version.

"Happy Days" debuted in January 1974, and it had a highly successful 10-year run. Interestingly, on the "Happy Days 30th Anniversary Show" that aired on February 3, 2005, "Rock Around The

Clock" was prominently heard, both in the replay of the jukebox scene used for the opening credits and during the cast's alumni softball game. Fifty years later and "Rock Around The Clock" was still primetime!

DOCUMENTED CONCERT PERFORMANCES OF "ROCK AROUND THE CLOCK"

As of May 1, 2024, *Setlist.fm* documented that "Rock Around The Clock" has been performed in concert 304 times by 84 different artists. In addition to Bill Haley, artists who have included "Rock Around The Clock" on their set lists on five or more occasions include The Replacements (14), Sha Na Na (12), Cliff Richard (10), NRBQ (7), and Tom Jones (5). Even Elvis sang "Rock Around The Clock" in concert twice, the first on September 22, 1955, at the Kingsport Auditorium in Kingsport, Tennessee, and the second on November 19, 1955, at the Gladewater High School Gymnasium, in Gladewater, Texas.

HONORS AND ACCOLADES FOR "ROCK AROUND THE CLOCK"

- Inducted into the Grammy Hall of Fame in 1982
- Selected in 2017 for inclusion on National Recording Registry of the Library of Congress by the National Recording Preservation Board, which annually selects songs that are "culturally, historically or aesthetically significant"
- Ranked #12 by the National Endowment for the Arts (NEA) and the Recording Industry Association of America (RIAA) on its list of the top 365 songs of the 20th century; it was the first Rock 'n' Roll song to be listed, unless you consider "You've Lost that Lovin' Feelin'" or "American Pie" to be Rock 'n' Roll songs
- Chosen by the Rock & Roll Hall of Fame as one of the "500 Songs That Shaped Rock and Roll," an unranked list that included songs from all eras
- Ranked #2 on Joel Whitburn's *Honor Roll of Hits*
- Ranked #159 on the *Rolling Stone*'s 2004 list of "The 500 Greatest Songs of All Time"
- Ranked #37 on the 2004 VH1 list of the "100 Greatest Rock Songs"
- Ranked #50 in the American Film Institute's "100 Years… 100 Songs" based on its appearance in *Blackboard Jungle*; the only other true Rock 'n' Roll songs to make the list were "Jailhouse Rock," "Born To Be Wild," and "Old Time Rock & Roll" (by Bob Seger, which was heard in the film *Risky Business*)
- Voted the #1 song of 1955 in poll conducted by *Cash Box*
- Ranked #46 on the BBC's list of the "100 Favourite Songs of the 20th Century"
- Selected by music preservationist Roger Lee Hall as one the "100 Essential Songs of the Twentieth Century"

ALSO WORTH NOTING . . .

- Chuck Berry in his autobiography said that "Rock Around The Clock" was his inspiration for "Reeling and Rocking."
- Subway's late 2017-early 2018 ad campaign for its Subway Reuben Sandwich used "Rock Around The Clock" as the soundtrack and included brief images of Haley/Comets and scenes from the 1950s.
- The Yardbirds said, "Over Under Sideways Down" came about "after we heard 'Rock Around The Clock' on the radio and somebody… probably Jeff, who loved that kind of music… suggested we give fifties rock 'n roll our own Yardbirds twist."
- Graham Nash still proudly carries a Bill Haley concert ticket stub in his wallet, about which he commented:

> I've still got the ticket stub in my wallet from when I went to see Bill Haley and the Comets play in Manchester in February 1957—my first-ever concert. Over the years I've lost houses… I've lost wives… but I've not lost that ticket stub. It's that important to me.

- Scotty Moore in his book, *That's Alright Elvis*, noted that "Bill Haley had a great jazz guitarist [Danny Cedrone] whose "solo on 'Rock Around The Clock' will stand forever. The only thing I came close to with that type of feel was the solo on 'King Creole.'"
- The lyrics to Elton John's "Crocodile Rock" from 1972 include the following:
  While the other kids were rocking 'round the clock
  We were hopping and bopping to the Crocodile Rock
- In his 2004 review of the re-release of the Decca album, *Rock Around The Clock*, music critic Seth Limmers commented, "If Bill Haley is gone, he is hardly forgotten. He is alive in every one of Clarence Clemons's solos, he breathes into every scale Brian Setzer fingers on his majestic Gretsch. By the way, I'd pay serious money to hear Setzer release a cover version of this entire album."
- The very first sentence of Bob Dylan's autobiography, *Chronicles, Volume One* (2004), reads as follows:
  LOU LEVY, top man of Leeds Music Publishing company, took me up by taxi to the Pythian Temple on West 70th Street to show me the pocket sized recording studio where Bill Haley and His Comets had recorded "Rock Around The Clock"…

■ In 1975 the Isley Brothers released an album entitled "Rock Around The Clock."

■ "Rock Around The Clock" has been sampled by more than a few rap artists, most notably by L.L. Cool J. on "Go Cut Creator Go" on Def Jam 38-07620 (1987).
■ In a July 27, 2016, article in *The New Yorker* titled "The Startling Blast of 'Rock Around the Clock,' Sixty Years Later," David Cantrell observed:

> It's a youthful grandfather to any number of rock party anthems: "Rock and Roll Music" [Chuck Berry], "Rock and Roll All Nite" [Kiss], "I Love Rock and Roll" [Joan Jett & The Blackhearts]. And when something of the early rebellious rock spirit is sought, it's Haley's record that people often reach for.

ADDITIONAL SOURCES

Dawson, Jim, *Rock Around the Clock: The Record That Started the Rock Revolution* (Backbeat Books, 2005)

Dylan, Bob, *Chronicles, Volume One* (Simon & Schuster, 2004)

Haley, John W. & John von Hoelle, *Sound and Glory* (Dyne-American, 1990)

Kochakian, Dan, Bob McGrath, Steve Gronda, and Chris Bentley, "The Wally Mercer Story," *Rhythm & Blues*, Vol. 371, August 2021 (UK)

Limmers, Seth, *PopMatters*, 05 Apr. 2004, https://www.popmatters.com/haleybill-rockaround-2495933450.html.

The Paul McCartney World Tour, at p. 36 (1989)

McDonough, John, "Bill Haley's Truly Golden Oldie," *The Wall Street Journal*, April 8, 2004

Swenson, John, *Bill Haley* (Star Books, 1982)

CHAPTER 4

"BO DIDDLEY"

BO DIDDLEY (APRIL 1955)

"BO DIDDLEY"—THE BASIC FACTS

Label: Checker 814 (both 45 and 78); Reo 8022X (Canada)

Writer: Bo Diddley (as E. McDaniels)[16]

Date recorded: March 2, 1955

Date released: April 1955

B side: "I'm A Man"

Producers: Leonard and Phil Chess, with assistance from Willie Dixon

Billboard chart:

R&B Chart

- Debut: 5/07/55
- Peak: #1 (2 weeks)
- Duration: 18 weeks

---

16 Although his name at birth was Otha Ellas Bates, he was raised by his mother's first cousin, Mrs. Gussie McDaniel. His name changed to Ellas McDaniel when he was six or seven years old, when Gussie McDaniel took legal custody of Ellas. On the labels of his records and the labels of the artists who covered songs he penned, his last name is listed either correctly as McDaniel or incorrectly as McDaniels.

THE SONG AND ITS IMPACT

Bo Diddley's eponymous song started life as "Uncle John," a risqué tune with strong sexual overtones. It and "I'm A Man" were among the four songs that Bo, at the urging of Billy Boy Arnold, recorded as a demo in February 1955. With the demo in hand, Bo and Billy Boy first went to United Records, where they rehearsed for several days. After United passed on their songs, Bo visited Vee Jay Records in the hopes of getting a recording contract, but Vee Jay turned him down.

Bo's next stop was Chess Records. Little Walter, who was behind the counter, told Bo that they didn't need anything at that time and perhaps he could return in a few weeks. Fortuitously, Phil Chess appeared and asked Bo what he had. After listening to the dub of "I'm A Man," he told Bo to come back the next day so his brother Leonard could weigh in on whether Chess might be interested in his songs. When Bo and his group returned, the Chess brothers were impressed, in part because Muddy Waters said he wanted to record "I'm A Man." As for "Uncle John," Leonard Chess said he couldn't record it because "the old folks ain't gonna dig it, and the dee jays ain't gonna play it." So he told Bo to go home and rewrite the lyrics. As Bo related to writer George R. Wright (italics in original)[17]:

> Man, it took me *all night* to figure out how to say: *"Bo-Didd'ly bought his babe a-di'mond-ring"*, because that's where it got *tricky*! At first, I was sayin': *"Bo Diddley, he bought his baby…."*, you know, an' that just didn't fit. Took *all damn night* before I stumbled upon it.

Bo's rewrite mimicked the rhythm of, as well as borrowing some lines from, "Hambone," a 1952 song by Red Saunders that was released on Coral 4-6862.[18] The following is a comparison of some of the lyrics from "Hambone" and "Bo Diddley":

"HAMBONE" LYRICS (1952)	"BO DIDDLEY" LYRICS (1955)
Papa's gonna buy me a mockingbird / And if that mockingbird don't sing / Papa's gonna buy me a diamond ring / And if that diamond ring don't shine / Papa's gonna take it to the five and dime / I just skinned an alley cat / To make my wife a Sunday hat / Took the hide right off a goat / To make my wife a Sunday coat	Bo Diddley bought his babe a diamond ring / If that diamond ring don't shine / He gonna take it to a private eye / If that private eye can't see / He'd better not take the ring from me / Bo Diddley caught a nanny goat / To make his pretty baby a Sunday coat / Bo Diddley caught a bear cat / To make his pretty baby a Sunday hat

17 In his 2021 book titled, *The Blues Dream of Billy Boy Arnold*, Arnold claimed that he wrote some of the verses "right there in rehearsal," including "Bo Diddley, Bo Diddley, have you heard, my baby is a bird." As the adage goes, "Success has many authors."

18 This record featured The Hambone Kids, one of whom was Delecta Clark. He later shortened his first name to Dee and became a successful singer in his own right, with such charted hits as "Hey Little Girl" and "Raindrops."

The lyrics to "Bo Diddley" also bear a strong resemblance to the traditional lullaby, "Hush, Little Baby," which the following side-by-side comparison shows:

"HUSH, LITTLE BABY" LYRICS (CIRCA EARLY 20TH CENTURY)	"BO DIDDLEY" LYRICS (1955)
Hush, little baby, don't say a word / Papa's gonna buy you a mockingbird / And if that mockingbird don't sing / Papa's gonna buy you a diamond ring / And if that diamond ring turns brass / Papa's gonna buy you a looking glass / Papa's gonna buy you a billy goat / And if that billy goat don't pull / Papa's gonna buy you a cart and bull / And if that cart and bull turn over / Papa's gonna buy you a dog named Rover	Bo Diddley bought his babe a diamond ring / If that diamond ring don't shine / He gonna take it to a private eye / If that private eye can't see / He'd better not take the ring from me / Bo Diddley caught a nanny goat / To make his pretty baby a Sunday coat / / Bo Diddley caught a bear cat / To make his pretty baby a Sunday hat

When questioned about the relationship between "Bo Diddley" and "Hambone," Diddley responded:

I guess I could have been influenced in some way, but I was playin' on street corners when Hambone came out, an' I was already doin' this: I was playin' this "Uncle John" beat around Chicago on street corners when Red Saunders made the record.

Chess initially intended to call Bo by his real name, Ellas McDaniel (born Otha Ellas Bates), but Billy Boy Arnold, a member of Bo's band,[19] suggested, "Why don't you call him Bo Diddley?" After being assured that Bo Diddley wasn't a discriminatory name, Leonard Chess agreed to call him Bo Diddley, and that is the name that Ellas McDaniel used for his entire recording and performing career.[20]

"Bo Diddley" was recorded on March 2, 1955, at the Universal Recording Studio in Chicago where the Chess brothers recorded most of their records. With Bo on rhythm guitar, Jerome Green on maracas, and Fred Kirkland on drums, the infused African rhythms that they produced soon became

19 While Billy Boy Arnold was a member of Bo's band before the release of "Bo Diddley," he did not play on the record, but it is believed he did play harmonica on the flip, "I'm A Man." Some sources, however, state that Lester Davenport played the harmonica on the flip. Subsequently, Billy Boy Arnold signed with Vee Jay Records, for whom he recorded several excellent Chicago blues songs.

20 The source of the name "Bo Diddley" has been variously attributed to, among others, a nickname Bo picked up in high school, the name of a comedian who was regularly on the bill at a local theatre where he occasionally performed, and the name given to a homemade one-string guitar popular in the Mississippi Delta and the Southside of Chicago, i.e., a "Diddley Bo."

known as the "Diddley Beat." Willie Dixon, who helped supervise the session, noted that "[t]he drums are speaking, and [Bo will] tell you what the drums are saying." Trying to determine the genre of "Bo Diddley" has eluded many critics over the years. Consider the following from *Rough Guide to the Blues*:

> Not exactly the blues, or even straight R&B—although it owed allegiance to both— this was a new kind of earthy, funky, jive-talking, guitar-based rock 'n' roll that was every bit as revolutionary as the sound being forged by his fellow Chess artist and rival Chuck Berry around the same time.

Even though it was Bo's first record, *Billboard* made it a "Review Spotlight" R&B pick on April 2, 1955, noting that it was "mainly instrumental, with really driving, down-to-earth rattling rhythm." The review also observed that the flip, "I'm A Man," had "a tremendous primitive beat." The following week, on April 9, 1955, *Cash Box* made "Bo Diddley" an "Award O' The Week," commenting that it had "an intriguing reading of a calypso flavored item and a sharp danceable beat."

Interestingly, Chess initially advertised "I'm A Man" as the A-side. It didn't take long, however, for Chess to recognize that "Bo Diddley" was the more popular side.

Cash Box, April 2, 1955

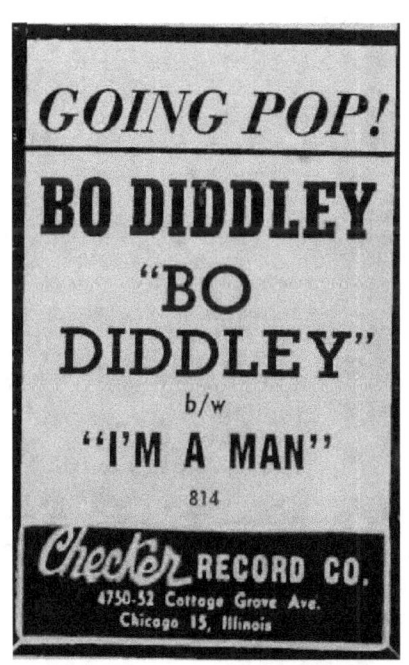

Cash Box, April 23, 1955

On May 7, 1955, "Bo Diddley" debuted on *Billboard's* R&B chart on its way to its two-week stint at #1 amidst its 18 weeks on the chart. It made its first appearance on the *Cash Box* "Rhythm and Blues Top 15" chart on May 14, 1955, rising to #2 during its 15 weeks on that list.

Given that "Bo Diddley" was definitely aimed at the R&B market, it is surprising that two major labels issued contemporaneous pop covers, the Harmonicats on Mercury 70629, and Joe Reisman and His Orchestra and Chorus on RCA 47-6121. Concerning Reisman's cover, one person on *YouTube* remarked, "One of the absolute worst pop covers of an 'R&B' classic, and that's saying a lot. Even Pat Boone never sounded this clueless!" As they say, "Stay in your lane."

Of more interest, however, is Jean Dinning's pop cover on Essex 395, the Philly label that Bill Haley and His Comets recorded for pre-Decca (e.g., "Crazy Man Crazy" and "Rock The Joint"). Essex sought the permission of Chess to use Bo's band for the cover. While Chess didn't allow Essex to use Diddley's band, it did accommodate Essex by arranging for a recording session in Chicago at which the backing for Dinning's vocal was provided by Willie Dixon on bass, Billy Boy Arnold on harmonica, Clifton James on drums, and two unknown artists on guitar and saxophone.[21] *Billboard's* April 30, 1955, review noted that it was "an exciting reading of the interesting ditty," on which "Dinning sings all out…, and is backed with an ingenious arrangement." Indeed!

Bo Diddley's signature song was not released in the UK until June 1956, and then only as one of four songs on an EP titled *Rhythm and Blues with Bo Diddley* on London REU-1054. But, like all but one of his other releases in the UK, it did not chart. Finally, the fiftieth anniversary re-release in 2005 of "Bo Diddley" backed with "I'm A Man" managed to crack the UK charts at #99.

A subsequent cover of "Bo Diddley" by Buddy Holly, however, did much better in the UK. Holly's cover, which had been recorded on his home tape recorder in 1956, was released in the U.S. on Coral 62352 in March 1963, and in the UK on Coral Q.72463 in June 1963. While it "Bubbled Under" at #116 in the U.S. , in the UK it peaked at #4 during its 12 weeks on the chart. Mention should also be made to Ronnie Hawkins' cover on Roulette 4483, which "Bubbled Under" at #117.[22]

Bo mined the popularity of "Bo Diddley" on more than a few subsequent releases, including the following:

- "Diddley Daddy" on Checker 819 (1955)
- "Diddy Wah Diddy" on Checker 832 (1956)
- "Hey, Bo Diddley" on Checker 860 (1957)
- "Monkey Diddle" on Checker 1058 (1963)
- "The Story of Bo Diddley" on NEP-44019 (1964, UK)
- "Bo Diddley 1969" on Checker 1213 (1969) (not the same song)
- "Bo Diddley-Itis" on Chess 2129 (1972)

Only "Diddley Daddy" charted, making *Billboard's* R&B chart for four weeks.

While it is clear that the "Bo Diddley Beat," which is sometimes called a "shave-and-a-haircut-two-bits," did not originate entirely with Bo,[23] he unquestionably put his indelible imprimatur on

---

21 This wasn't entirely gratuitous on the part of Chess Records as Chess owned the publishing rights for "Bo Diddley" and thus would get royalties from the sales of Dinning's cover.

22 Jimmie Rodgers, a pop singer with 1950s top 10 hits like "Honeycomb" and "Kisses Sweeter Than Wine," released a song titled "Bo Diddley" on Roulette EPR-1-315 (1958), but it is not the same song.

23 Jim Allen in his internet article, "Tracing the Bo Diddley Beat," noted, "Hambone, also known as the juba dance,"

it. The "Bo Diddley Beat" can be heard on countless 45s released over the years. The most famous is "Not Fade Away" by Buddy Holly and The Crickets. *See* Chapter 15. Among the other prominent examples are:

- "Chicken In Basket" by Billy Bland on Old Town 1016 (1955)
- "Willie And The Hand Jive" by Johnny Otis on Capitol F3966 (1958), covered by Eric Clapton on RSO 503 (1973)
- "Cannonball" by Duane Eddy on Jamie 1111 (1958)
- "Jungle Hop" by Kip Tyler on Challenge 59008 (1958)
- "Hey Little Girl" by Dee Clark on Abner 1029 (1959)
- "Clara" by Ronnie Hawkins on Roulette 4228 (1960)
- "Buzz Buzz A-Diddle-It" by Freddy Cannon on Swan S-4071 (1961)
- "Bo-Da-Ley Didd-Ley" by Little Willie John on King 5571 (1962) (instrumental)
- "A-B-C 1-2-3" by the Tokens on RCA 47-8210 (1963)
- "Mickey's Monkey" by The Miracles on Tamla 54083 (1963)
- "Mockingbird" by Inez and Charlie Foxx on Symbol 919 (1963)
- "Mystic Eyes" by Them on Parrot 45-9796 (1965)
- "Magic Bus" by The Who on Decca 32362 and in the UK on Track 602024 (1968)
- "1969" by The Stooges on Elektra 45664 (1969)
- "Panic In Detroit" by David Bowie on RCA PB-10105 and on RCA 2466 in the UK (1976)
- "I Want Candy" by the Strange Loves (AKA Strangeloves) on Bang B-501 (1965), covered by Bow Wow Wow on RCA JH-13204 and in the UK on RCA 238 (1982)
- "How Soon Is Now?" by The Smiths on Sire 7-29007 (1985)
- "Faith" by George Michael on Columbia 38-07623 (1987)
- "Desire" by U2 on Island 7-99250 (1988)
- "Water Fountain" by The Tune-Yards on 4AD 3421 (UK, 2014)

Since a musical beat cannot be copyrighted, Bo never was able to monetize his signature beat, one that has been copied by multiple artists over the years as noted immediately above. As author Lee Cotton observed, "Eric Burdon and the Animals, The Beatles, Buddy Holly, Elvis Presley, the Yardbirds (especially guitarists Jimmy Page and Eric Clapton), and The Rolling Stones all bear testimony to the powerful influence of Bo Diddley."

---

derived from the rhythm African Americans brought "from their homeland to the plantations of the American South. It came from the Yoruba people of West Africa, but the Yoruba diaspora had long since extended to Cuba as well, where the beat evolved into the rhumba clave crucial to Afro-Cuban music," sometimes also referred to as 3-over-2 clave rhythm. Allen further observed: "In place of the drums, the transplanted Africans developed a series of dances based around slapping their hands against each other and against other body parts. In a development not dissimilar to the way capoeira came about in Brazil, the practice of 'pattin' Juba' was born."

Moreover, the following 45s use "Bo Diddley" in the song's title:

- "The New Bo Diddley" by Johnny Otis on Eldo 106 (1960) (same song)
- "I Ain't Bo Diddley" by Mickey Gilley on San 1513 (1963)
- "Bo Diddley Bach" by Sonny Curtis on Liberty 55710 (1964), which was later covered by the Kingsmen on Wand 1164 (1967)
- "Bo Diddley Goes East" by King Kurt on Stiff BUY 206 (1984, UK)
- "Bo Diddley is Jesus" by The Jesus and Mary Chain on blanco y negro SAM 360 (1987)

Also worth noting is Seasick Steve's 2010 RSD record on Atlantic Ryko 8606 (UK) titled "Diddley Bo," which is sung to a strong Bo Diddley beat.

"I'm A Man," the B-side, charted for 11 weeks. Other artists who have covered "I'm A Man" include the Yardbirds on Epic 5-9857, which rose to #17 on the *Billboard* pop chart in 1965. Five years later, it was covered by the Yellow Payges on Uni 5522, which "Bubbled Under" for three weeks, and by Dr. Feelgood on UA UP 35857 (UK). Etta James also recorded an answer record—"W-O-M-A-N"—on Modern 972 (1955).

Muddy Waters' "Manish Boy," on Chess 1602, is both an arrangement of, and an answer to, Bo's "I'm A Man," with writing credits given to Bo, Muddy, and Mel London.[24] It rose to #5 on *Billboard's* R&B chart. Muddy's answer adopts Bo's beat, but, unlike Bo, in the words of rock critic Dave Marsh, Muddy "isn't kidding around; he *is* a man and his sexual boasts and demands aren't fantasies, they're real."

Caveat emptor. The Spencer Davis Group released a record in 1967 titled "I'm A Man" on UA 50144 and in the UK on Fontana TF 785, but it is a song penned by Steve Winwood and Jimmy Miller.[25] It, in turn, was later covered by Chicago in 1969 in the UK on CBS 4715 and two years later in the U.S. on Columbia 4-45467. Wynder K. Frog also released a cover of the Winwood/Miller penned "I'm A Man" on UA 50320 and in the UK on Island WIP-6014 (1968). And, Doc Pomus and Mort Shulman penned "I'm A Man" for Fabian that was issued on Chancellor C-1029 (1958) and in the UK on HMV POP 587 (1959). Yet another different "I'm a Man" was released in 1966 by Joe Tex on Dial 4028 and in the UK on Atlantic 584016.

---

24 Mel London was a Chicago songwriter, producer, and the owner of several record labels, including Age, Chief, and Profile.

25 Other than the shared title, it bears no resemblance either lyrically or rhythmically to the song that Bo Diddley penned and recorded.

CONTEMPORANEOUS COVER VERSIONS OF "BO DIDDLEY"

ARTIST	LABEL	COMMENTS
Jean Dinning	Essex 395	B/w "Baby, We're Through"; Dinning is the younger sister of Mark Dinning of "Teen Angel" fame, a song that she co-penned.
Bonnemere and His Piano	Royal Roost 608	Instrumental; b/w "The Man In The Raincoat"; Bonnemere was a jazz pianist
Reisman, Joe	RCA 47-6121	B/w "Bubble Boogie"
Jerry Murad's Harmonicats	Mercury 70629	B/w "Southern Cross"; both sides are instrumentals

Harmonicats on Mercury 70620

Jean Dinning on Essex 395

CONTEMPORANEOUS BUDGET LABEL COVERS OF "BO DIDDLEY"

A thorough review of releases on budget labels in 1955 turned up nary one budget label cover of "Bo Diddley." From checking a large cross section of releases on more than a dozen budget labels between 1955 and 1959, the number of R&B songs that were released on budget labels were few and far between, and virtually all that did were songs that crossed over to the pop market, such as "Ain't That A Shame," "Johnny B. Goode," and "Kansas City."

LATER RELEASES OF "BO DIDDLEY" BY BO DIDDLEY

LABEL	YEAR	COMMENTS
London RE-U 1054 (UK)	1956	EP with "I'm A Man"/"Pretty Thing"/"Bring It Home Jerome"
Chess 5125	1958	EP with "I'm A Man"/"Billie And Lillie"/"Bo Meets The Monster"
Checker 997	1961	B/w "I'm A Man"
Pye Int'l 7N 25210 (UK)	1963	B/w "Detour"
Eric 239	1979	B/w "Susie-Q" by Dale Hawkins
Chess CHES 4001 (UK)	1980	Chess "Mini Masters" EP with "Pretty Thing"/"Say Man"/"Road Runner"
Checker CCKGT 315X (Canada)	1981	B/w "I'm A Man"; "Golden Treasures" series
Chess CH-104	1982	B/w "I'm A Man"
Chess CH-91003	1984	B/w "I'm A Man"
Chess CH-9031	c. 1980s	B/w "I'm A Man"; Chess "Blue Chip Series"
Collectables 3455	c. 1984	B/w "I'm Sorry"; "Back to Back Hit Series"
Old Gold OG 7704 (UK)	1990	EP with "Pretty Thing"/"You Can't Judge A Book By Its Cover"/"Road Runner"
Chess 9830034 (UK)	2005	B/w "I'm A Man"; "50th anniversary limited edition single"
Sleazy SR-163 (Spain)	2019	Alternate take recorded on March 2, 1955, the same date as the original; b/w "Little Girl"

1967 re-release on Checker 997

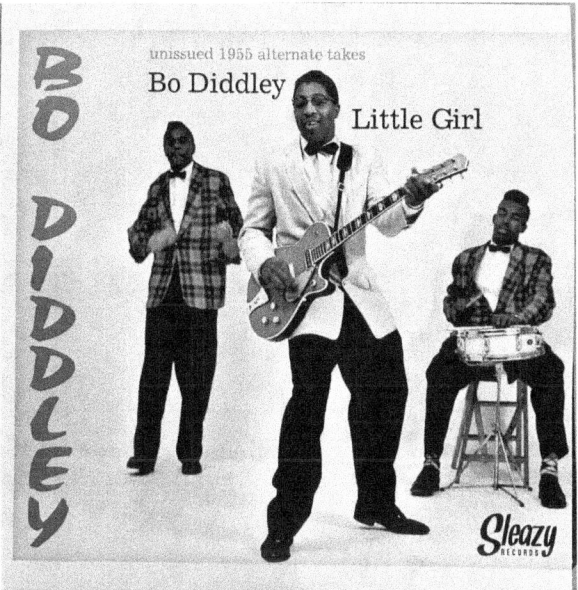

2019 release on Sleazy SR-193

SUBSEQUENT COVER VERSIONS OF "BO DIDDLEY"

ARTIST	LABEL	YEAR	COMMENTS
American Way	Sound 277	1960s	Garage version; b/w "Just One More Time With Me"; Detroit, MI, label
Bad Bascomb	Paramount 0209	1973	The promo release has both mono and stereo versions; b/w "Give The Bass A Taste"
Les Carle	Embassy WB-572 (UK)	1963	B/w "Nature's Time For Love"
Carroll Brothers	Cameo C-213	1962	B/w "Slippin' An Slidin'"; on some records the B-side is "Don't Knock The Twist"
The Cavemen	Capitol Star Artist matrix nos. 18285/18286	1966	Garage version; Rochester, NY, label with address; b/w "All About Love"; Rite pressing

Classics	Ram 66037	1966	EP with "Mean Woman"/"I Don't Want To Be Around"/"Pink Cats"; Chatham, NY, group
Count Drac (AKA Bobby Saver)	Arzee 501	1965	B/w "The Trance," a Philly garage song; "A Rex Zario Production"
Jerry Dee and The Intruders	Sara 6352	1963	B/w "Sugar Corsage"; Sauk City, WI, label; RCA pressing
Early Dawn	Club 200	1974	B/w "Sittin' and Thinkin'"
Jimmy Elledge	RCA 47-8042	1962	Surprisingly good; b/w "Diamonds"; produced by Chet Atkins
Jimmy Elledge	RCA RCX 7132 (UK)	1963	EP with "Funny How Time Slips Away"/"Penny's Worth Of Happiness"/"I Miss You Already"
Ronnie Hawkins	Roulette 4483	1963	"Bubbled Under" at #117; b/w "Who Do You Love," another cover of a Bo Diddley song; produced by Henry Glover
Ronnie Hawkins	Columbia DB 7036 (UK)	1963	B/w "Who Do You Love"
Ronnie Hawkins With The Band	Roulette RO 512 (UK)	1970	B/w "Who Do You Love"
Ronnie Hawkins	Monument ZS7 8573	1973	B/w "Lonely Hours"
Ronnie Hawkins	Monument ZS7 8573	1973	Mono long version; b/w "Bo Diddley" (stereo long version); promo only
Buddy Holly	Coral 62352	1963	"Bubbled Under" at #116; b/w "True Love Ways"
Buddy Holly	Coral EC 81193	1963	EP with "Brown Eyed Handsome Man"/"True Love Ways"/"Wishing"

Buddy Holly	Coral Q.72463 (UK)	1963	B/w "It's Not My Fault"
Buddy Holly	Coral FEP 2065 (UK)	1964	EP with "Umm, Oh Yeah"/"Brown-Eyed Handsome Man"/"Slippin' and Slidin'"
Buddy Holly	MCA BH-10 (UK)	1983	B/w "Brown-Eyed Handsome Man"
Buddy Holly	Old Gold OG 7701 (UK)	1990	EP with "Brown-Eyed Handsome Man"/"Reminiscing"/"Wishing"
The Ivymen	Twin Town TT 720	1966	B/w "La-Do-Dada," a cover of Dale Hawkins' song; Minneapolis, MN, label
Janis Joplin and The Kozmik Blues Band	Columbia 88697 97969 7-3	2011	Part of an RSD boxset of four previously unreleased singles
The Juveniles	Jerden 770	1965	Garage version; b/w "Yes I Believe"
The Juveniles	Pye Int'l 7N 25349 (UK)	1966	Garage version; b/w "Yes I Believe"
Mighty Manfred & The Wonderdogs	Paris Tower 140	c. 1960s	The promo release has both mono and stereo versions of "Bo Diddley"; b/w "By The Time I Get To Phoenix"
Stu Mitchell	Capitol 72361 (Canada)	1966	B/w "What Am I"; Norman Petty produced both sides; not released in the U.S. ; collectable garage record
Jim Mundy	Hickory K-1621	1972	B/w "I Wish I Hadn't Brought My Face Home Last Night"
Mystery Train	Mystery Train 7121-31	1977	B/w "That's Allright [sic] Mama"; Livonia, MI, label

Art Neville	Sansu 481	1968	B/w "Bo Diddley, Part 2"; arranged by Allen Toussaint; two different takes of the same song
New York City Band	American International 4101	1979	B/w "Sometimes"; promo release has both mono and stereo versions
Johnny Otis	Eldo 106	1960	Same song, but titled "The New Bo Diddley"; b/w "The Jelly Roll"
Raw Pony	Heel Turn 003	2015	B/w "Shattered"
Emil Richards & The Factory	Uni 55027	1967	Group later became Little Feat; b/w "No Place I'd Rather Be," with vocal by Lowell George
Billy Lee Riley	Mercury 72314	1964	Instrumental version; b/w "Memphis," likewise an instrumental
The Rovin' Flames	Tampa Bay 1111	1966	B/w "Seven Million People"; Tampa, FL, label; rare garage record
The Royal Guardsmen	Festival FX-11,260 (Australia)	1967	EP with "The Return Of The Red Baron"/"Road Runner"/ "Sweetmeats Slide"
Bob Seger	Reprise REP 1117	1972	Titled "Who Do You Love (Bo Diddley)," a medley of both songs; b/w "Turn On Your Love Light"
Tony Steven	Cannon EP 013; also on Crossbow XB-305 (both UK)	1963	Budget label EP with "If You Gotta Make A Fool Of Somebody"/"It's My Party"/"Falling"/"Atlantis"/"I like It"
J.M. Van Eaton and "The Untouchables"	Nita 127	1960	Rockabilly version; b/w "Midnite Blues"; Memphis label; Van Eaton was a Sun label session drummer

Bobby Vee and The Crickets	Liberty LEP 2116 (UK)	1963	EP with "Peggy Sue"/"Someday"/"I Gotta Know"
Link Wray	Norton 801	1995	B/w "Jack The Ripper"; produced by Ray Vernon
None listed	Hit Parade 6011 (UK)	1963	EP with five other songs
None listed	Top 6 T6504 (UK)	1963	EP with five other songs

1963 Buddy Holly cover

1966 Rovin' Flames garage cover

"BO DIDDLEY" IN THE MOVIES

"Bo Diddley" made it onto the soundtracks of several movies, including the following:

MOVIE TITLE	YEAR	COMMENTS
John Lennon and the Plastic Ono Band: Sweet Toronto	1971	Performed by Bo Diddley; D. A. Pennebaker produced documentary about the 1969 Toronto Rock and Roll Revival 1969 concert the featured John Lennon and included performances by Little Richard, Jerry Lee Lewis, and Chuck Berry; the opening prologue included the comment, "John could at last introduce Yoko to the heroes of his childhood"
Fritz the Cat	1972	Performed by both Bo Diddley and Billy Boy Arnold; animated satiric comedy about the 1960s; Robert Crumb created Fritz the Cat; Crumb is famous for his blues album covers
Stealing Home	1988	Performed by Bo Diddley; romantic drama starring Mark Harmon and Jodie Foster
Short Circuit 2	1988	Performed by Bo Diddley; family comedy and drama
Who Shot Pat?	1989	Performed by Bo Diddley; nostalgic drama set in the mid-1950's in Brooklyn, NY, starring Sandra Bullock
Flight of the Intruder	1991	Performed by Bo Diddley; military action drama
The Life and Times of Guy Terrifico (Canada)	2005	Performed by Ronnie Hawkins; faux comedy documentary about the rise and fall of a country singer with Kris Kristofferson, Merle Haggard, Ronnie Hawkins, among others
Hollywoodland	2006	Performed by Bo Diddley; crime drama with Ben Affleck
The Roaring 20's: Mick Jagger's Glory Years (UK)	2011	Performed by Buddy Holly and The Crickets; documentary explores Jagger's musical influences
Not Fade Away	2012	Performed by both Bo Diddley and Jack Huston; friends form a rock band hoping to score big; Steven Van Zandt was the film's musical director

DOCUMENTED CONCERT PERFORMANCES OF "BO DIDDLEY"

As of May 1, 2024, *Setlist.fm* documented that "Bo Diddley" has been performed in concert 169 times by 51 different artists. In addition to Bo Diddley (56), artists who have included it on their set lists on more than five occasions include Kenny Rodgers (13), Bob Seger (12), The Rolling Stones (6), and Little Richard (6).

HONORS AND ACCOLADES FOR "BO DIDDLEY"

- Inducted into the Grammy of Fame in 1998
- Both "Bo Diddley" and "I'm A Man" were selected in 2011 to be permanently included in the Library of Congress' National Recording Registry by the National Recording Preservation Board, which annually selects songs that are "culturally, historically, or aesthetically significant"
- Ranked #155 on the National Endowment for the Arts (NEA) and the Recording Industry Association of America (RIAA) on its list of the top 365 songs of the 20th century
- Chosen by the Rock & Roll Hall of Fame as one of the "500 Songs That Shaped Rock and Roll," an unranked list of songs from all eras
- Ranked #62 on the 2004 *Rolling Stone* list of the "500 Greatest Songs of All Time"; the flip, "I'm A Man," ranked 378 on the same list
- Ranked #2 on Joel Whitburn's list of "Non-Pop or R&B Chart Honorees"
- Inducted into the Blues Hall of Fame in 2017, and in 2022 Bo's self-titled 1958 Chess LP "Bo Diddley" was likewise inducted into the Blues Hall of Fame as the album of the year

ALSO WORTH NOTING . . .

- Bo Diddley appeared on the Ed Sullivan TV show on November 20, 1955, where he reprised "Bo Diddley," much to the chagrin of Sullivan who had requested that he play "16 Tons." Sullivan never invited him to appear again.
- Bo Diddley performed "Bo Diddley" with Eric Clapton and Robbie Robertson at the Rock & Roll Hall of Fame's 20th annual induction ceremony on March 14, 2005.
- In their cover of Bo Diddley's "Pretty Thing," the Pretty Things acknowledged their debt to Bo with the following lines:
    We thank you Bo
    For the name
    We thank you all
- One week after his death on June 2, 2008, the United States House of Representatives adopted without objection a resolution, H. Res. 1251, honoring Bo Diddley's life, which included the statement that "Bo Diddley reshaped the sound of popular music, recording such tracks as "Bo Diddley" and "I'm A Man," both becoming number 1 hits," and also noting that his "music continues to influence generations of musicians."

ADDITIONAL SOURCES

Allen, Jim, "Tracing the Bo Diddley Beat," https://www.udiscovermusic.com/stories/bo-diddley-beat-feature (retrieved February 1, 2022)

Arnold, Billy Boy with Kim Field, *The Blues Dreams of Billy Boy Arnold* (The University of Chicago Press, 2021)

Ratliff, Ben, Obituary, *"Bo Diddley, Who Gave Rock His Beat, Dies at 79," New York Times (June 3, 2008)*

White, George, *Bo Diddley: Living Legend* (Castle Communications PLC, 1995)

Williamson, Nigel, *Rough Guide to the Blues* (Rough Guides, 2007)

CHAPTER 5

"AIN'T IT A SHAME" AKA "AIN'T THAT A SHAME"

FATS DOMINO (APRIL 1955)

Original first press 78 red script label

Original first press 45 red script label

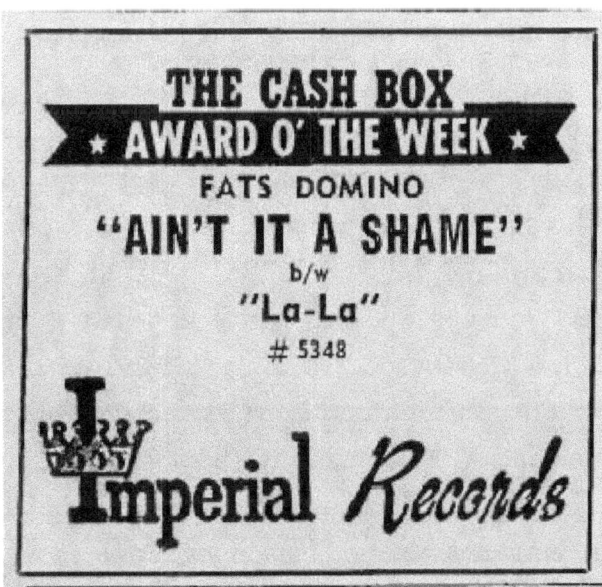

FATS DOMINO
    Ain't It a Shame (Commodore, BMI)
    La-La (Commodore, BMI) — Imperial 5348 — The great
blues singer socks over two showmanly sides with a
personable rendition of the blues rocker "Ain't It a
Shame," and an amusing interpretation of the novelty
"La-La." Both sides are wrapped up in Domino's inimitable style and a pounding ork beat.

Billboard Spotlight review, April 23,
1955

"AIN'T IT A SHAME" — THE BASIC FACTS

Label: Imperial X5348 (45) and Imperial 5348 (78)

Writers: Antoine "Fats" Domino and Dave Bartholomew

Date recorded: March 15, 1955

Date released: April 14, 1955

B-Side: "La-La"

Producer: Dave Bartholomew

Billboard charts:_

  <u>R&B Chart</u>

  - ■ Debut: 5/14/55
  - ■ Peak: #1 (11 weeks)
  - ■ Duration: 26 weeks

  <u>Pop Chart</u>

  - ■ Debut: 7/16/55
  - ■ Peak: #10
  - ■ Duration: 13 weeks

THE SONG AND ITS IMPACT

"Ain't That A Shame" is a relatively common phrase that has been used as the title of a song as early as 1900 when Dan Quinn recorded "Ain't That A Shame" or "Ain't Dat A Shame" on Victor 923, as well as on Monarch 923. Quinn was one of the first popular American recording artists who recorded such well-known songs as "A Hot Time in the Old Town," "Bill Bailey Won't You Please Come Home," and "The Beer That Made Milwaukee Famous." Parenthetically, the latter song is not an earlier version of the Jerry Lee Lewis 1969 top ten country song, "What Made Milwaukee Famous (Has Made A Loser Out Of Me)," although both songs are about beer.

Fats Domino's original version of "Ain't That a Shame" was penned by Fats and Dave Bartholomew, his longtime composing partner. It was recorded in Hollywood on March 15, 1955, when Fats was on tour in Los Angeles, and it was his first hit that was not recorded at Cosimo Matassa's New Orleans studio. Like nearly all Domino recordings, Imperial Records tweaked the song a bit before issuing the record. The sound was compressed to make it punchier and speeded up slightly to make Fats seem more youthful and less bluesy. Cosimo Matassa speculated that the intent behind speeding up the songs recorded by Fats was to make it more difficult for other artists to copy. Concern about the issuance of cover versions was legitimate in the 1950s, as many R&B songs were being covered by white artists whose versions were often deemed more palatable to the mainstream public.

As originally released on Imperial, the title was "Ain't It A Shame." Pat Boone's cover changed it to "Ain't That A Shame," and that's how virtually all versions since then have been titled, including most later reissues of Fats' original version. In the song itself, Fats sang "Ain't that a shame" rather than

"Ain't it a shame."[26] And, the title submitted to the Library of Congress and published in its *Catalog of Copyright Entries* was "Ain't That A Shame!":

> BARTHOLOMEW, DAVE.
> Ain't that a shame! Words and music by
> Antoine Domino and Dave Bartholomew.
> 50¢   © Commodore Music Corp., Holly-
> wood; 23Jun55; EP90764.

On April 23, 1955, *Billboard* placed a "Review Spotlight" on the release, noting that "both sides are wrapped up in Domino's inimitable style and pounding ork beat." A week later, *Billboard* commented that "first week reports on this Domino release indicate that it is a powerhouse" and that "Ain't It a Shame" is the more popular of the two sides at this stage, tho the action is good on both." For its part, on April 30, 1955, *Cash Box* gushed that "it has all the earmarks of a hit," noting further that "Fats rocks along in lilting style as the supporting band sets a strong beat to accompany the top-flight blues artist." "Ain't That A Shame" entered the *Billboard* R&B chart on May 14, 1955, and spent a half year there, including 11 weeks at #1. It also crossed over to the pop chart on July 16, 1955, and peaked at #10 during its 13-week stay. As author Larry Birnbaum noted, Fats Domino, based on his original version, "became the first black rock 'n' roll artist to connect with a mass white audience, preceding Chuck Berry and Little Richard."

As was customary in the mid-1950s, in addition to a slew of budget label covers, "Ain't That A Shame" attracted two covers from major labels, the first by Ronnie Gaylord on Wing 90000, the label's first release, and the second by Pat Boone on Dot 15377. It was Boone's cover, however, that captured a lion's share of the market. It debuted on *Billboard's* pop chart on July 9, 1955, the same day that "Rock Around The Clock" became the first rock and roll record to top the chart. It eventually peaked at #1 for two weeks and spent 20 weeks on the pop chart. Somewhat surprisingly, Boone's cover version even crossed over to the R&B chart for two weeks in late September 1955.

Most music critics have been quite critical of white artists like Pat Boone, who covered the original versions of R&B songs by black artists and, in the process, frequently enjoyed greater chart success. But those covers by white artists often brought attention to the black artists who released the originals, something that some black artists came to appreciate. For example, Fats and Dave Bartholomew, as the writers of "Ain't That A Shame," collected writers' royalties for both versions. As Jack Doyle noted in his internet article about Fats, it "resulted in a pretty good payday thanks in part to Boone's successful No. 1 version, as well as their own." Fats acknowledged as much during one of his concerts with Pat Boone in the audience. After inviting Pat to the stage, he showed off his big gold ring and said, "Pat Boone bought me this ring."

---

26 It's possible that an error was made in titling the song for initial release, given that the phrase "ain't it a shame" is not used either by Fats in the song or in the published lyrics.

Interestingly, on the other side of the pond, both versions were issued in September 1955, on consecutively-numbered London releases, Pat on London 45-HL-D.8172, and Fats on London 45-HL-U.8173, as shown below:

Boone's cover made the UK charts for 11 weeks, reaching #7, while Domino's cover did not chart in the UK until January 1957, and then it only reached #23 during its short two weeks on the chart. Parenthetically, the titles for both UK releases are the same, i.e., the word "That" is used rather than "It."

Over the years, there have been numerous subsequent cover versions, perhaps most notably by John Lennon on Apple P-1883, a promo-only release of one of the rarest Apple 45s.[27] Cheap Trick recorded its cover version in 1978, and it reached #35 on the *Billboard* pop chart. Rick Nielsen, Cheap Trick's guitarist, said that the idea to record the song came from hearing John Lennon's cover version. It is, therefore, not surprising that Cheap Trick's version sounds more like Lennon's version than Domino's version. In other words, it was a cover of a cover.

The other 45 releases that made at least one of the *Billboard* charts are The Four Seasons in 1963 on Vee Jay 512 (pop chart peak #22) and Hank Williams, Jr., in 1972, on MGM 14317 (country chart peak #7). The Four Seasons version also charted in the UK.

As noted below, "Ain't That A Shame" gathered its share of honors and accolades, including being inducted into the Grammy Hall of Fame and included on National Public Radio's list of the 20th century's 100 most important musical works. As NPR's Nick Spitzer put it in his May 1, 2000, broadcast about "Ain't That A Shame":

> This enduring hit showcases Domino's powerful blues piano and stop-time, swamp-pop texture with an abundance of saxophones, plus that warm Creole-accented voice telling the simple but sincere story of romance found and lost.

27 Reportedly, "Ain't That A Shame" was the first song that John Lennon learned to play.

Spitzer added, "The piano communicates so much, it never drowns out the sadness of the lyric in its own sweetness." While Fats Domino had more than sixty *Billboard* charted songs, rock critic Dave Marsh observed that "one of the most characteristic of a style that never rocked harder than it needed to but never relented a whit, either" was "Ain't That A Shame."

CONTEMPORANEOUS COVER VERSIONS OF "AIN'T THAT A SHAME"

ARTIST	LABEL	COMMENTS
Pat Boone	Dot 15377	B/w "Tennessee Saturday Night"; reached #1 on the *Billboard* pop chart
Ronnie Gaylord	Wing 90000	First release on Wing, a subsidiary of Mercury Records; b/w "Che [*sic*] Sera Sera"
Rosemary Gaynor	Columbia SCM 5196 (UK)	B/w "A Happy Song"
The Southlanders	Parlophone MSP 6182 (UK)	B/w "Have You Ever Been Lonely"; Jamaican/British male quartet whose sound is like the Ink Spots

Pat Boone's cover on Dot 15377

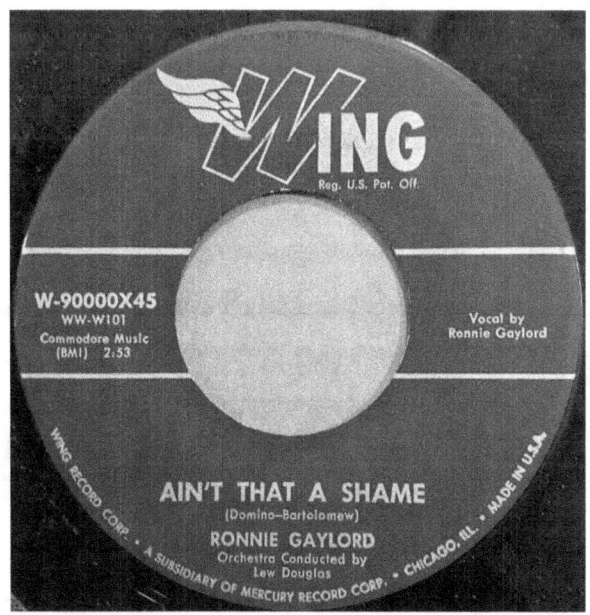

Ronnie Gaylord's cover on Wing 90000

CONTEMPORANEOUS BUDGET LABEL COVERS OF "AIN'T THAT A SHAME"

ARTIST	LABEL	COMMENTS
Loren Becker	18 Top Hits 155 and 18 Top Hits 160	EP with "Rock Around The Clock"/"Autumn Leaves"/"If I May"/"Song Of The Dreamer"/ "House Of Blue Lights"
Tony Benson & The Toppers	Tops R-263-49	EP with "Hard To Get"/"Wake The Town"/ "Yellow Rose Of Texas"
Ken and Tina	Broadway BR-2002	B/w "Be-Bop-Baby" by Jack Richards
Bill Marine	Prom 1122	B/w "Yellow Rose Of Texas" by the Prom Orchestra and Chorus
Sy Oliver	Bell 1102	B/w "Seventeen"
Jack Richards	Broadway 307	Titled "Ain't It A Shame"; b/w "Wake The Town And Tell The People"
Art Rouse, with The Four Jacks	Gateway 1129	Like Fat's original, titled "Ain't It A Shame"; b/w "The House Of Blue Lights" by Dick Warren and Jack Daniels
Art Rouse	Big 4 Hits	EP with "The Man In The Raincoat"/ "Seventeen"/"The House Of Blue Lights"
The Three Guys	RCA Camden CAE 303	EP with "Wake The Town And Tell The People"/"Seventeen"/"The Yellow Rose Of Texas"
None Listed	Variety EPV-6025	EP with "Hound Dog"/"Rock Around The Clock"/"Long Tall Sally"/"Blue Suede Shoes"
None Listed	Variety 1812	EP with "Hound Dog"/"Rock Around The Clock"/"Long Tall Sally"

None Listed	Popular PO-9	EP with "Tina Marie"/"The House Of Blue Lights"/"Rock Around The Clock"/"The Longest Walk"/"Want You To Be My Baby"
None Listed	EP 327	EP with "Wake The Town And Tell The People"/"Love Is A Many Splendored Thing"/"The Yellow Rose Of Texas"

Art Rouse on Gateway

Sy Oliver on Bell

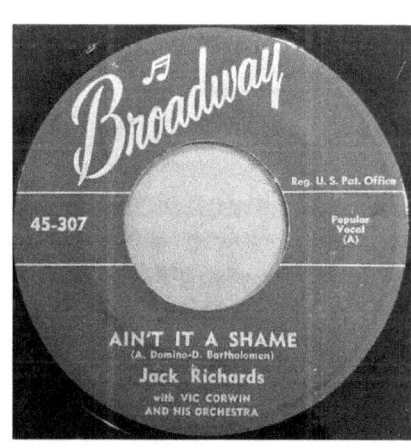
Jack Richards on Broadway

LATER RELEASES OF "AIN'T THAT A SHAME" BY FATS DOMINO

LABEL	YEAR	COMMENTS
Imperial IMP-140	1956	EP with "Poor Me"/"Bo Weevil"/"Don't Blame It On Me"
London REP 1116 (UK)	1958	EP with "Please Don't Leave Me"/"Poor Me"/"All By Myself"
Imperial 002	1962	B/w "Going To The River"; "Golden" series; still titled "Ain't It A Shame," the same as the original
Mercury SR-659-C	1965	7" small hole 33 1/3; with "Blueberry Hill"/"So Long"/"Let The Four Winds Blow"/"I'm Gonna Be A Wheel Someday"/"Oh, What A Price"; re-recorded for Mercury

United Artists XW001	1972	B/w "Goin' Home": "Silver Spotlight Series"; titled "Ain't That A Shame"
UA ROCK 602 (UK)	1972	EP titled "Rock Samples," with "Great Balls of Fire" by Jerry Lee Lewis, "Three Steps To Heaven" by Eddie Cochran, and "Let There Be Drums" by Sandy Nelson; "Maxi-Rock Single"
Hammer HB 609 (UK)	1979	7-inch 33 1/3 EP titled "The Big Six" with "My Blue Heaven"/"Kansas City"/"Heartbreak Hill"/"Jambalaya"/"When The Saints Go Marching In"
Liberty G45 17 (UK)	1984	B/w "The Fat Man"
SMP SKM 6 (UK)	1984	B/w "The Fat Man"
Collectables COL 6050	1992	B/w "I'm In Love Again"; "CEMA Special Markets"
American Pie 9071	1990s?	Titled "Ain't It A Shame"; b/w "Blueberry Hill"
Demon 45001/9 (UK)	2016	B/w "Blueberry Hill"; reissue of original Imperial sides

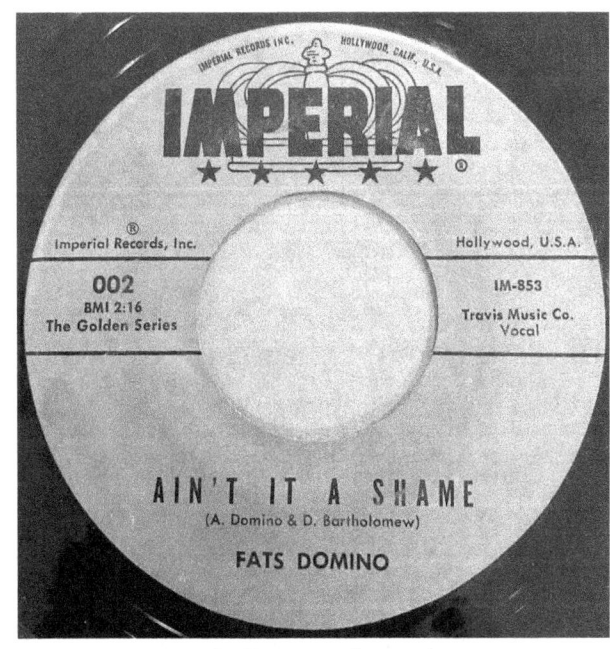

1962 Imperial reissue

1992 Collectables reissue

SUBSEQUENT COVER VERSIONS OF "AIN'T THAT A SHAME"

ARTIST	LABEL	YEAR	COMMENTS
Ken Berry	Barnaby ZS7 2020	1970	B/w "Lonely Street"; produced by Dick Glasser
Pat Boone	Dot DEP-1049	1955	EP with "At My Front Door"/"Two Hearts"/"Tennessee Saturday Night"
Pat Boone	Dot 45-16028	1959	B/w "I'll Be Home"
Pat Boone	Dot 45-108	1965	B/w "Friendly Persuasion (Thee I Love)"
Pat Boone	Collectables COL 3718	1980s?	B/w "I Almost Lost My Mind"; "Back to Back Hit Series"
Pat Boone	Dot GT-002X (Canada)	1990s?	B/w "Don't Forbid Me"
Connie Francis	MGM X 1693	1959	EP with "Silhouettes"/"I'm Walking"/ "It's Only Make Believe"
The Belles	Giant 9005	1963	B/w "If You Wanna Be Happy"; Nashville label; Four Seasons sound, unquestionably a cover of the Four Seasons' version
Cheap Trick	Epic 9-50743	1979	Peaked at #35 on the *Billboard* pop chart; b/w "ELO Kiddies";
Cheap Trick	Epic 15-2390	1980	B/w "I Want You To Want Me"; "Memory Lane" series
Cheap Trick	Epic E4 1056 (Canada)	1980	B/w "I Want You To Want Me"
Cheap Trick	Collectables 15-2390	1990s?	B/w "I Want You To Want Me"
Cheap Trick	Epic E-1056 (Canada)	1990s?	B/w "I Want You To Want Me"; "Hall of Fame" series

The Chellows	Hit 64	1963	B/w "If You Want To Be Happy"; Hit was a 1960s budget label
Earl Dixon	Decca DFE 8626 (UK)	1965	EP titled "Earl Sings Fats" with "My Blue Heaven"/"Blueberry Hill"/"Whole Lotta Loving"
The Four Seasons	Vee Jay 512	1963	Reached #22 on the *Billboard* pop chart; b/w "Soon (I'll Be Home Again)"
The Four Seasons	Stateside SS-194 (UK)	1963	B/w "Soon (I'll Be Home Again)"
The Four Seasons	Reo 8716X (Canada)	1963	B/w "Soon (I'll Be Home Again)"
The Four Seasons, "Featuring the 'Sound' of Frankie Valli"	Four Seasons LM 0016	c. mid-70s	B/w "Marlena"
Sammy Harps	Jin 411	1989	B/w "Whiskey Drinking, Foolish Thinking"
Bobbi Lynn Kelly	American Sound AS-3169	Late 70s-early 80s	B/w "Have I Told You Lately (That I Love You)"
Ronnie Hawkins	Monument MNT S-8292 (UK)	1972	B/w "Cora Mae"; produced by Fred Foster
Bill King	Change 45034 (Canada)	1980	B/w "Nothin's Gonna Stand"; distributed by MCA
John Lennon	Apple P-1883	1975	Mono/stereo versions; arranged and produced by John Lennon; only issued as promo, no stock copies issued
Rebecca Lynn	Elka 309	1976	B/w "Once In A While"

Paddy Manna	USA S-1776	1962	B/w "I'm In Love Again"; distributed by Smash
Paul McCartney	MPL PRO-2/004 (Spain)	1988	B/w "Crackin' Up"; unofficial release
Paul McCartney	Parlophone 12R 6213 (UK)	1989	12" 45 rpm EP with "My Brave Face"/"I'm Going To Be A Wheel Someday"/"Flying To My Home"
Ella Mae Morse	Capitol EAP-1-9126	1955	EP with "Razzle Dazzle"/"Seventeen"/ "Piddley Patter Patter"
Ella Mae Morse	Capitol CL 14341 (UK)	1955	B/w "Razzle Dazzle," a cover of Bill Haley
O'Keefe, Johnny, and The Dee-Jays	Festival FX-5002 (Australia)	1958	EP with "Wild One"/"Silhouettes"/ "Little Bitty Pretty One"; O'Keefe was one of the composers of "Wild One," which was later covered by Buddy Holly, Jerry Lee Lewis, Iggy Pop, among others
Earl Palmer	Liberty F-55356	1961	Medley with "I'm Walkin,'" "Honky Tonk," and "Blueberry Hill," titled "New Orleans Medley"; b/w "Honky Tonk, Part II"; Palmer was a session on drummer on many of Fats' records, but not on "Ain't That A Shame"
Pretenders	Sahara 1001	c. mid 60s	B/w "You Don't Fool Me"
Raphael Exchange	Much CH 1014 (Canada)	1972	B/w "Alky Jones"; Montreal band
Joe Reed	Dawn DNS-1012 (UK)	1971	B/w "Follow Me"

Tanya Tucker	MCA 40540	1976	B/w "You've Got Me To Hold On To," which rose to #3 on the *Billboard* country chart
Hank Williams, Jr.	MGM 14317	1971	Spent 14 weeks on *Billboard's* country chart and peaked at #7 in 1972; b/w "The End Of A Bad Day"
None listed	Hit Parader HP-23	1963	EP with "Da Doo Ron Ron"/"Killer Joe"/ "Hot Pastrami"/"Take These Chains From My Heart"/"This Little Girl"; budget label

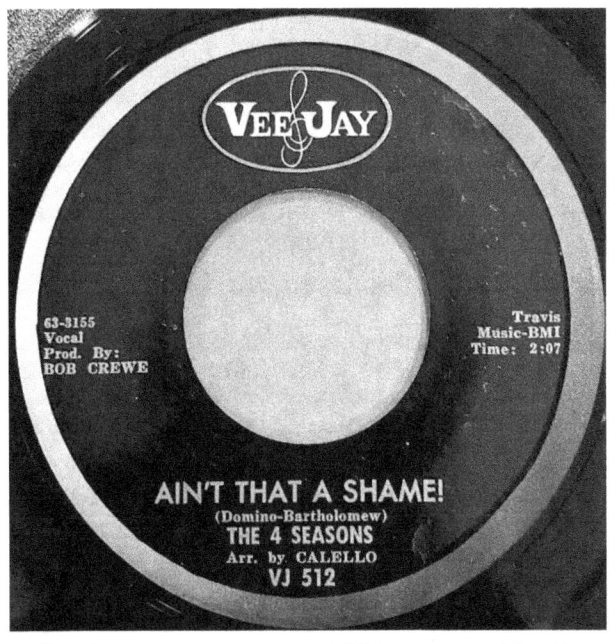

The 4 Seasons cover 1964 cover on Vee Jay 512

John Lennon 1975 cover on Apple P-1883

SAME TITLE, DIFFERENT SONG

One of the problems collectors of cover records encounter from time to time is that the same title is used for a totally different song. This is particularly true in collecting covers of Fats Domino's "Ain't That A Shame," as the following releases of songs with the same title that are **not** covers of Fats can attest:

ARTIST	LABEL	YEAR	COMMENTS
Ashford and Simpson	WB 8775	1979	B/w "Flashback"
The Butler & Just Us	Peppermint PP 1407	1986	B/w "Navy Beans"; "Parental Discretion Advised"
Roy Brown	King 4731	1954	B/w "Gal From Kokomo"
Leroy Carr	RCA Victor RCX 7168 (UK)	1968	EP with "Big Four Blues"/"Rocks In My Bed"/"Six Cold Feet In The Ground"
The Dells	20th Century Fox TC-2602	1982	B/w "Stay In My Corner"; produced by Carl Davis
Roy Eldridge	Decca 23523	1946	B/w "All The Cats Join In"
Shawn Elliott	Diamond D-113	1962	B/w "Goodbye My Love"; big band pop sound
Shawn Elliott	Stateside 45-SS-124 (UK)	1962	B/w "Goodbye My Love"; big band pop sound
Forbidden Fruit	Playboy P 6012	1974	B/w "Tutsi '74"
Guys & Dolls	Astrophe 37114	1968	B/w "Pretty, Pretty Baby"; Illinois group
Brian James	IRC 9501	1973	B/w "Living In Sin"; James was The Damned's original guitarist
Dennis Knight	Chrystal Clear CC-11309 (Australia)	1976	B/w "If I Didn't Have A Dime"

Major Lance	Okeh 4-7223	1965	Reached #20 on the *Billboard* R&B chart; penned by Curtis Mayfield; b/w "Gotta Get Away"
Lonnie Lester & Chuck Danzy	Nu-Tone 1209	1960s	B/w "I Know"; scarce soul record
Conrad Pierce	Cape 001	1965	B/w "A World I Can't Live In"; FL label
Lloyd Price	Specialty 452	1953	Reached #4 on the *Billboard* R&B chart; b/w "Tell Me Pretty Baby"
Question Mark & The Mysterians	Tangerine 45-TRC-989X	1969	B/w "Turn Around Baby (Don't Ever Look Back)"
Alan Ross	Ebony EYE 13 (UK)	1978	B/w "Kamina" and "Restless Nights"
Sensational Saints of Ohio	Message 1235	1963	B/w "Come On"; label is a short-lived gospel subsidiary of the Tri-Phi and Harvey labels
The Singing Mellerairs	Impel 309 and Maple 309	1971	B/w "Western Union Man"; gospel
Leroy Smalley	Golden World 107	1962	B/w "Girls Are Sentimental"; soul
Marvin Smith	Contempo 6603	1974	Composed by Curtis Mayfield and produced by Major Lance; b/w "Let The Good Times Roll"
Marvin Smith	Contempo CS-2034 (UK)	1974	Composed by Curtis Mayfield and produced by Major Lance; b/w "Let The Good Times Roll"
Don Thomas	Probe 466	1969	B/w "He Knew (That He Was Dying)"
Kenny Vernon	Epic 5-10192	1967	B/w "Miles And Miles"
Albert Washington	DeLuxe 45-135	1971	B/w "Somewhere Down The Line"
The Wave-Riders	Tener TC 154	1966	B/w "Thing In G"; garage record

Sarge and Shirley West	Jack 'O Diamonds 1039	1969	B/w "We're Gonna Have A Good Time Tonight"

"AIN'T THAT A SHAME" IN THE MOVIES

"Ain't That A Shame" has appeared in the following movies:

MOVIE TITLE	YEAR	COMMENTS
Shake, Rattle & Rock!	1956	Played and performed by Fats Domino; a low budget "musical jukebox" in which rock 'n' roll is put on trial
American Graffiti	1973	Performed by Fats Domino; movie about a group of high school grads' last night before heading off to college to the sounds of many 1950s Rock 'n' Roll classics
Mischief	1985	Performed by Fats Domino; romantic teen comedy
L.A. Story	1991	Performed by Fats Domino; fantasy drama/comedy
School Ties	1992	Performed by Fats Domino; star quarterback must hide his Jewish identity to attend an elite prep school
Judgment Night	1993	Performer is not identified by *IMDbpro*; crime drama
Shake, Rattle, and Rock	1994	Performed by Fats Domino; TV movie about two young females, one of whom is played by Renee Zellweger, who seek to prove that Rock 'n' Roll is not a fad; essentially a remake of the 1956 movie of the same name
The Climb	1997	Performed by Pat Boone; drama about a crusty old civil engineer and his relationship with a neighborhood kid

Shake, Rattle and Roll: An American Love Story	1999	Performed by Randy Jackson; TV mini-series; won Golden Reel Award for best sound editing for TV movies
October Sky	1999	Performed by Fats Domino; true story about Homer Hickum (played by Jake Gyllenhaal), who took up rocketry against his father's wishes after the 1957 Russian launch of Sputnik
Hearts in Atlantis	2001	Performed by Fats Domino; mystery drama starring Anthony Hopkins
Till	2022	Performed by Fats Domino; biopic about a mother's effort to obtain justice over the brutal lynching of her son, Emmett Till

Poster for the 1956 movie *Shake, Rattle and Rock!*

DOCUMENTED CONCERT PERFORMANCES OF "AIN'T THAT A SHAME"

As of May 1, 2024, *Setlist.fm* documented that "Ain't That A Shame" has been performed in concert 1,479 times by 43 different artists. In addition to Fats Domino (26), artists who have included it on their set lists include Cheap Trick (1,262), Paul McCartney (108), Jon Batiste (4), Pat Boone (4), and Bruce Springsteen (2). In both 2019 and 2023 it was on 79 set lists.

HONORS AND ACCOLADES FOR "AIN'T THAT A SHAME"

- Inducted into the Grammy Hall of Fame in 2002
- Included on NPR's list of the 20th century's 100 most important musical works
- Ranked #120 on Joel Whitburn's *Honor Roll of Hits*
- Ranked #438 on the *Rolling Stone*'s 2004 list of "The 500 Greatest Songs of All Time"
- Chosen by the Rock & Roll Hall of Fame as one of the "500 Songs That Shaped Rock and Roll"
- Ranked #660 in Dave Marsh's 1989 book, *The Heart of Rock & Soul: The 1,001 Greatest Singles Ever Made*

ALSO WORTH NOTING . . .

- "Ain't That A Shame" was performed at the 60th Annual Grammy Awards by Gary Clark, Jr., Jonathan Batiste, and Joe Saylor.
- When Cheap Trick was inducted into the Rock & Roll Hall of Fame in 2016, they, along with the other inductees and assorted musicians, performed "Ain't That A Shame" as the final song to conclude the induction ceremony.
- In 1979 Fats Domino gave the gold record he received for "Ain't It A Shame" to Cheap Trick, whose version he loved. Guitarist Rick Nielsen ended up with the gold record after the group drew straws to see who would get it.
- "Ain't That A Shame" was sampled by Buchanon & Goodman on the 1956 hit novelty song, "Flying Saucers, Part 2," on Luniverse 101.
- "Cousin Brucie" Morrow noted that Fats Domino's "piano-style reportedly inspired Paul McCartney's "Lady Madonna."

ADDITIONAL SOURCES

Doyle, Jack, "Fats Domino: 1950s-2000s," *PopHistoryDig.com*, March 20, 2017, accessed July 23, 2021

Morrow, "Cousin Brucie," with Rich Maloof, *Rock & Roll … And The Beat Goes On* (Charlesbridge Publishing, 2009)

CHAPTER 6

"TUTTI FRUTTI"

LITTLE RICHARD (OCTOBER 1955)

Original Specialty 45 release

Original Specialty 78 release

Cash Box ad, 1/14/56

Original UK release on London label

"TUTTI FRUTTI" — THE BASIC FACTS

Label: Specialty 561 (both 45 and 78)

Writers: Dorothy La Bostrie and Richard Penniman (AKA Little Richard)

Date recorded: September 14, 1955

Date released: October 1955

B-Side: "I'm A Lonely Guy"

Producer: Robert "Bumps" Blackwell

Billboard charts:

Pop Chart
- Debut: 1/14/56
- Peak: #17
- Duration: 12 weeks

R&B Chart
- Debut: 1/14/56
- Peak: #2
- Duration: 16 weeks

THE SONG AND ITS IMPACT

"Wop bop a loo bop wop bam boom." In many respects, this nonsensical primal scream ushered in the Rock 'n' Roll era. Yes, there were other songs before "Tutti Frutti" that suggested the arrival of Rock 'n' Roll, but none of them did so with so much energy and sexual innuendo. Nor by a singer as outlandish as Little Richard. His recording career, however, began four years earlier in 1951.

Little Richard was first signed to RCA by Steve Sholes, the same RCA executive who later purchased Elvis Presley's Sun Records contract from Sam Phillips. He released four records for RCA in the early 1950s but when none of them sold well, RCA let his contract lapse. He next signed with Peacock, and four sides were released by him as a member of the Tempo Toppers or Duces of Rhythm. Once again, no chart success. (He also recorded four sides with Johnny Otis's band backing him, but those sides were not released until after the success of "Tutti Frutti").

Then in 1955 Little Richard, at the suggestion of Lloyd Price, sent a tape to Specialty Records. As Billy Vera recounts in his book about Specialty Records, Art Rupe, although not initially impressed with what he had heard, "… relented and shelled out the $600 pittance Robey [the owner of the Peacock label] was asking and had himself an artist." Thereafter, Rupe dispatched Bumps Blackwell, a West Coast arranger and band leader, to set up a September 1955 recording session at Cosimo Matassa's famed J&M New Orleans recording studio. During a lunch break at the Dew Drop Inn, Little Richard broke into a salty ditty that he had performed live numerous times. Blackwell believed it could be a hit, but he realized that the lyrics needed to be cleaned up. To accomplish that task he enlisted Dorothy La Bostrie,[28] a tunesmith who happened to be at a table nearby. For example, the

---

28 La Bostrie penned the B-side, "I'm Just A Lonely Man," and that is the likely the reason why her talents as a tunesmith

original lyrics that had strong gay overtones were removed and new lyrics were written to take their place. Example:

ORIGINAL LYRICS	CLEANED UP LYRICS
Tutti Frutti, good booty / If it don't fit, don't force it / You can grease it, make it easy	Tutti Frutti, oh rooty / Tutti Frutti, oh rooty / Tutti Frutti, oh rooty

According to Blackwell, with the new lyrics in hand, Little Richard recorded the song in three takes in less than twenty minutes. The cream of New Orleans's session musicians backed up Little Richard: Lee Allen on tenor saxophone, Alvin "Red" Tyler on baritone saxophone, Frank Fields on double bass, Earl Palmer on drums, and Justin Adams on guitar. Although Huey Smith was listed as one of the musicians for the session, it was Little Richard on the keyboards on "Tutti Frutti" and not Huey Smith. Smith, however, did play piano on the other songs recorded during that session.

Released in October 1955, "Tutti-Frutti" was reviewed by *Billboard* on October 29, 1955, but it only received a numerical ranking of 76 based on its rating scale of 90 to 100 = tops, 80 to 89 = excellent, and 70 to 79 = good. *Billboard* noted that the song was a "cleverly styled novelty with nonsense lyrics delivered rapid-fire" and that Little Richard "shows a compelling personality and an attractive vocal style," concluding: "On performance rather than material, this disk is strong." A month later on November 26, 1955, it debuted on the *Billboard* R&B chart and subsequently entered the pop chart on January 14, 1956. It eventually peaked at #2 on the R&B chart and at #17 on the pop chart. As one critic observed, "One thing for sure, 'Tutti Frutti' has nothing to do with the ice-cream-and-chopped fruits dessert; the song is a sexual anthem in Richard's unique language: raving, speaking-in-tongues, R&B Esperanto."[29]

The same day that Little Richard's original version debuted on its R&B chart, *Billboard* spotlighted Pat Boone's cover version, noting that it "is an extremely spirited and exciting job on the fast-moving [Little Richard] r.&b. hit." Boone had recorded both "Tutti-Frutti" and the B-side—"I'll Be Home"— in Chicago in December 1955, with Billy Vaughn leading the orchestra and Randy Wood, the owner of Dot Records, producing. The lyrics of Boone's version, however, were further sanitized by Joe Lubin, an Englishman who had moved to the United States in 1947,[30] as the following demonstrates:

---

were used to clean up Little Richard's racy ditty. During the same time frame she also co-penned several songs for other Specialty artists, including "Rich Woman" by Li'l Millet and "His Creoles" on Specialty 565.

29 A song likewise titled "Tutti Frutti" was a #2 R&B hit in 1938 for Slim [Gaillard] and Slam [Stewart] on Vocalion 4225, but it is an entirely different song, although it does have the lyric "Tutti Frutti, Frutti."

30 The original lyrics by D. LaBostrie and R. Penniman were copyrighted on October 2, 1955; subsequently, Joe Lubin's name was added as a writer in the copyright entry dated January 30, 1956. The later adding of Lubin seems to confirm that Lubin was brought in further sanitize the lyrics for Pat Boone's cover version.

LITTLE RICHARD'S LYRICS	PAT BOONE'S LYRICS
She rocks to the East, she rocks to the West / But she's the gal that I love best / I've been to the East, I've been to the West / But she's the gal that I love best / Got a gal named Daisy / She almost drives me crazy / She knows how to love me, yes indeed / Boy you don't know what she do to me	I got a gal, her name's Daisy / She almost drives me crazy / She's a real gone cookie, yes sirree / But pretty little Suzy is the gal for me

Boone's version spent 18 weeks on *Billboard's* pop chart, peaking at #12, five spots higher than Little Richard's original version. As author Larry Birnbaum noted, "Pat Boone's toned-down version helped raise awareness of Richard's original, even as it cut into Richard's sales."

Interestingly, the B-side of Boone's record, a cover of the Flamingo's "I'll Be Home" on Checker 830, did significantly better on *Billboard's* pop chart, peaking at #4.[31] In 1959 Dot reissued several of Boone's cover hits, including "I'll Be Home," but "Tutti Frutti" was not one of them. "Ain't That A Shame" was the flip of the "I'll Be Home" release on Dot 16028. Dot also did not include "Tutti Frutti" as any of Boone's records that were released on Dot's 100 series. Finally, although many of Boone's hits can be found on both the Goldies 45 and Collectables reissue labels, "Tutti Frutti" is not one of them. Perhaps, Randy Woods and Dot realized that Boone's cover version simply did not measure up to Little Richard's original.

Boone's version was released in the UK in March 1956 on London HL-D 8253, followed by Little Richard's original version nearly a year later in February 1957 on London HL-O 8366 backed with "Long Tall Sally." On Boone's UK version, Joe Lubin is not listed as a writer even though he was the person who further cleaned up the lyrics for Boone, but Lubin is listed as one of the writers on Little Richard's raunchier version along with La Bostrie and Penniman (AKA Little Richard). Go figure!!! Parenthetically, only Little Richard's original version made the UK charts, but only for one week in late February 1957.

---

31 As a commentator (goodiesguy) noted on *45cat.com*: "The ballad is the worthwhile tune here. Pat was fantastic with that type of material, and he knew it, but the record company had him record Little Richard material, which he never felt comfortable with as he just didn't have the voice for it. This unfortunately gives him an unfairly bad reputation."

Using Little Richard's more suggestive lyrics, Elvis Presley sang "Tutti Frutti" on the *Dorsey Brothers Stage Show* on February 4, 1956, his second appearance on national TV. He recorded the song on January 31, 1956, but for reasons unknown it was not released as a single, even though he sang it again on the *Stage Show* on February 18, 1956. But it was one of the songs issued on RCA EPA-747 on March 26, 1956. The EP's other three cuts were "Blue Suede Shoes," "I Got A Woman," and "Just Because." It was only later issued as a single on August 31, 1956, on RCA 47-6636, backed with "Blue Suede Shoes." "Tutti Frutti" was, however, issued as a single in Canada in March 1956 on RCA 47-6466, backed with "One Sided Love Affair."

Among the many artists who recorded subsequent cover versions are Jerry Lee Lewis, Carl Perkins, Sting, and the Swinging Blue Jeans, all of which is documented below. Given Little Richard's frenetic original version, it is somewhat surprising that so many artists recorded cover versions. But perhaps the strangest version is the one by Michael Reed, albeit with Pat Boone's lyrics and not Little Richard's racier lyrics, on the Peter Pan label, a kiddie budget label. Why it was released is anybody's guess.[32]

Rock writer Paul Williams correctly observed that "Tutti Frutti" "helped tear the roof of the self-satisfied edifice called American popular music, to let in the light of unrestrained sexuality, spirituality, and musicality." And, in summarizing the importance of "Tutti Frutti," he noted that "[v]inyl means immortality. The screams of Little Richard leap joyously off the turntable to this day." Referring to the opening shout—"Wop bop a loo bop wop bam boom"—*Rolling Stone* declared in 2012 that the song "still has the most inspired rock lyric on record."

Arnold Shaw observed that Little Richard's "gospel dynamism, showy exhibitionism, and sheer animal vitality 'spoke' to artists as different as Elvis Presley, Otis Redding, Jerry Lee Lewis…, Bill Haley, Marty Balin of The Jefferson Airplane, The Rolling Stones, and The Beatles."

---

32 *45cat* lists nearly 500 releases on the Peter Pan label, almost all of which are songs that are in the public domain, including numerous nursey rhymes, Christmas songs, cartoon songs, etc.

CONTEMPORANEOUS COVER VERSIONS OF "TUTTI FRUTTI"

ARTIST	LABEL	COMMENTS
Pat Boone	Dot 15443	Released January 1956; *Billboard* pop charted for 18 weeks, peaking at #12
Art Mooney	MGM K12165	Vocal by Ocie Smith; b/w "You Can Take My Heart"; first record release by Ocie Smith (AKA O.C. Smith)

Original Boone release on Dot

Billboard ad, February 4, 1956

CONTEMPORANEOUS BUDGET LABEL COVERS OF "TUTTI FRUTTI"

ARTIST	LABEL	COMMENTS
Loren Becker	18 Top Hits 185	EP with "Theme From 'Three Penny Opera'"/"See You Later, Alligator"/"The Little Child"/"Chain Gang"/"No, Not Much"/ "Lisbon Antigua"
Danny Daniels	Gilmar 119	EP with "Why Do Fools Fall In Love"/"No, Not Much"/"A Tear Fell"/"The Poor People Of Paris"/ "Band of Gold"

Danny Daniels	Tops R276-49; Record -of -the-Month Club 45-RG276	EP with "Little Child"/"The Poor People Of Paris"/"Ninety-Nine Years"
Jack Daniels	Gateway 1157	B/w "Are You Satisfied"
Steve Marks	Broadway 321	B/w "Theme From Three Penny Opera" by Kenneth Wayne
Artie Marvin and The Zig Zags	18 Top Hits 169	EP with "If I Didn't Care"/"Theme From 'Three Penny Opera'"/"See You Later, Alligator"/"The Little Child"/"Chain Gang"
Artie Marvin and The Zig Zags	18 Top Hits 188	EP with "Moonglow"/"A Tear Fell"/ "To Love Again"/"The Saints Rock And Roll"/"Standing On The Corner"
None Listed	Value 120	EP with "Lisbon Antigua"/"See You Later, Alligator"/"Theme From The Three Penny Opera (Moriat)"

Budget label cover by Loren Becker

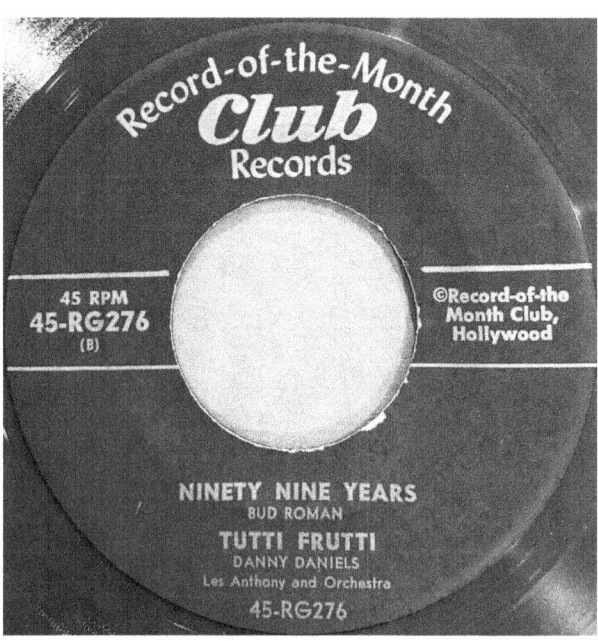

Budget label cover by Danny Daniels

LATER RELEASES OF "TUTTI FRUTTI" BY LITTLE RICHARD

LABEL	YEAR	COMMENTS
Regency 571X (Canada)	1957	B/w "I'm Just A Lonely Guy"; from the Specialty masters
London HLO.8366 (UK)	1957	B/w "Long Tall Sally"; released in February 1957
Specialty SEP-402	1957	EP with "Rip It Up"/"True Fine Mama"/"Jenny, Jenny"
Oldies 45 OL-187	1964	B/w "Going Home Tomorrow"; reissues of Vee Jay remakes
Collectables 1447	1964s	B/w "Long Tall Sally"
Modern Oldies 39	1967-68	Medley with "Ready Teddy"; remake; b/w "Do You Feel It Pt. 1"
Trip 33	1969-70	B/w "Baby Face"; reissue of Specialty originals
Kama Sutra SP 17	1970	7" small hole 33 1/3 LP sampler with "Good Golly Miss Molly"/"The Girl Can't Help It"/"Keep A Knockin'"
Goldies 45 D-2531	1973	Reissue of Vee Jay remake; b/w "Going Home Tomorrow"
Specialty SON 5002 (UK)	1973	B/w "Keep A Knockin'"
Quality QGT-295X (Canada)	1979	B/w "Long Tall Sally"; Quality "Golden Treasures" series
GRT GG-21 (Canada)	1960s?	B/w "Going Home Tomorrow"
JB 13 (UK)	1980	B/w "Good Golly Miss Molly"; re-recordings
K-Tel 7913	1981	EP titled "Class of '55," with "Rock Around The Clock" by Bill Haley, "Blue Suede Shoes" by Carl Perkins," and "Earth Angel" by the Crew Cuts

Quality GC 373X Canada	1982	B/w "Long Tall Sally"
Epic A 4593 (UK)	1984	From his remake for Okeh, not the Specialty original; b/w "Long Tall Sally," likewise an Okeh remake
Epic A4593 (UK)	1984	B/w "Long Tall Sally"; reissued from an earlier Okeh remake; part of the CBS "Back Tracks" series
Old Gold OG 9493	1985	B/w "Long Tall Sally"; licensed from Specialty Records
Lost-Nite LN-309	1980s?	B/w "Long Tall Sally"; remakes, not the originals
Elektra 7-69370	1988	B/w "Rave On" by John Cougar Mellencamp; from the movie *Cocktail*
Elektra 7-69385	1988	B/w "Kokomo" by The Beach Boys; from the movie *Cocktail*
Elektra 7-69384	1988	B/w "Powerful Stuff" by the Fabulous Thunderbirds, which made the lower reaches of the *Cash Box* "Top 100 Singles" chart; from the movie *Cocktail*
Elektra 7-65937	1990	B/w "Kokomo" by The Beach Boys and produced by Terry Melcher; "Elektra Spun Gold"; from the movie *Cocktail*
Vee Jay 241	???	Titled "Tutti Fruitti [*sic*]"; a rather obvious bootleg complete with a misspelling; b/w "Long Tall Sally"
Collectables COL 10561	c. 2008	B/w "I'm Just A Lonely Guy"; from the original Specialty masters; note that last 3 digits of the release number match the Specialty release number
Vipvop 45001 (UK)	2018	B/w "Ready Teddy"; limited edition of 500

2018 reissue on Vipvop 45001   **Picture sleeve for Vipvop 45001**

SUBSEQUENT COVER VERSIONS OF "TUTTI FRUTTI"

ARTIST	LABEL	YEAR	COMMENTS
Lee Austin (The Burner)	Polydor 14195	1973	Soul/funk version arranged and produced by James Brown; the promo has both mono and stereo versions; the stock copy is backed with "Moonlight"
Marc Bolan and T. Rex featuring Elton John and Ringo Starr	Demon BOOGIE 001	2016	B/w "Children Of The Revolution" and "Born To Boogie"; all titles from movie *Born to Boogie*, a documentary about T. Rex produced and directed by Ringo Starr
Pat Boone	London RE-D 1112	1958	EP with "Love Letters In The Sand"/"Just As Long As I Am With You"/"Bernardine"
Pat Boone	Dot DEP-1064	1958	EP with "Chattanooga Shoe Shine Boy"/"Harbor Lights"/"I'll Be Home"

Big Wheelie & The Hubcaps	Scepter 12375	1973	Medley with "Long Tall Sally" and "Ready Teddy"; b/w "Over The Mountain"
Mike Evola and Country Fever	Gap SA83-201	1983	Medley with "Country Pictures"; b/w "Walkin' In Hank's Shoes" and "Workin' Man's Blues"
Fair Weather	RCA 2040 (UK)	1970	Great version with honking saxes and guitar runs; b/w "Road To Freedom"
The Jesters	Winley 248	1960	B/w "That's How It Goes"; produced by Paul Winley, the label's owner
The Jones Boys	Decca 45-F 10717 (UK)	1956	B/w "Are You Satisfied"
Mickey Lee Lane	Mala 12,032	1968	Same song, but titled "Tutti Fruitti" [sic]; b/w "With Your Love (I'll Make It Through)"
Mickey Lee Lane	Rollercoaster RCEP 120 (UK)	1995	EP with "Shaggy Dog"/"The Zoo"/ "Rock The Bop"
The Late Show	Decca FR 13851 (England)	1979	Medley with "Peppermint Twist"; b/w "I Saw Your Picture In The Subway"; produced by Tommy Boyce & Richard Hartley
Jerry Lee Lewis	Mercury 73374	1973	Medley with "Long Tall Sally"/"Good Golly Miss Molly"/"Jenny Jenny"/ "Whole Lotta Shakin' Goin' On"; b/w "Drinking Wine Spo-Dee-O'dee"
Jerry Lee Lewis	Mercury 652 260 (UK)	1973	Same as immediately above
Los Teen Tops	Columbia EPC-155 (Mexico)	1960	EP with three other songs
Jim Lucus	Republic 7123	1955-56	B/w "My Favorite Doll"

Art Mooney	Cover 002	1960s???	EP with "Don't Knock The Rock"/ "Juke Box Baby"/"Sh-Boom"
Morris Brothers	Tyger 7103-17	???	Medley with "Long Tall Sally"/ "Slippin' and Slidin'"/"Good Golly Miss Molly"; b/w Chuck Berry medley
Lidia Morales	Lidia 102378	???	B/w "Rock And Roll Music," a cover of Chuck Berry
Moose & Da Sharks	Butterscotch 6969	1975???	B/w "Way Down Yonder (In New Orleans)"; Detroit, MI, area label
O'Keefe, Johnny	Festival FX-11,692 (Australia)	1971	EP with "Whole Lotta Shakin' Goin' On"/ "Rip It Up"/"Brown Eyed Handsome Man"
Carl Perkins	Columbia B-12341	1958	EP with "That's All Right"/"I Gotta Woman"/"Whole Lotta Shakin' Goin On"
Elvis Presley	RCA 47-6636	1956	B/w "Blue Suede Shoes"
Elvis Presley	RCA EPA 747	1956	EP with "Just Because"/"Blue Suede Shoes"/"I Got A Woman"
Elvis Presley	His Maser's Voice 7M 405 (UK)	1956	B/w "Blue Suede Shoes"; released in June 1956; Presley's second release in the UK
Elvis Presley	RCA 447-0609	1959	B/w "Blue Suede Shoes"; "Gold Standard Series"; original dog on top label; reissued on a variety of RCA labels over the years, e.g., dog on side, dog at 1 p.m., etc.)
Elvis Presley	Sun 523	1973	B/w "I'll Never Let You Go (Little Darlin')"; bootleg tracks from the *Dorsey Brothers Stage Show*
Elvis Presley	RCA PB-11107	1977	B/w "Blue Suede Shoes"

Elvis Presley	RCA PP-11370	1977	B/w "Blue Suede Shoes"; "Collector's Series" box set of 10 separate 45s of Elvis hits
Elvis Presley	RCA PB-13885	1984	B/w "Blue Suede Shoes"
Elvis Presley	RCA 2715 (Canada)	1978	B/w "Blue Suede Shoes"; "Collector Series"
Michael Reed	Peter Pan 45-434	1959	Boone lyrics; b/w "Dwarf's Yodel Song"; kiddie label
Georgie Saint and The Dragons	York SKY 544 (UK)	1973	Medley with "Bony Moronie" and "Hound Dog"; b/w medley of "Sweet Little Sixteen" and "High School Confidential"
Lawrence Shaul and The Aristocrats	Reed RR 1049	1960	B/w "True Fine Mama," another cover of Little Richard; Birmingham, AL, label
Sting	A & M PARTY 2	1982	B/w "Run Rudolph Run" by Dave Edmunds; promo release; one of six promos issued in connection with the movie *Party Party*
The Sunset Boys	Gimp GIM-1234 (UK)	1979	EP with" Wreck My Bed"/"Wreck My Bed (Hippy Version)"/"Copy Cat Blues"
Swinging Blue Jeans	Imperial 66059	1964	B/w "Promise You'll Tell Her"
Larry Taylor	Cozy PR-1122	Early 1970s	Described as "mood music"; b/w "Baby Face"; Chicago, IL, label
Trio	Mercury MER 149 (UK)	1983	B/w "Boom Boom"; produced by Klaus Voorman
Vibrashions	Duck 6073-22	1976	B/w "I'd Like To Teach The World To Sing"

Lee Austin (The Burner) on Polydor   The Swinging Blue Jeans on Imperial

"TUTTI FRUTTI" IN THE MOVIES

"Tutti Frutti" can be heard in numerous movies, starting with *Don't Knock the Rock* in 1956:

MOVIE TITLE	YEAR	COMMENTS
Don't Knock the Rock	1956	Performed by Little Richard; "juke box" musical featuring Bill Haley, Little Richard, and others
The London Rock and Roll Concert	1973	Filmed on location at London's Wembley Stadium on August 5, 1972; performed by Little Richard; also features Chuck Berry, Bo Diddley, Bill Haley, Jerry Lee Lewis, among others

American Hot Wax	1978	Performed by Little Richard; biopic loosely based on Rock 'n' Roll DJ Alan Freed's career
The Year of Living Dangerously	1982	Performed by Little Richard (Vee Jay version); military drama starring Mel Gibson and Linda Hunt
Party Party	1983	Performed by Sting; comedy about a teen having a New Year's Eve party at his parents' house while they are out celebrating elsewhere
Top Secret!	1984	Performed by Val Kilmer; musical comedy starring Val Kilmer as a R&R singer seeking to rescue an imprisoned scientist being held by East Germany during the cold war
Heaven Help Us	1985	Performed by Little Richard; coming-of-age film about a Catholic boy's school in Brooklyn, NY
The Brave Little Toaster	1987	Performed by Little Richard; animated family film that has become a cult classic; it tells the story of old abandoned appliances that seek to find their master
Police Academy 6: City Under Siege	1989	Performed by Little Richard; comedy about bumbling rookie cops
Listen to Me	1989	*IMDbPro* does not identify who performs the song; a coming-of-age film about a group of college debaters
Her Alibi	1989	Performed by Little Richard; criminal mystery comedy starring Tom Selleck
Flirting (Australia)	1991	*IMDbPro* does not identify who performs the song; romantic drama starring Thandive Newton and Nicole Kidman
I.Q.	1994	Performed by Little Richard; romantic comedy about a mechanic courting the niece of Albert Einstein, starring Meg Ryan, Tim Robbins, and Walter Matthau
It Takes Two	1995	Performed by Little Richard; family romantic comedy about two identical but unrelated girls who try to prevent one of their father's from marrying the wrong woman

Why Do Fools Fall In Love	1998	Performed by Little Richard; movie about the three women who claim to be Frankie Lymon's wife and thus entitled to his estate
Ginger & Rosa	2012	Performed by Little Richard; story of two teenage girls and the impact of the Cuban Missile Crisis on their lives
The Smurfs 2	2013	Performed by Buckwheat Zydyco; animated kiddie adventure comedy
Get On Up	2014	*IMDbPro* does not identify who performs the song; biopic about James Brown's rise to fame
Elvis	2022	"Tutti Frutti" was sung by Les Greene portraying Little Richard; biopic about Elvis Presley starring Austin Butler as Elvis and Tom Hanks as Colonel Parker

DOCUMENTED CONCERT PERFORMANCES OF "TUTTI FRUTTI"

As of May 1, 2024, *Setlist.fm* documented that "Tutti Frutti" has been performed in concert 570 times by 106 different artists. In addition to Little Richard (66), artists who have included "Tutti Frutti" on their set lists on more than five occasions include Johnny Hallyday (147), Jerry Lee Lewis (49), Queen (28), AC/DC (16), Fleetwood Mac (8), and Elvis Presley (7).

HONORS AND ACCOLADES FOR "TUTTI FRUTTI"

- Inducted into the Grammy Hall of Fame in 1998, which "honor recordings of lasting qualitative or historical significance that are at least 25 years old"
- Selected in 2009 for inclusion on the National Recording Registry of the Library of Congress by the National Recording Preservation Board, which noted that Little Richard's "unique vocalizing over the irresistible beat announced a new era in music"
- Ranked #130 in the RIAA/NEA list of the 365 "Top Songs of the 20th Century"
- Chosen by the Rock & Roll Hall of Fame as one of the "500 Songs That Shaped Rock and Roll"
- Ranked #43 on the *Rolling Stone's* 2004 list of "The 500 Greatest Songs of All Time"
- Ranked #38 on Joel Whitburn's *Honor Roll of Hits*
- Ranked #15 on the VH1 2004 list of the "100 Greatest Rock Songs"
- Ranked #1 on *Mojo* magazine's "Big Bangs: 100 Records That Changed the World" (June 2007), described as a list of "[t]he most influential & inspirational recordings ever made, they changed music - the way it was played, bought or even imagined"
- Ranked #9 in Dave Marsh's 1989 book, *The Heart of Rock & Soul: The 1001 Greatest Singles Ever Made*

ALSO WORTH NOTING . . .

- It has been suggested that Little Richard's wailing falsetto "Oooh!" was appropriated by The Beatles, who were his opening act on a 1963 European tour.
- "Tutti Frutti" provided the title for Nik Cohn's *"Awopbopaloobop Alopbamboom"* (1969), one of the earliest books exploring the emergence of Rock 'n' Roll in the 1950s.
- "Tutti Frutti" was sampled by Buchanon & Goodman on the 1956 hit novelty song "Flying Saucers, Part 1," on Luniverse 101: "And now I believe we are about to hear the words of the first spaceman ever to land on earth, 'wop bop a loo bop wop bam boom.'"
- In 1984 a record titled "Tutti Frutti Oh Flutie" by T.D. and the Extra Points mimicked in many ways Little Richard's "Tutti Frutti," although not credited to him. The label touted: "A Rockin Tribute to the Miami Miracle," which referenced Doug Flutie's successful "Hail Mary" pass that propelled Boston College to a win over defending National Champion University of Miami 47-45 on the last play of the game.
- "Tutti Frutti" was even appropriated as the name for a group produced by Richard Perry that issued a 45 on Reprise 0866 in 1969 ("Don't You Just Know It," a cover of Huey Smith and Clowns b/w "Honeysuckle Workout").
- In 1955 Mel Torme issued a record on Coral 9-61263 titled "Tutti Frutti," but, blessedly, it is not the same song.

ADDITIONAL SOURCES

Vera, Billy, *Rip It Up: The Specialty Records Story* (BMG, 2019)

White, Charles, *The Life and Times of Little Richard: The Authorized Biography* (Omnibus Press, 2003)

Williams, Paul, *Rock and Roll: The 100 Best Singles*, Ch. 3 ("Tutti Frutti") (Carroll & Graf, 1993)

CHAPTER 7

"BLUE SUEDE SHOES"

CARL PERKINS (JANUARY 1956)

Original release on Sun 234 (West Coast pressing with Delta Nos.)

Original B-side of Sun 234 (West Coast pressing with Delta Nos.)

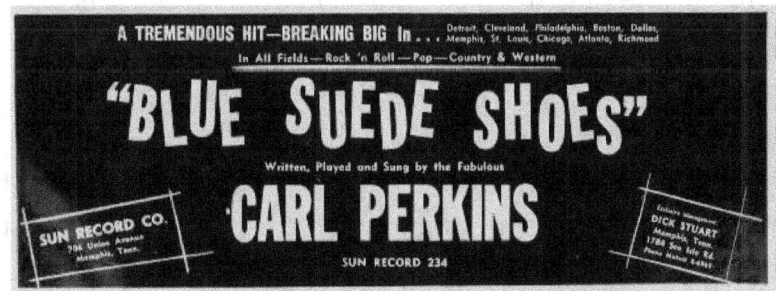

Cash Box ad, March 3, 1956

"BLUE SUEDE SHOES" — THE BASIC FACTS

Label: Sun 234 (both 45 and 78)

Writer: Carl Perkins

Date recorded: December 19, 1955

Date released: January 5, 1956 (although possibly in late December 1955)

B-Side: "Honey, Don't!"

Producer: Sam Phillips

Billboard charts:

Pop Chart
- Debut: 3/03/56
- Peak: #2
- Duration: 21 weeks

R&B Chart
- Debut: 3/10/56
- Peak: #2
- Duration: 16 weeks

Country Chart
- Debut: 3/10/56
- Peak: #1 (3 weeks)
- Duration: 24 weeks

THE SONG AND ITS IMPACT

The inspiration for "Blue Suede Shoes" came initially from Johnny Cash who in the fall of 1955 suggested to Carl Perkins that he should write a song about blue suede shoes based on a comment he heard from an army buddy, C.V. White, a flashy dresser who had admonished Johnny, "Don't step on my blue suede shoes." Carl seemingly ignored the suggestion until one night in October 1955, at one of his performances he overheard a young male angrily telling his date, "Don't step on my suedes." He was taken aback by how upset the male was at having his suede shoes stepped on. Later that night when he couldn't get to sleep, he got up and in the span of several hours before dawn he penciled out the lyrics to "Blue Suede Shoes" on a brown paper potato bag.

As related in his biography, *Go, Cat, Go! The Life and Times of Carl Perkins*, when he told Sam Phillips about his new song, which he called "Don't Step On My Blue Suede Shoes," Sam was interested, but told Carl, "Sounds good, but the title's too long; it'll take up the whole label. We'll call it 'Blue Suede Shoes.'" Some time passed before Carl and his band returned to Sun Studios on December 19, 1955, to record "Blue Suede Shoes." During the session, Perkins first altered the lyrics from "Go, man, go" to "Go, boy, go," and then on the second take to "Go, cat, go." When Perkins pleaded to do another take because he had mistakenly said "Go, cat, go," Sam Phillips response was adamant, "You ain't changin' nothin'." As they say, the rest is history.[33]

As a possible B-side, Carl suggested "Honey Don't," a song that he said he improvised and perfected while playing the honky tonks in and around Memphis. Phillips paired it with "Blue Suede Shoes," cut the masters, and shipped the acetates to Superior Records in Los Angeles with the direction to rush shipment of the 45 and 78 stampers to Plastic Products, the Memphis record plant that Phillips used to press Sun records.[34]

Released on January 1, 1956, *Billboard's* review on January 21 was lukewarm at best, calling it "a lively reading on a gay rhythm ditty with strong r. & b. styled backing. Fine for the jukes." It gave the record a rating of 76, which in *Billboard's* rating terminology was "Good," but not "Tops" (90-100), or even "Excellent" (80-89). Despite its initial unenthusiastic review of "Blue Suede Shoes," a few weeks later on February 18, 1956, *Billboard* listed it as one of the week's "Best Buys" in the C&W field:

In addition to C&W record buyers, *Billboard* presciently noted that "the disk has a large measure of appeal for pop and R&B customers." As set forth in the info above, "Blue Suede Shoes" rose to #1 on the country chart, and #2 on both the pop and R &B charts, and in the process became the

• This Week's Best Buys

BLUE SUEDE SHOES (Hi Lo, BMI)--Carl Perkins--Sun 234
Difficult as the country field is for a newcomer to "crack" these days, Perkins has come up with some wax here that has hit the national retail chart in almost record time. New Orleans, Memphis, Nashville, Richmond, Durham and other areas report it a leading seller. Interestingly enough, the disk has a large measure of appeal for pop and r.&b. customers. Flip is "Honey, Don't" (Hi Lo, BMI).

first record to be a three-market hit, preceding Presley's "Heartbreak Hotel" by several weeks.

Of all the records selected for this book, "Blue Suede Shoes" attracted the most contemporaneous cover versions issued by mainline record labels, including Capitol (Bob Roubian), Columbia (Sid King), Decca (Roy Hall), Dot (Jim Lowe), King (Boyd Bennett), Mercury (Jerry Mercer), MGM (Sam "The Man" Taylor), and RCA (Pee Wee King), each of which is documented below. Only Boyd Bennett's cover version made any of the *Billboard* charts.

Not surprisingly, "Blue Suede Shoes" attracted numerous budget label covers. Typical of the budget labels of the 1950s, there were multiple examples of the same song by the same artist released on two or more different budget labels. For instance, Delbert Barker's cover of "Blue Suede Shoes" was released on the Big 4 Hits (two different releases with a different mixture of hits), Gateway, and Worthmore. And Barker used the name Buzz Williams for his release of "Blue Suede Shoes" on the Hep label.

---

33 Acclaimed Sun Record Label chroniclers Colin Escott and Martin Hawkins, in their book *Good Rockin' Tonight* (1991), assert that after the first take, "Phillips suggests that Perkins change it [from "go, boy, go"] to ' go cat go.'" While I have found Escott/Hawkins normally to be quite reliable, on this point I have to credit the accounts of both Perkins in his book, *Go, Cat, Go* and Peter Guralnick in his book, *Sam Phillips, The Man who Invented Rock 'n' Roll*, that it was Perkins who on his own used the phrase "go, cat, go" on the second take.

34 For information on what acetates and stampers are and how they are used in the production of vinyl records, *see* htts://blog.discogs.com/en/how records-are-made.

The best known of the subsequent cover versions is Elvis Presley's. Steve Sholes recorded his version of "Blue Suede Shoes" on January 30, 1956. Several days later he called Sam Phillips to inquire whether Sam would have any objections if RCA released Elvis' version. When Phillips objected, Sholes backed off (although he didn't legally have to), telling Sam that RCA would only put in on an EP, which would not directly compete with Perkins' version on the 45 singles' chart. Released on March 23, 1956, the EP (RCA EPA-747) entered the *Billboard* pop chart on April 7, 1956, where it remained for 12 weeks, peaking at #20. It also appeared on *Elvis Presley*, his first RCA album that was released in the same timeline. At the same time it was included as one of the eight songs on a double-pocket EP (RCA EPB-1254). It was also one of the 12 songs on the rare triple-pocket promotional EP that was released sometime in 1956 on RCA SPD-23. Finally, on August 31, 1956, RCA released "Blue Suede Shoes" as a single on RCA 47-6636, backed with "Tutti Frutti."

Rare paper sleeve for RCA EPA-747

August 1956 release on RCA 47-6636

Interestingly, four months earlier in April 1956, RCA Records in Canada released "Blue Suede Shoes" as a single on RCA 47-6492, backed with "I'm Counting On You," a song that Presley recorded on January 11, 1956. Of interest to collectors is that "I'm Counting on You" was not released as a single in the U.S. until August 1956 on RCA 47-6637, backed with "I Got a Woman." As noted above, it had been released in the U.S. on single-pocket, double-pocket, and triple-pocket EPs.

In the UK, Perkins' original version was released in April 1956, on London HLU 8271. It debuted on the UK charts on May 24, 1956, peaked at #10, and remained on the charts for nine weeks. On the other hand, Presley's version was released in the UK on HMV 7M 405 in late May,[35]

---

35 It is likely that the UK 78 on HMV POP.213 was released before the 45 was released on HMV HLU 8271. The introduction of 45s in the UK occurred much later than it did in the U.S.

backed with "Tutti Frutti." It first hit the UK charts on May 31, 1956, and reached #9 during its 10 weeks on the UK charts. One *45Cat* commentator noted that "[b]oth versions only just made it into the Top Ten. Had there been only one version, it might have been Number One."

Over the years, people have identified "Blue Suede Shoes" more with Elvis Presley than Carl Perkins. As Bob Dylan observed, "Carl wrote the song, but if Elvis was alive today, he'd be the one to have a deal with Nike."

In addition to Elvis Presley, Buddy Holly, Bill Haley, and Eddie Cochran all covered it soon after. Evidence of its continuing impact are the later 45 versions by Johnny Rivers (1973), Lemmy and the Upsetters (Lemmy was the former front man for Motorhead) (1990), and Chris Robinson Brotherhood (Chris was the former lead singer of The Black Crowes) (2012). Rivers' cover peaked at #38 on *Billboard's* pop chart.

The Beatles were big fans of Carl Perkins. They recorded "Blue Suede Shoes" in a medley (along with "Rip It Up" and "Shake, Rattle and Roll") during The Beatles' *Get Back* sessions in January 1969, at Apple Studios in London. It was later released as an LP on *The Beatles –Anthology 3* on Capitol C1 7243. And, of course, it is well known that The Beatles released three different Carl Perkins songs as 45s: "Matchbox" on Capitol 5255, "Honey, Don't" and "Everybody's Trying to Be My Baby," both on the *4-By The Beatles* EP on Capitol R-5365.

The impact that Carl Perkins had on all four Beatles, collectively and individually, and a host of other musicians, as well as the reverence with which he is held, is especially evidenced by the 1996 "Go Cat Go!" CD on which the contributing artists were in alphabetical order: Bono, Johnny Cash, Eric Clapton, Clarence Clemons, Rick Danko, Dr. John, John Fogerty, George Harrison, Levon Helm, Jimi Hendrix, Paul McCartney, Willie Nelson, Tom Petty, Lee Rocker, Paul Simon, Ringo Starr, and Joe Walsh. One of the songs, "Rockabilly Music," was co-penned and sung by Carl Perkins and Paul Simon. Fifteen of the 17 songs were specifically recorded for this CD, but the remaining two are cover versions of "Blue Suede Shoes," one by John Lennon, which was taken from the *Live Peace Toronto 1969* LP, and the other by Jimi Hendrix, which had been recorded live in Berkeley, CA, on May 30, 1970.

A special tip of the hat should also be given to "Honey, Don't!," the B-side of "Blue Suede Shoes," making it a great two-sider!!! As already noted, it was covered by The Beatles, as well as by numerous other artists, including Mac Curtis on Epic 5-10574, Ronnie Hawkins and the Hawks on Ozark 9002/3 (UK), and Wanda Jackson on Capitol EAP-1-21005 (Australia).

CONTEMPORANEOUS COVER VERSIONS OF "BLUE SUEDE SHOES"

ARTIST	LABEL	COMMENTS
Boyd Bennett and His Rockets	King 4903	B/w "Mumbles Blues"; peaked at #63 on the *Billboard* pop chart
Roy Hall	Decca 9-29880	BB C&W rev. 3/31/56; b/w "Luscious"
Roy Hall	Brunswick 05555 (UK)	B/w "Luscious"
Homer & Jethro (titled "Two Tone Shoes")	RCA 47-6542	Parody version; b/w "Hart Brake Motel," another parody version
Pee Wee King and His Band	RCA 47-6450	BB C&W rev. 3/3/56; vocal by Walter Hayes; b/w "Tennessee Dancin' Doll"
Sid King & The Five Strings	Columbia 4-2104	BB C&W rev. 3/10/56; b/w "Let 'Er Roll"
Jim Lowe	Dot 15456	B/w "(Love Is) The $64,000 Question"
Jim Lowe	London HLD 8276 (UK)	B/w "Maybelline," a cover of Chuck Berry
Jerry Mercer	Mercury 70805	B/w "The Ghost of My Love"; terrible big band pop version with vocal chorus
Bob Roubian	Capitol F3373	With Cliffie Stone & His Orchestra; BB pop rev. 3/3/56; b/w "Candy Coated Kisses";
Sam "The Man" Taylor	MGM K12197	Taylor does the vocal on "Blue Suede Shoes"; b/w "To A Wild Rose"

Roy Hall on Decca

Boyd Bennett on King

Billboard ad, June 16, 1956

While the *Billboard* publisher's ad lists Lawrence Welk as having released a version of "Blue Suede Shoes" on Coral, I have found no evidence that it exists. The *Billboard* list of available versions also lists Lawrence Welk on Coral, but unlike all the other versions, no Coral release number is provided. Searches on *Google, eBay, Discogs*, and *45cat* did not turn up anything. The *Google* search, however, did establish that Buddy Merrill, a Welk vocalist, sang "Blue Suede Shoes" on the Lawrence Welk Show that aired on May 11, 1956.

CONTEMPORANEOUS BUDGET LABEL COVERS OF "BLUE SUEDE SHOES"

ARTIST	LABEL	COMMENTS
Delbert Barker	Big 4 Hits 185	4-song EP with "Heartbreak Hotel"/"Juke Box Baby"/"I'll Be Home"
Delbert Barker	Big 4 Hits 187; Worthmore 187	4-song EP with "Heartbreak Hotel"/"Glad Rags"/"These Hands"; Worthmore label: "Country & Western Series"
Delbert Barker	Gateway 1162	B/w "Heartbreak Hotel"; "Parade of Hits" series
Loren Becker	Waldorf Music Hall 212	4-song EP with "Rock And Roll Waltz"/"Rip It Up"/"Saints Rock And Roll"
Loren Becker	Rock 'n Roll T7A-X45	EP with six other songs including "Hound Dog"
Loren Becker	Waldorf Music Hall WH 4547	EP with "Hot Diggity"/"Poor People Of Paris"/"Rock And Roll Rag"
Loren Becker	18 Top Hits 175	With The Zig Zags; five other songs are on the EP
Jerry Dodge and The Lazy Ranch Boys	Broadway 324	B/w "Why Baby Why" by Tommy Loftin and the Lazy Ranch Boys
Four Angels featuring Judy Lynn and Paul Bean	Today's 507	B/w "Heart Break [sic] Hotel"/"Jute [sic] Box Baby"/"I'll Be Home"
Terry Hall	Hep 285	AKA Delbert Barker; EP with "Heart Break [sic] Hotel"/"Juke Box Baby"/"I'll Be Home"; Michigan label
Thumper Jones	Dixie 502	AKA Leon Payne; 6-song EP including "Heartbreak Hotel" by Thumper Jones (AKA George Jones); part of a Dixie label mail order series
Bill Marine	Prom 45-712	B/w "A Tear Fell"/"I'll Be Home"/"Hot Diggity"

Hank Smith & The Nashville Playboys	Hollywood 280; Tops R280-49	AKA Leon Payne; b/w "Heartbreak Hotel"/"Juke Box Baby"/"Rock Island Line"; also released on Record-of-the Month Club 280;
Hank Smith	Tops 45-R279-79	AKA Leon Payne; EP with "Yes, I Know Why"/"Heartbreak Hotel"/"So Doggone Lonely"; "Western Series"
Buzz Williams	Worthmore 185	AKA Delbert Barker; b/w "Heartbreak Hotel"/"Juke Box Baby"/"I'll Be Home"
None listed	EP 334	B/w "Juke Box Baby"/"Heartbreak Hotel"/"I'll Be Home"
None listed	Value 199	B/w "Heartbreak Hotel"/"A Tear Fell"/"No Not Much"
None listed	Variety EPV-6025	B/w "Rock Around The Clock"/"Long Tall Sally"/"Ain't That A Shame"/"Hound Dog"/"See You Later Alligator"

 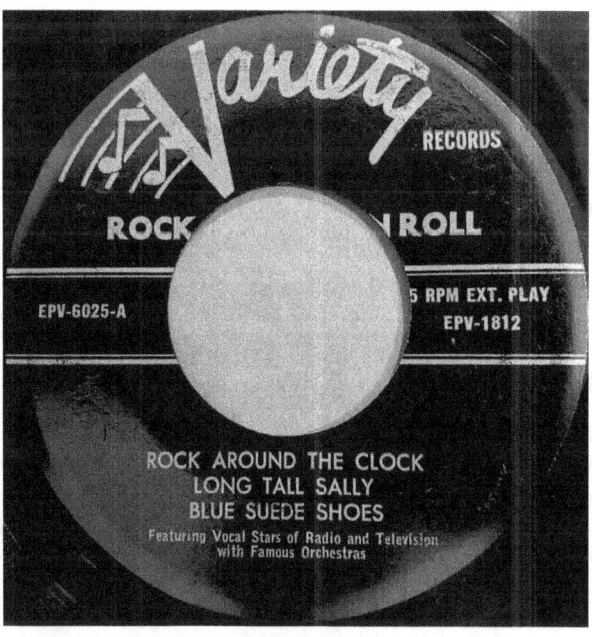

Budget cover versions on the Today's and Variety labels

LATER RELEASES OF "BLUE SUEDE SHOES" BY CARL PERKINS

LABEL	YEAR	COMMENTS
Sun EP-115	1958	B/w "Movie Magg"/"Sure To Fall"/"Gone Gone Gone"
London HLS-10192 (UK)	1968	B/w "Matchbox"; reissue of the Sun originals
Sun 6094 002 (UK)	1970	B/w "Only You," Perkins' cover of the Platters hit
Sun 4	c. 1971	B/w "Honey Don't!"; Sun "Golden Treasure Series"
Charly Pye CYS 1014 (UK)	1976	7" small hole 45; b/w "Matchbox"
Jet ZS8 5054	1978	Re-recorded; b/w "Rock On Around The World" and "That's All Right"; produced by Felton Jarvis
K-TEL 7913	1981	EP titled "Class of '55" with "Tutti Frutti" by Little Richard, "Earth Angel" by The Crew Cuts, and "Rock Around The Clock" by Bill Haley and His Comets
Ripete R45-126	Early 80s	B/w "Be-Bop-A-Lula" by Gene Vincent
Ripete R45-165	Early 80s	B/w "Holy Cow" by Lee Dorsey
Collectables 3088	1984	B/w "Honey Don't!"
Original Sound 4549	1986	B/w "Honey Don't!"; "Oldies But Goodies" series
Old Gold OG-9737 (UK)	1987	B/w "Raunchy" by Bill Justis; licensed from Charly Records; from the Sun original masters
Demon 45001/8 (UK)	2016	B/w "Bopping The Blues"; from the Sun originals

Rockinitis Records (no record number)	2017	The so-called "The Lost Acetate," a four song EP that was allegedly taped by one of the musicians on a 1964 UK tour and sent to Deroy Sound Service to be custom pressed; it captures unreleased "live" performances from Perkins' May 1964, tour of England backed by the Nashville Teens; the other three songs are "Lonely Hearts," "High Heel Sneakers," and "Matchbox"
Sun 234 (TMR 361 reissue)	2017	B/w "Honey Don't"; issued with replica Sun label sleeve with the Third Man Record logo

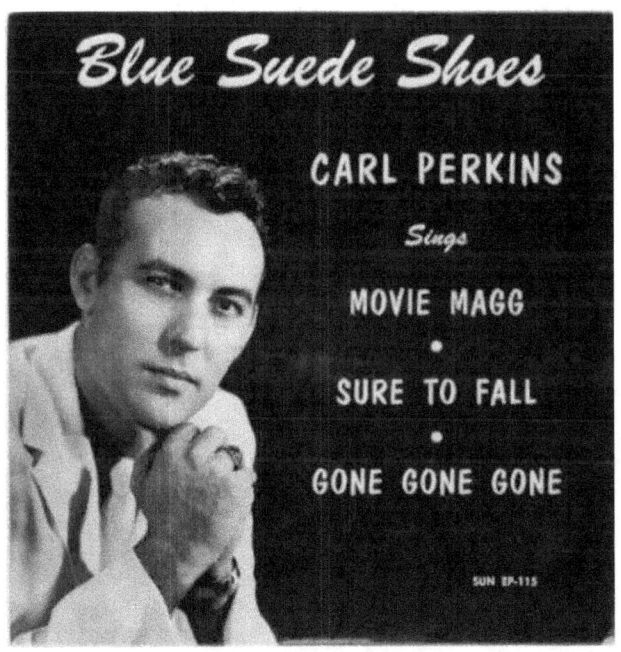

Sun EP-115

Sun "Golden Treasure Series"

SUBSEQUENT COVER VERSIONS OF "BLUE SUEDE SHOES"

ARTIST	LABEL	YEAR	COMMENTS
Beacon Street Union	MGM K13935	1968	B/w "Four Hundred And Five"; group named for the street in their native Boston, MA; psychedelic band
The Birdwatchers	Tara 1001	1964	Garage version; b/w "She Tears Me Up"; "A Gary Stites Production"; Florida label; wild version
Tom Birg and The Rockin' Ghosts	Thunder 1	1960s	B/w "Midnight Special"; San Mateo, CA, label; comped on LP *Let's Go Rockabilly* on Lonely Records 2219 (France, 1979)
Eddie Bond	Rock-It 104	1979	B/w "One Way Ticket"; Deer Park, TX, label
Eddie Cochran	Liberty LEP 2052 (UK)	c. 1962	7" small hole EP with "Long Tall Sally"/"Little Angel"/"Milk Cow Blues"
Paul Dragon	Star Fire 109, Dragon 200	1975	B/w "Mean Woman Blues"; produced by Paul Dragon and Rip Lay
Cova Elkins	Cova 133	1975	Promo with "Blue Suede Shoes" on both sides; produced by Harold Bradley; South Nashville, TN, label
Marc Ellington	Ampex X 11030	1971	DJ copy has mono/stereo versions of "Blue Suede Shoes"; b/w "Rains/Reins Of Change"
Charlie Feathers	Feathers 1	1979	B/w "We're Getting Closer To Being Apart"; "Jukebox Rockabilly Series"
Shane Greer	Quadrille Q-913	???	Instrumental version; b/w "Blue Suede Shoes (called)"; square dance record
Cecil Hadden	Studio Four 103	1960s ???	B/w "Holding Things Together"; Dothan, AL, label

Bill Haley and His Comets	Warner Brothers WEP-1633 (UK)	1964	EP with "Stagger Lee"/"I Almost Lost My Mind"/"Blueberry Hill"
Dora Hall	Cozy 71000	1971	B/w "Rock Medley," which includes "Long Tall Sally"; Solo Cup "Once Upon A Tour" promotion; Dora was the wife of the founder of Solo Cup
Jimi Hendrix	Barclay 61550 (France)	1972	B/w "Johnny B. Goode"; extended classic Hendrix distorted guitar break; PS titled "Jimi Hendrix Story Vol. 11"
Don Hinton	GMA 11	1964	B/w "The Way You Are Tonight"; Chicago label
Buddy Holly	Coral FEP 2069 (UK)	1964	EP with "Shake, Rattle and Roll"/"Come on Baby"/"Love's Made A Fool Of You"
Charlie Ingram	Char-Mart 7172	c. late 60s or early 70s	Energetic Elvis-like version; b/w "Match Box"; Meridian, MS, label with address and phone number; artist's name is written in ink on label; perhaps a vanity release, since there is no reference to this release on the internet
Jerry (Big Bear) Jones	Fan 11329	???	Secretary, MD, label; b/w "We Love You Uncle Sam"; nothing could be found on the internet about this release
Johnny G	Beggar's Banquet 344	1980	Titled "Blue Suede Shoes (Leave Me Alone)" and credited to Perkins, with lyrics from "Blue Suede Shoes" supplemented by phrases added by Johnny G, primarily "Leave Me Alone"; b/w "Highway Shoes (Put 'Em On)"
Jim Kirby with Jinx Jones and The Jaguars	Devoid DV041181	1981	B/w "Enough is Enough (When There's All That Stuff)"

Aaron Lee	BKY 315 (France)	1982	B/w "Treat Her Nice"
Lemmy & The Upsetters	Sunnyside STYLE 777 (UK)	1990	Heavy metal version with Mick Green on guitar; Lemmy is the former front man for Motorhead; b/w "Paradise"; 7" small hole 45; taken from the New Musical Express double album *The Last Temptation Of Elvis*
Long John and His Ballroom Kings	Rydell's Records RR 721 (France)	2015	Featuring Huelyn Duvall; b/w "It Is True What They Say About Dixie"
Jim Marlboro	Jim M G-1748	???	7" small hole 33 1/3 mini-album; b/w "Jambalaya"/"A Long Time In The Mountain"/"Sometimes"; Delaware Gap, PA, label; other than the label info, nothing further was found about this artist and release
Ricky Martin and The Tyme Machine	Olga OLE 004 (UK)	1968	B/w "Something Else," a cover of Eddie Cochran
Jim Matthews and The Traditions	Shoe 3672	1972	B/w "Goin' Out Of My Mind"; Piscataway, NJ, label
Glenn Mead	Ponzi 100	???	B/w "Baby I Don't Care," a cover of Presley
Sandy Nelson	Imperial IRK-2548 (Australia)	1968	B/w "Summertime Blues"; both sides are instrumentals
Mark Papousek	Snocan 225 (Canada)	1986	B/w "The Comb Song"; Papousek was a long time DJ at CKBY-FM in Ottawa, Canada
Buddy Porter	Scamp NR8938	1970s	B/w "Splish Splash," a cover of Bobby Darin's hit; Roanoke, VA, label; Elvis sound-a-like

Elvis Presley	RCA 47-6636	1956	BB pop rev. 9/8/56; b/w "Tutti Frutti";
Elvis Presley	RCA EBP-1254 (547-0793)	1956	A two-pocket EP with 4 songs on each of the EP's; the EP with "Blue Suede Shoes" includes "I'm Counting On You"/"I'm Gonna Sit Right Down And Cry"/"I'll Never Let You Go"
Elvis Presley	HMV 7M 213 (UK)	1956	B/w "Tutti Frutti"
Elvis Presley	RCA 1095 (UK)	1958	B/w "Hound Dog"
Elvis Presley	RCA 447-0609	1959	B/w "Tutti Frutti"; "Gold Standard Series"
Elvis Presley	Sun 521	1970s	B/w "My Baby's Gone"; repro/bootleg
Elvis Presley	RCA 2715 (Canada)	1978	B/w "Tutti Frutti"; "Victor Collector Series"
Elvis Presley	RCA PB-13929	1984	B/w "Promised Land"
Elvis Presley	RCA PB-13885	1984	B/w "Tutti Frutti"; gold vinyl 50th Presley Anniversary reissue
Elvis Presley	Collectables 4522 (DPE1-1022)	1986	B/w "Fools Fall In Love"; "Back to Back Hits Series"
The Radio	Fader Kat 101	1969	Rock; b/w "Border Town"
Ricky and The Memphis Beat	American 010 (Belgium)	???	Medley with "Whole Lotta Shakin' Goin' On"; b/w "I Can Sing You (Lonely Man)"
Bob Riley and His Magic Guitar	Vikim 7661	1965	B/w "Red Roses For A Blue Lady"; Riley was known as "The Elvis of New England" and was a regular of the Boston-aired "Hayloft Jamboree"
Johnny Rivers	UA XW198-W	1973	On the *Billboard* "Hot 100" chart for 10 weeks and peaked at #38 during its 10 week run; b/w "Stories To A Child"

Johnny Rivers	United Artist XW-522	1974	B/w "Rockin' Pneumonia – Boogie Woogie Flu"; "Silver Spotlight Series"; also issued on Capitol X 522 (Silver Spotlight Series)
Chris Robinson Brotherhood	Silver Arrow	2012	RSD release; b/w "Girl I Love You"; 7" small hole colored 45
Jack Scott	Underground C-387	1979	Canadian release recorded "live" in Toronto on 4/4/79; b/w "I Knew You First"
Norman Seldin & The Joyful Noyze	Pandora's Box PB1A	c. 1970s	Medley with "Chantilly Lace"; b/w "Johnny B. Goode"
Stampeders	MWC PR 1X (Canada)	1974	B/w "Devil You"; "Special Promotion—Not For Sale"
Sully	Bunny 810104	1981	Accompanied by "The Northern Review Band & The Tender Touch"; b/w "Pledging My Love," a cover of Johnny Ace; an internet search yielded no info on this artist or release, but the picture sleeve strongly suggests that Sully was an Elvis tribute artist
Tumbleweed Band	Comanchero 104	1976-77	B/w "Spanish Pipe Dream"
Conway Twitty	MGM EP-752 (UK)	1960	EP with "Shake, Rattle and Roll"/"Diana"/"Treat Me Nice"
Bert Weedon	Polydor 2058 832 (UK)	1977	Medley titled "Rocking Guitar," which also includes "Guitar Boogie Shuffle"/"Shake, Rattle and Roll"/"See You Later, Alligator"/"What'd I Say"/"Rock Around The Clock"; b/w "Bella Ciao"
Johnnie White	M-S 242	1973	Medley with "Long Tall Sally"/"Party Doll"/"Johnny B. Goode"/"Whole Lotta Shakin' Goin' On"

Whitson Hollow, featuring Fred Huber	Whitson Hollow 333	1970s	Recorded at Malaco Studios, Jackson, MS; b/w "Hard Rain's Gonna Fall," a Dylan cover

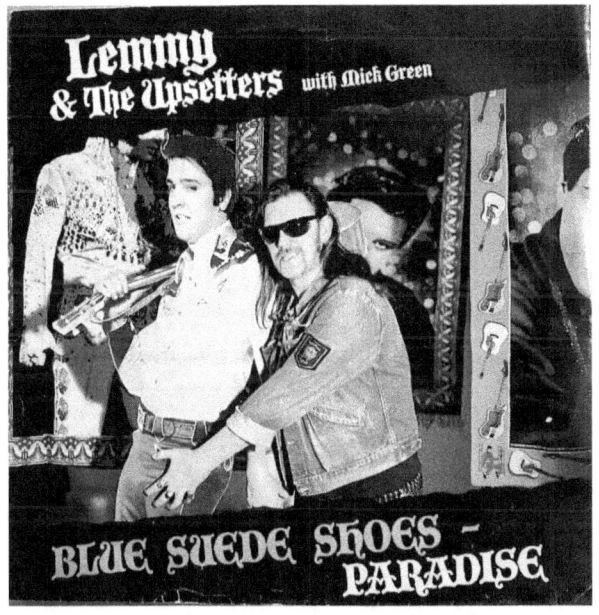

Lemmy & the Upsetters 1990 release on Sunnyside (UK)

Chris Robinson Brotherhood 2012 RSD release on Silver Arrow

"BLUE SUEDE SHOES" IN THE MOVIES

"Blue Suede Shoes" has appeared on a number of movie soundtracks over the years, including over the opening credits to the 1980 UK film, *Blue Suede Shoes,* that documents England's Rock & Roll revival, and prominently features Bill Haley and His Comets. The movies where "Blue Suede Shoes" can be heard include the following:

MOVIE TITLE	YEAR	COMMENTS
G.I. Blues	1960	Performed by Elvis Presley, who re-recorded it in stereo, closely following his original mono version; while it is on the soundtrack for the film, it was not issued as a single
Blue Suede Shoes	1980	Performed by Carl Perkins; movie features Bill Haley, Eddie Cochran, Gene Vincent, Crazy Cavan, Ray Campi, among others; it can be found on *YouTube*
Porky's Revenge!	1985	Sung by Perkins and backed by Lee Rocker and Slim Jim Phantom of The Stray Cats; *see* below
Heaven Help Us	1985	Performed by Elvis Presley; a coming-of-age movie
The Pick-up Artist	1987	*IMdbpro* does not state who performs the song; Molly Ringwald and Robert Downey, Jr., star in this crime/comedy drama
Rock Odyssey	1987	Performed by Robert Jason; a jukebox narrated by Scatman Crothers documents a woman's search for true love based on four decades of rock music; animated by Hanna/Barbera
Salsa	1988	Performed by Draco Rosa
Pink Cadillac	1989	Performed by Carl Perkins; stars Clint Eastwood and Bernadette Peters; a crime/comedy/action flick
New York Stories	1989	Performed by Carl Perkins; both Woody Allen and Mia Farrow star in this movie
The Last of the High Kings (Ireland)	1996	Performed by Elvis Presley; coming-of-age flick starring Catherine O'Hara, Christina Ricci, and Jared Leto
Man on the Moon	1999	Comedy starring Jim Carrey, with Danny DeVito who was the producer; the film is about the life and career of legendary comedian Andy Kaufman

The Roaring 20s: Mick Jagger's Golden Years	2011	Performed by Elvis Presley; documentary exploring the musical influences of Mick Jagger during the period 1963 to 1972
Battleship	2012	Performed by Josh Max; film marked Rihanna's acting debut
Jim & Andy: The Great Beyond	2017	Performed by Jim Carrey; a documentary about how Jim Carrey adopted the persona of comedian Andy Kaufman
Rocketman	2019	A musical fantasy about the life of Elton John; performed by Elvis Presley, which was taken from a clip of the *Dorsey Brothers Stage Show*
Elvis	2022	Performed by Elvis and taken from footage of his *1969 Comeback Special;* biography of Elvis Presley who is played by Austin Butler, as seen through the eyes of Colonel Thomas Parker played by Tom Hanks.

The soundtrack for the 1985 movie, *Porky's Revenge,* contains a newly recorded version of "Blue Suede Shoes" by Carl Perkins, with backing by Lee Rocker and Slim Jim Phantom of The Stray Cats. Produced by Dave Edmunds, the soundtrack also includes songs by Willie Nelson, Jeff Beck, and George Harrison. There is a substantial difference in the quality of the soundtrack and the film, with the latter receiving a nomination for "The Stinkers Bad Movie Awards." *New York Times* critic Janet Maslin called it "just another brand-name teenage movie.... Some of it is funny, but it's also entirely predictable."

DOCUMENTED CONCERT PERFORMANCES OF "BLUE SUEDE SHOES"

As of May 1, 2024, *Setlist.fm* documented that "Blue Suede Shoes" has been performed in concert 1,641 times by 237 different artists. In addition to Carl Perkins (63), the other artists include Johnny Hallyday (368), Elvis Presley (356), Chris Robinson Brotherhood (65), Paul McCartney (58), Cliff Richard (47), Jerry Lee Lewis (33), AC/DC (14), John Fogerty (10), and Fleetwood Mac (7).

HONORS AND ACCOLADES FOR "BLUE SUEDE SHOES"

- Inducted into the Grammy Hall of Fame in 1986
- Selected in 2006 for inclusion on the National Recording Registry of the Library of Congress by the National Recording Preservation Board, which annually selects songs that are "culturally, historically, or aesthetically significant"
- Included on the National Public Radio's *NPR 100*, an unranked list compiled by NPR's editors of the "most important musical works of the 20th century"
- Ranked #68 on the NEA/RIAA 2001 list of the top 365 songs of the 20th century
- Ranked #95 on the *Rolling Stone*'s 2004 list of "The 500 Greatest Songs of All Time"; Presley's cover version ranked #423
- Ranked #9 on Joel Whitburn's *Honor Roll of Hits*
- Listed by the Rock & Roll Hall of Fame as one of "The 500 Songs That Shaped Rock and Roll"
- Ranked #77 on the VH1 2004 list of the "100 Greatest Rock Songs"
- Ranked #93 in Dave Marsh's 1989 book, *The Heart of Rock & Soul: The 1001 Greatest Singles Ever Made*

ALSO WORTH NOTING . . .

- When "Blue Suede Shoes" broke fast and quickly made it to the charts, Steve Sholes, RCA's head of A&R, called Sam Phillips and asked if he had signed the wrong artist; Sam assured Sholes that Elvis would do well.
- In discussing "Blue Suede Shoes," one of 66 songs in his 2022 book, *The Philosophy of Modern Song*, Bob Dylan commented:

  > This song is the handwriting on the wall, loaded with menacing meaning—a signal to gate crashers, snoops, and invaders—keep your nose out of here, mind your own business and whatever you do stay away from my shoes.

- John Lennon regularly performed the song in concert with The Plastic Ono Band; his rendition of "Blue Suede Blues" is included on the album *Live Peace in Toronto 1969*.
- "Blue Suede Shoes" has been quoted in other songs, including Chuck Berry's "Roll Over Beethoven" ("Early in the mornin', I'm-a givin' you the warnin', don't you step on my blue suede shoes").

- Jimi Hendrix performed "Blue Suede Shoes" at the 1970 Atlanta Pop Festival in Byron, Georgia, on July 4, 1970.
- A 2001 bootleg release of "Blue Suede Shoes" performed as a duet by Van Morrison and Bob Dylan exists.
- *Blue Suede Shoes: A Rockabilly Session* was a televised concert that was taped "live" at Limehouse Studios in London, England on 21 October 1985, a show featuring Carl Perkins along with guest stars, including Eric Clapton, George Harrison, and Ringo Starr, as well as Dave Edmunds who served as musical director.
- George Harrison spoke at Perkins' funeral. In addition to Harrison, Garth Brooks, The Judds, and many other music business luminaries attended his funeral in a small town on short notice, which said a lot about his musical influence, and the type of person he was.
- Paul McCartney performed "Blue Suede Shoes" at the 1999 Rock & Roll Hall of Fame induction ceremony on March 3, 1999, at the Waldorf-Astoria Hotel, NYC.
- "Blue Suede Shoes" is referred to by the Rockabilly Hall of Fame as "the first true rock 'n' roll hit, in the sense that it was an 'all market' hit." On the *Billboard* charts it peaked at #1 on the country chart and at #2 on both the pop and R&B charts.
- Perkins does a great version of his song on Johnny Cash's *Madison Square Garden* album.
- "Blues Suede Shoes" was sampled by Buchanan & Goodman on the 1956 hit novelty song "Flying Saucers, Part 2," on Luniverse 101.
- Playing off the "Blue Suede Shoes" motif, country artists Con Hunley and Mel McDaniel both recorded a song titled "Blue Suede Blues," Hunley in 1986 on Capitol B-5586 and McDaniel in 1989 on Capitol B-44358.

ADDITIONAL SOURCES

Dylan, Bob, *The Philosophy of Modern Song* (Simon & Schuster, 2022)

Escott, Colin and Martin Hawkins, *Sun Records: The Brief History of the Legendary Record Label* (Quick Fox, 1980)

Escott, Colin, with Martin Hawkins, *Good Rockin' Tonight: Sun Records and the Birth of Rock 'N' Roll* (St. Martin's Press, 1991)

Guralnick, Peter, *The Last Train to Memphis: The Rise of Elvis Presley* (Little, Brown, 1994)

Guralnick, Peter, *Sam Phillips: The Man Who Invented Rock 'n' Roll* (Little, Brown, 2015)

Guralnick, Peter, and Colin Escott, *The Birth of Rock 'n' Roll: The Illustrated Story of Sun Records* (Weldon Owen, 2022)

Hilburn, Robert, *Johnny Cash: The Life* (Back Bay Books, 2013)

Perkins, Carl, and David McGee, *Go, Cat, Go!: The Life and Times of Carl Perkins* (Hyperion, 1986)

The Elvis Presley Canadian 45 Discography at elvisrecords.com/the-elvis-presley-canadian-45-discography

CHAPTER 8

"WHY DO FOOLS FALL IN LOVE"

FRANKIE LYMON AND THE TEENAGERS (JANUARY 1956)

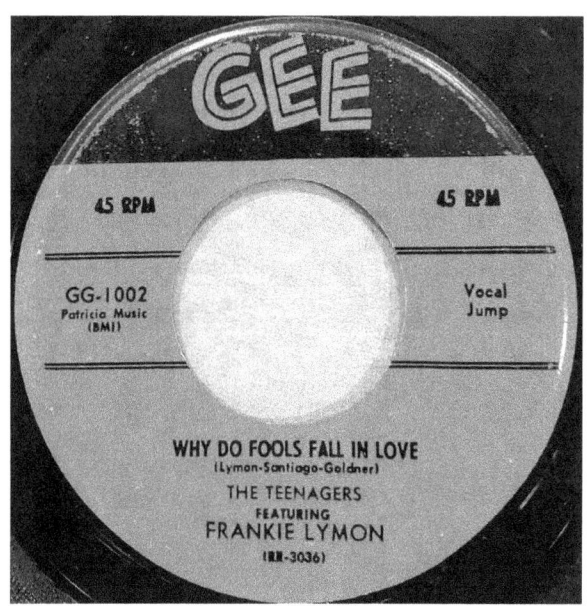

Original release with three writers

Rare label with two writers

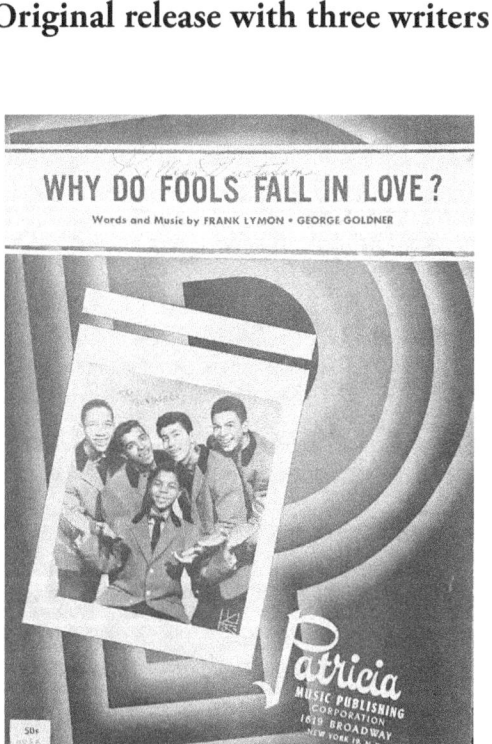

U.S. Sheet Music

Cash Box, January 21, 1956

"WHY DO FOOLS FALL IN LOVE" — THE BASIC FACTS

Label: Gee GG-1002 (both 45 and 78)

Writers: Frankie Lymon, Herman Santiago, and Jimmy Merchant (see comments below)

Date recorded: November 1955

Date released: January 10, 1956

B-Side: "Please Be Mine"

Producer: George Goldner

Billboard charts:

> Pop Chart
> - ■ Debut: 2/11/56
> - ■ Peak: #6
> - ■ Duration: 21 weeks
>
> R&B Chart
> - ■ Debut: 2/18/56
> - ■ Peak: #1 (5 weeks)
> - ■ Duration: 17 weeks

THE SONG AND ITS IMPACT

The story behind the writing of "Why Do Fools Fall In Love" is far from the fantasy version set forth on the back side of the EP released in the UK in 1957 on Columbia SEG 7662:

> It was originally written for his [Frankie Lymon's] school as a poem, but turned out to be so good that music was written by the manager of "The Teenagers" [George Goldner] and put onto record.

The writer credits on the original Gee 1002 release are somewhat closer to the facts; in addition to Lymon and Goldner, [Herman] Santiago is listed. Later releases, however, only gave writers' credit to Lymon and George Goldner who owned the Gee label. When Goldner sold Gee and its catalog, along with other recording assets, to Morris Levy, Levy's name started appearing as the co-author with Lymon on subsequent releases of "Why Do Fools Fall In Love."

Many years later in 1987 a lawsuit was filed by Jimmy Merchant and Herman Santiago, two of the original members of The Teenagers, seeking to establish that they were co-authors of the song and for which they were seeking damages. Following a jury trial, the federal magistrate judge set forth the essential facts upon which the jury's favorable verdict for them was as based (*Merchant v. Lymon*, 828 F. Supp. 1048 (S.D.N.Y. 1993):

Plaintiffs testified that in April of 1955, Santiago, Merchant, [Sherman] Garnes and [Joe] Negroni formed a singing group, eventually known as The Teenagers, that rehearsed at a local junior high school and at other locations around Washington Heights. At first, the group sang popular songs written by other musicians, but they later began to create their own music. Inspired by love letters given to the group by a neighbor, plaintiffs, neither of whom had any formal musical training, developed the melody and lyrics for *Fools* [the court's shorthand reference to "Why Do Fools Fall In Love"], a song that the group initially called *Birds Sing So Gay*. In the original arrangement of *Fools,* Santiago sang the lead voice and the other group members sang back up. Three witnesses for plaintiff, Gigi Merchant, Howard Bobo and Elder Henix, testified that they heard the original four group members rehearse *Birds Sing So Gay* prior to Lymon's joining the group. Not until June of 1955, approximately two months after the plaintiffs began to write and rehearse this early version of *Fools,* did Lymon join the group.

Due in part to Lymon's presence, a member of another local singing group [Richard Barrett, lead singer of the Valentines] introduced The Teenagers to Goldner, who invited them to audition in September of 1955 at Gee Records. After hearing the group perform *Fools,* Goldner suggested that the group rehearse the song with Lymon replacing Santiago as the lead singer. In December of 1955, the group returned to Gee Records' studios and, accompanied by a band of studio musicians, recorded *Fools.* At the time *Fools* was recorded, plaintiffs were fifteen years old and Lymon was twelve.

The plaintiffs also testified that Goldner told them that he would handle registering the song's copyright but that only two of their names could appear and that "they chose to include the names of the two lead singers Lymon and Santiago, thus accounting for the absence of Merchant's name" on the copyright form.

The jury credited the plaintiffs' version of the facts, with the court rejecting the defendants' numerous challenges. As a result, the court declared that Merchant and Santiago, in addition to Lymon, were co-authors of "Why Do Fools Fall In Love." It then awarded Merchant and Santiago an undivided one-half interest in the copyright and damages that had accrued for the three years prior to the filing of the lawsuit. On appeal, however, the Second District Court of Appeals reversed the jury verdict, holding in agreement with the Defendants that Plaintiffs' copyright co-ownership claim was "time-barred by the three-year statute of limitations." *Merchant and Santiago v. Morris Levy et al.,* 92 F.3d 51 (2d Cir. 1996). As The Bobby Fuller Four sang, "I fought the law and the law won."

Parenthetically, there was a related legal proceeding involving the question of who was Frankie Lymon's wife, who would have the legal right to his estate following his death by a heroin overdose in 1967. Surprisingly, there were three contenders, Zola Taylor, a member of the original Platters; Ethel Waters (no relation to Ethel Waters, the famous singer and actress); and Elmira Eagle. At the time Waters married Lymon she was separated from her first husband but was not yet officially divorced.

On the other hand, Eagle produced documentation of her marriage to Lymon in Augusta, Georgia, in 1967, even though Lymon had not yet divorced Waters. The courts were left to sort all of this out. Initially, the trial court determined that Waters was the rightful claimant to Lyman's estate. However, on appeal, the appellate court overturned the trial court's decision and finally determined that Elmira Eagle was the rightful heir to Lymon's estate. This confusing narrative of three women each seeking to be named Mrs. Frankie Lymon led to the movie *Why Do Fools Fall in Love*, a movie that featured Halle Berry portraying Zola Taylor.

For the purposes of posterity, however, it is appropriate to state with some conviction that the real writers of "Why Do Fall In Love" were Frankie Lymon, Herman Santiago, and Jimmy Merchant.[36] It is also fair to list George Goldner as the producer. Thus, Marv Goldberg in his *R&B Notebooks* recounts that Jimmy Merchant told him that what happened at the recording session was a combination of "Frankie's singing ability with George Goldner's special ability to bring out the best in Frankie." Goldner is also said to be the person who suggested changing the name of the song from "Birds Sing So Gay" to "Why Do Fools Fall in Love." The lyrics, however, do include the phrase, "Why do birds sing so gay." Parenthetically, the BMI website as of March 1, 2021, lists Morris Levy, Elmira E. Lyman, and Frank Joseph Lymon as the "composers" of "Why Do Fools Fall In Love."

"Why Do Fools Fall In Love" was recorded in late November 1955, and released on January 10, 1956. Shortly thereafter on February 4, 1956, it was a *Billboard* "Spotlight" pick, with the notation that it was…

> a hot new disk, which has already sparked a couple of covers in the pop market. The appealing ditty has a frantic arrangement, a solid beat and a sock lead vocal by 13-year-old Frankie Lymon.

It spent 21 weeks on the *Billboard* pop chart, peaking at #6. It took the top spot on the *Billboard* R&B chart for five weeks. It did even better on the *Cash Box* R&B chart where it spent eight weeks in the top spot. Although not released in the UK until six months later on Columbia SCM 5265, it topped the *New Music Express* (NME) chart for three consecutive weeks in July/August 1956 and was in the top three on the British charts for a remarkable eight straight weeks, which helped to establish Frankie Lymon as a major rock star in England.

Continuing a practice that had been in place for many years of major labels issuing covers of promising R&B records put out by small independent labels, several major labels immediately covered "Why Do Fools Fall In Love." The major competitors were Gale Storm's version on Dot and the Diamonds version on Mercury, which both spent nearly 20 weeks on *Billboard*'s pop chart, peaking at #9 and #12, respectively. Even Gloria Mann's version on Decca hit #59 on the *Billboard* pop chart. And, in England Alma Cogan released a cover on HMV that made the lower reaches of the NME

---

36 Being the writer of a song is not synonymous with who gets the credit on the record label. A song is an asset that, like other assets, can be sold. When the rights to a song are sold, the person getting the credit on the record label is usually the name of person who bought or otherwise acquired the rights to the song.

music charts at #25. While these major label covers enjoyed considerable chart success, they did not eclipse the original in either sales or chart position.

Over the years, "Why Do Fools Fall in Love" has been covered by numerous major artists, including The Beach Boys ("Bubbled Under" at #120), The Four Seasons, the Happenings, Joni Mitchell, and Diana Ross. The covers by both the Happenings in 1967 and Diana Ross in 1981 made the *Billboard* pop chart, peaking at #41 and #7, respectively. Ross's cover also rose to #4 on the UK charts. The Ponderosa Twins' cover in 1972 reached #40 on the *Billboard* R&B chart and it also made *Billboard's* "Bubbling Under" chart at #102. Also making the "Bubbling Under" chart was Summer Wine's 1973 version at #103.

The 2017 cover of "Why Do Fools Fall In Love" by the popular R&B boy band Boyz II Men is of interest because it features Jimmy Merchant, one of the co-composers and an original member of The Teenagers. Unfortunately, it is only available as one of 10 cuts on the CD *Under the Streetlight*. It can also be accessed on *Spotify* and the album can be downloaded on *iTunes*.

Despite the numerous covers over the years, including many that charted, in the estimation of virtually everyone, the original version by Frankie Lymon and the Teenagers was and remains "the best version." As Dave Marsh commented, Lymon's "version is the only memorable rendition, a scorching example of what one precocious teenager can accomplish without much ammunition except a huge voice and unwavering ambition."

CONTEMPORANEOUS COVER VERSIONS OF "WHY DO FOOLS FALL IN LOVE"

ARTIST	LABEL	COMMENTS
Alma Cogan	HMV 7N 415 (UK)	B/w "The Same Thing Happens (With The Birds And The Bees)"
The Diamonds	Mercury 70790	Credits Lymon, Goldner, and Santiago; on the *Billboard* pop chart for 19 weeks, peaking at #12; b/w "You Baby You"
The Diamonds	Mercury 70790X-45 (Canada)	B/w "You Baby You"
Gloria Mann	Decca 9-29832	B/w "Partners For Life"
Gloria Mann	Brunswick 05569 (UK)	B/w "Partners For Life"

Gale Storm	Dot 15448	Credits just Lymon and Goldner; on the *Billboard* pop chart for 18 weeks, peaking to #9; b/w "I Walk Alone"
Gale Storm	London HLD 8286 (UK)	B/w "I Walk Alone"

Cash Box, February 4, 1956

Cash Box, March 3, 1956

Billboard, February 11, 1956

Cash Box, February 11, 1956

CONTEMPORANEOUS BUDGET LABEL COVERS OF
"WHY DO FOOLS FALL IN LOVE"

ARTIST	LABEL	COMMENTS
Jack Daniels	Gateway Top Tune/ Parade of Hits 1159	B/w "Flowers Mean Forgiveness"
Barry Frank	Bell 1123	B/w "I'll Be Home"
Ceci Julian	Broadway 45-328	B/w "Eleventh Hour Melody"
New Notes	Remington R-45-79	B/w "A Tear Fell," by Mattie Marshall
Dolly Nunn	Worthmore 183	B/w "Theme From The Three Penny Opera"/"The Poor People Of Paris"/"Flowers Mean Forgiveness"
Eileen Scott	Big 4 Hits 183	B/w "Flowers Mean Forgiveness" / "Theme From The Three Penny Opera" / "Poor People of Paris"
Eileen Scott	Gateway Top Tune 1159	B/w "Flowers Mean Forgiveness," by Jack Daniels
The Teeners, featuring Laura Leslie	Prom 45-710	B/w "The Poor People Of Paris"/"Ninety Nine Years"/"Lullaby Of Birdland"
Benn Zeppa with The Four Jacks	Gilmar RX 119	B/w "No, Not Much"/"A Tear Fell"/"The Poor People Of Paris"/"Tutti Frutti"/"Band Of Gold"
Benn Zeppa with The Four Jacks	Tops R278X45	B/w "No, Not Much"/"A Tear Fell"/"I'll Be Home"; under the name Ben/Benn Joe Zeppa, he recorded several collectable rockabilly records for labels such as Award, Era, and Metrol
The Zig Zag Quartet	Waldorf Music Hall MH-4545	B/w "No, Not Much"/"I'll Be Home"/"Lipstick, Candy and Rubber Soled Shoes"

The Zig Zags	18 Top Hits 174	B/w "Eleventh Hour Melody"/"I'll Be Home"/ "Lipstick, Candy and Rubber Soled Shoes"/"Mr. Wonderful"/"Forever Darling"
The Zig Zags	18 Top Hits 181	B/w "Eleventh Hour Melody"/"I'll Be Home"/ "Rock And Roll Waltz"/"Poor People Of Paris"/ "Juke Box Baby"
None Listed	Variety EP-1812	B/w "When My Dream Boat Comes Home"/"Don't Be Cruel"/"Ready Teddy"/"I'm In Love Again"/"Love, Love, Love"
None Listed	EP 4 Hits 333	B/w "Poor People Of Paris"/"Theme From The Three Penny Opera (Moritat)"/"Flowers Mean Forgiveness"

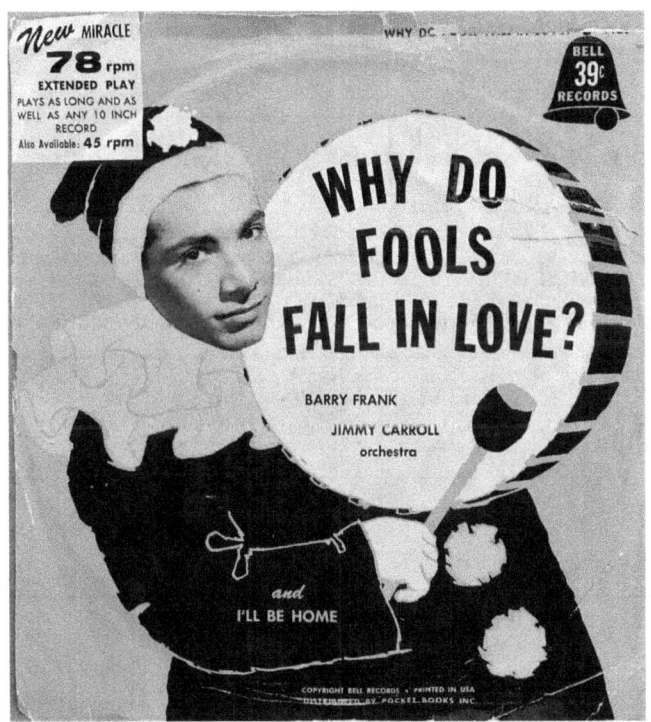 

Budget covers on the Bell and Gilmar labels

LATER RELEASES OF "WHY DO FOOLS FALL IN LOVE" BY FRANKIE LYMON & THE TEENAGERS

LABEL	YEAR	COMMENTS
Gee GEP-601	1956	EP with "Teenage Love"/"I Want You To Be My Girl"/"Love Is A Clown"
Apex 9-76083 (Canada)	1956	B/w "Please Be Mine"; probably released in Canada at about the same time as the original in the U.S.
Columbia SEG 7662 (UK)	1957	EP with "I'm Not A Know It All"/"I Want You To Be My Girl"/"I Promise To Remember"
Gee 1002	1962	B/w "My Girl"; label mentions "A Division of Roulette Records Inc"
Roulette GG 30	1963	B/w "I'm Not A Juvenile Delinquent"; "Golden Goodies Hit Series"
Rama GG 30	1963	B/w "I'm Not A Juvenile Delinquent"; "Golden Goodies Hit Series"
King KG 1042 (UK)	1966	Credited to Lymon/Levy; b/w "I'm Not A Juvenile Delinquent"
Goldies 45 D-2522	1973	B/w "Please Be Mine"; distributed by ABC/Dunhill Records
Polydor PC 1073 (Canada)	1974	B/w "Goody Goody"; "Pop Classics" series; credited to Lymon/Levy
Pye 7N 25773 (UK)	1978	B/w "I'm Not A Juvenile Delinquent" and "Goody Goody"
Precision PRT 7N 25773 (UK)	1981	B/w "I'm Not A Juvenile Delinquent"/"Goody Goody"; licensed from Roulette; a "maxi-single"
Old Gold OG 8411 (UK)	1983	B/w "I'm Not A Juvenile Delinquent"
Musicor MU-1951	1984	Credited to Lymon & Goldner; b/w "Sincerely" by the Moonglows; "Startime Series"

Maybelline 24 (Europe)	1987	B/w "Jailhouse Rock"; 7-inch picture disc
Roulette RLTE 1 (UK)	1989	B/w "Goody Goody"
Old Gold OG 9986 (UK)	1991	B/w "I'm Not A Juvenile Delinquent"
Collectables COL 0100	???	Credited to Lymon & Levy; b/w "Please Be Mine"; "Back to Back Hit Series"

SUBSEQUENT COVER VERSIONS OF "WHY DO FOOLS FALL IN LOVE"

ARTIST	LABEL	YEAR	COMMENTS
The Beach Boys	Capitol 5118	1964	Some but not all releases credit Santiago as well as Lymon and Goldner; b/w "Fun, Fun, Fun"
The Beach Boys	Capitol CL 15339 (UK)	1964	Only credits Lymon and Goldner; b/w "Fun, Fun, Fun"
The Beach Boys	Capitol EAP 1-20603 (UK)	1964	EP with "Fun, Fun, Fun" / "Little Deuce Coupe" / "In My Room"
The Beach Boys	Capitol 6106	1967	B/w "Fun, Fun, Fun"; "Star Line" series
The Beach Boys	Capitol CL 16043 (UK)	1979	Only credits Lymon and Goldner; b/w "Fun, Fun, Fun"
The Beach Boys	Collectables COL 6283	1990s?	B/w "Heroes and Villains"; "Back to Back Hit Series"
Fred Bergin	Rinx 45-226	1950s?	B/w "I'll Be Home" by Jimmy Caro; label noted for releasing organ music for skating rinks
Big Ben Accordion Band	Columbia DB 3835 (UK)	1956	EP with "Rock Around The Clock"/ "Rock Island Line" / "Blue Suede Shoes" / "See You Later, Alligator"/ "The Saints Rock 'N' Roll"

Jimmy Briscoe & The Little Beavers	Atlantic 2822	1971	Writer credits list only Frank Lymon and Morris Levy; b/w "Sugar Brown"
California Music	RCA NB-10363	1975	Produced by Brian Wilson; b/w "Don't Worry Baby"
Johnny Cameron	RCA 47-8065	1962	B/w "The Crying I'm Doing Alone"
The Catalinas	Jayne J500	1973	B/w "I'm So Tired"; Connecticut label; possibly a boot
The Chesterfields	A&M 2041	1978	B/w "That Is Rock And Roll," a Leiber/Stoller penned song
The Chesterfields	A&M AMS 7364 (UK)	1978	From the soundtrack of *American Hot Wax*, the biopic about Alan Freed; b/w "Mister Blue" by Timmy and The Tulips, also from the soundtrack
Lou Christie	Buddah 2011-127 (UK)	1972	B/w "I'm Gonna Get Married"
The Danes	Charay C-303	c. 1965	B/w "Teresa"; Fort Worth, TX, label
The Diamonds	Mercury EP-1-4038	1961	EP with "Church Bells May Ring" / "The Stroll" / "Little Darlin'"
The Fabulous Four	Chancellor C-1078	1961	B/w "The Sounds Of Summer"; this group sang background for many Fabian releases
The Four Seasons	Vee Jay EP 1-902	1963	EP with "Silhouettes" / "Since I Don't Have You" / "Alone"
The Fourmost	Parlophone R 5379 (UK)	1965	B/w "Girls, Girls, Girls"; recorded in England
The Fourmost	Capitol 5591	1966	B/w "Girls, Girls, Girls"; recorded in England

The Fuller Brothers	Monument 925	1966	Credited to Lymon/Levy; b/w "Judge Me With Your Heart"; produced by Ray Stevens and Fred Foster
The Gallahads	Rendezvous R-153	1961	B/w "Gone"; a Seattle, WA, group
Darren Green	RCA APBO-0294	1974	B/w "Dream World"; good modern remake with a teen male lead singer
The Happenings	Apex 9-78063 (Canada)	1966	B/w "My Mammy"; produced by The Tokens
The Happenings	B.T. Puppy 532	1967	Reached #41 on the *Billboard* pop chart; b/w "When The Summer Is Through"; produced by The Tokens
The Happenings	B.T. Puppy BTS 45532 (UK)	1967	B/w "When The Summer Is Through"; produced by The Tokens
The Happenings	Virgo V-503	1972	B/w "See You In September"
The Happenings	Collectables COL 0312	1990s?	B/w "I Got Rhythm"; "Back to Back Hit Series"
Derrick Harriott	Harry J HJ-6671 (UK)	1974	Credited to only F. Lymon; b/w "Why Do Fools Fall In Love—Version"
Derrick Harriott	Trojan TR.7981 (UK)	1976	Reggae version; b/w "Dancin' the Reggae"
The Heaters	Columbia 1-11347	1980	B/w "Put One Foot In Front Of The Other"
Eddie Holman	Parkway P-157	1967	B/w "Never Let Me Go"
Eddie Holman & The Larks	Popular Request 114	1990s?	B/w "Never Let Me Go"; bootleg/repro
Honey Dreamers with Earl Sheldon and Orch.	Camden CAE 330	1956	EP with "The Campus Rock" / "Molly-O" / "Rock Island Line"

The Hullaballoos	Columbia DB 7392 (UK)	1964	B/w "I'm Gonna Love You Too," a cover of Buddy Holly
Joker's Wild	No label; matrix # JW-001 (country of issuance unknown)	1980s?	Songs on this record date from 1964-65 with David Gilmour signing vocals and on lead guitar, which was pre-Pink Floyd; limited numbered unofficial edition; b/w "Don't Ask Me Why"
Wally Jones	Baby 1111		Credited to M. Levy and L. Barry; b/w "The ABC's"; also incorrectly credits M. Levy as the producer
The Keytones	Red Sky KEY 1 (UK)	1984	EP with "Coastin' Along" / "Lonely Road" / "The Munsters"
Annette Klooger with The Four Jones Boys	Decca F 10738 (UK)	1956	B/w "Lovely One"
Philip Leo & C.J. Lewis	Fashion FAD 065 (UK)	1989	Reggae version; b/w "I Wanna Be Loved"
Magnificent Mercury Brothers	Transatlantic BIG 536 (UK)	1976	B/w "(I'm Not A) Juvenile Delinquent"
Gloria Mann	Decca ED 2399	1956	EP with "Partners For Life" and two songs by the Mello-Tones
Joni Mitchell	Asylum E-47038	1980	B/w "Black Crow"
Joni Mitchell	Asylum K 12478 (UK)	1980	B/w "Black Crow"
Mud	RCA PB 5129 (UK)	1978	Medley with "Book Of Love"; b/w "Run, Don't Walk"
The Newlanders	Tank BSS 301 (UK)	1978	EP with "Diana" / "When Will I See You Again" / "All I Have To Do Is Dream"; club/cabaret band

Ponderosa Twins	Astroscope A-104	1972	Made the *Billboard* R&B chart for three weeks, peaking at #40; b/w "The Bitter With The Sweet"
Kenny Rankin	Little David LD-727	1974	B/w "Berimbau"
The Don Rose Band	Philwood P-239	Early 1970s	Featuring Dave Chapman; b/w "Whamboogie"; Memphis, TN, label
Diana Ross	RCA PB-12349	1981	On the *Billboard* pop and R&B charts, peaking at #7 and #6, respectively; b/w "Think I'm In Love"
Diana Ross	Capitol CL 226 (UK)	1981	B/w "Think I'm In Love"
Diana Ross	RCA GB-13479	Mid-late 1980s	B/w "Mirror, Mirror"; "Gold Standard Series"
Diana Ross	EMI EM 332 (UK)	1994	Peaked at #36 on the UK charts; b/w "I'm Coming Out (Joey Negro 1994 Remix)"
Diana Ross	Collectables DRE-11929	1996	B/w "Mirror, Mirror"; "Back to Back Hit Series"
The Shondelles	Selsom 102	1964	CB rev. 12/26/64; b/w "Upsetter Of Her Heart"; New Jersey group;
Gale Storm	Underground URC 1138 (Canada)	1988	B/w "Dark Moon"
Summer Wine	Sire SAA-701	1972	Credited to Lymon/Levy; b/w "Ode To A Steel Guitar"
Summer Wine	Philips 6006 217 (UK)	1972	B/w "Ode To The Steel Guitar"

Summer Wine	EMI 2634 (UK)	1977	B/w "The Sound Of Summer's Gone"
The Symbols	Columbia DB 7664 (UK)	1965	B/w "You're My Girl"; produced by Mickie Most
Teen Angel and The Rockin' Rebels	Hellroaring HRM-102 (Canada)	1975	B/w "Greasy Spoon"
The Track	Columbia DB 7987 (UK)	1966	B/w "Cry to Me"; female group, featuring Eve Graham (pre-The New Seekers) and Sandra Stevens (pre-Brotherhood of Man)

The Fuller Brothers on Monument 925

The Beach Boys on Capitol 5118

"WHY DO FOOLS FALL IN LOVE" IN THE MOVIES

"Why Do Fools Fall in Love" is the name of a 1998 movie in which three women, each of whom claims to be Frankie Lymon's widow, assert their right to his estate. "Why Do Fools Fall In Love" can also be heard in the following movies:

MOVIE TITLE	YEAR	COMMENTS
That'll Be The Day (UK)	1973	Performed by Frankie Lymon & The Teenagers; David Essex, of "Rock On" fame, plays the lead and the cast also includes Ringo Starr, Billy Fury, and Keith Moon; movie loosely based on John Lennon's early years
American Graffiti	1973	Performed by Frankie Lymon & The Teenagers; this George Lucas produced movie contains a soundtrack of 1950s songs and was a huge box office hit
The Big Fix	1978	Performed by Frankie Lymon & The Teenagers; comedy mystery thriller
American Hot Wax	1978	Performed by The Chesterfields; biopic about DJ Alan Freed
Hollywood Knights	1980	Performed by Frankie Lymon & The Teenagers; comedy about a car club's Halloween pranks
Eddie Murphy: Raw	1987	Performed by Frankie Lymon & The Teenagers; live recorded standup performance; among the best box office concert films

Havana	1990	Performed by Frankie Lymon & The Teenagers; a romantic war drama starring Robert Redford and Alan Arkin
Calendar Girl	1993	Performed by Frankie Lymon & The Teenagers; comedy about three men seeking to meet Marilyn Monroe
'Til There Was You	1997	Performed by Frankie Lymon & The Teenagers; a romantic comedy
Why Do Fools Fall in Love	1998	The soundtrack includes both Lymon's and Diana Ross's versions of "Why Do Fools Fall in Love"; also performed by Gina Thompson featuring Mocha
October Sky	1999	Performed by Frankie Lymon & The Teenagers; true story about Homer Hickum (played by Jake Gyllenhaal), who took up rocketry against his father's wishes after the 1957 Russian launch of Sputnik

DOCUMENTED CONCERT PERFORMANCES OF "WHY DO FOOLS FALL IN LOVE"

As of May 1, 2024, *Setlist.fm* documented that "Why Do Fools Fall In Love" has been performed in concerts 1,484 times by 27 different artists. In addition to Frankie Lymon and The Teenagers, artists who have included it on their set lists on more than five occasions include The Beach Boys (1,127), Diana Ross (244), Cliff Richard (41), Joni Mitchell (13), and Sha Na Na (12). As recently as 2017, it was on 145 set lists, the most for any year captured by *Setlist.fm* statistics.

HONORS AND ACCOLADES FOR "WHY DO FOOLS FALL IN LOVE"

- Inducted in 2001 into the Grammy Hall of Fame
- Ranked #182 by the NEA/RIAA on its list of the top 365 songs of the 20th century
- Chosen by the Rock & Roll Hall of Fame as one of the "500 Songs That Shaped Rock and Roll"
- Ranked #314 on *Rolling Stone's* 2004 list of "The 500 Greatest Songs of All Time"
- Ranked #98 on Joel Whitburn's *Honor Roll of Hits*
- Ranked #192 in Dave Marsh's 1989 book, *The Heart of Rock & Soul: The 1001 Greatest Singles Ever Made*

ALSO WORTH NOTING . . .

- It was the session sax man, Jimmy Wright, who suggested that the group be called The Teenagers.
- When Frankie Lymon topped the bill at the London Palladium in April 1957, he was the youngest performer ever to do so.
- Ronnie Spector, who as the lead singer of the Ronettes had such hits as "Be My Baby" and "Walkin' In The Rain," said that her first 45 was "Why Do Fools Fall In Love" (*Wall Street Journal*, 3/29-30/2019).

CHAPTER 9

"HEARTBREAK HOTEL"

ELVIS PRESLEY (JANUARY 1956)

Original 1956 RCA 45 release

Original 1956 RCA 78 release

HMV 7M 385 UK 1956 release. Credit: *Discogs*

U.S. Sheet music

"HEARTBREAK HOTEL" — THE BASIC FACTS

Label: RCA 47-6420 (45) and RCA 20-6420 (78)

Writers: Mae Axton, Tommy Durden, and Elvis Presley

Date recorded: January 10, 1956

Date released: January 27, 1956

B-Side: "I Was The One"

Producer: Steve Sholes

Billboard charts:

Pop Chart
- Debut: 3/3/56
- Peak: #1 (8 weeks)
- Duration: 27 weeks

R&B Chart
- Debut: 3/31/56
- Peak: #3 (2 weeks)
- Duration: 13 weeks

Country Chart
- Debut: 3/3/56
- Peak: #1 (17 weeks)
- Duration: 27 weeks

THE SONG AND ITS IMPACT

"Heartbreak Hotel" was penned by Mae Boren Axton[37] and Tommy Durden after Durden showed her a newspaper article about a man whose suicide note said, "I walk a lonely street." Mae suggested let's put "Heartbreak Hotel" at the end of a lonely street. Mae first met Elvis while he was on tour in Florida and interviewed him for a country music magazine.[38] Subsequently, in the second week of November 1955, Mae saw Elvis at a DJ convention in Nashville and urged him to listen to her song. As Presley biographer Peter Guralnick noted, she told him that "he could have it if he would just make it his first single on RCA." Later in a hotel room with Bob Neal (Presley's manager before Colonel Parker), Mae, and Elvis, a demo of the song was played over and over.[39] Finally, according to Guralnick, Elvis said, "That's gonna be my next record." Mae said she gave Elvis credit as one of the

---

37 If her maiden name—Boren—sounds familiar, it is probably because her nephew, David Boren, represented Oklahoma in the U.S. Senate 1979 to 1994 and subsequently served as President of the University of Oklahoma from 1994 to 2018.

38 By at least one account, it was Mae Axton who first introduced Colonel Parker to Elvis, supposedly after a concert in Jacksonville, Florida.

39 A demo had been made by Glen Reeves, a Jacksonville, FL, DJ and musician. Reeves is remembered by R&R aficionados as a rockabilly artist who recorded songs released on such labels as TNT, Atco, and Decca. In 2011 Bear Family Records issued a compilation album of his songs, including his demo of "Heartbreak Hotel."

composers since he made some lyrical adjustments and helped create the song's arrangement that was used in the recording studio.[40]

Parenthetically, since Mae had previously worked with Colonel Parker and given that Parker was about to take over as Presley's manager, it is well within the realm of possibility that he had a hand in Presley being cut in as a co-composer. Interestingly, Tommy Durden was quoted in *Mind Over Matter* as saying "Mae Boren [Axton] shouldn't have had her name on that song, she never wrote a damn word of it." It has been reported, however, that Durden was enormously pleased with the songwriting royalties he received for being a co-author of "Heartbreak Hotel."

"Heartbreak Hotel" was recorded on January 10, 1956, at RCA's Nashville studios. As Peter Guralnick observed, "Elvis clearly believed in it and put everything he had into it, and despite whatever Sholes' [the RCA A&R head who had signed Elvis away from Sun Records] or Chet's [Atkins] personal reservations were, the heavy overlay of echo and D.J.'s [Fontana] rim shots created a powerful, emotion-laden atmosphere of upbeat despair." Scotty Moore on guitar and Bill Black on bass provided superb accompaniment.

Although "Heartbreak Hotel" was released on January 27, 1956, it did not immediately take off. So much so that Steve Sholes called Sam Phillips to say, "Man I don't know whether I bought the wrong person or not. That damn 'Blue Suede Shoes' [by Carl Perkins] is breakin' all over New York and everywhere I go." After Phillips reassured him he had not made a mistake, Sholes asked Phillips if he could release Presley's version of "Blue Suede Shoes" as a single because "he couldn't get 'Heartbreak Hotel' to do a damn thing." Phillips demurred and Sholes agreed that he wouldn't release "Blue Suede Shoes" as a single. In lieu thereof, on March 23, 1956, RCA released "Blue Suede Shoes" as one of the four cuts on an EP (RCA EPA-747). Then, on August 31, 1956, after Perkin's original version had completed its chart run, RCA released it as a single on RCA 47-6636, coupled with "Tutti Frutti."

For some unknown reason Presley did not sing his new song the day after it was released on the first of his six appearances on the nationally televised *Dorsey Brothers Stage Show* on January 28, 1956.[41] Instead, he sang two Joe Turner songs, "Shake, Rattle and Roll" and "Flip Flop and Fly," as well as Ray Charles' "I Got A Woman." For his second appearance on February 4, 1956, he sang "Baby, Let's Play House" and "Tutti Frutti." On his third appearance on February 11, 1956, he sang "Blue Suede Shoes" and, finally, "Heartbreak Hotel," but this performance was lackluster at best and was marred by the backing provided by the Dorsey Brothers' big band musicians. Next, on February 18, 1956, he reprised a particularly energized version of Little Richard's "Tutti Frutti," as well as "I Was The One," the B-side of "Heartbreak Hotel." Finally, on his fifth appearance on March 17, 1956, Elvis sang "Heartbreak Hotel" with Bill Black and Scotty Moore providing the backing, which was an immensely superior performance. He also did "Blue Suede Shoes." On his sixth and

40 The Library of Congress *Catalog of Copyright Entries* shows that it was filed on January 3, 1956, listing words and music by "Mae Boren Axton [*sic*], Tommy Durden, and Elvis Presley."

41 All six appearances can be seen on faded video but with good audio at Elvis Presley—The Complete *Dorsey Brothers Dorsey Stage Shows* [1956., Rock 'N' Roll] (ok.ru). To begin to understand all the excitement that these performances caused, this video is a must see.

final appearance on March 24, 1956, Elvis sang "Money Honey" and another energized reprise of "Heartbreak Hotel" with lots of leg shaking and pelvic gyrations. The last 1956 nationally televised performance of "Heartbreak Hotel" occurred on April 3 on the *Milton Berle Show*.

"Heartbreak Hotel" did not enter the *Billboard's* pop and country charts until March 3, 1956,[42] and the R&B chart until four weeks later on March 31. Unquestionably, Presley's nationally televised performances ultimately helped propel "Heartbreak Hotel" to the top of the charts. It spent 27 weeks on both *Billboard's* pop and country charts, including 8 weeks and 17 weeks, respectively, at #1. It was on the R&B chart for 13 weeks, peaking at #3. It turned out to be *Billboard's* top selling pop record of 1956.

"Heartbreak Hotel" was not released in the UK until March 1956. It debuted on the UK charts on May 17, 1956, peaked at #2, and spent 22 weeks on the charts. What is more amazing is that it returned to the UK charts, as documented by the Official Chart Company, on two different occasions. The first was in 1971 when RCA released its "MaxiMillion Series" that included three "Golden Oldies" per 45 rather than the normal two. In this instance the A-side was "Heartbreak Hotel" and the B-side included both "Hound Dog" and "Don't Be Cruel." This release appeared on the UK charts for 10 weeks and reached #10. The second was in 1996 on the fortieth anniversary of its initial chart appearance when RCA reissued the record in the UK with the A-side coupled with the original B-side, "I Was The One," and with the B-side containing previously unreleased alternate takes of both songs. It peaked at #45.

Unlike "Blue Suede Shoes" with its multiple contemporaneous cover versions, the only competing non-budget label version of "Heartbreak Hotel" was by the Cadets on Modern, whose very next release would be "Stranded in the Jungle," a top 15 hit in the summer of 1956. There were two parody versions, one by Homer and Jethro and the other by Stan Freberg. There were also more than a few budget label covers, many of which also included a cover of "Blue Suede Shoes" on the same disc. Of particular interest are the covers of "Heartbreak Hotel" by Thumper Jones and by Hank Smith and the Nashville Playboys. That's because it was George Jones, the future country all-time great, who reluctantly sang the song using the pseudonyms of Thumper Jones for the Dixie label release and Hank Smith for the Gilmar, Tops, Hollywood, and Record-of-the-Month label releases. Then head of Starday Records, Pappy Dailey, wanting to break into the emerging Rock 'n' Roll market, had Jones and others use pseudonyms to record current Rock 'n' Roll hits for release on either his Dixie label or on other budget labels to whom he licensed the songs. The use of a pseudonym was designed to not jeopardize their budding careers as country artists.

Over the years, there has been considerable confusion over whether the artist listed as either Thumper Jones or Hank Smith was in fact George Jones or some other artist such as Leon Payne. Part

---

42 On that same March 3, 1956, Presley's last Sun release, "I Forgot to Remember to Forget" coupled with "Mystery Train" on Sun 223, which had also been released on RCA 47-6357 following RCA's purchase of Presley's contract and his Sun recordings, sat at #1 on *Billboard's* C&W's "Best Sellers in Stores" and "Most Played on Jukeboxes," and at #4 on "Most Played by Jockeys."

of this confusion was resolved when George Jones in his bio confessed that he was indeed Thumper Jones. As a result, it is now generally agreed by knowledgeable record people that the "Heartbreak Hotel" recording attributed to either Thumper Jones or Hank Smith was sung by George Jones and that the "Blue Suede Shoes" recording, also attributed to Thumper Jones or Hank Smith, was done by Leon Payne, another Starday artist.

The subsequent artists who have released 45 vinyl versions of "Heartbreak Hotel" include Blues Magoos, John Cale, Connie Francis, Frijid Pink, Roger Miller, Willie Nelson and Leon Russell, the Orlons, and Joe Tex. The Willie Nelson/Leon collaboration topped the country charts in 1979. Both the Frijid Pink and Roger Miller covers made the pop chart, with Miller also making the country chart. It also attracted more than a few garage covers, of which the version on Wildwood 005 by the Tremolons, a Michigan all-girl band, is highly collectable.

An interesting sidenote is that Tommy Durden, one of the co-authors, and Hoyt Axton, Mae Axton's son, both recorded covers of "Heartbreak Hotel," Tommy in 1969 on Sound 272 and Hoyt in 1990 on DPI 5000, a record label owned by his mother Mae Axton. Hoyt was both a singer and songwriter. In the latter capacity he wrote "Joy To The World," a #1 hit in 1971 for Three Dog Night, and the "No, No Song," a #3 hit for Ringo Starr in 1975. He has also appeared in dozens of movies and TV shows.

"Heartbreak Hotel" raked in its fair share of honors, including being inducted into the Grammy Hall of Fame and selected by the NEA/RIAA as one of the 20th century's top 365 songs. As rock author Paul Williams summarized, "Heartbreak Hotel" is "a performance that still resonates today with all the spine-tingling power and dignity and mystery of a classic rock and roll single."

Caveat Emptor. Both The Jacksons and Whitney Houston released records titled "Heartbreak Hotel," but they are definitely not the same song. Both, however, enjoyed considerable chart success. The Jacksons' 1980 recording on Epic 50959 spent 17 weeks on the *Billboard* R&B charts, including five weeks at #2. It also was on the *Billboard* pop chart for 16 weeks, peaking at #22. The Whitney Houston 1998 song rose to #2 on *Billboard's* "Hot 100" chart and #1 on *Billboard's* "Hot R&B/ Hip-Hop Songs" chart. It was initially released as a single only on cassette or CD, but in 2000 Arista released a 7-inch vinyl jukebox version.

CONTEMPORANEOUS COVER VERSIONS OF "HEARTBREAK HOTEL"

ARTIST	LABEL	COMMENTS
Cadets	Modern 985	Yes, the same group that gave us "Stranded In The Jungle"; b/w "Church Bells May Ring," a cover of the original by The Willows (Melba 102), on which Neil Sedaka played the chimes

Stan Freberg and His Sniffle Group	Capitol F3480	Charted to two weeks, peaking at #79; parody version; BB review: "Excellent novelty that'll tickle the funny bones of jockeys and the public"; b/w "Rock Island Line," likewise a parody version
Stan Freberg and His Sniffle Group	Capitol CL14609 (UK)	Charted in the UK for two weeks, peaking at #24; parody version b/w "Rock Island Line," likewise a parody version
Homer & Jethro	RCA 47-6542	Titled "Hart Brake Motel," a parody version; b/w "Two Tone Shoes," a parody version of "Blue Suede Shoes"

CONTEMPORANEOUS BUDGET LABEL COVERS OF "HEARTBREAK HOTEL"

ARTIST	LABEL	COMMENTS
Delbert Barker	Big 4 Hits 185	EP with "Blue Suede Shoes"/"Juke Box Baby"/"I'll Be Home"
Delbert Barker	Big 4 Hits 187	EP with "Blue Suede Shoes"/"Glad Rags"/"These Hands"
Delbert Barker	Gateway 1162	B/w "Blue Suede Shoes"
Delbert Barker	Worthmore 187	EP with "Blue Suede Shoes"/"These Hands"/"Glad Rags"; "Country & Western Series"
Loren Becker	18 Top Hits 175	EP with five other songs
Jerry Dodge & The Lazy Ranch Boys	Broadway 325	At least one release on Broadway 325 lists Tommy Collins as the artist; b/w "Yes, I Know Why" by Tommy Loftin & The Lazy Ranch Boys
Bob Eberly	Waldorf Music Hall MH 45-211	EP with "I Want You, I Need You, I Love You"/"Stranded In The Jungle"/"Rock And Roll Rag"

Bob Eberly	Waldorf T8-X45	EP with "Shake, Rattle And Roll"/"Ready Teddy"/"Fever"/"I Want You, I Need You, I Love You"/"My Baby Left Me"
Bob Eberly	18 Top Hits 187	B/w "I've Grown Accustomed To Your Face"/"Theme from 'The Man With the Golden Arm'"/"Port-Au-Prince"/"Magic Touch"/"Ivory Tower"
The Four Angels	Today's 507	B/w "Blue Suede Blues"/"Jute [sic] Box Baby"/"I'll Be Home"; "featuring Judy Lynn and Paul Bean"
Thumper Jones	Dixie 502	AKA George Jones; six song EP, reportedly part of a Dixie label mail order series
Bill Marine	Promenade NNR-2	B/w "Tutti Frutti"/"Sweet Old-Fashioned Girl"/ "Treasure Of Love"
Hank Smith & The Nashville Playboys	Tops 45-R279-49	AKA George Jones; b/w "Blue Suede Shoes"/"Yes, I Know Why"/"So Doggone Lonesome"
Hank Smith & The Nashville Playboys	Hollywood 280; Record-of-the Month Club 280; Tops 280	AKA George Jones; EP with "Blues Suede Shoes"/"Juke Box Baby"/"Rock Island Line"
Hank Smith & The Nashville Playboys	Gilmar RX 120	AKA George Jones; EP with "Dungaree Doll"/"Go On With The Wedding"/"Bayou Baby"/"Trouble In Mind"/"You're Free To Go"
Terry Wall	Hep 185	AKA Delbert Barker; same as Big 4 Hits 185, with the same matrix numbers; b/w "Blue Suede Shoes"/"Juke Box Baby"/"I'll Be Home"

Buzz Williams	Worthmore 185	AKA Delbert Barker; b/w "Blue Suede Shoes"/"Juke Box Baby"/"I'll Be Home"
None listed	EP 334	B/w "Juke Box Baby"/"Blue Suede Shoes"/"I'll Be Home"
None listed	Prom 45-600W	B/w "Why, Baby, Why"/"So Doggone Lonesome"/"You And Me"
None listed	Value 199	B/w "Blue Suede Shoes"/"A Tear Fell"/"No Not Much"

Classic example of the same songs released on different but affiliated budget labels

LATER RELEASES OF "HEARTBREAK HOTEL" BY ELVIS PRESLEY

LABEL	YEAR	COMMENTS
RCA EPA-821	1956	EP with "I Was The One"/"Money Honey"/"I Forgot To Remember To Forget"; rose to #5 on *Billboard's* EP chart
RCA 1088 (UK)	1958	B/w "All Shook Up"
RCA 477-0605	1959	B/w "I Was The One"; original gold standard release with dog on the top; released multiple times in subsequent years with same release number but with different label designs, e.g., dog on side, red label, dog at 1 p.m., etc.

RCA 2104 (UK)	1971	B/w "Hound Dog" and "Don't Be Cruel"; "MaxiMillion Golden Oldies Series," which featured three songs per 45
RCA 2694 (Canada and UK)	1977	B/w "All Shook Up"
RCA PB-11105	1977	B/w "I Was The One"; "RCA Collectors' Series"
RCA RCX-7189 (UK)	1981	EP with "I Was the One"/"Money Honey"/"I Forgot To Remember To Forget"
RCA PB-13892	1984	B/w "Jailhouse Rock"; Presley's 50th Anniversary release
Old Gold OG 9704 (UK)	1987	B/w "All Shook Up"; licensed from RCA
RCA 8760-7-R	1988	Two versions of "Heartbreak Hotel," one by Elvis and B-side by David Keith Schlattner with "Zulu Time"; both from the 1988 movie *Heartbreak Hotel*
RCA 07863-62449-7	1992	B/w "Hound Dog"; critically acclaimed remastered version
RCA 07863-64476-7	1996	A-side coupled with "I Was The One"; the B-side includes previously unreleased alternate takes of both songs
RCA 74321 33686 7 (UK)	1996	A-side coupled with "I Was The One"; the B-side includes previously unreleased alternate takes of both songs
Collectables COL 80009	1997	B/w "I Was The One"; "Back to Back Hit Series"
Sun 227	???	With the Tommy and Jimmy Dorsey Band; b/w "Shake, Rattle and Roll," with the Jordanaires; bootleg/repro unofficial release

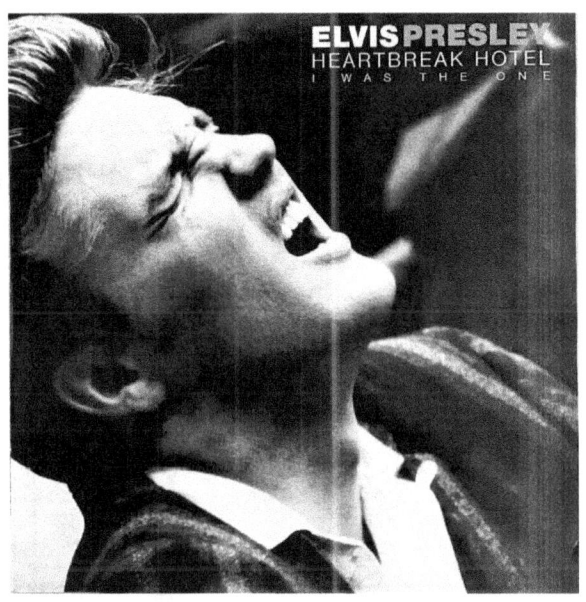

RCA 2104 UK MaxiMillion 1971 Reissue   Picture sleeve for 1996 RCA 07863-64476-7

SUBSEQUENT COVER VERSIONS OF "HEARTBREAK HOTEL"

ARTIST	LABEL	YEAR	COMMENTS
Bobby Angel and The Hillsiders	Astra 300; Nova 300	1962	Hillside, Illinois, labels; instrumental garage version; b/w "Submarine Races," likewise an instrumental
Ann-Margret	RCA RCX-7848 (UK)	1964	E.P with "Oh Lonesome Me"/"I Just Don't Understand"/"Let Me Go Lover"
Hoyt Axton	DPI 5000	1990	Hoyt is the son of Mae Axton, one of the penners of "Heartbreak Hotel"; b/w "Mountain Right"; also issued on DPI 5001 with both sides being stereo versions of "Heartbreak Hotel," probably issued for promo purposes
Blues Magoos	ABC 11226	1969	B/w "I Can Feel It (Feelin' Time)"
Delaney Bramlet	G.N.P. Crescendo 328x	1964	B/w "You Never Looked Sweeter"; produced by Jackie DeShannon

Delaney Bramlet	Vocalion V-N-9227 (UK)	1964	B/w "You Never Looked Sweeter"; produced by Jackie DeShannon
John Cale	Island IXP-3	1975	B/w "Dirtyass Rock 'N' Roll"; supposedly only issued as a promo
Vilas Craig & The Viscounts	International Artists 6336	1963	Titled "Heart Break Hotel"; Sheldon pressing; b/w "Black-Out," a good surf instrumental
Roger Alan Dennis & Pure Pleasure	Sojourner 777	???	B/w "The Love We Had"; Streamwood, IL, label; no internet info on this band
Johnny Devlin and The Devils	ATA K-6632 (Australia)	1976	B/w "I Can't Go, I Can't Stay"
Doug Dillard Band	Flying Fish FF 4539	1988	B/w "G-String Boogie"; Chicago, IL, label
Dread Zepplin	I.R.S. EIRS 146 (UK)	1990	Medley with "Heartbreaker"; b/w "Your Time Is Gonna Come"
Paul Dragon	Dragon 45-100	1974	B/w "Johnny B. Goode"
Tommy Durden	Sound 272	1969	One of the writers of "Heartbreak Hotel"; Detroit, MI, label; b/w "Ride The Thunder (Sound Of The Astronauts)"
Bob Eberly	Sparton 4-277R (Canada)	1956	B/w "Moonglow"
Chuck Fowler	Future Earth FEK 022 (UK)	1985	B/w "Cry" and "Killamarsh Killa"
Connie Francis	MGM SB-8	1959	B/w "There's No Tomorrow ('O Sole Mio)"; 7-inch 33 1/3
Connie Francis	MGM X1691	1959	EP with "Tweddle Dee"/"I Almost Lost My Mind"/"I Hear You Knockin'"

Ernie Freeman	Imperial X5716	1960	Instrumental version; b/w "Hawaiian Eye"
Frigid Pink	Parrot 45-352	1970	Garage version; promo copy has mono and stereo versions; on *Billboard* pop chart for five weeks, but only reached #72; b/w "Bye Bye Blues"; released in England on Deram 321
Frijid Pink	Parrot SN-59042	c. mid-70s	B/w "House Of The Rising Sun," a cover of The Animals; greatest hits reissue
Guns N' Roses	Pro-004	???	With PS; heavy metal version; blank labels, obviously a bootleg
The Grand-Prees	Go Go 101-45	1967	Garage version; b/w "Four Winds"; FL group
Grump	Magic Carpet 45-901	1969	Heavy psych garage version; b/w "I'll Give You Love"
The Individuals	Tequila 101	1961	CB rev. 11/25/61; b/w "La Bamba"; label affiliated with Chuck "Tequila" Rio
J. Harrison B.	Anawim 101	1980s	Fond du Lac, WI, label; b/w "Crazy," a cover of the Patsy Cline and Willie Nelson songs; female lead; Wisconsin band originally formed in Fremont, Nebraska, in 1962.
Bert Jansch	Logo G0 409 (UK)	1982	B/w "Up To The Stars"
Donald Johnson with The Debonaires	Waynette 1400	1966	Country/RAB version; b/w "Four Lives"; Dallas, TX, label with address; RCA custom pressing
Reesa Kay Jones	Bravado BRA 103	1980	EP with "A Hurtin' Memory"/"Good-Hearted Woman"/"Someday Soon"; Tullahoma, TN, label

Billy Kidd and His Band	Q QE.104 (Ireland)	1974	B/w "Jailhouse Rock," likewise a cover of Presley
Kurt Knudsen	Triodex 109	1961	Slow tempo version; BB review 5/15/61; b/w "Jimmy Crack Corn"; NYC label
Leppo & The Jooves (AKA The Soft Boys)	Black Snake 16806	1987	Live version with a new lead-in to a demented slow hard rock dirge; EP with "Give It To The Soft Boys"/"Which Of Us Is Me"/"Salamander"; repro/boot
Buddy Love	Proud 101	1964	Punk/garage version; b/w "High School Days"; RCA custom pressing; *Rockin' Country Style* website lists 10 LPs/CDs on which Love's version has been comped; reissue on Hent PR-101 is a boot
Lee Marlow	RCA PB-50800 (Canada)	1984	B/w "The Freeze Is On"
Roger Miller	Smash 2066	1966	B/w "Less And Less"
Willie Nelson and Leon Russell	Columbia 3-11023	1979	An up-tempo country version; b/w "Sioux City Sue"
Willie Nelson and Leon Russell	Columbia 13-33404	1980	B/w "Help Me Make It Through The Night," a Kris Kristofferson cover; "Hall of Fame" series
Mayf Nutter	Laguna 103/104	1968	B/w "The Grass Is Greener (In L.A.)"
The Orlons	Cameo C-319	1964	B/w "Rules Of Love"
Buck Owen Studio Buckaroos	Fine Tune FT-112		Instrumental version; b/w "Heartbreak Hotel," called for a square dance; Kingsburg, CA, label
Cavril Payne	Pulse P-102	1965	B/w "Cry"

Die Rock 'N Rollers	Tell T 292 (Switzerland)	c. 1956	B/w "Minor Rock"; instrumentals; said to be among the first Swiss Rock 'n' Roll records
The Scoundrelz	Red Leaf TTM 626 (Canada)	1966	Reached as high as #60 on the Canadian "RPM Top 100 Singles" chart; b/w "Poor John"
Sector Four	Destroy 003	1983	EP with "Jump On You"/"No Revenge"/ "Time"/"Table Leg"; Florida label
Shadow of Fear	St. Valentine SVR-008	1986	Punk version; b/w "In The Flesh"; Cleveland, OH, label
Shammy—Sydney—Sheryl	S*S*S 29030	???	Vocal by Sheryl Ronin; an EP b/w "Diamond Girl"/"Lady Marmalade"/"Someday Soon"; El Cajon, CA, label, with address and phone no.
Sheiks of Shake	Mystic M-45-109	1978	B/w "Bullets In My Gun"
Bill Smith Combo	Le Bill 305; Chess 1773	1960	Instrumental version; original release was on Le Bill 305, a Fort Worth, TX, label, that was picked up by the Chess brothers and released on their Chess label; b/w "Lonely" by James Bradley and The Caravells
Billie Jo Spears	Liberty UP 636 (UK)	1980	B/w "Your Good Girl's Gonna Go Bad"
Bruce Springsteen	Bootleg, no labels	c. 1978	Maybe from Springsteen's 1978 tour where "Heartbreak Hotel" was on his set list; b/w "Night Train" and "Santa Claus Is Coming To Town"
Staggerwing	Magic Wand 001	1980s?	B/w "Doin It"

Joe Tex	Atlantic SD 78124	1966	7-inch 33 1/3 small hole EP; b/w "The Love You Save (May Be Your Own)"/"Build Your Love (On A Solid Foundation)"/"Funny Bone"/"I'm A Man"/"Don't Let Your Left Hand Know (What Your Right Hand Is Doing)"
The Topsiders	Josie 45-907	1963	Folk sounding group, certainly not a Rock 'n' Roll version; b/w "Let The Good Times Roll"
Diana Trask	Dot 45-17342	1970	Country; Trask is from Australia; produced by Buddy Killen; b/w "Beneath Still Waters"
The Tremolons	Wildwood 005	1965	B/w "Whole Lotta Shakin' Goin' On"; Michigan all girl garage band; Benton Harbor, MI, label; group later signed with Dunwich Records and changed their name to The Luv'd Ones
The Tremolons	Sundazed SEP 121	1996	Incorrectly credited to Leiber/Stoller; EP with "Whole Lotta Shakin' Goin' On"/"Theme for a 'D.J.'"/"Please Let Me Know"
Barbara Trent	Red Label 35	1970	Soul/funk version; b/w "The Man I Love"
Barbara Trent	Funk 45.025 (UK)	2007	B/w "A Woman Was Made For A Man"
Frank Wilcox, Jr.	Pro-Gress 8825	1972	Titled "Good Times Medley" with "Josephine," "That'll Be The Day" and "Heartbreak Hotel," prefaced by "Where did all the good times go"; b/w "First Lonely Night"

None Listed	Statler 661	???	Instructional dance record; b/w "Shoeless Joe From Hannibal Mo"; instrumentals
None Listed	Statler S-9011	???	B/w "Dim All The Lights"

The Orlons cover on Cameo C-319

"HEARTBREAK HOTEL" IN THE MOVIES

"Heartbreak Hotel" is the name for two movies, one released in 1988, and the other in 2006 in Sweden. The following are the more significant movies in which "Heartbreak Hotel" can be heard:

TITLE	YEAR	COMMENTS
This Is Elvis Presley	1977	Performed by Elvis Presley; low budget documentary about Elvis with a lot of archival footage
This Is Spinal Tap	1984	Performed by Michael McKean, Christopher Guest, and Harry Shearer, each of whom portrayed members of Spinal Tap in the picture; described as a musical comedy that chronicles a fateful U.S. Spinal Tap tour; produced by Rob Reiner
Volunteers	1985	*IMDbPro* does not identify the performer; adventure comedy starring Tom Hanks and Rita Wilson, who Hanks later married
Heartbreak Hotel	1988	Preformed by both Elvis Presley and David Keith & Charles Schlatter with Zulu Time; David Keith portrays Elvis in this romantic comedy with plenty of Elvis tunes sung by Elvis and others
Hot to Trot	1988	*IMDbPro* does not identify the performer; fantasied comedy that was nominated for five Razzies, an award for the worst movie as opposed to an Oscar
Honeymoon in Las Vegas	1992	Performed by Billy Joel; romantic comedy starring Nicolas Cage and James Caan that features numerous Elvis songs song by Elvis and others; Little Elvis played by a six-year old Bruno Mars
True Romance	1993	Performed by Val Kilmer, who portrayed Presley in the film; crime drama produced by Quentin Tarantino
The Client	1994	Performed by Steve Tyrell; crime mystery drama based on the John Grisham book

Inventing the Abbotts	1997	*IMDbPro* does not identify the performer; romantic drama co-produced by Ron Howard
Cast Away	2000	Performed by Elvis Presley; adventure, romantic drama; Tom Hanks is in the cast
Elvis Has Left the Building	2004	Performed by Elvis Presley; comedy starring Kim Bassinger
Alien Autopsy	2006	*IMDbPro* does not identify the performer; a sci-fi comedy about the Roswell Incident
Heartbreak Hotel (Sweden)	2006	Performed by Jill Johnson; romantic comedy
Lilo & Stitch	2006	Performed by Elvis Presley; a Disney animated adventure comedy
Happy Feet	2006	Performed by Hugh Jackman; movie is about an Emperor Penguin, who, unlike the others, cannot sing, but proves he can tap dance
Hounddog	2007	Performed by both Elvis Presley and Dakota Fanning, the young girl who fantasizes Elvis
Promised Land: A Musical Roadmovie From Elvis in Memphis	2020	Performed by both Jason James, and Thomas Schreiber and Peter Tippelt; TV movie documentary
Elvis	2022	Performed by Elvis and taken from footage of his *1969 Comeback Special*; biography of Elvis Presley played by Austin Butler, as seen through the eyes of Colonel Thomas Parker played by Tom Hanks

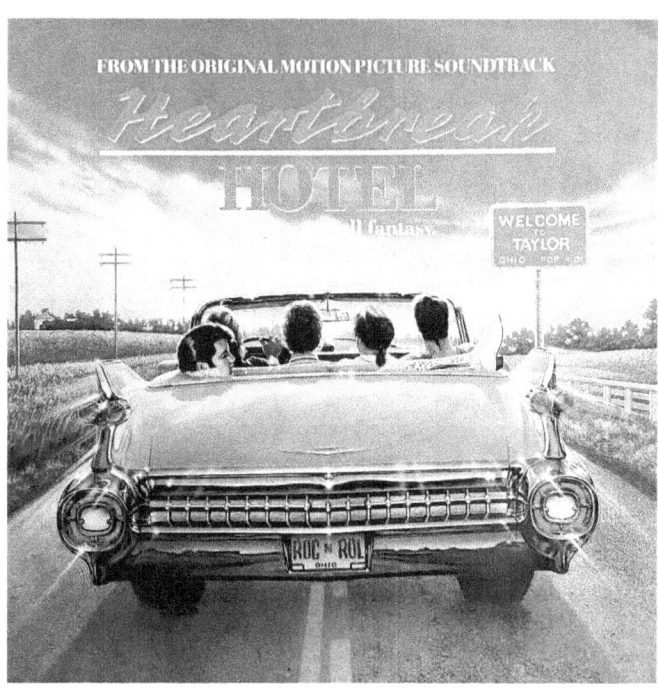

DOCUMENTED CONCERT PERFORMANCES OF "HEARTBREAK HOTEL"

As of May 1, 2024, *Setlist.fm* documented that "Heartbreak Hotel" has been performed in concert 1,527 times by 169 different artists. In addition to Elvis Presley (374), among the artists who have included it on their set list on more than 10 occasions are John Cale (217), Justin Timberlake (126), Cliff Richard (70), Roger McGuinn (34), Guns N' Roses (24), Wanda Jackson (21), AC/DC (20), Bruce Springsteen (20), The Cramps (19), and Elton John & Billy Joel (11). As recently as 2014, it was on 116 concert set lists, the most of any year documented by *Setlist.fm*.

HONORS AND ACCOLADES FOR "HEARTBREAK HOTEL"

- Inducted into the Grammy Hall of Fame in 1995
- Ranked #87 on the NEA/RIAA's list of the top 365 songs of the 20th century
- Chosen by the Rock & Roll Hall of Fame as one of the "500 Songs That Shaped Rock and Roll," an unranked list that included songs from all eras
- Ranked #2 in the 2015 book *The Top 500 Songs of the Rock Era: 1955-2015*
- Ranked #45 on *Rolling Stone's* 2004 list of "The 500 Greatest Songs of All Time"
- Ranked #71 on the VH1 2004 list of the "100 Greatest Rock Songs"

- Ranked #3 on *Mojo* magazine's "Big Bangs: 100 Records That Changed the World" (June 2007); described as a list of "The most influential & inspirational recordings ever made, they changed music, the way it was played, bought or even imagined"
- Listed by *Billboard* as the bestselling pop record of 1956
- Won a *Billboard* pop "Triple Crown Award" for ranking #1 as the bestselling record, the most played on jukeboxes, and the most played by DJs; also won a *Billboard* country "Triple Crown Award" for ranking #1 in the same three categories
- Ranked #26 on the BBC's list of the "100 Favourite Songs of the [20th] Century"

ALSO WORTH NOTING...

- "Heartbreak Hotel" was Presley's first release of a song he recorded for RCA rather than Sun. Sam Phillips was not impressed, commenting that it was a "morbid mess."
- "Heartbreak Hotel" was certified double platinum by the Recording Industry Association of America (RIAA).
- Presley first performed "Heartbreak Hotel" live while on tour with the Louisiana Hayride in December 1955.
- Keith Richards: "When I heard 'Heartbreak Hotel,' I knew what I wanted to do in life. It was as plain as day. All I wanted to do in the world was to be able to play and sound like that. Everyone else wanted to be Elvis, I wanted to be Scotty."
- References to "Heartbreak Hotel" have been used in the titles of other records including "A Room At The Heartbreak Hotel" by U2 on Island 7-99254 and "Heartbreaker (At The End of Lonely Street)" by Dread Zeppelin on I.R.S. EIRS 146 (UK).
- During an appearance on *The Arsenio Hall Show* on June 3, 1992, then candidate and future President Bill Clinton performed "Heartbreak Hotel" on his saxophone.
- "Heartbreak Hotel" was sampled by Buchanan & Goodman on the 1956 hit novelty song "Flying Saucers, Part 1" on Luniverse 101.

ADDITIONAL SOURCES

Goldman, Albert, *Elvis* (McGraw-Hill, 1981)

Guralnick, Peter, *Last Train to Memphis: The Rise of Elvis Presley* (Little, Brown, 1994)

Jones, George, with Tom Carter, *I Live to Tell It All* (Dell Paperback ed., 1997)

Miller, Billy, and Michael Hurtt, *Mind Over Matter: The Myths and Mysteries of Detroit's Fortune Records* (Kick Books, 2020).

Williams, Paul, *Rock and Roll: The 100 Best Singles*, Ch. 4 ("Heartbreak Hotel") (Carroll & Graf, 1993)

CHAPTER 10

"LONG TALL SALLY"

LITTLE RICHARD (MARCH 1956)

U.S. sheet music for "Long Tall Sally"

Little Richard original 45 on Specialty

Little Richard original 78 on Specialty

"LONG TALL SALLY" — THE BASIC FACTS

Label: Specialty 572 (both 45 and 78)

Writers: Enotris Johnson, Robert 'Bumps' Blackwell (as Robert Blackwell), and Little Richard (as Richard Penniman) (see below)

Date recorded: February 10, 1956

Date released: March 1956

B-Side: "Slippin' and Slidin' (Peepin' and Hidin')"

Producer: Robert "Bumps" Blackwell

Billboard charts:

Pop Chart

- ■ Debut: 4/07/56
- ■ Peak: #6
- ■ Duration: 19 weeks

R&B Chart

- ■ Debut: 4/07/56
- ■ Peak: #1 (8 weeks)
- ■ Duration: 16 weeks

THE SONG AND ITS IMPACT

According to Bumps Blackwell, a well-known West Coast arranger and bandleader,[43] the following lines written by a young girl who wanted to raise money to help her ill Aunt Mary were the origin of the song:

Saw Uncle John with Long Tall Sally
They saw Aunt Mary comin'
So they ducked back in the alley

According to this account, the girl gave the lines to a popular DJ, who gave them to Blackwell, along with her wish. After being given the lines, Little Richard and Bumps Blackwell are said to have added verses and a chorus. Initially, credit for writing the song was given to Enotris Johnson, as shown on the sheet music and on the original release by Little Richard, as well as on early covers by Pat Boone and Marty Robbins, among others. Indeed, the copyright entry registered with the Library of Congress on April 10, 1956, lists Enotris Johnson as the only composer:

JOHNSON, ENOTRIS.
Long tall Sally; arrangement, words and
music by Enotris Johnson. 3 p. 50¢
NM: arrangement. © Venice Music Corp.,
New York; 10Apr56; EP98361.

---

43 In addition to Little Richard, Robert "Bumps" Blackwell produced and worked with many A-list artists, including Ray Charles, Sam Cooke, Bob Dylan, Quincy Jones, and Ike & Tina Turner.

But exactly who was Enotris Johnson? Over the years, several different and conflicting accounts have emerged. As writer Mark Ribowski observed, "The genesis of this song is an enigma." The special note at the end of this Chapter documents my deep dive to solve this enigma and my, hopefully educated, conclusion concerning the identity of Enotris Johnson.

Within a year after "Long Tall Sally" was released, however, both Little Richard (as R. Penniman) and Bumps Blackwell (as R. Blackwell) were added as co-writers on both Little Richard's first EP (Specialty SEP-400) and his first LP (*Here's Little Richard*, Specialty SP-100). Since it was Little Richard who presumably credited Enotris Johnson, he apparently decided to add both himself and Blackwell as co-writers.

Little Richard's first attempt at recording "Long Tall Sally" with his band was produced by Art Rupe, the owner of Specialty Records, in November 1955, in Los Angeles, the rough cut of which was titled "The Thing," supposedly, as Billy Vera noted, "… in hopes of getting it into an upcoming movie by that name." Not satisfied with this take, Rupe had Blackwell reassemble the same A-list New Orleans musicians that backed Little Richard on "Tutti Frutti," which included, among others, Earl Palmer on drums and Lee Allen on tenor sax. With Little Richard on piano, the song was committed to tape on February 10, 1956, at Cosimo Matassa's New Orleans' J&M studio. Bumps wanted "the lyrics going so fast that [Pat] Boone wouldn't be able to get his mouth together to do it."

The song, with "Slippin' and Slidin'" on the flip, was released in March 1956. On March 17, *Billboard* spotlighted the record, noting that "Little Richard has a sock follow-up to 'Tutti Frutti' in this two-sided hit, which should grab plenty of play in both the r.&b. and pop markets." One week later on March 24 it made the record a "Best Buy of the Week," observing that "both sides of this disc have been showing spectacular strength in the market." "Long Tall Sally" debuted on *Billboard's* pop chart on April 7, 1956, and rose to #6 in its 19-week stay on that chart. On *Billboard's* R&B chart "Long Tall Sally" did even better. On May 5, 1956, it not only topped the "Best Sellers in Stores" chart, but it also topped the "Most Played by Jockeys" and "Most Played in Juke Boxes" charts, thereby earning *Billboard's* "Triple Crown Award."

Concerning the B-side, "Slippin' and Slidin'," Little Richard in a May 1970 *Rolling Stone* interview stated:

> A fellow in my band, Lee Diamond, gave me some of the words and I changed them
> around. Another cat had "Slippin' and Slidin'" out before me, Eddie Bo, and it was a hit
> by him in New Orleans, and they put mine out the following week, and it killed him,
> because he didn't have the rhythm, you see, he didn't have that thing I have.

Although Little Richard (as R. Penniman) was credited as the sole composer of "Slippin' and Slidin'" on the record's original release, following litigation composer credits were also given to Eddie Bo (as Bocage), Al Collins (as Collins), and James Smith (as Smith).[44]

44 Billy Vera in his 2019 book, *Rip It Up: The Specialty Records Story*, asked whether "James Smith could have been the same James Smith who was the disk jockey Okey Dokey? Vera then observed that "it was not unknown for a DJ to demand that their name be on song in return for airplay. Ask Alan Freed."

On the *Billboard* R&B and pop charts, "Slippin' and Slidin'" rose to #2 and #31, respectively. Significantly, "Slippin' and Slidin'" has itself been covered numerous times on 45s by such artists as Buddy Holly and John Lennon.

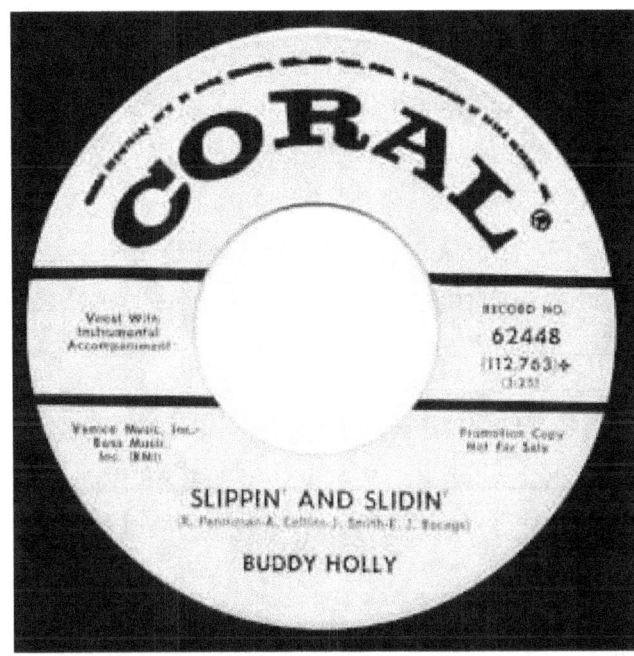

Buddy Holly on Coral 62448   **John Lennon on Apple P-1883**

In this author's opinion, the B-side, "Slippin' and Slidin'," is one of best double-sided records ever released, rivaled by, among others, Elvis Presley's "Hound Dog" and "Don't Be Cruel" and Carl Perkins' "Blue Suede Shoes" and "Honey Don't."

Despite Bumps Blackwell's best efforts, like "Tutti Frutti," "Long Tall Sally" attracted a cover by Pat Boone on Dot 15457. *Billboard* noted in its review that "Boone's stylings of outstanding r.&b. tunes continue to find an enormously receptive market." Boone only deviated from the original version by changing the lyric "Well, long tall Sally she's built for speed," presumably because of its sexual connotation, to "Well, long tall Sally, she's built sweet." However, this time his cover did not do as well as Little Richard's original, only making it to #8 on *Billboard's* pop chart. As *Billboard* perceptively commented on May 5, 1956, "… the public has discovered the real thing and that's what the kids want."[45]

In the UK, Pat Boone's cover was released in June 1956, on London 45-HL-D8291. It hit the UK charts in the first week of August 1956, where it spent seven weeks, but it only rose to #18. On the other hand, Little Richard's version, backed with "Tutti Frutti," which had not been previously released in the UK, was released eight months later in early February 1957, on London 45-HL-O 8366. It did much better on the UK charts, entering the charts on February 14, 1957, and peaking at #3 during its 16-week chart run.

---

45 In an interview, Bumps Blackwell said, "I give credit to Elvis Presley and Pat Boone for helping break Little Richard over the Mason-Dixon Line," i.e., with the white market.

"Long Tall Sally" attracted a fair number of budget label covers, all but one of which are lame imitations of Little Richard's original. The exception is the cover by Rufus Gordon that appeared, as noted below, on three different but affiliated budget labels. In record collector parlance, it is a collectable "Black rocker." While not as great as Little Richard's release, it is, nevertheless, well worth checking out.

Beyond the contemporaneous and budget label covers, there have been a slew of subsequent covers, as documented in detail below. The first notable cover was by Elvis Presley. His second album, *Elvis*, on RCA LPM-1382, included "Long Tall Sally," along with two other Little Richard songs, "Rip It Up" and "Ready Teddy." It was also included as one the four songs on his 1957 EP, *Strictly Elvis*, on RCA EPA-994. Other excellent covers of "Long Tall Sally" that were released before the "British Invasion" include those by Eddie Cochran, Barbara Greene, and Shirley Jean Wiley.

COVERS BY THE BEATLES AND THE KINKS

The Beatles really got to know Little Richard In 1962 when they opened several shows for him in Liverpool and for two weeks at the Star Club in Hamburg, Germany. As Mark Ribowski remarked in his 2020 bio of Little Richard:

> Spending long hours together The Beatles followed him like lap dogs, breathing in his chatter about the industry and rock, making mental notes of the advice he handed down about stage craft and the art of singing without losing spontaneity or honest emotion. They couldn't get enough of him.

"Long Tall Sally" was a staple for The Beatles dating from their earliest days as the Quarry Men, including their Star Club days in Hamburg, Germany, and continuing to their last concert in 1966. As John Lennon commented:

> Little Richard was one of the all-time greats. The first time I heard him a friend of mine had been to Holland and brought back a 78 with "Long Tall Sally" on one side, and "Slippin' and Slidin'" the other. It blew our heads—we'd never heard anybody sing like that in our lives and all those saxes playing like crazy.

In all their performances of "Long Tall Sally," either in concert or on record, Paul sings the vocal because of his ability to mimic Little Richard's singing style. However, in the 1994 movie *BackBeat* about The Beatles' early days in Hamburg, Germany, "Long Tall Sally" was sung by the actor portraying John Lennon, much to Paul McCartney's dismay:

> One of my annoyances about the film *Backbeat* is that they've actually taken my rock 'n' rollness off me. They give John "Long Tall Sally" to sing and he never sang it in his

life. But now it's set in cement. It's like the Buddy Holly and Glenn Miller stories. *The Buddy Holly Story* does not even mention Norman Petty, and *The Glenn Miller Story* is a sugarcoated version of his life. Now *Backbeat* has done the same thing to the story of The Beatles.

Because they had played it so many times,[46] it took only one take for The Beatles' producer, George Martin, to get the song on tape. It was recorded on March 1, 1964, during the sessions for *A Hard Day's Night*. While it was not used for either the album or movie of the same name, it was first released in the U.S. on the unimaginably titled LP, *The Beatles' Second Album*, on April 10, 1964. In Canada, the LP was titled *The Beatles' Long Tall Sally*, and was released on May 11, 1964. It was finally released as a 45 in the UK on June 19, 1964, as one of the four songs on the *Long Tall Sally* EP. In the U.S., The Beatles' cover of "Long Tall Sally" did not appear as a 45 until 1982 when it was released on Collectables COL 1513.[47] It was not the version they recorded in 1964, but rather it was a version recorded live in 1962 at Hamburg, Germany's Star Club.

In Europe, proof of the popularity of The Beatles' cover of "Long Tall Sally" was documented by *Cash Box's* music charts for August 15, 1964: "Long Tall Sally" topped the singles record charts in Denmark and Sweden and was #4 in Norway. Not surprisingly, their *Long Tall Sally* EP was #1 on England's EP chart.

"Long Tall Sally" will also be remembered as the first release by The Kinks both in the UK on PYE 7N.15611 (February 4, 1964) and in the U.S. on Cameo 308 (April 1, 1964). Neither release charted. As John Mendelssohn, author of *The Kinks Kronikles*, noted, "Ray's [Ray Davies] vocal wasn't likely to make listeners who'd recently thrilled to Paul McCartney's superb rendition of Little Richard's classic reach for their coin purses." Ray, however, did contribute a memorable harmonica solo. Nevertheless, it was re-released on Cameo 345 in December 1964, perhaps in the wake of the huge success of the Kinks' "You Really Got Me" on Reprise 0306. This time it made the very lower reaches of *Billboard's* "Bubbling Under" chart at #129.

Even after the British Invasion, "Long Tall Sally" continued to be covered by a wide variety of artists, including Jerry Lee Lewis, the Swinging Blue Jeans, and more than a few garage bands. Special mention should also be made to Paul McCartney's 1987 limited edition release for "The Prince's Trust 10th Anniversary Birthday Party."

As BMI noted in its tribute to Little Richard following his passing in May 2020, "… while the world mourns the loss of a true icon, his singular creativity and musical impact [in songs such as "Long Tall Sally']" will endure."

---

46 Between April 1963, and July 1964, The Beatles recorded "Long Tall Sally" seven times for BBC radio broadcasts.
47 It did, however, appear on a promo only 33 1/3 jukebox EP on Capitol SX4-2080 that was released in April 1964. This release is titled *The Beatles Second Album*, and it is quite rare.

CONTEMPORANEOUS COVER VERSIONS OF "LONG TALL SALLY"

ARTIST	LABEL	COMMENTS
Pat Boone	Dot 15457	Charted for 15 weeks, peaking at #8; b/w "Just As Long As I Am With You"; released in Canada in April 1956 on Reo 8092X and in the UK in June 1956 on London 45-HL-D 8291
Marty Robbins	Columbia 4-40679	RAB version; b/w "Mr. Teardrop"

Pat Boone's cover on Dot

Marty Robbins' cover on Columbia

CONTEMPORANEOUS BUDGET LABEL COVERS OF "LONG TALL SALLY"

ARTIST	LABEL	COMMENTS
Loren Becker	Waldorf T-9-X45	EP with seven other songs including "Don't Be Cruel" and "Rock Around The Clock"
Danny Daniels	Tops R282-49; Record-Of-The-Month Club 45-RG-282; Hollywood Hit Club R282-49	EP with "Ivory Tower"/"The Magic Touch"/"Standing On The Corner"
Rufus Gordon	Gateway Parade of Hits 1167	B/w "Ivory Tower"
Rufus Gordon	Big 4 Hits 188; Worthmore 188	EP with "Ivory Tower"/"Hot Diggity"/"The Magic Touch"
Artie Marvin and The Zig Zags	18 Top Hits 188	EP with "A Tear Fell"/"To Love Again"/ "Moonglow"/"The Saints Rock And Roll"/"Standing On The Corner"
The Rockets	Prom 715	EP with "To Love Again"/"I Want You To Be My Girl"/ "Ivory Tower"
None Listed	EP 335	EP with "Main Title-Molly-O ('Man With The Golden Arm')"/"Magic Touch"/"Ivory Tower"
None Listed	Value 123	E. Johnson credited as the writer; EP with "Magic Touch"/"Ivory Tower"/"Moonglow"

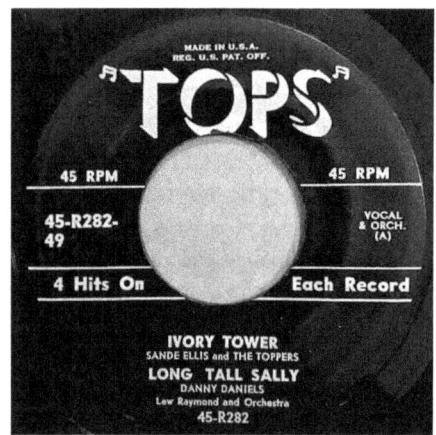 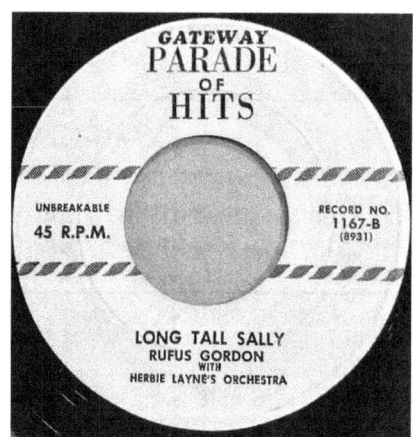 

Budget label covers on Tops, Gateway Parade of Hits, and EP 4 Hits

LATER RELEASES OF "LONG TALL SALLY" BY LITTLE RICHARD

LABEL	YEAR	COMMENTS
Specialty SEP-400	1957	EP with "Miss Ann"/"She's Got It"/"Can't Believe You Wanna Leave"
London HLO.8366 (UK)	1957	B/w "Tutti-Frutti"; released in February 1957
Oldies 45 OL-186	1964	B/w "Only You," a cover of the Platters; Vee Jay recordings
Collectables 1447	Mid-60s	B/w "Tutti-Frutti"
Modern MX 40	Late 60s	Medley with "Jenny Jenny"; re-recordings; "Oldies Series"; b/w "I'm Back"
Trip 35	Early 70s	B/w "Slippin' And Slidin'"; from Little Richard's remakes for the Vee Jay label, i.e., not taken from the Specialty masters
Lost-Nite LN-309	60s/70s???	B/w "Tutti Frutti"; remakes, not the originals
Goldies 45 D-2530	1973	B/w "Only You," a cover of the Platters; Vee Jay remakes, not the originals on Specialty, contrary to what the label says
Specialty SON 5015 (UK)	1974	B/w "Heebie Jeebies"
GRT GG-80	1976	B/w "Only You," a cover of the Platters

Specialty SONE 1 (UK)	1977	EP with "Lucille"; b/w "Dizzy Miss Lizzy" and "Bony Maronie" by Larry Williams; reissues of their Specialty originals
Epic A 4593 (UK)	1984	B/w "Tutti Frutti"; both sides are Okeh remakes, not the Specialty originals
Old Gold 9493 (UK)	1985	B/w "Tutti-Frutti"; licensed from Specialty Records
Vee Jay 241	???	B/w "Tutti Fruitti [*sic*]"; a rather obvious bootleg complete with misspellings
Ripete R45-248	c. 1989	B/w "Keep A Knockin'"
Collectables 10572	2009	B/w "Slippin' And Slidin'"; from the Specialty masters; "Back to Back Hit Series"
Vipvop 45004 (UK)	2018	B/w "Lucille"

1964 re-recording on Oldies 45

2018 UK reissue of original on Vipvop

SUBSEQUENT COVER VERSIONS OF "LONG TALL SALLY"

ARTIST	LABEL	YEAR	COMMENTS
The 5, 6, 7, 8's	Planet Pimp 005	1993	Japanese girl band; San Francisco, CA, label; b/w "I Need A Man"
Danny Adams	JEK 6902	1969	B/w "It Hurts My Heart"; recorded in Kennett, MO
The Backbeat Band	Virgin VS 1502 (UK)	1994	Medley with "C'mon Everybody"; b/w "Please Mr. Postman"; from the movie *BackBeat*, which is about The Beatles' early days in Hamburg, Germany
Dennis Wayne Bass	Camaro 718S-1179	1968	B/w "You Win Again"; Memphis, TN, label
The Beatles	Capitol SXA-2080	1964	Promo only 7-inch 33 1/3 "Second Album"; EP with "Thank You Girl"/"Money (That's What I Want)"/"Please Mister Postman"/"I Call Your Name"/"Devil In Her Heart"
The Beatles	Parlophone GEP 8913 (UK)	1964	EP with "I Call Your Name"/"Slow Down"/ "Matchbox"; when re-released as a "Record Store Day Exclusive" in 2014, it topped *Billboard's* "Vinyl Albums" chart
The Beatles	Collectables COL 1513	1982	B/w "I Remember You"; "British Import Series"; recorded live in 1962 at the Star Club in Hamburg, Germany
The Beatles	BEAT 12-142 (UK)	???	Alternate take recorded April 1, 1964; b/w "A Hard Day's Night"; unofficial UK release

The Beatles	Baktobak 1001, Stab 2008 (UK)	1988	Recorded live 12/31/1962 at Hamburg, Germany's Star Club; b/w "I Wish You Would Shimmy Like My Sister Kate"; boxset of 15 45s labeled Stab 2001 through Stab 2015
The Beatles	Collectables 10572	2009	B/w "Slippin' And Sliddin'"; "Back to Back Hit Series"
The Beatles	1960s Records REP 038 (UK)	2019	EP titled "NME Poll Winners 1964" with "She Loves You"/"Twist and Shout"/"Can't Buy Me Love"/"You Can't Do That"; live recordings from NME concert on 4/26/1964; unofficial release
The Beatles	REP 040 (UK)	2020	EP titled "NME Poll Winners 1965" with "I Feel Fine"/"She's A Woman"/"Baby's In Black"/"Ticket To Ride"; unofficial release
Big Wheelie & The Hubcaps	Scepter 12375	1973	Medley with "Tutti-Frutti" and "Ready Teddy"; b/w "Over The Mountain"
Bobby and The Troubadours	Bronko 504	1963	B/w "Hallelujah I Love Her So," a cover of Ray Charles and Eddie Cochran; Chicago, IL, label
Cactus	Atco 6811	1971	The promo 45 has both mono and stereo versions; b/w "Rock N' Roll Children"
Danny Carl	Skyrocket 1009	1962	Wild RAB version, comped twice per *Rockin' Country Style*; b/w "Pretty Baby"; Philadelphia, PA, label

The Chantells	Bece 110	1960s	Fast female garage version; b/w "Rockin' Reveille"; Benton Harbor, MI, label
Eddie Cochran	Liberty LEP-2052 (UK)	1962	EP with "Blue Suede Shoes"/"Little Angel"/ "Milk Cow Blues"
Eddie Cochran	Liberty LYX 11,508 (Australia)	1968	EP titled "Long Tall Sally" with "Blue Suede Shoes"/"Little Angel"/"I Almost Lost My Mind"
Graham Desmond	SRTS 82 CUS 1375 (UK)	1982	B/w "My Sweet Lord," a cover of George Harrison's song
Expros	Magnum 00114	1977	B/w "In The Mood"
Barbara Greene	Atco 6250	1963	B/w "Slippin' and Slidin'"
Dora Hall	Cozy 71000	1972	Medley with many other songs; b/w "Blue Suede Shoes"
Cash Holiday (AKA Neil Baron)	Corlyn 67-102	1967	B/w "I'm In Love"; rare garage version
The Interns	Paradise 1019	1965	Titled "Sally Met Molly," medley with "Good Golly Miss Molly" and other Little Richard songs; b/w "Have Mercy"; energetic garage record
E. L. Jones	Goldust 45-5057	1974	B/w "Welcome To My World"; Mesilla Park, NM, label
Tom Jones	Parrot DPAS 49/50	1970s?	Medley with "Johnny B. Goode"/"Good Old Rock 'n Roll"/"Bony Morony"; "Radio Demonstration Record—Not For Sale"; b/w medley of four Tom Jones hits

The Keymen	ABC-Paramount C-258	1958	EP with "Goggles"/"Like Help Man"/ "Sentimental Journey"; EP titled "Dance with Dick Clark"; all are instrumentals
King Bees	No label no.; matrix #134607	1965	Garage; b/w "Karen"
The Kinks	Cameo 308	1964	B/w "I Took My Baby Home"; released April 1, 1964; first U.S. release
The Kinks	Cameo 345	1964	"Bubbled Under" in 1965 at #129; re-released with same flip in December 1964
The Kinks	Pye 7N 15611 (UK)	1964	B/w "I Took My Baby Home"
The Kinks	Pye 727 (Canada)	1964	B/w "I Took My Baby Home"
The Kinks	Pye AMEP 1001 (UK)	1978	Pye "Yesterday Series" EP that also includes "I Took My Baby Home"/"You Still Want Me"/ "You Do Something To Me"; pressed solely for export to the USA
Jerry Lee Lewis	Mercury MF 1105 (UK)	1969	B/w "Jenny Jenny"
Jerry Lee Lewis	Mercury 73374	1973	Medley with "Tutti Frutti"/"Good Golly Miss Molly"/"Jenny Jenny"/"Whole Lotta Shakin' Goin' On"; b/w "Drinking Wine Spo-Dee-O'dee"
Jerry Lee Lewis	Mercury 652 260 (UK)	1973	Same as immediately above

Jerry Lee Lewis	Hammer HB 607 (UK)	1979	Small hole 7-inch 33 /13 with "Roll Over Beethoven"/"Flip, Flop and Fly"/"I Believe In You"/"Herman the Hermit"/"Breathless"; manufactured and distributed by Pye Records
Los Teen Tops	Columbia 4730 (Mexico)	1960	Titled "La Larguirucha Sally"; b/w "Tutti Frutti"
Cat Mother and The All Night News Boys	Polydor PD 14002	1969	Medley titled "Good Old Rock 'N' Roll," which includes "Blue Suede Shoes"/"Sweet Little Sixteen"/"Whole Lotta Shakin' Goin' On"; b/w "Bad News"
Cat Mother and The All Night News Boys	Polydor 56543 (UK)	1969	Same as immediately above
Eddie McCall	Bowling Green 100	Pre-1964	Decent guitar break; b/w "Welcome To The Party Of Broken Hearts"; Dallas, TX, label
Paul McCartney	A&M FREE 21 (England)	1987	B/w "I Saw Her Standing There"; 7-inch small hole 45; "Limited Edition, Not for Sale"; "The Prince Trust's 10th Anniversary Birthday Party"
Paul McCartney and Wings	Heavy 101 (boot)	1973	B/w "Hound Dog" by John Lennon with Elephant's Memory
The Merseybeats	Fontana TE.17422 (UK)	1964	EP with "I'm Gonna Sit Right Down And Cry"/"Shame"/"You Can't Judge A Book By Its Cover"
Amos Milburn, Jr.	Le Cam 961	c. 1962	B/w "Dearest Darling"; Fort Worth, TX, label

The Mod IV	Poe 1221	1968	Garage version; b/w "It's Not The Same"
The Morris Brothers	Tyger 7103-17	???	Chuck Berry/Little Richard medley; includes, among others, "Johnny B. Goode" and "Good Golly Miss Molly"
Neon	Columbia 4-44893	1969	B/w "Back To Brooklyn"
The Paupers	Roman DR 1111 (Canada)	1966	Garage; b/w "Sooner Than Soon"
Elvis Presley	RCA EPA-994	1957	EP with "How Do You Think I Feel"/"How's The World Treating You"/"First In Line"
Elvis Presley	RCA RCX 7143 (UK)	1964	Same as immediately above
Lincoln Rand with The Reveliers	Adona AD-1444	1961	B/w "(I Love You) For Sentimental Reasons"; East Chicago, IN, label
Marty Robbins	Columbia B-2134	1957	EP with "Mean Mama Blues"/"Grown-Up Tears"/"A White Sport Coat And A Pink Carnation"
Marty Robbins	Fontana TFE 17167 (UK)	1959	EP with "The Hanging Tree"/"The Story Of My Life"/"She Was Only Seventeen (He Was One Year More"
The Rocky Fellers	Parkway 836	1962	B/w "South Pacific Twist"; Philippines band
Smiley and Co.	Jet 759 (UK)	1975	Medley with "Johnny B. Goode" and "Bony Maronie"; b/w "You Got Me Runnin'"

Robert Smith	Air 5006	1960	B/w "Roll On"; Miami, FL, label; Rite pressing
Little Arnie Stone	BC 45-354	???	B/w "Left Without A Woman"; 11-year old kiddie rocker; Sikeston, MO, label
Swinging Blue Jeans	EMI EM 83 (UK)	1989	Coupled with "It's Too Late Now" on the same side; b/w "The Hippy Hippy Shake"
Cy Tucker & The Friars	Amazon AR 7012S (UK)	1976	EP with "Funny Face"/"Gifts"/"Leavin' On Your Mind"
Thundermug	Avco Embassy 4557	1970	B/w "Carry All I Own"; Massachusetts based band
Bobby Lee Trammell	Sims 254	1965	B/w "Saints Go Marching In"
Gene Vincent	Columbia ESRF 1649 (France)	c. early 1960's	EP with "You Are My Sunshine"/"Private Detective"/"La Den-Da-Den-Da-Da"
Shirley Jean Wiley	Myrl 408	1961	Great female RAB version; b/w "Evening Shadows"; Ferriday, LA, label
David Wills	Epic 8-50188	1975	B/w "Queen Of The Starlight Ballroom"; co-produced by Charlie Rich
The Wreck-A-Mended	United Artists 50122	1967	Medley with "Sally's The One"; b/w "Dirty Old Man"

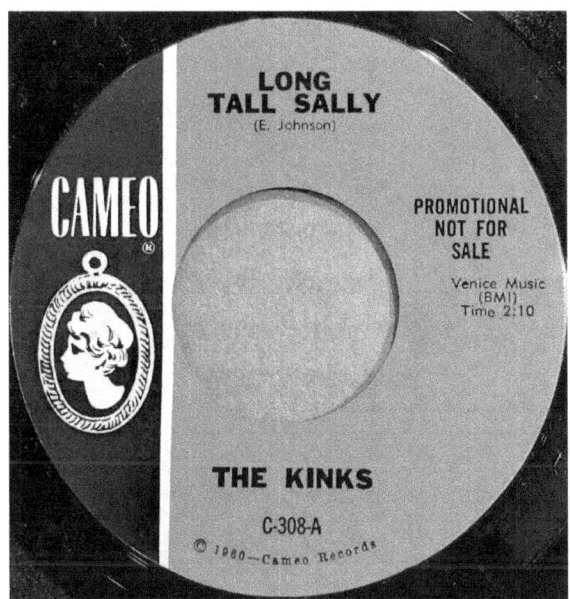

The Kinks on Cameo 308
(First American release, 1964)

The Beatles (1964 Parlophone UK EP)

A&M FREE 21 Picture Sleeve

A&M FREE 21 7-inch 45

"LONG TALL SALLY" IN THE MOVIES

"Long Tall Sally" has appeared in many movies, starting with *Don't Knock the Rock* in 1956:

MOVIE TITLE	YEAR	COMMENTS
Don't Knock the Rock	1956	Performed by Little Richard; musical jukebox headlined by Bill Haley and His Comets who sing three songs in addition to the title track
John Lennon and the Plastic Ono Band: Sweet Toronto	1971	This D. A. Pennebaker produced documentary is about the Toronto Rock and Roll Revival 1969 concert that featured John Lennon and included performances by Little Richard, Jerry Lee Lewis, Chuck Berry, and Bo Diddley; the opening prologue included the comment, "John could at last introduce Yoko to the heroes of his childhood"
The Year Living Dangerously	1982	Performed by Little Richard; war drama starring Mel Gibson and Linda Hunt
Predator	1987	Performed by Little Richard; war movie starring Arnold Schwarzenegger; the film clip of the helicopter scene in which "Long Tall Sally" is heard can be found on *YouTube*
Red Scorpion	1988	Performed by Little Richard; action-adventure film
Road House	1989	Performed by The Jeff Healey Band; Patrick Swayze stars as a tough bouncer hired to bring order to an unruly bar

BackBeat (UK)	1994	Performed by Dave Pirner who is best known as lead singer for the group Soul Asylum; produced by Dan Was; dramatization of The Beatles' days in Hamburg, Germany, in the early 1960s
Shake, Rattle and Roll: An American Love Story	1999	TV mini-series; performed by Billy Porter; Golden Reel Award for best sound editing for TV movies
Planet 51	2009	Performed by John Sloman; animated sci-fi adventure comedy; Dwayne Johnson and Jessica Biel are among the voices heard in the movie.
Predators	2010	Performed by Little Richard; sci-fi action adventure starring Adrien Brody
The Roaring 20s: Mick Jagger's Golden Years (UK)	2011	Performed by Little Richard; documentary exploring Mick Jagger's musical influences of during the period 1963 to 1972
A House With A Clock In Its Walls	2018	Performed by Little Richard; played once during the movie and again over the credits; fantasy family comedy

DOCUMENTED CONCERT PERFORMANCES OF "LONG TALL SALLY"

As of May 1, 2024, *Setlist.fm* documented that "Long Tall Sally" has been performed in concert 1,142 times by 152 different artists. In addition to Little Richard (54), artists who have included "Long Tall Sally" in their set lists on more than five occasions include The Beatles (256), Elvis Presley (135), Wings (53), Cliff Richard (47), Jerry Lee Lewis (31), Scorpions (22), Fleetwood Mac (14), John Fogerty (9), Led Zeppelin (7), and Bruce Springsteen (6).

HONORS AND ACCOLADES FOR "LONG TALL SALLY"

- Inducted into the Grammy Hall of Fame in 1990
- Chosen by the Rock & Roll Hall of Fame as one of the "500 Songs That Shaped Rock and Roll"
- Ranked #55 on the *Rolling Stone*'s 2004 list of "The 500 Greatest Songs of All Time"
- Ranked #278 on Dave Marsh's 1989 book *The Heart of Rock & Soul: The 1001 Greatest Singles Ever Made*

ALSO WORTH NOTING . . .

- "Long Tall Sally" was Specialty Records' largest selling record.
- "Long Tall Sally" was the last song sung by The Beatles before a paying audience, which was on August 29, 1966, at San Francisco's Candlestick Stadium.
- Little Richard returned the favor of The Beatles covering his "Long Tall Sally" with his 1970 cover of "I Saw Her Standing There" on Reprise 0942, which was recorded at the Fame Studios in Muscle Shoals, Alabama.
- "Long Tall Sally" was sampled by Buchanan & Goodman on the 1956 hit novelty song "Flying Saucers, Part 1," on Luniverse 101.
- Larry Williams makes a reference to "Long Tall Sally" in the opening lyrics of his hit "Short Fat Fannie": "I was slippin' and slidin' with a long tall Sally; Peekin' and a hidin', duck back in the alley."
- Reportedly, Little Richard's recording of "Long Tall Sally" was on the juke box owned by John Lennon.
- Jerry McCain's "Run Uncle John! Run" on Excello 2081 is his answer to Little Richard's "Long Tall Sally."

ADDITIONAL SOURCES

Clifford, Mike, Consultant Editor, *The Harmony Illustrated Encyclopedia of Rock* (Harmony Books, 7th ed., 1992)

Dalton, David, "Little Richard: Child of God," *Rolling Stone* (May 28, 1970)

Enotris Johnson Bio, Wiki 2017 - Musician Biographies at https://muscianbio.org/enotris.johnson/

Kirby, David, *Little Richard: The Birth of Rock 'n' Roll* (Continuum International Publishing Group, 2009)

Levinson, Mark, *The Complete Beatles Chronicle* (Pyramid Books, 1992)

Long Tall Sally—song facts, recording info and more! (beatlesbible.com)

Mendelssohn, John, *The Kinks Kronikles* (Quill, 1985)

Ribowski, Mark, *The Big Life of Little Richard* (Diversion Books, 2020)

Rolling Stone Encyclopedia of Rock & Roll (Patricia Romanowski and Holly George Warren eds.) (Fireside, 1995)

Vera, Billy, *Rip It Up: The Specialty Records Story* (BMG, 2019)

White, Charles, *The Life and Times of Little Richard: The Authorized Biography* (Omnibus Press, 2003)

SPECIAL NOTE

Exactly who is Enotris Johnson? Over the years, several different and conflicting accounts have emerged. Depending on the source, it was:

- The man, identified as Enotris Johnson, who Little Richard's mother remarried after the death of her husband, Charles "Bud" Penniman
- The man, identified as Enotris Johnson, who with his wife Ann, both white and devout Seventh Day Adventists, took in and raised about 12 black and white children, including Little Richard
- Little Richard's adoptive father, Johnny Johnson, who along with his wife Ann, ran Macon's Tick Tock Club [sic], and took Little Richard in after he was kicked out of his house at age 13
- Alternatively, Ann Howard who, along with her husband Johnny Howard, owned Macon's Ann's Tic Toc Club, and took Little Richard in after he was kicked out of his house at age 13
- The young girl, identified by Bumps Blackwell as Enortis [sic] Johnson, who purportedly gave the lyrics to a DJ who, in turn, gave them to Blackwell

Unfortunately, as far as currently known, none of the many persons who interviewed Little Richard during his lifetime, including his authorized biographer, Charles White, ever asked Little Richard to identify who "Enotris Johnson" was, i.e., the person initially credited as being the sole composer of "Long Tall Sally."

Trying to sort facts from fiction is difficult if the events occurred a decade ago, but it is nearly impossible when the events occurred more than six decades ago. However, it may be possible to reconcile some of the asserted facts and develop a hypothesis concerning Enotris Johnson's identity.

At the outset, it is possible to rule out that Enotris Johnson was the man who Little Richard's mother married shortly after her husband was murdered in 1952, as Mark Ribowski wrote in his 2020 Little Richard bio.[48] First, he did not identify his source or any evidence that Little Richard's mother, Leva Mae Penniman, ever remarried. To the contrary, all available evidence strongly supports the conclusion that she never remarried. Both Leva Mae and Richard are quoted extensively in Charles Wright's authorized Little Richard bio, and there is nary a suggestion that she remarried. Moreover, official government death records show that Leva Mae Penniman died on January 11, 1984, in Riverside, CA, where she had lived in Little Richard's house since 1956. Those records list her spouse as "Charles Penniman," i.e., Little Richard's father.

---

48 Ribowski is a recognized biographer of numerous artists and musicians, including The Supremes, Phil Spector, Stevie Wonder, The Temptations, Otis Redding, James Taylor, and Hank Williams. He has also written for such magazines as *TV Guide* and *Playboy*. Although Ribowski appended a lengthy bibliography, amazingly he did not reference Charles White's authorized biography that contains numerous quotes from Little Richard, his mother Leva Mae Penniman, Bumps Blackwell, among numerous others.

Likewise highly suspect is Eugene Chadbourne's bio of Little Richard that he penned for *Allmusic.com*,[49] in which he stated:

> Enotris Johnson and his wife, Ann, devout white Seventh Day Adventists, adopted
> and raised a total of a dozen Johnson children, both black and white. One of these was
> Richard Penniman, who took on the stage name of Little Richard in the '50s.

The Harmony Illustrated Encyclopedia of Rock (7th ed. 1992), in somewhat similar fashion states, that Little Richard was "[a]dopted by white Macon couple Ann and Enotris Johnson." These two accounts assert that Enotris Johnson was a man, but all the other accounts, other than Ribowski's discussed immediately above, state that Enotris was a woman, which I believe is accurate.[50] Since neither Chadbourne nor the *Harmony Encyclopedia* cite any source or evidence to support their account, it is easy to dismiss them.

Next, it is necessary to discuss the following comment in the *Rolling Stone* biography of Little Richard:

> He moved in with a white family, Ann and Johnny Johnson, who ran Macon's Tick
> Tock Club, after his own family kicked him out at age 13.

This account was repeated virtually verbatim in an article entitled "Little Richard in Macon" posted on the *Visit Macon* website at www.maconga.org. In similar fashion, identical articles about Little Richard's comeback authored by Joan Engels, a *Newsweek Feature Service* contributor, were published in multiple newspapers in 1970,[51] that state that "Richard was taken in by a local white woman, Ann Johnson, who still runs Ann's Tic-Toc Tavern on Macon's Broadway."

Exhaustive *Google* and *Ancestry.com* searches failed to locate any information on an Ann and/or Johnny Johnson who lived in Macon, Georgia, and ran a club or tavern. Nor was there any information on *Google* or *Ancestry.com* that would provide evidence of an Enotris Johnson who lived in Macon. The problem with this oft repeated scenario is that while the existence of Ann's Tic Toc Club is well-documented,[52] that same documentation establishes beyond reasonable doubt that the owners were

---

49 Eugene Chadbourne is a guitarist whose recording career includes innumerable releases, many of which are self-released. His primary genre is avantgarde jazz, but he has explored many other genres ranging from Cajun to rockabilly. As an author, he has been a reviewer for the *All Music Guide* (AMG) and a contributor to *Maximum RocknRoll* and *Allmusic.com*.

50 An *Ancestry.com* search establishes that "Enotris" has been used as the first name for both women and men, although the sample size is very small.

51 The newspapers included *The Kenosha News* (Kenosha, WI, 4/8/70), *The Ithaca Journal* (Ithaca, NY, 4/18/70), *The Dayton Daily News* (Dayton, OH, 4/19/70), *The Rochester Democrat and Chronicle* (Rochester, NY, 4/26/70), *The Pensacola News Journal* (Pensacola, FL, 4/30/70), and *The Mercury* (Pottstown, PA, 6/6/70).

52 Although some sources refer to the establishment owned by Ann and Johnny Howard as "Ann's Tick Tock Club," period pictures of the bar on the internet establish that the correct name is "Ann's Tic Toc Club." Among other entertainers who are said to have performed at Ann's Tic Toc Club are James Brown and Otis Redding, both of whom were raised in Macon, Georgia.

Johnny and Ann Howard. For example, when Ann Howard died, the *Macon Telegraph's* January 17, 2007, obituary, read, in relevant part, as follows:

> Ann Howard, 82, was the owner of Ann's Tick-Tock Club [*sic*] and gave a young Little Richard the opportunity to perform in her Macon nightclub as well as a place to stay in the mid-1950s. "She allowed Little Richard to do what he did," said Joseph Johnson, curator at the Georgia Music Hall of Fame. "She was almost like a second mama to him."
>
> ****
>
> In a telephone interview Wednesday, Little Richard, whose real name is Richard Penniman, recalled Howard and her late husband, Johnny, with fond memories. "She was a good lady," he said. "When racism was real strong down there, she was always real nice. Her husband was a good man, and she was a good woman who opened the door for a lot of black people."
>
> ****
>
> "He would come after (the bus station) closed down to work for me," Howard told *The Telegraph* in a 1990 interview. "He would work in the kitchen, and then he would go on stage and play for 45 minutes or an hour and then go back in the kitchen."

In that same interview, Little Richard's one-time manager, Percy Welch,[53] recalled the singer's relationship with Howard. "We started playing at Ann's Tick-Tock, and (Howard) was crazy about him," Welch said in that interview. "She wanted to bring him home with her. Of course, he was bringing all these people into the place.... Six nights a week it was packed from 6 o'clock to whenever they went home.... He was singing 'Tutti Frutti' right there."

In a 1990 *Rolling Stone* interview, Little Richard said he wrote "Miss Ann" to express his appreciation of Ann Howard.[54]

This reported information on Ann Howard would seemingly suggest that she *might* be the person who Little Richard was trying to benefit, but how do you get from Ann Howard to Enotris Johnson? Despite an exhaustive search, I have found no information that would suggest that Ann Howard somehow morphed into Enotris Johnson.

Next is Bumps Blackwell's oft-repeated account that he got the three lines on "just a piece of paper with a few words written on it" from Honey Chile, a New Orleans DJ, the latter of whom said she got it from a young girl, Enortis [*sic*] Johnson, from Appaloosa, Mississippi, who asked that it be given to Little Richard in the hopes of raising some money for her ailing Aunt Mary.[55] This account has been disputed by many, primarily on the grounds that nobody has been able to identify a 1950s

---

53 An UPI article dated February 15, 2004, reported that "Little Richard returned home to Macon, Ga., for the funeral of Melvin C. "Percy" Welsh and told how Welsh literally gave him the shirt off his back."

54 Puterbaugh, Parke, "Little Richard: 'I Am the Architect of Rock 'n' Roll,'" *Rolling Stone* (April 19, 1990).

55 Blackwell's account is based on what he is quoted as telling Charles White for his authorized Little Richard bio.

New Orleans DJ who went by the handle "Honey Chile" [56] or establish that the town of Appaloosa, Mississippi, exists.

With the foregoing helping set the context, we next encounter Enotris Johnson, a woman whose official birth records show was born in Hammond, Tangipahoa Parish, Louisiana, on October 3, 1935. [57] At some point in time she moved to Bogalusa, Louisiana, which is about 45 miles from Hammond. A now deleted comment about Enotris Johnson that was posted in May 2009, on the *Who's Dated Who* celebrity website by a person only identified as "Betty" reads as follows[58]:

> *What happened to Enotris Johnson, the song writer that almost became a star? She loved the music industry very much and still does. She says that Little Richard was her brother back then. She married a preacher back on September 10, 1956; that ended all of her musical dreams because he was a man of God and he could not have his wife singing the blues. You can only think of what was expected of a housewife back in the 1950s. Enotris now lives in Bogalusa, Louisiana. She is now 72 years old. She has one daughter, Wilma Dunn, [who] resides in Asheville, North Carolina, with her husband.[59] Enotris is a warm loving mother and friend and still supports her husband. Every once in a while, you can hear her wailing on that piano and singing in the middle of the night. You would just love to sit around her and hear her tell all the stories from back in the day when all of the old singers were at their humble beginnings. Enotris Johnson has lived a full and happy life with her husband and being the ideal preacher's wife.* [Edited slightly.]

Betty's comment that "Little Richard was her brother back then" is open to both question and interpretation. Given that Little Richard was born and raised in Macon, Georgia, it is hard to believe that the Enotris Johnson, who was living in either Hammond or Bogalusa, Louisiana, was Little Richard's brother, unless the word "brother" was used in a loose, colloquial sense and not intended to be taken literally. While Little Richard came from a large family, none of the biographies of Little Richard list a sister named Enotris.[60]

---

56 In his account, Blackwell said that the DJ was a female. As a result, it is possible that "Honey Chile" was the name that Blackwell used when referring to the DJ. "Honey Chile" is a term of endearment, especially in the American South. Assuming some validity to Blackwell's account, it would seem logical that a young female would seek out a female DJ to whom to give the lyrics.

57 While some reports state Enotris Johnson was born in Tangipahoa, Louisiana, and not Hammond, Louisiana, both accounts are accurate in that Hammond is in Tangipahoa Parish. Tangipahoa is not a town but rather is a parish, akin to a county in other states.

58 *Echoes In The Wind Archives: Rock 'n' Roll For Aunt Mary,* at echoesinthewind2.blogspot.com.

59 *Ancestry.com* documents the accuracy of this information about Enotris Johnson's daughter, Wilma Dunn.

60 The obituary for Lafayette Marquis Penniman, one of Little Richard's brothers, listed all twelve of Leva Mae Penniman's children, including six sisters, none of whom was named Enotris, albeit one was named Elnora. A Google search of Elnora Penniman, or Elnora Connor, her married name, did not turn anything up that would suggest that she was ever called Enotris.

Bumps arguably misspoke when he said the girl was from Appaloosa when in fact it may have been Bogalusa. Although not the same name, it is somewhat similar sounding.[61] Bogalusa is where on September 12, 1956, she married Willie J. Johnson, a minister at the Tree of Life Baptist Church. She would have been 20 when Bumps said a girl 16 or 17 years old gave him the three lines that he said led to "Long Tall Sally." While the age difference is not insignificant, perhaps Enotris appeared to Bumps to be younger than she was. Thus, Blackwell told Charles White that Enotris was "about sixteen, seventeen, with plaits, who reminded you of one of these little sisters at a Baptist meeting, all white starched collars and everything." Was this the Enotris Johnson to whom Bumps was referring? Maybe.

Supportive of this hypothesis is the information that the organizers of the Bogalusa Blues & Heritage Festival provided in 2015, i.e., that a person who knew Enotris Johnson said that she "kept silent about her early successes in the pop industry for decades because she was married to a preacher in Bogalusa." It was also reported that relatives of Johnson confirmed that she had received songwriting royalties. Then, in a web posting on August 25, 2015, the Festival made the following announcement that one of the two women it was honoring was Enotris Johnson:

> The second lady that we discovered after her death, August 2 of this year, astounded us all. This well-kept secret was revealed by her family, and we are so thrilled to honor her this year! Enotris Johnson was born on October 3, 1935, in Hammond, LA. Enotris loved songwriting and was a gifted musician. Early in her music career she met Rev. Willie J. Johnson and put her music career on hold for the love of her life. They were married in September 1956 and lived in Bogalusa. Enotris supported her husband's ministry, and never claimed her fame publicly for all the wonderful music she wrote and contributed to the cultural world of music. In the end of her life, she began to speak of her writings with her great sense of humor.

Ancestry.com documents that Enotris Johnson was the daughter of Thomas J. and Doretha Johnson and that her name prior to her marriage to Willis J. Johnson on September 12, 1956, was Enotris Olivia Johnson. This is therefore consistent with the information on the Library of Congress Copyright Entry dated March April 10, 1956, that lists Enotris Johnson as the sole composer of "Long Tall Sally."

But perhaps the best evidence that Enotris Johnson is the person who was credited with composing "Long Tall Sally" is the following information that was included on the copyright application filed with the Copyright Office of the Library of Congress on March 8, 1956[62]:

---

61 In the third edition of White's Little Richard bio, the name of the town was changed to "Opelousas, Mississippi, but that town is in Louisiana. Like Appaloosa, Opelousas sounds somewhat similar to Bogalusa, at least in terms of the last two syllables.

62 This exceedingly helpful information was provided on June 27, 2018, in a comment posted on the *45cat.com* website by a person identified as "Mickey Rat."

Claimant: Venice Music, Inc. 8508 Sunset Blvd, Hollywood 46 California[63]

Composer: Enotris Johnson, 212 Washington Ave., Hammond, Louisiana

In this author's opinion, the listing of her address as being in Hammond, Louisiana, is consistent with documentation that Enotris Johnson was born in Hammond, Louisiana, and presumably lived there at the time the copyright application was filed in March 1956.[64] Significantly, official Census Records available on *Ancestry.com* list the address of Enotris' father, Thomas J. Jefferson, as Washington Avenue in Hammond, Louisiana. By September of 1956 she had moved to Bogalusa. Louisiana, where she married Willis Johnson, a preacher at the Tree of Life Baptist Church.

Admittedly, there is tension between saying that she was living in Hammond when she gave the lyrics to a New Orleans DJ as opposed to being from a town that sounds similar to the town mentioned by Blackwell in his account. One possible explanation might be that Enotris told the DJ she was from Bogalusa knowing that she was going to be married in Bogalusa in the not too distant future and that she listed the Washington Avenue address on the copyright application in order to hide her involvement in writing R&B songs from her soon to be preacher husband.[65]

How can one make sense of all these conflicting accounts? Since Little Richard was fond of both his birth mother, Leva Mae Penniman,[66] and Ann Howard, the woman who took him in at age 13 and helped raise him, it would seem to logically suggest that the woman he was trying to help out with his newfound wealth by crediting her as a writer of "Long Tall Sally," as well as giving her credit for two other songs recorded in essentially the same time frame, was either Leva Mae or Ann Howard. But this leaves out the third woman, i.e., Enotris Johnson, who was born in Hammond, Louisiana, and who later lived in Bogalusa, Louisiana, and for whom supportive information was found on the internet that pretty much establishes that she is the person credited as one of the writers of "Long Tall Sally," "Miss Ann," and "Jenny, Jenny." Thus, my educated conclusion is that Enotris Johnson from Hammond and Bogalusa, Louisiana is the person who was initially credited as the sole composer of "Long Tall Sally."[67]

My conclusion that it was Enotris Johnson from Hammond and Bogalusa, Louisiana, adds strength to some elements of Bumps Blackwell's account. Given the reports of her songwriting and musical background, one can speculate that she journeyed to New Orleans with more than just three

---

63 Venice Music was the publishing company for Specialty Records.

64 Little Richard first recorded "Long Tall Sally" (AKA "The Thing") in Los Angeles, CA, in late November of 1955. Since lyrics for this November 1955, recording session are the same as the lyrics from the February 1956 recording session that resulted in the released version of "Long Tall Sally," Enotris Johnson must have composed and delivered the lyrics, or at least a portion of them, sometime prior to the November 1955 recording session.

65 Since neither Appaloosa, Mississippi, nor the town mentioned in third edition of White's Little Richard bio, Opelousas, Mississippi, exist, it is probably a fool's errand to try to reconcile the facts we know about Enotris Johnson with Blackwell's account of where Enotris hailed from.

66 Little Richard was deeply attached to his mother. Indeed, one of songs he penned that appeared on RCA 47-4582 is titled "Thinkin' 'Bout My Mother."

67 Alas, I was unable to uncover information that Enotris Johnson had an "Aunt Mary," although her funeral home obituary reported that she had "a host of nieces, nephews and other relatives."

lines on a small piece of paper,[68] i.e., that she provided the New Orleans DJ with the words and perhaps the music for "Long Tall Sally," and perhaps the other two songs attributed to her. In giving his account, Blackwell was probably spinning a story that downplayed the role of Enotris Johnson in order to take more credit for himself. The need to help out "Aunt Mary" as told by Blackwell is very likely more fiction than fact. It certainly wouldn't have been the first time that a musician has embellished the facts.

POST-SCRIPT

The BMI website lists 16 songs that Enotris Johnson composed or co-composed, but several of the songs listed are clearly in error. For example, "Eating and Sleeping" and "I'm Your Best Bet Baby" are songs that Earl King composed and recorded. His real name is Earl Silas Johnson IV; hence, for the songs he composed, the composer was listed as "E. Johnson."

---

68 The distance between Hammond, Louisiana and New Orleans, Louisiana is approximately 62 miles.

CHAPTER 11

"ROLL OVER BEETHOVEN"

CHUCK BERRY (MAY 1956)

Original Chess release

Original 1957 UK London tri-center release
(Image: *45cat*)

Cash Box ad, 6/16/56

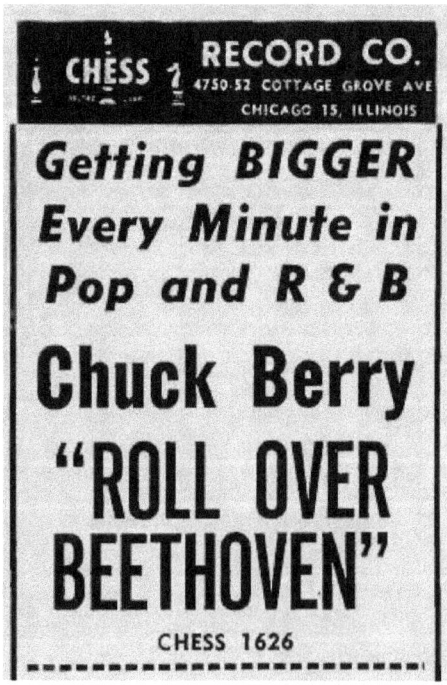

Billboard ad, 5/26/56

"ROLL OVER BEETHOVEN" — THE BASIC FACTS

Label: Chess 1626 (both 45 and 78)

Writer: Chuck Berry

Date recorded: April 16, 1956

Date released: May 1956

B-Side: "Drifting Heart"

Producers: Leonard and Phil Chess

Billboard charts

Pop Chart
- Debut: 6/30/56
- Peak: #29
- Duration: 5 weeks

R&B Chart
- Debut: 6/09/56
- Peak: #2
- Duration: 7 weeks

THE SONG AND ITS IMPACT

In his autobiography, Chuck Berry said that the inspiration for "Roll Over Beethoven" was his sister Lucy's monopolization of the family's piano to practice classical music. As Chuck related, "most of the words were aimed at Lucy instead of Maestro Ludwig Van Beethoven," asserting—tongue in cheek—that "Lucy was the culprit that delayed rock 'n' roll music by twenty years." Complaining to his mother wouldn't have worked, "but writing a letter and mailing it to a local DJ might have, as stated in the opening of the song." He said that out of his "sometimes unbelievable imagination, the rest of the self-explanatory lyrics came forth."

Recorded on April 16, 1956, at the Chess Records' Chicago studio with Johnnie Johnson on piano, Willie Dixon on bass, and Fred Below on drums, "Roll Over Beethoven" was released in May to good reviews. *Billboard* on May 19, 1956, put a "Review Spotlight" on it, noting it was "a natural for action" in light of its "humor, a driving beat and most of all, Berry's own distinctive and wailingly primitive style." Two weeks later on June 2, *Billboard* listed "Roll Over Beethoven" as one of the week's "Best Buys," observing that Berry had come up with "another powerhouse" and that it "should be on the national charts in a week or so." On May 26, 1956, *Cash Box* listed "Roll Over Beethoven" as a "Sleeper of the Week." Then, on June 2, *Cash Box* named it as a "R&B Sure Shot." By June 16, it was #2 on *Billboard's* R&B list of "Most Played in Juke Boxes" and #9 on its "Best Seller" list. Ultimately, it peaked at #2 on *Billboard's* R&B chart and #4 on *Cash Box's* R&B chart.

Unlike "Maybelline," Berry's first big hit that attracted multiple major label contemporaneous covers, including Jim Lowe on Dot 15407, Ralph Marterie on Mercury 70682, and Marty Robbins on Columbia 4-21446, "Roll Over Beethoven" was covered by only one major label artist, Helen Dixon on Vic 4X-0212, an RCA subsidiary. It, however, proved to be a weak competitor, despite *Billboard's* suggestion to the contrary. Its release did not have a material impact on the sales of Berry's original and, in any event, he received writer royalties and Chess received publisher royalties for both versions.

HELENE DIXON
Roll Over Beethoven 86
   VIK 0212—The comely chirp, who has moved to the label from Epic, belts out the Chuck Berry material in potent, growling rock and roll style to strong backing. This would seem a certain money-maker for the label. (Arc, BMI)
A Teen-Ager Sings the Blues....84
   This side is an extremely torchy lament with a feeling similar to that of "Teen-Age Prayer." The thrush renders it with great warmth, and this side also could catch hold. (Iris-Trojan, BMI)

"Roll Over Beethoven" was not released in England until 1957 on London HLU 8428. Although it did not chart in the UK, it is clear that it caught the ears of four lads from Liverpool who later became The Beatles. It was in their repertoire from the earliest days. And it was on their set list during their engagements at the Star-Club, as evidenced by its inclusion on a double album titled *Live! At the Star-Club in Hamburg, Germany; 1962*, released on Lingasong LS-2-7001 in 1977. Back in England with George Martin producing, they recorded it on July 30, 1963, but it was only released as a single in Canada on Capitol Records of Canada 72133.[69] Nevertheless, in the midst of Beatlemania in the U.S. in 1964, the Canadian release of "Roll Over Beethoven" found its way to the U.S. where it hit #30 on the *Cash Box* singles chart and #68 on the *Billboard* "Hot 100" chart. The song was later included on the EP "Four By The Beatles" on Capitol EAP 1-2121 that was released on May 11, 1964.

---

69 According to *45cat.com*, "Roll Over Beethoven" was released in Canada on December 23, 1963, and peaked on the Toronto Radio Station CHUM's chart at #2 on January 20, 1964.

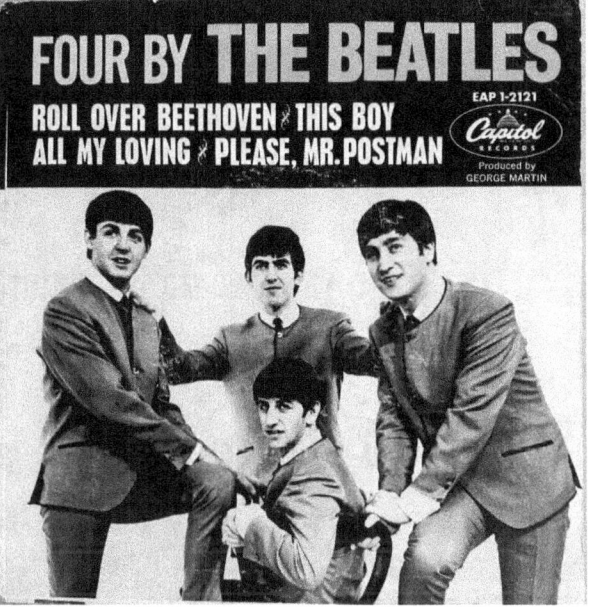

1963 Canadian release on Capitol 72133   **1964 U.S. EP on Capitol EAP 1-2121**

A live version recorded on February 28, 1964, was aired by the BBC on March 30, 1964, as part of the BBC's Beatles series, *From Us to You.* It was this version that was used in the movie *Superman III* (1983), which was directed by Richard Lester. Nearly two decades earlier Lester had directed The Beatles' first two movies, *A Hard Day's Night* (1964) and *Help!* (1965).

The Beatles were not the only British band aware of Chuck Berry's "Roll Over Beethoven." The Electric Light Orchestra, founded by Jeff Lynne and Roy Wood in 1970, issued its version in 1973. It included an element of Beethoven's "Fifth Symphony" and was released in England on Harvest HAR 5063 and in the U.S. on United Artists XW173-W. It was the band's second charted record in England, peaking at #6, and its first in the U.S. It eventually became one of the band's signature songs and one that they frequently ended concerts with. At their Rock & Roll Hall of Fame induction ceremony on April 7, 2017, it was the first performance of the evening following a video tribute to Chuck Berry, who had died less than a month earlier. *Setlist.fm* documents that ELO, as the band is sometimes known, has performed "Roll Over Beethoven" 533 times in concert as of May 1, 2024, which is more times than any other song performed in concert by ELO.

"Roll Over Beethoven" was a favorite of the mid-1960s garage bands. Versions well worth checking out include The Princetons Five on Princeton PF-1001, Ryells Combo on Orlyn 5511, and The Velaires on Jamie 1198 (originally released as by the Flairs on Palms 726).

"Roll Over Beethoven" was Chuck Berry's brash proclamation that helped usher in the era of Rock 'n' Roll music in the mid-1950s. His electrifying opening guitar riff, which was largely replicated in his later masterpiece "Johnny B. Goode," is one of the most famous riffs in the history of rock music, copied countless thousands of times by guitarists worldwide. "Roll Over Beethoven" still reverberates today.

CONTEMPORANEOUS COVER VERSIONS OF "ROLL OVER BEETHOVEN"

Other than Helene Dixon's version Vik 4X-0212, the only other contemporaneous cover version was by The Four Chaps on Rama 199, b/w "Wrong Number."

CONTEMPORANEOUS BUDGET LABEL COVERS OF "ROLL OVER BEETHOVEN"

Surprisingly, only one budget label cover was found, despite an exhaustive internet search.

ARTIST	LABEL	COMMENTS
Joe Fortunato	Waldorf T9X45	EP by various artists with "Long Tall Sally"/"I'm In Love Again"/"I Want You To Be My Girl"/"Love, Love, Love"/"Rock Around The Clock"/"Rip It Up"/"Don't Be Cruel"

LATER RELEASES OF "ROLL OVER BEETHOVEN" BY CHUCK BERRY

LABEL	YEAR	COMMENTS
Pye Int'l NEP 44009 (UK)	1963	EP titled "Chuck & Bo" with Chuck's "Our Little Rendezvous" and Bo Diddley's "Pills Or (Love's Labour's Lost)" and "The Greatest Lover In The World"
Pye Int'l NEP 44018 (UK)	1964	EP titled "The Best of Chuck Berry," with "Memphis, Tennessee," "I'm Talking About You," and "Sweet Little Sixteen"
Mercury MF 1102 (UK)	1969	B/w "Back to Memphis"; recorded by Mercury, not the Chess originals

Philco Hip Pocket HP-34	1969	B/w "Maybelline"; reissues of his Mercury sides, not the original versions on Chess; Hip Pocket records were 3 7/8 inch 45 rpm flexi-discs; approximately 40 Hip Pocket discs of old hits were released between 1967 and 1969
Chess 9010	1972	B/w "Nadine (Is That You?)"; Chess "Blue Chip Series"; issued by GRT after purchasing the Chess catalogue in 1969
Mercury C-30145	1970's?	B/w "Back In The U. S. A."; Mercury "Celebrity Series"; re-recorded versions, not the Chess originals
Eric 227	1979	B/w "Maybelline"
Chess CHES 4000 (UK)	1985	EP with "Sweet Little Sixteen," "School Days," and "Johnny B. Goode"; "Chess Mini Masters" series
Ripete R45-202	c. 1989	B/w "Nadine"
Old Gold OG-9847 (UK)	1989	B/w "Johnny B. Goode"
Collectables COL 3404	???	B/w "My Ding-A-Ling"; "Back to Back Hit Series"

Philco Hip Pocket HP-34

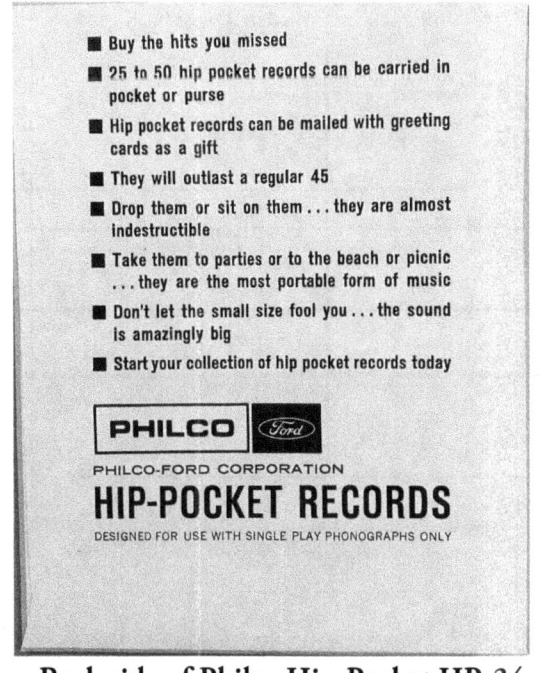

Back side of Philco Hip-Pocket HP-34

SUBSEQUENT COVER VERSIONS OF "ROLL OVER BEETHOVEN"

ARTIST	LABEL	YEAR	COMMENTS
The Astronauts	RCA 5-WLP-5-100	1964	Small hole 7" 33 1/3 compact stereo; b/w "It's So Easy"/"Johnny B. Goode"/"If I Had A Hammer"/"Dream Lover"/"Shortnin' Bread"; "Wurlitzer Discotheque Music"
The Beatles	Capitol 72133 (Canada)	1963	B/w "Please Mister Postman"; although only released in Canada in December 1963, it made the U.S. *Billboard* pop chart for four weeks in 1964, reaching #68 amid Beatlemania
The Beatles	Capitol EAP 1-2121	1964	EP titled "Four By The Beatles"; b/w "This Boy," "All My Loving," and "Please, Mr. Postman"
The Beatles	Eva-Tone 8464	1964	5 3/4" flexi disc b/w "Little Deuce Coupe" by The Beach Boys and "The Saints" by the Kingston Trio; freebie with LP purchase
The Beatles	Capitol 6065	1965	B/w "Misery"; "Starline" series; green swirl label; reissued in 1971 on the Capitol target label as noted immediately below
The Beatles	Capitol 6065	1971	B/w "Misery"; target label; reportedly pressed in limited quantity
The Beatles	Collectables COL 1501	1982	B/w "I'm Gonna Sit Right Down And Cry Over You"; Hamburg Star Club tracks; "British Import Series"

The Beatles	Baktobak 1001, Stab 2009 (UK)	1988	Live recording from December 31, 1962, at Hamburg, Germany's Star Club; b/w "Your Feets Too Big"; boxset of 15 45s numbered Stab 2001 through Stab 2015
The Beatles	Reel-to-Reel Music Company, Covers 8 (Europe)	2020	Live recording from 1963; 7-inch 45 rpm picture disc EP titled *The Beatles Play Chuck Berry*, with "Rock And Roll Music," "Memphis Tennessee," and "Too Much Monkey Business"; unofficial
Benny and The Bedbugs	DCP 1008	1964	Instrumental version with some vocal shouts; b/w "The Beatle Beat," likewise an instrumental with some background "Yeah, Yeah, Yeahs," written by Don Costa
Bill Black	London SBG 22	1964	7" 33 1/3 EP with "School Days"/"Little Queenie"/"Brown Eyed Handsome Man"/"Thirty Days"/"Memphis Tennessee"; EP titled "Bill Black Plays Chuck Berry"
The Continentals	Wind Mill NR 2251	???	B/w "For The Love Of A Women"; "Featuring Gary Batchelder"
Harold Cox	C.M.W. 457	1974	B/w "She Had All The Dreaming (She Could Stand)"; produced by Buck Owens
The Dovells	Event 3310	1970	B/w "Something About You Boy"
Electric Light Orchestra	Harvest HAR 5053 (UK)	1972	Original release backed with "Manhattan Rumble (49th Street Massacre)"; quickly withdrawn, supposedly because Roy Wood's name appeared on the B-side

Electric Light Orchestra	Harvest HAR 5053 (UK)	1972	Reached #6 on the UK charts in January 1973; b/w "Queen Of The Hours"; recorded at Abbey Road in September 1972; version with new B-side released two weeks after the original version was withdrawn
Electric Light Orchestra	United Artists XW173-W	1973	B/w "Queen Of The Hours"; promo issue has mono/stereo versions of "Roll Over Beethoven"
Electric Light Orchestra	United Artists XW-513-X	1974	B/w "Slowdown"; "Silver Spotlight Series"
Electric Light Orchestra	Harvest HAR 5121 (UK)	1977	B/w "Slowdown"
Electric Light Orchestra	Harvest HAR 5179 (UK)	1979	B/w "Slowdown"; re-released to promote the release of Electric Light Orchestra's LP *The Light Shines On, Vol. 1*
Electric Light Orchestra	Jet ZS8 5152	1980	B/w "Slowdown"; Jet "Golden Oldies"
Electric Light Orchestra	EMI G45 22 (UK)	1984	B/w "10538 Overture"; EMI "Golden 45's" series
Electric Light Orchestra	Collectables ZS8 5152	1991	B/w "Slowdown"
Charlie Feathers	Feathers 8	1981	B/w "Swinging Doors"; "Rockabilly Juke Box Series"
Charlie Feathers	Feathers 12	1982	Same song but titled "Roll Over Beethoven #2"; b/w "What Da Say"; "Rockabilly Juke Box Series"
Narvel Felts	Lobo XI	1982	Peaked at #64 on the *Billboard* country chart; b/w "I'd Love You To Love Me"

The Flairs	Palms 726	1961	B/w "Brazil"; Phoenix, AZ, label, but band is from Iowa; master sold to Jamie and released as by the Velaires; see entry below
Dora Hall	Cozy 71006	c. early 70s	B/w "All Shook Up," a cover of Elvis Presley
The Johnson Brothers	No label name; matrix 106242	1971	B/w "The Windmill Song"
Sleepy LaBeef	Charly CYS 1049 (UK)	1979	B/w "Send Me Some Lovin'"
Larry and Teri	Peppermint Productions 1181	1980s	B/w "Ode To Billy Joe"; Youngstown, OH, label
Billy M. Lawrie	Polydor 56363 (UK)	1969	B/w "Please Comeback Joanna"; Billy was Lulu's sister who married Maurice Gibb of the Bee Gees, who produced the record; he and Lawrie co-wrote several songs for the Bee Gees
Linda Gail Lewis and Jerry Lee Lewis	Smash S-2254	1969	*Billboard* 11/22/69 "Spotlight Single," noting that the "vocal and piano performance are tops"; b/w "Secret Places"
Jerry Lee Lewis and Linda Gail Lewis	Mercury CC-35022	1971	B/w "Don't Let Me Cross Over"; Mercury "Celebrity Country Series"
Margaret Lewis	RAM A-2331	1961	EP with "Birmingham Valley Blues"/"Love Is A Fortune"/"You Can't Break My Heart No More"; Louisiana label
The Look Outs	Seeburg 3012	1965	B/w "Northern Lights"; "Discoteen Series"

Mountain	Windfall 536	1971	*Billboard* "Special Merit Spotlight" selection 12/11/71, noting that "the Chuck Berry classic gets a wild revival"; b/w "Crossroader"
Mountain	Island WIP 6119 (UK)	1971	B/w "Crossroader"
Joey Paige	Vee Jay 704	1965	B/w "Goodnight My Love"
Powder Blues	RCA PB-50765 (Canada)	1983	B/w "Your Daddy"
The Princetons Five	Princeton PF-1001	1964	B/w "Passing By"; St. Joseph, MI, label
Rattles	Decca F-11873 (UK)	1964	B/w "Bye Bye Johnny"
Rockers	CBS A3929 (UK)	1983	Medley titled "We Are The Boys (Who Make All The Noise)," with excerpts from six oldies, including "Great Balls of Fire" and "Johnny B. Goode"; group included Ron Wood and Chas Hodge; b/w "Rockin' On The Stage"
Roscoe and His Little Green Men	Pontiac 105	1960	B/w "Bye Bye Blues"
Bobby Russell and The Beagles	Spar 740	1964	Decent version with good guitar work; b/w "Right Or Wrong"; Nashville, TN, label
Ryells Combo	Orlyn 5521	1965	B/w "Only As Long As You Want It" and "Hank's Big Chance"; rare garage version
The Damien St. Thomas Show	Harbor HB 307	1969	B/w "I Never Complain"

Enoch Smokey	Pumpkin Seed 83-4010	1969	B/w "It's Cruel"; Iowa group; recorded in 1969 in Chicago, IL
Warren Storm	Showtime 1026	1977	B/w "Please Santa (Bring My Baby Back To Me)"; Crowley, LA, label
Carmol Taylor	Elektra E-45446	1977	B/w "You're Looking At A Happy Man"
Thirteenth Floor Elevators	Austin RE 1 (UK)	1978	EP with "Word" and "You Really Got Me"; recorded live in Austin, TX, in 1967
The Trashmen	Sundazed S-105	1992	B/w "Betty Jean"; recorded in 1964 but previously unreleased
Vanguards	No label name; matrix U-9271	c. 1960s	B/w "What's Wrong With You"; Mendota, IL, label
The Velaires	Jamie 1198	1961	B/w "Brazil" on the first pressing and "Frankie and Johnny" on the second pressing
Gene Vincent	Rollin' Danny RD 1 (UK)	1980	EP with "Rainyday Sunshine"/"Green Grass"/ "Mister Love"; recorded in Los Angeles, CA, in 1969, but previously unreleased
Gene Vincent	Magnum Force MFEP-003 (UK)	1981	EP with "Rainyday Sunshine"/"Green Grass"/ "Mister Love"
Gene Vincent	Pye BEEB 001 (UK)	1974	B/w "Be-Bop-A-Lula" and "Say Mama"; taken from an October 1971 Johnny Walker radio show
Pat Wayne with The Beachcombers	Columbia DB 7182 (UK)	1963	B/w "Is It Love?"; recorded at Abbey Road Studios before The Beatles cut their version; contrary to some reports, Geoff Roberts, a member of The Beachcombers, stated on the band's website that he played guitar and that "Jimmy Page had nothing to do with the band"

None Listed	Seeburg D-110	1965	7" 33 1/3 EP with "Everybody Loves Somebody"/"Nadine"/"Taste of Honey"/"In A Little Spanish Town"; "Discotheque Series"
None Listed	Seeburg DN-304-B	1965	7" 33 1/3 EP with "Ram Charger"/"Maybelline"/"Watusi '64"/"What's Easy For Two"/"A Hard Day's Night"; "Discoteen A Go Go Series"
None Listed	Seeburg DN-309-A	1965	7" 33 1/3 EP with "Supersonic"/"Rinky Dink"/ "Boney Moronie"/"Mother-In-Law"/ "Tomorrow's Love"; "Discoteen Series"
None Listed	Seeburg DN-315	1965	7" 33 1/3 EP with "Tequila"/"Up On The Roof"/"Walkin' Mr. Sax"/"Forty Miles Of Bad Road"/"C'mon and Swim"; "Discoteen Series"

  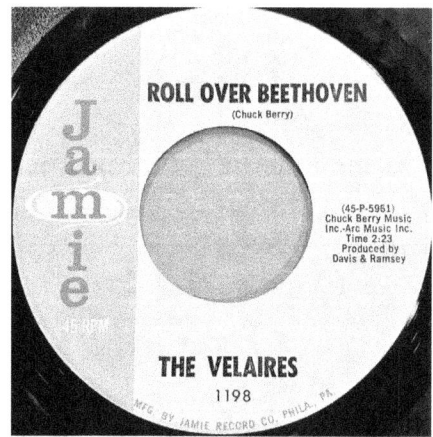

Subsequent covers by The Princetons Five, The Ryells Combo, and The Velaires

"ROLL OVER BEETHOVEN" IN THE MOVIES

The following are the movies in which "Roll Over Beethoven" can be heard:

MOVIE TITLE	YEAR	COMMENTS
Rock, Rock, Rock!	1956	Disappointingly, only performed by Chuck Berry on the soundtrack album (Chess LP 1425), but not in the film; film debut of Tuesday Weld (but her singing voice was dubbed by Connie Francis), as well as Valarie Harper
American Hot Wax	1973	Performed by Chuck Berry; the story is loosely based on the career of pioneering DJ Alan Freed
Superman III	1983	Performed by The Beatles; not credited
Rock Odyssey	1987	Performed by Robert Jason; a jukebox narrated by Scatman Crothers documents a woman's search for true love based on four decades of rock music; animated by Hanna/Barbera
Beethoven	1992	Paul Shaffer and The World's Most Dangerous Band recorded this version of the song that was the main theme for the film; the movie is about a St. Bernard dog named Beethoven
Beethoven's 2nd	1993	Sequel in which Beethoven becomes a father; likewise performed by Paul Shaffer
Rock & Roll Hall of Fame Live: Feelin' Alright	2009	Performed by Chuck Berry, Jerry Lee Lewis, and the Rock Hall Jam Band; film features highlights from past annual induction ceremonies, with speeches, performances, etc.

George Harrison: Living in the Material World	2011	Directed by Martin Scorsese; performed by The Beatles
Chuck Berry (UK)	2018	Performed by Chuck Berry, as well as The Beatles, Electric Light Orchestra (ELO), Alvin Lee, Gene Vincent, and Jimi Hendrix; Chuck Berry's story as told by friends and relatives

DOCUMENTED CONCERT PERFORMANCES OF "ROLL OVER BEETHOVEN"

As of May 1, 2024, *Setlist.fm* documented that "Roll Over Beethoven" has been performed in concert 2,452 times by 230 different artists. In addition to Chuck Berry (283), artists who have played "Roll Over Beethoven" in concert five or more times include Electric Light Orchestra (533), The Beatles (217), Jerry Lee Lewis (105), Byrds (52), The Rolling Stones (32), The Cliff Richards (25), and Eric Clapton (5). In addition, Bruce Springsteen (3) and John Fogerty (2) have sung it in concert.

HONORS AND ACCOLADES FOR "ROLL OVER BEETHOVEN"

■ Inducted into the Grammy Hall of Fame in 1990
■ Selected in 2003 for inclusion on National Recording Registry of the Library of Congress by the National Recording Preservation Board, which annually selects songs that are "culturally, historically, or aesthetically significant"
■ Chosen by the Rock & Roll Hall of Fame as one of the "500 Songs That Shaped Rock and Roll"
■ Ranked #97 on the Rolling Stone's 2004 list of "The 500 Greatest Songs of All Time," with the comment that it "became the ultimate rock & roll call to arms, declaring a new era"
■ Ranked #107 on Joel Whitburn's *Honor Roll of Hits*
■ Ranked #60 in Dave Marsh's book, *The Heart of Rock & Soul: The 1001 Greatest Singles Ever Made*

ALSO WORTH NOTING . . .

■ Rock artist and writer, Cub Koda, said "Roll Over Beethoven" was a "masterpiece" that helped to define rock 'n' roll.
■ Arthur Alexander used the lyric "a shot of rhythm and blues" as the title for a song he penned, which was released in 1961 on Dot 45-16309, the A-side of which was "You Better Move On," a song later covered by The Beatles.
■ According to *Setlist.fm*, "Johnny B. Goode" and "Roll Over Beethoven" were the two songs that Chuck Berry played the most in concert.

- The song has been used in other song titles, including Sonny Curtis' "Do You Remember Roll Over Beethoven" on Elektra E-46568 (1979) and Wizzard's "Bend Over Beethoven" on Harvest 5050 (UK, 1973), the latter being the group formed by Roy Wood after leaving the Electric Light Orchestra in 1972.
- "Roll Over Beethoven" is one of only two covers that ELO recorded on studio albums, the other being "Little Town Flirt," a cover of Del Shannon, another one of Jeff Lynne's heroes.
- The Electric Light Orchestra's 1983 hit "Rock 'n' Roll Is King" alludes to their earlier cover of "Roll Over Beethoven" with the lyric, "she rolled over Beethoven and she gave Tchaikovsky back."
- Cliff Richard issued a promo single of "Roll Over Beethoven" in 2016, albeit on a CD, to promote his new album, *Just… Fabulous Rock n' Roll*, released via Sony Music on November 11, 2016.

Cliff Richard 2016 Release

2016 Cliff Richard Promo CD

ADDITIONAL SOURCES

Chuck Berry, *The Autobiography*, with Foreword by Bruce Springsteen (Harmony Books, New York, NY, 1987)

Kiste, John Van, *Electric Light Orchestra: Song By Song* (Fonthill Media Limited, 2017)

CHAPTER 12

"BE-BOP-A-LULA"

GENE VINCENT (JUNE 1956)

Original 45 on Capitol F3450

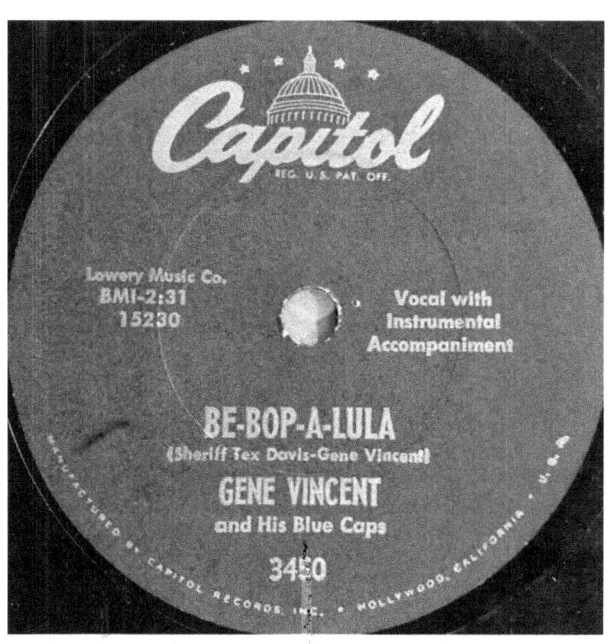

Original 78 on Capitol 3450

"Be-Bop-A-Lula" sheet music

Gold Record to commenorate the sales
of one million records

"BE-BOP-A-LULA" — THE BASIC FACTS

Label: Capitol F3450 (45) and Capitol 3450 (78)

Writers: Gene Vincent and Bill Davis (AKA Sheriff Tex Davis), but see below

Date recorded: May 4, 1956

Date released: June 6, 1956

B-side: "Woman Love"

Producer: Ken Nelson

Billboard charts

    <u>Pop Chart</u>

- Debut: 6/16/56
- Peak: #7
- Duration: 20 weeks

    <u>R&B Chart</u>

- Debut: 7/28/56
- Peak: #8
- Duration: 2 weeks

    <u>Country Chart</u>

- Debut: 7/7/56
- Peak: #5
- Duration: 17 weeks

THE SONG AND ITS IMPACT

In early 1956 Sheriff Tex Davis, a Norfolk, Virginia, DJ,[70] sent a three-song demo to Capitol Records, one of which was "Be-Bop-A-Lula." Capitol was eager at the time to find someone who could compete with RCA's Elvis Presley. Inspired by the Little Lulu comic strip character, the song was penned by Vincent and Don Graves who, like Vincent, was recuperating from a leg injury at the naval hospital in Portsmouth, Virginia. Grave's interest was subsequently bought out by Sheriff Tex Davis, reportedly for a mere $50, hence the reason for the listing of Davis as one of the song's writers.[71] Produced by Ken Nelson, the A & R head of Capitol, it was recorded by Vincent and The Blue Caps on May 4, 1956, at Owen Bradley's Nashville studio.

As Dave Marsh observed, "Vincent had a sulky country-blues baritone that fit the new rock and roll songs.... [Cliff Gallup, The Blue Caps'] guitarist turned in a pair of concise, cutting guitar breaks that rivaled Scotty Moore's work with Elvis." Although not planned, the Blue Cat's drummer, Dickie Harrell, can be heard screaming in the background. He later explained that he did so to make sure his family would know it was him on the record.

---

70 Davis became Vincent's manager. He is also listed as the co-author of other Vincent songs, including "Race with the Devil," "Who Slapped John," and "Important Words."

71 This summary is based on my analysis of multiple sources and my judgment as to the mostly likely account of the song's origin. The sources I used in making this judgment are included as a Special Note at the end of this Chapter.

As shown below, Capitol Records initially targeted "Woman Love" as the A-side, but when many radio stations banned it because of its supposedly sexual lyrics, Bill Lowery, the owner of Lowery Music and the publisher of "Be-Bop-A-Lula," stepped into the vacuum by mailing promo copies to numerous radio stations nationwide, helping to create grassroots support for "Be-Bop-A-Lula."

Billboard, **May 26, 1956**   *Billboard*, **June 23, 1956**

Billboard favorably reviewed "Be-Bop-A-Lula" as a "Best Buy" on June 16, 1956, commenting that it was showing "much of the sales excitement that Elvis stirs up."[72] It debuted on *Billboard's* pop chart that same week and later on the country and R&B charts on July 7, 1956 and July 28, 1956, respectively. It was on the pop chart for 20 weeks and peaked at #7. It peaked at #5 on the country chart and at #8 on the R&B chart. Vincent's performance of "Be-Bop-A-Lula" on the nationally televised Perry Como show on July 28, 1956, helped propel its ascent up the charts. Although it did not top any of the *Billboard's* national charts, "Be-Bop-A-Lula" did top *Billboard's* regional charts in both Denver and Milwaukee.

The song was released in England on Capitol CL 14599 in June 1956, and it rose to #16 on the UK charts in August 1956. A lengthy article in the *New Music Express* (*NME*) on July 20, 1956, commented:

> Gene Vincent is the new arrival. Make a note of same, because you're going to hear a great deal in the next few weeks. Make a note, too, of the titles of his first record"—"Be-Bop-A-Lula" and "Woman Love"—on the Capitol label.

72 Two weeks earlier on June 2, 1956, *Billboard* unenthusiastically reviewed "Be-Bop-A-Lula" as the B-side, commenting that it was "[a]nother blues … [that is] additionally gimmicked with echo." It gave the song a relatively low numerical rating of 77, one below the 78 it gave "Women Love."

Already, Gene has run into opposition, as the BBC has put "Woman Love" on their Restricted List. In other words, they have put a broadcasting ban on the record. But this could amount to good publicity, for nothing captures the attention of the public more than the banning of a record.

This was the beginning of England's love affair with Gene. Eventually, more Vincent 45s were issued in the UK than in the U.S. Thus, *45cat.com* lists 91 Gene Vincent records released in the UK compared to only 60 in the U.S. Moreover, while Vincent had four songs that charted in the U.S. , he had eight that charted in the UK. It is difficult to overstate the tremendous impact that Gene Vincent and "Be-Bop-A-Lula" had in England. It is more than fair to say that Vincent was and continues to be more revered in the UK than in the United States.

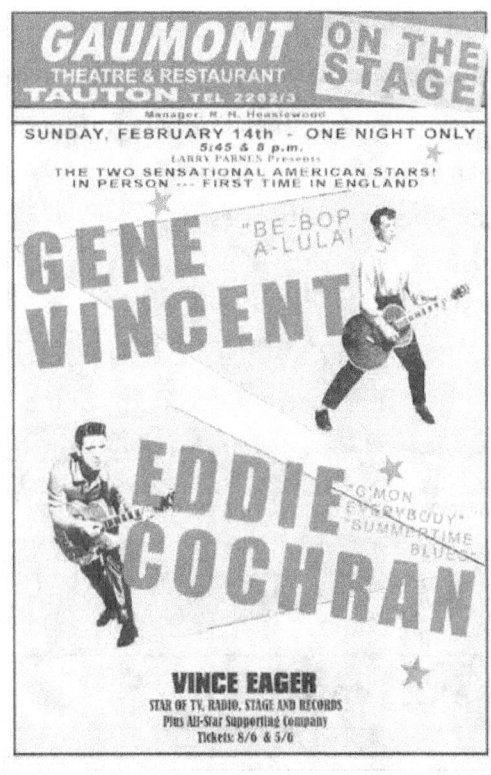

Prior to 1960 both Gene Vincent and Eddie Cochran had made numerous live performances in England and elsewhere in the UK, but it was the four-month tour throughout the UK that they headlined in 1960 that solidified their standing as Rock 'n' Roll royalty in the collective conscience of an entire generation of UK music fans.[73] After the last show in Bristol, they immediately left to go by cab to Heathrow for a flight back to the US, but the trip ended tragically when the cab crashed, killing Cochran and seriously injuring Vincent. The front page headline coverage of the accident in the British press indelibly etched their names in the memories of their UK fans.

---

73 John Collis' book, *Gene Vincent and Eddie Cochran: Rock 'n' Roll Revolutionaries,* meticulously documented the tour. The tour, which also featured English rocker Billy Fury, has been called the UK's first multi-artist tour.

Future members of The Beatles were among the attendees at one or more of those 1960 UK concerts. While The Beatles did not record a studio version of "Be-Bop-A-Lula," a live version of their rendition of the song at Hamburg, Germany's Star Club in 1962 was released as a 45 on Collectables 1510. And, interestingly, *Setlist.fm* documents a July 6, 1957, concert where the pre-Beatles Quarry Men sang "Be-Bop-A-Lula" at a Liverpool church. John Lennon also covered it as the opening song on his 1975 *Rock 'n' Roll* LP (Apple 8XK-3419). Other artists who were greatly influenced by Gene Vincent and "Be Bop A-Lula" include The Stray Cats and Johnny Hallyday, the French Rock 'n' Roll star who *Wikipedia* reports has sold 110 million records worldwide.

Among the numerous covers of "Be-Bop-A-Lula" were two that charted in subsequent years. The first was The Everly Brothers' 1960 cover on Cadence 1390 that was on *Billboard's* pop chart for five weeks, topping out at #74. Then, in 1986 Hank Chaney's cover on CHI HC-04 dented the *Billboard* country chart for one week at #98. Other notable covers were by Johnny Hallyday on Philips 40024, and Jerry Lee Lewis and Orion on Sun 1151. It also attracted numerous garage band covers that are detailed in the chart below of subsequent covers.

When John Fogerty inducted Gene Vincent posthumously into the Rock & Roll Hall of Fame in 1998 (Vincent died in 1971),[74] he sang a cappella a verse from "Be Bop A-Lula" and told the audience: "It doesn't get much better than that—I do believe this record is probably one of the greatest ever made."

CONTEMPORANEOUS COVER VERSIONS OF "BE-BOP-A-LULA"

There were no contemporaneous cover versions issued, continuing a trend wherein the major labels recognized that the record buying public, and especially teens, wanted to hear the original artist and not copycat versions of Rock 'n' Roll songs. Some budget labels, however, did issue covers.

CONTEMPORANEOUS BUDGET LABEL COVERS OF "BE-BOP-A-LULA"

ARTIST	LABEL	COMMENTS
"Scat Man" Crothers	Tops R289-49	B/w "I Want You, I Need You, I Love You"/ "Sweet Old-Fashioned Girl"/"Allegheny Moon"
Johnnie Desert	Gateway 1177	B/w "Treasure Of Love" (by Johnnie O'Neal), a cover of Clyde McPhatter

---

74 The Blue Caps, Gene Vincent's band, were subsequently inducted into the Rock & Roll Hall of Fame in 2012. The members inducted were Tommy Facenda, Cliff Gallop, Paul Peek, Jr., Jack Neal, Johnny Meeks, Dickie Harrell, Bobby Jones, and Willie Williams. As the Hall of Fame website accurately notes, "The Blue Caps and their revolving door of great guitarists were revered by the likes of John Lennon, Paul McCartney, Jeff Beck, Jimmy Page and more."

Bill Marine	Promenade 2	B/w "Treasure Of Love"/"I Almost Lost My Mind"/"Sweet Old-Fashioned Girl"
None Listed	Variety EPV-1801	B/w "Stranded In The Jungle"/"I Want You, I Need You, I Love You"/"Love, Love, Love"
None Listed	Royale 467	B/w "Born To Be With You"/"I Almost Lost My Mind"/"Sweet Old-Fashioned Girl"

Budget label cover versions on Tops and Gateway

LATER RELEASES OF "BE-BOP-A-LULA" BY GENE VINCENT

LABEL	YEAR	COMMENTS
Capitol CL 15264 (UK)	1962	A 1962 re-recording with twist lyrics like "She's a little twister," etc. ; b/w "The King Of Fools"
Capitol K 22 221 (Germany)	1962	B/w "Say Mama"
Capitol PRO-2276	1963	A 1962 re-recording with twist lyrics; b/w "The King of Fools" (Capitol PRO-2277); promo only

Capitol 6042	1963	"Star Line Series"; b/w "Lotta Lovin'"
Capitol CL 15546 (UK)	1968	B/w "Say Mama"
Dandelion S-4956 (UK)	1969	Titled "Be-Bop-A-Lula '69"; b/w "Ruby Baby"
Beeb 001 (UK)	1974	B/w "Roll Over Beethoven" and "Say Mama"; taken from a 1971 BBC Radio One session for the *Johnny Walker Show*
Capitol 3871	1974	B/w "Lotta Lovin'"
Ripete R45-126	c. 1981	B/w "Blue Suede Shoes" by Carl Perkins
EMI G45 8 (UK)	1984	B/w "Blue Jean Bop"; reissues of the original Capitol releases
Rockstar RSR-EP 2013 (UK)	1986	EP titled "On Tour with Gene Vincent & Eddie Cochran," with "Say Mama" and two Cochran songs, "C'mon Everybody" and "Twenty-Flight Rock," plus separate interviews with both artists
Nighttracks SFNT 451 (UK)	1987	B/w "Distant Drums"; labeled "For Radio Play Only"
Collectables 6029	1992	B/w "C'mon Everybody" by Eddie Cochran
Norton 45-114	2004	Recorded live on the *Alan Freed Show*, August 1956; b/w "Hound Dog"
Demon 45001/10 (UK)	2016	B/w "Blue Jean Bop"; reissues of the original Capitol recordings

1984 UK reissue of original [Image: *45cat*]

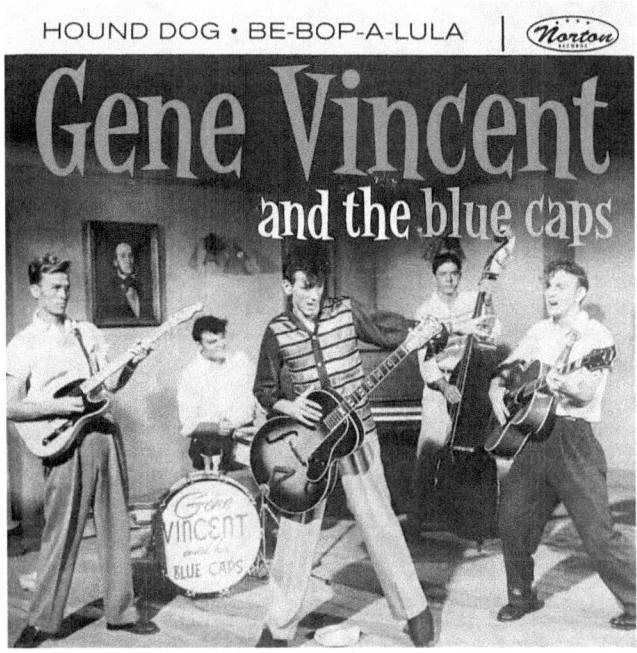

2004 Norton release of 1956 live recording from Alan Freed Show

SUBSEQUENT COVER VERSIONS OF "BE-BOP-A-LULA"

ARTIST	LABEL	YEAR	COMMENTS
The Aerovans	Winterhurst [No label number]	1965	B/w "Was It Meant To Be"; Ft. Lauderdale, FL, label
The Altar Boys	Sundance 002 (UK)	1982	B/w "Isn't It About Time"; 7" small hole 45
The Beatles	Collectables 1510	1982	B/w "Hallelujah I Love Her So"; recorded live in 1962 at the Star Club in Germany
The Beatles	Baktobak 1001, Stab 2006 (one of boxset of 15 45s (UK)	1988	Live recording from December 31, 1962, at Hamburg, Germany's Star Club; b/w "Reminiscing," a cover of Buddy Holly
Stan Lee Black	Almo International 222	1965	B/w "Raining In My Heart"

The Blue Cats	Gaity 674	1958	B/w "Oh Yeah"; Minneapolis, MN, label; group later became The Sonics
The Cannonballs	Bobby 222	1964	Great guitar break; b/w "Johnny B. Goode"; garage version; Erie, PA, band
Johnny Carroll	UK American USA 1 (UK)	1975	B/w "Black Leather Rebel"
Johnny Carroll	Roller Coaster 2002 (UK)	1979	B/w "Black Leather Rebel (Tribute to Gene Vincent)"; reissue of 1975 release on UK American Records
Hank Chaney	CMI HC-04	1986	Titled "Be-Bop-A-Lula '86"; same song on both sides; dented *Billboard's* country chart at #98
Barbara DeAnne	MBM NR8420	1977	B/w "Long Black Veil"; Colbert, WA, label; mastered at Nashville Record Productions
"Little" Jimmy Dempsey	Trend 662T-4909	1966	Guitar instrumental; b/w "Here Comes My Baby Again"; Smyrna, GA, label
David Essex	Mercury MER 72 (UK)	1981	B/w "Secret Lover"
The Everly Brothers	Cadence 1390	1960	B/w "When Will I Be Loved"; *Billboard* charted for 5 weeks, peaking at #74
The Everly Brothers	Apex 9-76685 (Canada)	1960	B/w "When Will I Be Loved"
The Everly Brothers	London HLA 9157 (UK)	1960	B/w "When Will I Be Loved"
The Everly Brothers	Barnaby 507	1974	B/w "When Will I Be Loved"

The Everly Brothers	Old Gold OG 9067 (UK)	1980	B/w "When Will I Be Loved"
Five Card Stud	Red Bird 10-082	1966	B/w "Everybody Needs Somebody"; produced by Richard Perry
Greaseball Boogie Band	GRT 1230-70 (Canada)	1973	B/w "Dr. Feelgood"
Johnny Hallyday	Phillips 40024	1962	B/w "I Got A Woman"
Jerry Lee Lewis & Orion	Sun 1151	1980	B/w "Breakup" by Charlie Rich & Orion
John Lennon	Apple 2C 004-05.899 (France)	1975	B/w "Move Over Ms. L"; produced and arranged by John Lennon
John Lennon	Apple 1C 006-05 924 (Germany)	1975	B/w "Ya Ya"; produced and arranged by John Lennon
Bobby Lowell & Jay Fremont	Roto 8506 (in dead wax)	1985	Lincoln, NE, label; b/w "Ice Cold Heart"
Marv Kary Exchange	Tri-Art 102	c. early 1980s	B/w "Love Is A Word"; Mastertonics pressing; North Dakota label
Ron McKee	American Sound 3090	c. 1977	B/w "Elvis, We Miss You Tonight"
Messendger [sic]	Jab 8888	1982	B/w "Strangers"; Tifton, GA, label
Chuck Owston	Bishop 1003	1980	B/w "Baby Let's Play House"
Pen and Ink	Charisma 400 (6000 866) (UK)	1982	B/w "Friday Night Flash Guy"
Phonics	Our Gang 1013	1983	B/w "You Ain't Got Me"

Rick and The Keens	Troy 1002	1963	B/w "You Can't Go"; Ft. Worth, TX, label
Johnny Rystl	Fox Fire 110	1979	B/w "Elvis' Greatest Show"; Nashville, TN, label
Hughie Scott & the Meteors	Tamarac TTM 607 (Canada)	1960s?	B/w "I Will"
Junior Shank and The Jesters	Madison 127	1960	B/w "Locked Out"
Hayden Thompson	Collector Item CI 001 (Sweden)	1984	EP with "Shake, Rattle and Roll" / "Good Rockin' Tonight" / "My Baby Left Me"
The Thundermen	Thundermen 612016	1980s?	Medley titled "Rock And Roll Medley" with "Claudette" / "Peppermint Twist"/ "Party Doll" / "Shake, Rattle And Roll"; b/w "Mule Skinner Blues"; Eau Claire, WI, label

Johnny Hallyday 1962 cover

The Beatles live cover recorded in 1962

"BE-BOP-A-LULA" IN THE MOVIES

"Be-Bop-A-Lula" has made frequent appearances in the movies, including the following:

MOVIE TITLE	YEAR	COMMENTS
The Girl Can't Help It	1956	Performed by Gene Vincent; starring Jayne Mansfield and Tom Ewell; in addition to Vincent, Eddie Cochran, Fats Domino, Little Richard, and the Platters, among others, performed in this picture; described by many as the best Rock 'n' Roll film ever; on September 18, 1969, amid a recording session at Abbey Road Studio, The Beatles left to go to Paul McCartney's house so they could watch the British premiere of the movie
Flaming Creatures	1963	Performed by The Everly Brothers; short 45-minute avant-garde movie directed by Jack Smith that featured, among other things, graphic sexual imagery; *IMDbPro* called it "one of the most controversial short films of all time"; *IMDbPro* also noted that "it was banned in 22 states and four countries"
The London Rock and Roll Concert (UK)	1973	Filmed on location at London's Wembley Stadium on August 5, 1972; performed by the Heartshakers; film also features Chuck Berry, Bo Diddley, Bill Haley, Jerry Lee Lewis, and Little Richard, among others
The Year of Living Dangerously	1982	Performed by Gene Vincent; romantic war drama set in Indonesia during the reign of President Sukarno starring Mel Gibson

Mischief	1985	Performed by Gene Vincent (uncredited); teenage coming-of-age movie
Sweet Dreams	1985	Performed by Gene Vincent; story of country star Patsy Cline, who is portrayed by Jessica Lange
The Delinquents	1989	Performed by Gene Vincent; parents try to break up two teenager lovers; movie debut for Kylie Minogue
Wild At Heart	1990	Performed by Gene Vincent; crime and comedy drama starring Nicolas Cage and Laura Dern
King Ralph	1991	Performed by John Goodman, albeit it is only a short snippet of the song; romantic comedy starring John Goodman and Peter O'Toole about someone who very unexpectedly becomes King of England
Pleasantville	1998	Performed by Gene Vincent; fantasy flick that is set for the most part in the 1950s
Planet 51	2009	Performed by Chris Cawte; animated comedy adventure
Nowhere Boy (UK)	2009	Performed by Gene Vincent; story of the childhood and teenage years of John Lennon (1944-1960)

DOCUMENTED CONCERT PERFORMANCES OF "BE-BOP-A-LULA"

As of May 1, 2024, *Setlist.fm* documented that "Be-Bop-A-Lula" has been performed in concert 809 times by 92 different artists. In addition to Gene Vincent (20), artists who have included it on their set lists more than five times include Johnny Hallyday (319), Cliff Richard (75), Queen (51), Van Morrison (23), Simon & Garfunkel (23), Stray Cats (22), Paul McCartney (13), The Everly Brothers (13), Little Richard (10), The Kinks (7), and Procol Harum (6).

HONORS AND ACCOLADES FOR "BE-BOP-A-LULA"

■ Inducted in 1999 into the Grammy Hall of Fame
■ Chosen by the Rock & Roll Hall of Fame as one of the "500 Songs That Shaped Rock and Roll"
■ Ranked #103 on the Rolling Stone's 2004 list of the "500 Greatest Songs of All-Time"
■ Ranked #626 in Dave Marsh's 1989 book, *The Heart of Rock & Soul: The 1001 Greatest Singles Ever Made*

ALSO WORTH NOTING . . .

- Paul McCartney has said that "Be-Bop-A-Lula" was the first record he purchased. He performed an acoustic version of the song on his 1991 live album *Unplugged (The Official Bootleg)*.
- It has been reported that Gene Vincent's recording of "Be-Bop-A-Lula" was on the jukebox owned by John Lennon.
- When Dickie Harrell, the original Blues Caps drummer, died in 2022, Brian Setzer, the lead singer for the Stray Cats, said that "Be-Bop-A-Lula" was "the best rock-n-roll song of all time."
- *Be Bop A Lula!* is the name of a *show* that first opened in Liverpool, England in 2014 and is still being scheduled at various UK venues following a COVID-19 interruption. In addition to Gene Vincent, the show is a tribute to Buddy Holly, Roy Orbison, Eddie Cochran, and Billy Fury.
- "Be-Bop-A-Lula" has been quoted in other songs, including the Dire Straits 1985 song "Walk of Life" (WB 7-28878), with the line, "Here comes Johnny singing oldies goldies, Be-Bop-a-Lula baby What'd I Say."
- The Blue Caps, Vincent's band, were named after the kind of hat that President Eisenhower wore when playing golf.

ADDITIONAL SOURCES

Collis, John, *Gene Vincent and Eddie Cochran: Rock 'N' Roll Revolutionaries* (Virgin Books (UK), 2004)

Farren, Mick, *There's One In Every Town* (Do-Not Press, 2004)

Hagarty, Britt, *The Day the World Turned Blue* (Blandfort Press (UK), 1984)

SPECIAL NOTE

The story behind the composition of "Be-Bop-A-Lula" varies depending on who is telling the story. Mick Farren, in his 2004 book about Gene Vincent entitled *Every Town Has One*, quotes Vincent:

> I come in dead drunk and stumble over the bed. And me and Don Graves were looking at this bloody book; it was called *Little Lulu*. And I said, "Hell, man, it's 'Be-Bop-A-Lula.' And he said, 'Yeah, man, swinging.' And we wrote this song."

This is partially corroborated by a person only identified by the initials "M.G" who told interviewers from the Rockabilly Hall of Fame:

> I can shed a bit of light on the origins of the song "Be Bop A Lula." In 1954, while serving in the US Navy, [following a motorcycle accident], I was sent to the US Naval Hospital in Portsmouth, Virginia, about February 1955. While there, I was in a ward with Don Graves, and we subsequently met Gene…. Once in braces, casts, etc., the three of us were basically ambulatory, and free to wander out of the ward. It was during one of these periods that Gene and Don worked out the song. Don was responsible for the lyrics, Gene the melody….
>
> [Vincent sang the song at a naval base concert and its attendant publicity] brought Gene to the attention of Sheriff Tex [Davis], who completely overwhelmed both boys. They had already scored a version of "Race With the Devil," and it looked like a partnership had been formed. Sheriff Tex quickly broke this up and got both to sign contracts. Don received a few dollars in "royalties" for his work to that date, but never received any more funds. On the original record release, Sheriff Tex was credited as the lyricist.

On the other hand, according to the write up of "Be-Bop-A-Lula" in *Wikipedia*, "Davis claimed that he wrote the song with Gene Vincent after listening to the song 'Don't Bring Lulu'."

The Library of Congress copyright registration for "Be-Bop-A-Lula" that was filed July 2, 1956, shows the following:

DAVIS, SHERIFF.
　Be-bop-a-lula; words and music by Gene
　　Vincent, pseud., and Sheriff Tex Davis.
　　3 p.　50¢　© Lowery Music Co., New
　　York; 2Jul56; EP100645.

Vincent's name was listed as a pseudonym because his real name is Vincent Eugene Craddock.

CHAPTER 13

"WHOLE LOTTA SHAKIN' GOIN' ON"

JERRY LEE LEWIS (APRIL 1957)

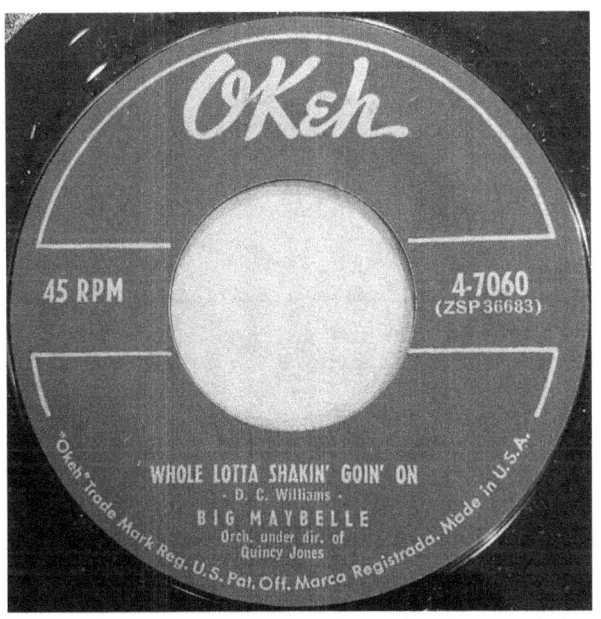

Big Maybelle original Okeh release

Jerry Lee Lewis original Sun 78 release

Jerry Lee Lewis original UK London release

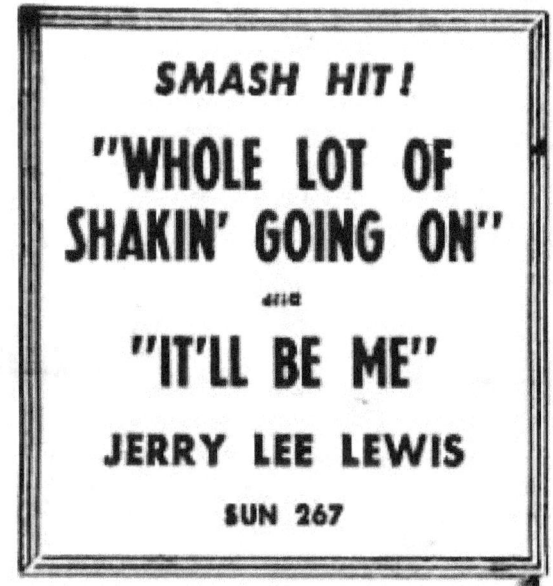

Billboard ad, October 7, 1957

"WHOLE LOTTA SHAKIN' GOIN' ON" — THE BASIC FACTS

Label: Sun 267 (both 45 and 78)

Writers: Roy Hall (using the pseudonym Sunny David) and Dave "Curly" Williams

Date recorded: February 1957

Date released: April 15, 1957

B-side: "It'll Be Me"

Producer: Sam Phillips

Billboard charts:

Pop Chart
- Debut: 6/24/57
- Peak: #3
- Duration: 29 weeks

R&B Chart
- Debut: 8/19/57
- Peak: #1 (2 weeks)
- Duration: 10 weeks

Country Chart
- Debut: 6/17/57
- Peak: #1 (2 weeks)
- Duration: 23 weeks

THE SONG AND ITS IMPACT

"Whole Lotta Shakin' Goin' On" was penned by Roy Hall and Dave "Curly" Williams in 1954. According to accounts by both Hall and Williams, it was composed while they were in a drunken state at a fishing camp on Lake Okeechobee in Florida. It was produced by Qunicy Jones and recorded by Big Maybelle on March 21, 1955. It was released in September 1955, on Okeh 4-7060. Surprisingly, a search of both *Billboard* and *Cash Box* for 1955 failed to turn up a single review of Big Maybelle's original version. Indeed, on October 8, 1955, *Billboard* listed it along with three other very collectable R&B records that were received by *Billboard* that week, but which were not deemed good enough to merit a review:

Rhythm & Blues

Annie Met Henry; Keep a Rockin'—The Champions, Chart 602

I Wish I Was a Catfish; I Believe My Time Ain't Long—Elmore James, Ace 508

One Monkey Don't Stop No Show; Whole Lotta Shakin' Goin' On—Big Maybelle, Okeh 7060

The Rocket; Night Life — Jesse Stone, Atco 6051

Subsequently, Hall recorded his version on September 15, 1955, and it was released later in September or in early October 1955, on Decca 9-29697 (and oddly, only credited to Dave Williams). This release by the song's co-composer did attract the following *Cash Box* review:

ROY HALL
(Decca 29697; 9-29697)

B+ "ALL BY MYSELF" [Commodore BMI—Domino, Bartholomew] Pianist Roy Hall displays a grand vocal talent as he belts out a captivating, rhythm and blues smash. Could head way up the country sales ladder.

B+ "WHOLE LOTTA SHAKIN' GOIN' ON" (2:55) [Marlyn BMI —D. Williams] Here's another solid, quick beat rhythmic piece that Hall waxes in contagious, ear-catching fashion.

Cash Box, **10/22/55**

Hall's release on Decca 9-29679

Billboard also reviewed Hall's version on October 8, 1955, noting that "Webb Pierce's pianist takes a stab in the vocal field and shows a highly distinctive, flavorsome voice, showcased in two rock 'n' roll type entries." Somewhat surprisingly, as Nick Tosches observed, "Though Hall was a powerful pianist, there was no piano on his recording of 'Whole Lotta Shakin' Goin' On,' and most of the record's hard-edged drive came from the burly licks of Sugarfoot Garland's electric guitar."

Hall's version led to two further covers. The first was by another Decca artist, Dolores Fredericks, on Decca 9-29716, which was common to the practice of major labels at that time of issuing multiple versions of the same song by different artists. Whereas Hall's was intended for the country & western market, Fredericks' version was intended for the pop market. The second cover version was by the Commodores in December 1955, on Dot 15429, backed with "Speedo" [*sic*], a cover of the Cadillac's original version. Neither of the covers by Hall nor Fredericks was released in the UK, but the Commodores' cover was released in March of the following year on London 45-HL-D 8251.[75]

How and when Jerry Lee Lewis first heard "Whole Lotta Shakin' Goin' On" varies considerably depending on the person or writer telling the story. The following versions are listed in the order of publication:

---

75 The May 2010 issue of the UK magazine, *Record Collector*, listed this London release as one of the 50 most collectable UK 45s and valued it at £1,000.

- The 1984 book *Great Balls of Fire* written by Myra Lewis, who Jerry married when she was just 13, states that Jerry Lee Lewis sang the song from lyrics he remembered while working for Roy Hall.
- The 1984 Nick Touches' book, *Hellfire*, relates that Johnny Littlejohn, a Natchez, Mississippi, DJ who owned a club where Lewis worked, regularly received copies of new records and that in October 1955, "Jerry Lee took a special liking to "'Whole Lotta Shakin' Goin' On,'" a Decca record by Roy Hall, the fellow who had hired Jerry Lee to work in his after-hours joint in Nashville several months before." Touches quotes Littlejohn as saying, "Jerry Lee liked the hell outa that damn record… and he sang the fire outa that sucker," with Littlejohn feeding him the lyrics.
- The 1992 account by famed Sun Records researcher Colin Escott (with Martin Hawkins) states that Lewis worked in a Nashville bar in 1955, owned by Roy Hall, a co-author of "Whole Lotta Shakin' Goin' On" and that "Roy Hall had probably taught him the song."
- The 2014 Rick Bragg book, *Jerry Lee Lewis: His Own Story* (2014), quotes Lewis as saying that he learned "Whole Lotta Shakin' Goin' On" from hearing Johnny Littlejohn singing the song and "took the song home with me," and that the next night he insisted on singing the song himself. As Lewis told Bragg, "I done it like Johnny done it."
- The 2015 Peter Guralnick book about Sam Phillips' life, *Sam Phillips—The Man Who Invented Rock 'n' Roll*, states that Jerry Lee Lewis heard the song sung by Johnny Littlejohn, a Natchez, Mississippi, disc jockey, at a club across the river from Ferriday, Louisiana, his hometown, and where he regularly performed. As Guralnick quotes Lewis, "I [started doing] it pretty close to exactly the way he done it," including "stand in one spot, wiggle it around a little bit." Lewis said, "I picked it up from—I didn't *steal* it. I just kind of took it."

In trying to reconcile these different accounts, perhaps the best assessment would be that Jerry Lee Lewis knew Roy Hall from when he worked for him at his nightclub in Nashville for a month or two in 1954 and he became aware of Roy Hall's version when he worked at Johnny Littlejohn's Wagon Wheel club in Natchez, Mississippi, in late 1955.

Whatever the inspiration may have been, Jerry Lee Lewis incorporated the song into his repertoire not later than the beginning of 1956. For example, Tosches related in his book, *Hellfire*, that Lewis sang the song at a club in Blytheville, Arkansas, in February 1956, wowing the females in the audience with multiple encores of the song, and that he sang it again at his debut on *The Big D Jamboree* in Dallas the very next night.

Lewis recorded "Whole Lotta Shakin' Goin' On" in February 1957, but what happened at that session is subject to debate. Tosches states that the first order of business was for Lewis to record a song that Jack Clement had penned, "It'll Be Me." Once that was done, Clement told Tosches that the band's drummer, James Van Eaton, suggested, "Hey, Jerry, why don't you do that thing you did the other night?" Clement further recalled:

I just turned on the machine, mixed it on the fly. We didn't even play it back at that point. We played it back later. Once we got to playin' it back, we played it again and again. Loved it.

This account essentially jibes with what Lewis told author Rick Bragg.

On the other hand, according to Guralnick's account, Lewis took "Whole Lotta Shakin' Goin' On" to Sam Phillips, who immediately realized it was "hit" material and that either that day or the next, it only took four or five takes to get it down. Needing a B-side, Jack Clement penned "It'll Be Me," the idea for which came to him while sitting on a toilet, which Clement explained:

I used to wonder about the forms of reincarnation and the song just came to me. "If you see a lump in a bowl, baby it'd be me and I'll be looking at you." We changed it to "sugar bowl" and the song came from there.

Clement further commented: "When we were short of hits Bill Justis [of 'Raunchy' fame] used to tell me, 'Why don't you go and take another of those $10,000 shits?'"

Regardless of whether "Whole Lotta Shakin' Goin' On" was recorded before or after "It'll Be Me,"[76] the result was a stunning success. As Guralnick noted, "…the final take exudes a sense of pure command and rumbling authority that as brilliant as all of his previous studio extemporizations may have been, had never been altogether realized before." In a similar vein, Colin Escott and Martin Hawkins in their book, *Sun Records: The Brief History of the Legendary Record Label*, assessed the record this way: "*Shakin'* is a masterpiece of power and energy remarkable for the way Lewis controls the ebb and flow of sound, lulling the beat before storming back in the final chorus."

Billboard reviewed the record on May 27, 1957, commenting that "Lewis comes thru with what should be a sure hit, in a driving blues shouter in the typical Sun tradition." Perhaps not surprisingly, it topped *Billboard's* Memphis regional chart on June 3, 1957. That same week, *Billboard* listed "Whole Lotta of Shakin' Goin' On" as a C&W "Best Buy," noting that "this platter by Lewis is taking off like wildfire," with the further astute observation: "It should also do well in pop and R.&B. markets." This coincided with *Cash Box's* assessment on June 8, 1957:

---

76 Interestingly, Cliff Richard, England's answer to Elvis Presley, recorded a particularly good rocking version of "It'll Be Me" that was released in the UK in 1962 on Columbia DB 4886; it spent 12 weeks on the UK charts, peaking at #2. For some unknown reason, it was not released in the U.S.

> **"WHOLE LOT OF SHAKIN' GOING ON"** [Marlyn BMI—Williams, David]
> **"IT'LL BE ME"** [Knox BMI—Clement]
> **JERRY LEE LEWIS** (Sun 267)
>
> ● Jerry Lee Lewis, who indicated that he's of star calibre with his rockin' record of "Crazy Arms," has in his latest release the material that will skyrocket him into the spotlight in the pop, country and rhythm & blues fields. The lad is a sensational performer out of the rock-a-billy school. He hands in an ultra commercial job as he belts out a house-rockin' side tagged "Whole Lot Of Shakin' Going On." Side has a great beat. It should be on the charts in all fields. Flip is another exciting side presented against a skiffle beat. Lewis has a great style the kids'll love.

It debuted on *Billboard's* country, pop, and R&B charts on June 17, 1957, June 24, 1957, and August 19, 1957, respectively. After rising to #34 on *Billboard's* "Top 100" songs on July 15, 1957, it stalled and fell to #39 the following week, and it totally dropped off *Billboard's* country chart. This was probably due to some radio stations banning the record due to its perceived risqué lyrics. To try to remedy this situation, Sam Phillips enlisted the promotional talents of one of his older brothers, Jud.

After seeing Lewis perform in person, Jud was convinced that he could be a hit on national TV. Despite Sam's initial objections, Jud eventually carried the day. He got Jerry Lee Lewis on *The Steve Allen Show* on July 28, 1957, which was announced by Sun Records in a large *Billboard* ad on July 15, 1957. Following the show, Sam confessed that Jud was right and reported that the orders were coming in by the boatload for "Whole Lotta Shakin' Goin' On."

Altogether, Jud arranged for Lewis to appear on four nationally televised shows between late July and August 1957:

- *The Steve Allen Show*, July 28, 1957
- Allen Freed's *Big Beat* show, August 2, 1957
- *The Steve Allen Show*, August 11, 1957
- *American Bandstand*, August 19, 1957

On each appearance Jerry Lee sang "Whole Lotta Shakin' Goin' On" to wildly enthusiastic audiences. These appearances, just as Jud Phillips had predicted, helped push the sales of "Whole Lotta Shakin' Goin' On" through the roof. By September 9, 1957, it was #1 on both the *Billboard* country and R&B charts, and #4 on *Billboard's* pop chart. It would eventually rise to #3 on the pop chart. While it was on *Billboard's* country and R&B charts for 23 weeks and 10 weeks, respectively, it remained on the pop chart for 29 weeks. Nothing today comes remotely close to the impact that national TV appearances had on record sales in the 1950s.

In the acknowledgement section of the book *Jerry Lee Lewis: His Own Story*, Lewis personally gave a shout out to "Steve Allen, the man who put me on television and made 'Whole Lotta Shakin' Goin' On' an overnight hit and made me a nationwide star." Interestingly, Allen, who just a year earlier had required Elvis to appear in tails and be televised from the waist up singing to a basset hound, allowed Lewis to sing "Whole Lotta Shakin' Goin' On" without any effort to tame his exuberant performance. In fact, in his second appearance on August 11, 1957, Allen even got into the act by tossing Lewis's chair back to him after he had kicked it to the back of the stage.

In the UK, "Whole Lotta Shakin' Goin' On" was released on London 45-H-LS 8457 in August 1957. It made the UK charts for 11 weeks, rising to #8. Shortly thereafter, a contemporaneous cover version was released in the UK by the Deep River Boys on HMV POP 395, backed with "There's a Gold Mine in the Sky," a cover of Pat Boone.

Over the years, "Whole Lotta Shakin' Goin' On" has attracted numerous subsequent covers on 45s by a wide variety of artists, including Chubby Checker, Mickey Gilley, Little Richard, Ricky Nelson, and Conway Twitty. Both the versions by Chubby Checker and Conway Twitty made the *Billboard* pop chart, peaking at #42 and #55, respectively. Paul McCartney and John Fogerty have frequently included "Whole Lotta Shakin' Goin' On" on their concert set lists.

"Whole Lotta Shakin' Goin' On" has picked up more than a few prestigious honors, including being inducted into the Grammy Hall of Fame and added to the National Recording Registry of the Library of Congress by National Preservation Board, which annually selects songs for permanent preservation that are "culturally, historically, or aesthetically significant."

"Whole Lotta Shakin' Goin' On" is one of the featured songs in the long-running Broadway musical *Million Dollar Quartet*, loosely based on the December 4, 1956, happenstance meeting of Lewis, Elvis, Carl Perkins, and Johnny Cash at Sun Records. Sam Phillips, ever alert to publicity, called the local newspaper, which ran a story the next day entitled "The Million Dollar Quartet." Lewis was portrayed by Levi Kreis in the musical, for which he won a Tony for "Best Featured Actor in a Musical."

As music writer Robert Gordon observed, "Jerry Lee began to show that in this new emerging genre called rock 'n' roll, not everybody was going to stand there with a guitar." And, in assessing "Whole Lotta Shakin' Goin' On," writer/critic, Paul Williams, asserted:

[It] is a testament to the power of charm, its ability to break down defenses and smuggle wild (sexual, musical, Dionysian) craziness into the homes and hearts of normal law-abiding citizens. "We ain't fakin'." You hear him say it, but you don't believe it—until it's much too late.

CONTEMPORANEOUS COVER VERSIONS OF
"WHOLE LOTTA SHAKIN' GOIN' ON"

Other than Big Maybelle's original version and the three covers discussed above that were released in 1955, none of which were listed by *Billboard* as records available, there were no contemporaneous cover versions of "Whole Lotta Shakin' Goin' On" released in 1957.

CONTEMPORANEOUS BUDGET LABEL COVERS OF
"WHOLE LOTTA SHAKIN' GOIN' ON"

ARTIST	LABEL	COMMENTS
Dave Burgess	Tops 45R-409-49	EP with "Send For Me" / "Rainbow" / "Tammy"
Allan Freed	Promenade RR 13	B/w "Diana" / "Jailhouse Rock"
Allan Freed	Promenade RR 19	B/w "Raunchy" / "Jailhouse Rock"
Allan Freed	Promenade RR 24	EP with "Why Don't They Understand" / "Only Because" / "Don't" / "Kisses Sweeter Than Wine" / "Great Balls Of Fire"
Steven Mark [*sic*]	Gilmar G-212	EP "Honeycomb" / "Fascination" / "Chances Are" / "Mr. Lee" / "That'll Be The Day"
Steven Marks	Value 146	EP with "Mr. Lee" / "Chances Are" / "Fascination"
Ray Wyatt	Top Tune Hits	EP with "Tammy" / "Fascination" / "That'll Be The Day" / "Diana" / "Honeycomb" / "Chances Are" / "That Reminds Me Of You"

Ray Wyatt	Country & Western CW-4	EP with "Four Walls" / "Too Much Water" / "My Special Angel" / "Teddy Bear" / "A Fallen Star"
None listed	Dixie DEP-308	EP with "The Twist" / "Guitar Twist" / "Twistin' In The USA" / "Searchin'" / "Jam Up Twist"
None listed	Popular PO-23-V6039	EP with "That'll Be The Day" / "Remember You're Mine" / "Rainbow" / "Diana" / "That Reminds Me Of You"
None listed	Variety EPV-6058	EP with "That'll Be The Day" / "Remember You're Mine" / "Rainbow" / "Diana" / "That Reminds Me Of You"

Budget label cover by Steve Marks on Value 45-146

LATER RELEASES OF "WHOLE LOTTA SHAKIN' GOIN' ON" BY JERRY LEE LEWIS

LABEL	YEAR	COMMENTS
London RES 1140 (UK)	1958	EP with "It'll Be Me"/"Great Balls Of Fire"/"You Win Again"
Smash SEP-2	1964	EP with "Great Balls Of Fire"/"Breathless"/"High School Confidential"; remakes, not the Sun originals
Smash S-1412	1965	B/w "Breathless"; both sides recorded and produced by Shelby Singleton, Jr.; not the original Sun versions; "All Time Smash Hits"
Mercury MF 1024 (UK)	1968	B/w "Great Balls Of Fire"; re-recordings
Mercury MF 1110 (UK)	1969	B/w "Great Balls Of Fire"; re-recordings
Sun 6094 007 (UK)	1971	Three song "Maxi Single" with "Great Balls Of Fire" and "High School Confidential"
Mercury 73374	1973	Medley with "Tutti Frutti"/"Good Golly Miss Golly"/"Jenny Jenny"/"Long Tall Sally"; b/w "Drinking Wine Spo-Dee-O'dee"; re-recordings
Mercury 6052 260 (UK)	1973	Same as immediately above
Goldies 45 D-2536	1973	B/w "Keep A Knockin'" by Little Richard; distributed by ABC/Dunhill Records
Charly CYS 1042 (UK)	1978	B/w "The Golden Rocket" by Warren Smith
Old Gold OG 9110 (UK)	1981	B/w "Great Balls Of Fire"
Columbia AE7 1505	1982	B/w "I Get Rhythm" by Johnny Cash; "Matchbox" by Carl Perkins," and "I Saw The Light," by Cash, Lewis and Perkins; recorded live in Stuttgart, Germany; 7-inch small hole 33 1/3

Scoop 33 7SR 5014 (UK)	1983	EP with "Great Balls Of Fire"/"What'd I Say"/"Breathless"/ Good Golly Miss Molly"/"High School Confidential"
Collectables 3091	1984	B/w "Break-Up"; "Back to Back Hit Series"
Original Sound OBG 4539	1985	B/w "High School Confidential"; "Oldies But Goodies" singles series
Sun #18	???	B/w "It'll Be Me"; "Golden Treasure Series"
Ripete R45-125	c. 1989	B/w "Great Balls Of Fire"
Demon 4500/5 (UK))	2016	B/w "Great Balls Of Fire"

1985 release on Original Sound

2016 Release on Demon (EU)

SUBSEQUENT COVER VERSIONS OF "WHOLE LOTTA SHAKIN' GOIN' ON"

ARTIST	LABEL	YEAR	COMMENTS
Tommy Adderley	Viking 156 (New Zealand)	1964	B/w "I Just Don't Understand"; with Max Merritt & His Meteors
Tommy Adderley	Mar-Mar 314; Chess matrix nos. 13385 & 13386	1964	Reissue of Viking release; b/w "I Just Don't Understand"; group is from New Zealand; Mar-Mar was a short-lived Chess subsidiary
Tommy Adderley	Chess M-314 (Canada); Chess matrix nos. 13385 & 13386	1964	With Max Merritt & His Meteors; b/w "I Just Don't Understand," which made several Canadian radio charts
Jim Breedlove (AKA Jimmy Breedlove)	Camden CAE 447	1958	EP with "Rock 'n' Roll Music" / "The Lonesome Road" / "Swanee River Rock"
Jimmy Breedlove	Bear Family BLE 007 (Germany)	2014	B/w "Killer Diller" by The Cues, whose lead singer was Jimmy Breedlove; his version of "Whole Lotta Shakin' Goin' On" is based on Big Maybelle's version
The Centurys	Mark C 101	1963	B/w "Gandy Dancer," an instrumental; Alamo, TX, label
Chubby Checker	Parkway 813	1960	B/w "The Hucklebuck"
Chubby Checker	Columbia 45-DB 4541 (UK)	1960	B/w "The Hucklebuck"
Cozy Cole	Columbia 4-43657	1966	Instrumental version by the artist whose big hit was "Topsy I" and "Topsy 2" from 1958; b/w "Watch It," likewise an instrumental

Dale Cook	Rocket 69811	1969???	B/w "Guitar Boogie"; Philadelphia, PA, label
Rick Covey	Hicklin D-12943	1960s???	Great crude R&B version; b/w "The Key's In The Mailbox" by Walt Covey; both sides backed by The Missouri City Troubadours
Cuddles	Pye 7N.45149 (UK)	1972	B/w "Good Golly Miss Molly"
The Deep River Boys	HMV 45-POP 395	1957	B/w "There's A Gold Mine In The Sky"
Johnny Devlin	Festival FK-644 (Australia)	1964	B/w "Blue Suede Shoes"
Sonny Flaharty	Alco 1003	1964	B/w "Please Be Real," a Beatles-like song; "and His Young Americans"; Ohio label
Mickey Gilley	Eric 7021	1962	Same basic lyrics but titled "Whole Lotta Twisting Going On"; b/w "Fraulein"; Conroe, TX, label
Barry Goldberg Blues Band	Epic 5-10033	1966	B/w "Ginger Man"; produced by Billy Sherrill
Tammy Graham	Soundwaves 4680	1982	B/w "Being Loved By You"
Wanda Jackson	Capitol K 22 880 (Germany)	1965	B/w "Yakety-Yak," a cover of the Coasters
Terry Lee and Poor Boys	Norton EP-064	1997	EP with "Hound Dog"/"My Little "Sue"/"Driftin'"
Little Richard	London HL 7085 (UK)	1959	B/w "All Around The World"

Little Richard	Specialty 680	1959	Same song, but titled "Whole Lotta Shakin'"; fast version with good guitar break; b/w "Maybe I'm Right"
Little Richard	Vee Jay 612	1964	Re-recorded; "Bubbled Under" at #126; b/w "Goodnight Irene"
Little Richard	Stateside SS 340 (UK)	1964	B/w "Goodnight Irene"; "A 'Vee Jay' Recording"
Little Richard	Oldies 45 OL-185	c. 1964	B/w "Keep A Knockin'"; reissues of Vee Jay remakes
Little Richard	President PT 201 (UK)	1968	B/w "Lawdy Miss Claudie"
Little Richard	Okeh 4-7325	1969	Re-recorded; b/w "Lucille"; produced by Larry Williams
Little Richard	Goldies 45 D-2536	1973	Reissue of Vee Jay remake; b/w "Keep A Knockin'"
Art Loranc or Rick Presley	Smash ARL-1001	???	B/w "Love Me Tender"; Presley impersonator; Corpus Christi, TX, label
Norma Lyn	Prime NL-657	1960s?	B/w "Band-Aid On My Heart"; rockin' female garage version; has been comped on collector CD's
McCarver Sisters	McCarver B-200	1974	B/w "Nashville Open Your Gates"; Memphis, TN, label with address and phone number; Plastic Products pressing
Doyle Nelson Trio	Coro 201	???	Same song, titled "Whole Lotta Shakin'"; b/w "Blueberry Hill," a cover of Fats Domino

Ricky Nelson	Imperial EP-154	1957	EP with "Baby I'm Sorry"/"Teenage Doll"/"If You Can't Rock Me"
Brenda Patterson	Epic 5-10843	1972	B/w "Jesus On The Mainline"
Carl Perkins	Columbia B-12341	1958	EP with "That's All Right"/"Tutti Frutti"/"I Gotta Woman"
Duffy Power	Fontana H 279 (UK)	1960	B/w "If I Can Dream"
Don Rader	Rock-A-Billy R-502	1994	B/w "Goodbye, I Hate To See You Go"; Edgewater, CO, label
The Reflections	Sonic 207	c. 1960s	B/w "Johnny Be Good" [sic]; vocals by Ken Driessen; Wisconsin label
Rivieras	Riviera 1405	1964	B/w "Rip It Up," a Little Richard cover; Michigan group whose big hit was "California Sun"
Royale Monarchs	Dell D-101	1962	"Featuring Roger Stafford"; b/w "Sombrero Stomp," an instrumental
Mike St. Shaw & Thee Neon	Atco 6648	1969	Medley with "Great Balls Of Fire"; b/w "Joint Meeting"
Jack Scott	Underground C-388	1979	B/w "Bella"
Sherree Scott	Robbins 101	1963	B/w "Unhappy Birthday"
Guy Shelborne	Jem 98J-513	1971	B/w "Eight Hours, Five Days A Week"; Nashville, TN, label
Tony Sheridan	Metronome M 25.551 (Germany)	1974	B/w "Skinnie Minnie Reprise," a Bill Haley cover; Sheridan recorded several records with The Beat Brothers, who later became The Beatles

Ray Smith	Wix 1002	1978	B/w "Me And Bobby McGee"; Smith is a former Sun label artist; Joliet, IL, label
Prentice Thomas & The Broken Hearts	Jin 253	1972	Rocking country version; b/w "I've Been Living A Bad Life"
Timmy Thomas	Goldwax 327	1967	Soul version; b/w "It's My Life," a scarce northern soul song; Memphis, TN, label
Terry Thompson	Ven-Jence No. 7	1960s	B/w "Shadow In The Window"; Carlisle, IA, label
Bobby Lee Trammell & The Jordanaires	Souncot 1113	1971	B/w "You're The Mostest Girl," a great RAB song that Trammell recorded for several different labels
The Tremolons	Wildwood 005	1965	B/w "Heartbreak Hotel"; Michigan all girl garage band; Benton Harbor, MI, label
The Tremolons	Sundazed SEP 121	1996	EP with "Heartbreak Hotel"/"Theme For A 'D.J.'"/"Please Let Me Know"; reissue of their Wildwood sides
Conway Twitty	MGM K12962	1960	B/w "The Flame"
Conway Twitty	MGM 1108 (UK)	1960	B/w "The Flame"
Vinegar Joe	Atco 6922	1973	B/w "Rock 'N Roll Gypsies"

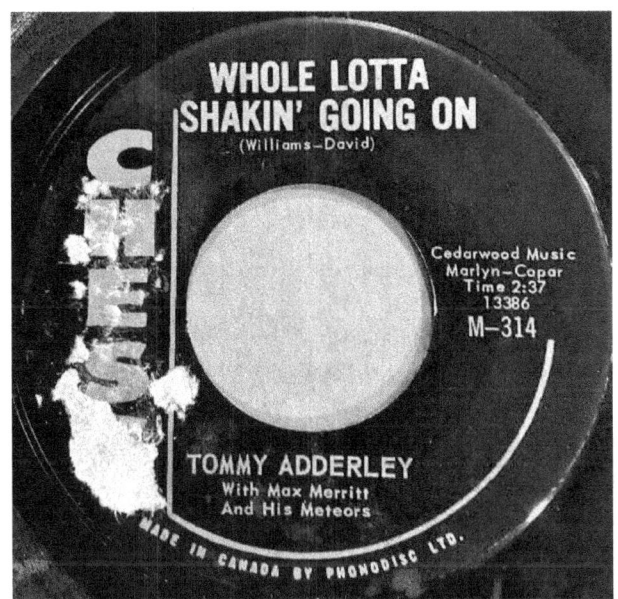

Tommy Adderley on Chess M-314
(Canadian release)

Royale Monarchs on Dell D-101

"WHOLE LOTTA SHAKIN' GOIN' ON" IN THE MOVIES

Most famously, "Whole Lotta Shakin' Goin' On" was front and center in the biopic "Great Balls of Fire" starring Dennis Quaid. The following are among the other flicks in which it can be heard:

MOVIE TITLE	YEAR	COMMENTS
Whole Lotta Shakin'	1964	A UK release featuring Jerry Lee Lewis, Eric Burdon, and Gene Vincent per *IMDbPro*, but *IMDbPro* provides scant details; it seems obvious that the film was a flop
The London Rock and Roll Concert (UK)	1973	Filmed on location at London's Wembley Stadium on August 5, 1972; performed by Jerry Lee Lewis; film also features Chuck Berry, Bo Diddley, Bill Haley, and Little Richard, among others
Grease	1978	Performed by Jerry Lee Lewis
The Buddy Holly Story	1978	Performed by Gary Busey and Jerry Zaremba; Busey portrayed Buddy Holly in the movie, for which he was nominated for an Oscar as best actor
Diner	1982	Performed by Jerry Lee Lewis; college-age friends struggle with moving on with their lives; set in Baltimore, MD
The Year of Living Dangerously	1982	Performed by Jerry Lee Lewis; Mel Gibson stars
Superman IV: The Quest for Peace	1987	Performed by Jerry Lee Lewis
Great Balls of Fire!	1989	Performed by Jerry Lee Lewis; Dennis Quaid portrayed Jerry Lee Lewis in this movie about the ups and downs of his career
Heavy Petting	1989	Performed by Ricky Nelson; documentary in which celebrities discuss their first sex experiences, some via archival footage
Jerry Lee Lewis: The Story of Rock 'n Roll	1991	Performed by Jerry Lee Lewis and taken from his performance on the *Steve Allen Show*; biopic about the Killer's career

| *Mr. Dynamite: The Rise of James Brown* | 2014 | Performed by Little Richard; HBO movie about James Brown's career |
| *Jerry Lee Lewis: Trouble in Mind* | 2022 | Performed by Jerry Lee Lewis; 73-minute Joel Coan produced documentary |

DOCUMENTED CONCERT PERFORMANCES OF "WHOLE LOTTA SHAKIN' GOIN' ON"

As of May 1, 2024, *Setlist.fm* documented that "Whole Lotta Shakin' Goin' On" has been performed in concert 1,609 times by 173 different artists. In addition to Jerry Lee Lewis (333), artists who have included "Whole Lotta Shakin' Goin' On" on their set lists on more than twenty occasions include Johnny Hallyday (492), Elvis Presley (124), Cliff Richards (67), Elton John (42), John Fogerty (34), and Paul McCartney (25). Other artists who have played it more than five times range from Prince (10) to Van Morrison (6).

HONORS AND ACCOLADES FOR "WHOLE LOTTA SHAKIN' GOIN' ON"

- Inducted into the Grammy Hall of Fame in 1999
- Added in 2005 to National Recording Registry of the Library of Congress by the National Recording Preservation Board, which annually selects songs for permanent preservation that are "culturally, historically, or aesthetically significant""
- Chosen by the Rock & Roll Hall of Fame as one of the "500 Songs That Shaped Rock and Roll"
- Ranked #61 on the *Rolling Stone*'s 2004 list of "The 500 Greatest Songs of All Time"
- Ranked #90 on the VH1 2004 list of the "100 Greatest Rock Songs"
- Ranked #14 on Dave Marsh's 1989 book, *The Heart of Rock & Soul: The 1001 Greatest Singles Ever Made*

ALSO WORTH NOTING . . .

- Jerry Lee along with Bruce Springsteen & The E Street Band sang it at the Concert for the Rock & Roll Hall of Fame in 1996.
- "Whole Lotta Shakin' Goin' On" was the first song performed on the inaugural national edition of *American Bandstand*. During the show's 37 years, Jerry Lee Lewis and B.B. King were the only performers who did not lip-synch their songs.
- Stephen King used some of the lyrics in his book *The Dead Zone*.
- The Miracles released a song titled "Whole Lotta Shakin' In My Heart (Since I Met You)" on Tamla 54134, which was titled "Whole Lotta Shakin' Goin' On" when it was reissued on Collectables COL-747, but it is not the same song.

ADDITIONAL SOURCES

Bragg, Rick, *Jerry Lee Lewis: His Own Story* (Harper/Collins, 2014)

Cain, Robert, *Whole Lotta Shakin' Goin' On* (Dial Press, 1981)

Escott, Colin and Martin Hawkins, *Sun Records: The Brief History of the Legendary Record Label* (Quick Fox, 1980)

Escott, Colin, with Martin Hawkins, *Good Rockin' Tonight: Sun Records and the Birth of Rock 'N' Roll* (St. Martin's Press, 1991)

Guralnick, Peter, *Sam Phillips: The Man Who Invented Rock 'n' Roll* (Little, Brown, 2015)

Guralnick, Peter, and Colin Escott, *The Birth of Rock 'n' Roll: The Illustrated Story of Sun Records* (Weldon Owen, 2022)

Lewis, Myra, with Murray Silver, *Great Balls of Fire: The Uncensored Story of Jerry Lee Lewis* (Quill, 1982).

Miller, Billy, and Michael Hurtt, *Mind Over Matter: The Myths and Mysteries of Detroit's Fortune Records* (Kick Books, 2020)

Palmer, Robert, *Jerry Lee Lewis Rocks!* (Delilah Books, 1981)

Tosches, Nick, *Hellfire* (Grove Press, 1982).

Williams, Paul, *Rock and Roll: The 100 Best Singles*, Ch. 8 ("Whole Lotta Shakin' Goin' On") (Carroll & Graf, 1993)

CHAPTER 14

"THAT'LL BE THE DAY"

BUDDY HOLLY AND THE CRICKETS (MAY 1957)

Original U.S. release on Brunswick

Original UK release on Vogue Coral

Cash Box, August 3, 1957

U.S. Sheet Music

"THAT'LL BE THE DAY" — THE BASIC FACTS

Label: Brunswick 9-55009 (45) Brunswick 55009 (78)

Writers: Jerry Allison, Buddy Holly, and Norman Petty (see below)

Date recorded: February 25, 1957

Date released: May 27, 1957

B-Side: "I'm Looking For Someone To Love"

Producer: Norman Petty

Billboard charts

<u>Pop Chart</u>

- Debut: 8/12/57
- Peak: #1 (1 week)
- Duration: 22 weeks

<u>R&B Chart</u>

- Debut: 9/09/57
- Peak: #2 (1 week)
- Duration: 14 weeks

THE SONG AND ITS IMPACT

Inspiration for Buddy Holly and Jerry Allison to write the song came from hearing John Wayne's utterance of "That'll be the Day" several times in the 1956 movie *The Searchers*. As recounted in Josh Gribbin's book about Holly, Buddy and Jerry "wrote the song in less than a half hour, making up alternating lines." Buddy first recorded "That'll Be the Day" for Decca on July 22, 1956, but it was not among the five 45s that Decca released prior to the release of the new version on Brunswick. It was produced by Owen Bradley in Nashville, Tennessee, who later reportedly said, "It was the worst song I've ever heard." In addition to Holly, participating in the July Decca session were Sonny Curtis, Don Guess, and J.I. Allison. In all, Holly recorded 17 songs for Decca, of which 11 were later issued on the 1958 Decca *That'll Be The Day* LP. Obviously, the decision to release the LP was made after the Norman Petty produced the version that rose to #1 on the *Billboard* pop chart and Buddy had become a major artist with a string of hits, including "Peggy Sue."

Decca let Holly's contract lapse on January 26, 1957. One month later on February 25-26, 1957, Holly re-recorded a demo of "That'll Be The Day" at Norman Petty's studios in Clovis, New Mexico, a town about 100 miles due west of Lubbock, Texas, where Holly lived. Holly was backed by Larry Welborn[77] on bass and J.I. Allison on drums, with Niki Sullivan, Gary Tollet, and Ramona Tollet doing the background vocals. Also recorded at the same session was a demo of "I'm Looking for Someone to Love,"[78] a song that Holly had written several nights before while they were practicing for

---

77 After the February 1957 Clovis sessions, Welborn was replaced as a member of The Crickets by Joe B. Mauldin.

78 As much as Greil Marcus loved "That'll Be the Day," he opined that "I'm Looking for Someone to Love" "might be better," observing that "it's internal rhythm is so strong."

the recording session and finished while driving to Clovis for the recording session. The demos of both songs were sent to Roulette Records in New York City, the same label that a year earlier had issued the Norman Petty produced hits "I'm Sticking With You" by Jimmy Bowen on Roulette 4001 and "Party Doll" by Buddy Knox on Roulette 4002, the first two releases on the Roulette label.[79] Roulette didn't like the demos but expressed interest in having Knox record "That'll Be the Day," a notion that Holly rejected. Norman Petty then shopped the two demos to various New York City labels and ultimately convinced Brunswick to pick them up.[80] Liking the demos as is, Brunswick released the two songs on Brunswick 9-55009. Since a clause in his contract with Decca prohibited Holly from re-recording any of the songs he did for Decca for five years, the song was listed by The Crickets without any reference to Holly other than in the writers' credits.

Parenthetically, Holly had separate contracts with both the Brunswick and Coral labels. The songs that he sang with The Crickets were primarily released on Brunswick (e.g., "That'll Be the Day," "Oh, Boy!," etc.) and songs that featured him as the solo vocalist were primarily released on Coral (e.g., "Peggy Sue," "Rave On," etc.). "Primarily" is the operative word because there was some randomness in terms of which songs were released on which label. As Jerry Allison, the drummer for The Crickets, commented, "We didn't know if it was going to be a Crickets record or a Buddy Holly record."

There is a decided difference in "That'll Be the Day" as recorded in Nashville in July 1956 and as recorded in Clovis, NM, seven months later. Holly biographer John Goldrosen observed that "the Decca version lacks the ease and humor of the Brunswick recording. The beat is more rigid." To rock critic Greil Marcus, the Decca version "was nothing," but the Brunswick version "takes your breath away, that anything could be this simple, and this complete." Writer Dave Laing in his book, *Buddy Holly* (1971), stated that "the main difference between 1956 Holly and 1957 Holly was, in fact, Norman Petty." He observed that "Petty, like George Martin, The Beatles' producer, was more willing to take risks and go further afield in the search for the new sounds necessary to achieve popular success." Summing up, Laing said Petty's "musical inventiveness matched his sensitivity to Buddy Holly's unique potential."

While Norman Petty's superb production assistance with the hit version of "That'll Be the Day" as released on Brunswick is uniformly acknowledged, the listing of him as one of the authors is not. In fact, Norman Petty had nothing to do with the writing of the song, the first version of which was recorded in Nashville with Owen Bradley—not Norman Petty—producing. Petty, however, told The Crickets that adding his name as one of writers would help assure that DJs would play the song since he was well-known in the music industry.[81] Allison was not pleased and has been quoted as

---

79 Both the Knox and Bowen songs had been initially recorded by Norman Petty at his studio in Clovis, NM, and released on Triple-D, a small Texas label. When the songs took off locally, the masters were purchased by Roulette and issued as two separate records, each with a new B-side.

80 The story about how the demos ended up with Brunswick is somewhat long and convoluted, but it is set forth at length in John Goldrosen's book, *The Buddy Holly Story*.

81 Petty had penned, among other songs, "Almost Paradise," a song by the Norman Petty Trio that spent 13 weeks on the *Billboard* pop chart in early 1957.

saying, "Well, that makes it look like I wrote a third of a tune, instead of half." As for Holly, he just let it go, not wanting to make a fuss over the issue. Parenthetically, the copyright entry filed with the Library of Congress on July 9, 1957, listed only Buddy Holly and Norman Petty as the composers of "That'll Be the Day." It should be noted that the practice of an artist's manager and/or the owner of the label taking credit for being one of a song's writers was rampant in the 1950s.

The record was released on May 27, 1957. *Billboard* in its June 10, 1957, review gave it only a "Good" rating with a numerical rating of 72, where 90 to 100 = excellent, 80 to 89 = very good, 70 to 79 = good. On the other hand, on June 22, 1957, *Cash Box* gave it a B+. Below are both reviews:

THE CRICKETS
That'll Be the Day **72**
BRUNSWICK 55009—Fine vocal by the group on a well-made side that should get play. Tune is a medium beat rockabilly. Performance is better than material. (Nor-Va-Jak, BMI)
I'm Lookin' for Someone to Love **72**
As with the flip, the material is inferior to the rendition. The up-tempo rockabilly gets bright, vigorous treatment, and should do as well as the flip. (Nor-Va-Jak, BMI)

Billboard review, June 10, 1957

THE CRICKETS
(Brunswick 9-55009)
B+ "THAT'LL BE THE DAY" (2:38) [Nor-va-jak Music BMI Allison, Holly, Petty] The Crickets make their initial try on Brunswick with a middle beat rock-a-billy tune of infectious quality. The Crickets handle the tune with a top-flight bit of chanting. Deck could stir up some action.
B "I'M LOOKIN' FOR SOMEONE TO LOVE" (2:37) [Nor-va-jak BMI — Holly, Petty] The Crickets up the tempo on the flip with a similar type of material. Good rocking wax that the kids will love.

Cash Box review, June 22, 1957

Despite these mixed reviews, a broad cross section of the record buying public, especially teenagers, clearly liked the song. It debuted on the *Billboard* pop chart on August 12, 1957, and on the *Billboard* R&B chart on September 9, 1957. It subsequently went to #1 on the pop chart and to #2 on the R&B chart.

In the wake of the success of the Brunswick release, on August 12, 1957, Decca released the version that had been recorded but not released a year earlier on Decca 9-30434. *Billboard's* review on August 19, 1957, was rather tepid. As *Billboard* noted, it was a cover of the hit by The Crickets, which had been released earlier on Brunswick, commenting that the Decca release "may be late to cop top loot." Ironically, *Billboard* gave the Decca release the same numerical ranking—72—that it gave for the Brunswick release.

As noted below, the song attracted two other contemporaneous cover versions,[82] the most interesting one being by The Ravens, who in the late 40s and early 50s released a string of important R&B vocal group records on such labels as National, Columbia, Jubilee, and Mercury. This latter-day Ravens were led by Joe Van Loan and included his brother, James. For some unexplained reason, the

82 Interestingly, on the covers by both The Ravens and Jeff Allen the writers' credit is only given to Holly and Petty, perhaps because they were the only two listed on the copyright entry. The original release on Brunswick and the later release on Decca listed Allison along with Holly and Petty as the writers.

Chess brothers issued it on both Argo 5276 and on Checker 871, with both records having the same B-side ("Dear One") and the same matrix numbers. The lead was sung by James Van Loan (formerly with the Dominoes) since Jimmy Ricks was no longer with the group. The Ravens' version, along with The Crickets' version, made the higher reaches of Chicago radio station WJJD's weekly top 40 chart. Although The Ravens' version has received decent reviews over the years, noted R&B chronicler Marv Goldberg strongly disagreed, stating that it was "the worst record the Ravens ever made (beating out 'Rooster' for the dubious honor)."

In the UK, "That'll Be The Day" was released on September 10, 1957. It entered the UK charts on October 10, 1957, and rose to #1 for three weeks during its 15-week chart run.[83] The song had an immediate impact on John Lennon and Paul McCartney. As Beatles biographer Mark Lewisohn observed:

> "That'll Be the Day" was the first song they absorbed and learned together—the right song with the right sound arriving at exactly the right time. They loved the performance, the electric guitar, the harmonies, the lead singer's distinctive vocal style (with a kind of hiccup on certain phrases), and they were impressed with the name "The Crickets."

Considering subsequent events, it is noteworthy that Buddy Holly and The Crickets toured England in March 1958.[84] On March 2 they performed "That'll Be The Day," "Peggy Sue," and "Oh Boy" for a British TV show. Mark Lewisohn in his epic book about The Beatles reported:

> John, Paul and George were well aware Buddy Holly and The Crickets were in the country because they'd been glued to TV the night of March 2 to watch them on *Sunday Night at the London Palladium*. As Paul says, "That was the big occasion—to watch his fingers, see what guitar he had, to see if he played the chords right, to see how he did the solo on 'Peggy Sue,' see whether he used the capo or not, all the various technical things—that was where you got the info."

Subsequently, Buddy Holly and The Crickets performed at the Philharmonic Hall in Liverpool on March 20, 1958. In all likelihood, their set included the same songs they played for the March 2 TV show. Beatle expert Mark Lewisohn says: "Given such enthusiasm [*for Buddy*], it is astounding they didn't go to see him when it was so easy to do so." No one has satisfactorily explained their non-attendance, but maybe they had other plans, or they simply couldn't get tickets as some have suggested.

---

83 Twenty-eight years later in 1986 it dented the lower reaches of the UK charts for another two weeks.

84 The NME chart of best-selling records in England as of March 14, 1958, included four songs by Buddy Holly and/or The Crickets ("Oh, Boy!" at #9, "Listen to Me" at #16, "Peggy Sue" at #19, and "Maybe Baby" at #28).

Four months later, "That'll Be The Day" was the first song ever recorded by The Quarry Men (frequently referred to as The Quarrymen), the group that later became The Beatles. While the date given for this historic recording session varies depending on the source, *Setlist.com* puts the date as July 12, 1958, at the Phillips Sound Recording Studio in Liverpool, England [Image: *Discogs*]. This version can be heard on the *Anthology 1* LP, Apple PCSB 727 (1995). As John Lennon is quoted on *The Beatles Bible* website, "The first thing we ever recorded was 'That'll Be The Day,' a Buddy Holly song." Concerning this same recording session, Paul McCartney recalled:

John did "That'll Be The Day," which was one of our stage numbers, and George played the opening guitar notes and I harmonised with John singing lead.

Nor should be forgotten that The Crickets were the inspiration for The Quarry Men changing their name to The Beatles. As Dave Marsh summed up his take on "That'll Be The Day": "This is the one where they prove they really were The Beatles' granddaddies."

In the years following its original release on Brunswick in May 1957, a wide variety of artists have covered "That'll Be the Day." Releases by The Everly Brothers, Pure Prairie League, Linda Ronstadt, and Kenny Vernon all charted in the U.S. and/or UK, as documented below in the chart of subsequent covers. A noteworthy cover that did not chart is on "Lucky" Token 112 by the Crossfires, the band that later became The Turtles who recorded such hits as "It Ain't Me Babe" and "Happy Together."

In selecting "That'll Be The Day" as one of the 100 most influential songs since the founding of *Time* in 1923, *Time* commented, "With that one song, Holly proved that rockin' music could take even a skinny, geeky boy with glasses and make him sound cool." Elvis Costello obviously took note. Induction into the Grammy Hall of Fame and selection for inclusion on the National Recording Registry of the Library of Congress are among the other honors accorded to "That'll Be the Day."

CONTEMPORANEOUS COVER VERSIONS OF "THAT'LL BE THE DAY"

ARTIST	LABEL	COMMENTS
Jeff Allen	Verve 10064	B/w "I'm Guilty"
Jeff Allen	His Master's Voice 45-JO 477 (UK)	B/w "I'm Guilty"
Buddy Holly and The Three Suns	Decca 9-30434	Recorded in Nashville, TN, on July 22, 1956, but only released after The Crickets' version on Brunswick became a smash hit; b/w "Rock Around Ollie Vee"
The Ravens	Argo 5276; Checker 871	Same pressing with same matrix numbers for both labels, both of which were subsidiaries of Chess Records; b/w "Dear One"
Tunettes	Embassy WB 259 (UK)	B/w "Whole Lotta Shakin' Goin' On"

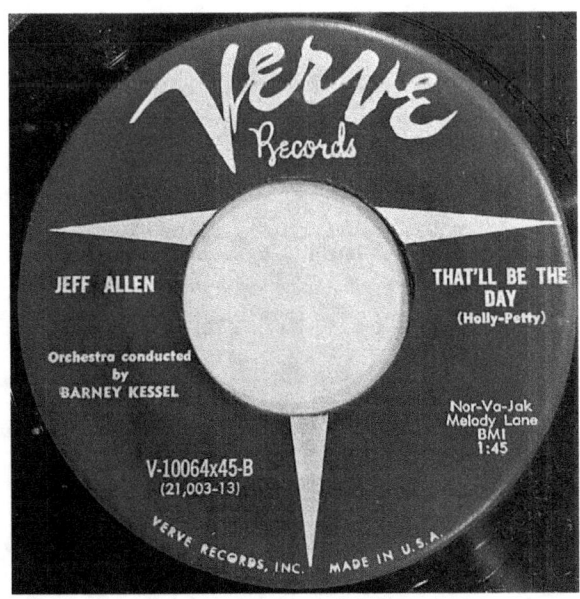

Jeff Allen on Verve 10064

The Ravens on Argo 5276

A usually reliable source for contemporaneous cover versions is *Billboard*. Thus, for charted pop hits in the 1950s *Billboard* listed the "Best Selling Record(s)," as well as "Record(s) Available," if there were any. But *Billboard* is not infallible. For "That'll Be the Day" it listed Connie Russell's release on Era 1020 as an available record, but it definitely is not a cover of The Crickets' "That'll Be The Day" despite having the same title.

CONTEMPORANEOUS BUDGET LABEL COVERS OF "THAT'LL BE THE DAY"

ARTIST	LABEL	COMMENTS
Jerry Case	Tops R410-49A	EP with "Diana"/"Love Me To Pieces"/"In The Middle Of An Island"
The Grasshoppers	Promenade Hit 16	EP with "My Heart Reminds Me (And That Reminds Me)"/"Tammy"/"Stardust"
The Grasshoppers	Promenade Hit 19	EP with "My Heart Reminds Me (And That Reminds Me)"/"Could This Be Magic"/"Melody Of Love"
Steven Mark [*sic*]	Gilmar G-212	EP with "Honeycomb" / "Fascination" / "Chances Are" / "Mr. Lee" / "Whole Lotta Shakin' Goin' On"
Steve Marks	Value 144	EP with "Honeycomb" / "Tammy" / "White Silver Sands"
Steve Marks	Value 146	EP with "Chances Are"/"Fascination"/"Honeycomb"
Steve Marks	Broadway 45-381	B/w "Honeycomb"

Artie Marvin with The Zig Zags	Top Hit Tunes DC-110	EP with "Tammy" / "Fascination" / "Diana" / "Honeycomb" / "Chances Are" / "My Heart Reminds Me" / "Whole Lotta Shakin' Goin' On"
Artie Marvin	Top Hit Tunes TH-14-3	EP with "Diana"/"Rainbow"/"Love Me To Pieces"/ "Jailhouse Rock"/"Honeycomb"/"Mister Lee"
Dave Remington	Gateway 1224; Big 4 Hits 222	B/w "Whole Lot Of Shakin' Goin' On"
Jack Richards	Broadway 2016	B/w "A Teenage Prayer"
Paul Wyatt	Country and Western CW-4B	EP with "Teddy Bear"/"A Fallen Star"/"Four Walls"/"Too Much Water"/"My Special Angel"
None listed	Popular V6039	EP with "Whole Lotta Shakin' Goin' On"/ "Remember You're Mine"/"Rainbow"/"Diana"/ "That Reminds Me Of You"
None listed	Variety EPV-6068	EP with "Whole Lotta Shakin' Goin' On"/ "Remember You're Mine"/"Rainbow"/"Diana"/ "That Reminds Me Of You"

Tops 45-R-410-49A

Gilmar G-212

LATER RELEASES OF "THAT'LL BE THE DAY" BY BUDDY HOLLY/CRICKETS

ARTIST	LABEL	YEAR	COMMENTS
The Crickets	Brunswick EB71036	1957	EP with "I'm Looking For Someone To Love"/"Oh, Boy!"/"Not Fade Away"
Buddy Holly	Decca ED 2575	1958	EP with "You Are My One Desire"/"Ting-A-Ling"/"Blue Days, Black Nights"
Buddy Holly	Coral CX-5329 (Australia)	1959	EP with "Fool's Paradise"/"It Doesn't Matter Anymore"/"Peggy Sue Got Married"
The Crickets featuring Buddy Holly	Coral FEP 2062 (UK)	1960	EP with "I'm Looking For Someone To Love"/"It's Too Late"/"An Empty Cup (And A Broken Date)"
The Crickets featuring Buddy Holly	MCA MU 1017 (UK)	1968	B/w "Oh, Boy!"

Buddy Holly & The Crickets	Coral 65618	1969	B/w "I'm Looking For Someone To Love"; "Silver Star Series"
Buddy Holly & The Crickets	MCA 60000	1973	B/w "I'm Looking For Someone To Love"; MCA rainbow label; the MCA tan label version was released in 1979
Buddy Holly	MCA MMU 1198 (UK)	1973	B/w "Well … Alright" and "Everyday"
Buddy Holly & The Crickets	MCA 254 (UK)	1976	EP with "It's So Easy"/"Maybe Baby"/ "Think It Over"
The Crickets	Buddy Holly Memorial Society 100	1978	EP with "Well All Right"/"Oh Boy"/ "Maybe Baby"; re-recorded by former members of The Crickets; produced by Bill Griggs, the longtime president of the Buddy Holly Memorial Society
Buddy Holly and The Crickets	The History of Rock 001 (UK)	1980	B/w "True Love Ways"; "Given away with the History of Rock Issue 1"
The Crickets	Pushbike PBF 0005 (UK)	1981	Single-sided free flexi from 7-Up
Buddy Holly & The Crickets	Old Gold OG 9208 (UK)	1982	B/w "I'm Looking For Someone To Love"
Buddy Holly	MPL 2 (UK)	1983	"Buddy Holly Week America '83"; EP with 5 other Holly songs; released by Paul McCartney, whose MPL Communications had purchased the publishing rights for Holly's songs in 1975

Buddy Holly & The Crickets	MCA BH 1 (UK)	1984	B/w "Rock Me My Baby," which was previously unreleased; one of ten 45s in "The Buddy Holly Box Set"
The Crickets	Memory Lane 771	1984	B/w "Peggy Sue"
Buddy Holly	MCA THAT 1 (UK)	1986	EP with "I'm Looking For Someone To Love"/"Raining In My Heart"/"It Doesn't Matter Anymore"; "50TH Anniversary Limited Edition"
Buddy Holly	Crosley B0000466-21	2003	This is the first version recorded in Nashville for Decca Records; b/w "Peggy Sue"; "Crosley Collector Vinyl Series"
Buddy Holly & The Crickets	Collectables 90093	2000s?	B/w "I'm Looking For Someone To Love"

Promo on Coral 65618 (1969)

Crosley Collectors Series (2003)

SUBSEQUENT COVER VERSIONS OF "THAT'LL BE THE DAY"

ARTIST	LABEL	YEAR	COMMENTS
Dave Baucom	Giant 1101	1957	Credited to only Holly-Petty; b/w "Whispering"; TX label
Pat Boone	Dot RED 1302 (UK)	1961	EP with "Moon River"/"A Thousand Years"/"Stagger Lee"
Bryan and Charlie	Hillside HIL EP4013 (UK)	1979	EP with five other songs
Charlie Boy	Gear 001	1980	EP with "Only Sixteen"/"Tequila Sunrise"/"It's So Easy"
The Crossfires	"Lucky" Token 112	1964	B/w "One Potato Two Potato"; the band later became The Turtles
Diamond Jym	Lucifer 202	???	B/w "Rock N' Roll Down Main Street"
Micky Dolenz	Romar 715	1974	Medley with "Peggy Sue," "Every Day," and "Maybe Baby"; b/w "Ooh She's Young"; Dolenz was a former member of The Monkees
Mike Elkins	Twin TRG 32	???	B/w "Sorry For The New Love You've Found"; Miami, FL, label
Emily and Midnite	Crashed CAR 32 (Ireland)	1982	B/w "Keep On Running"
The Everly Brothers	WB 5611	1963	"Bubbled Under" in 1965 at #111; b/w "Give Me A Sweetheart"
The Everly Brothers	WB 158 (UK)	1965	Reached #30 on the UK charts; b/w "Give Me A Sweetheart"
The Everly Brothers	WB WEP 604 (UK)	1965	EP with "The Price of Love"/"It Only Costs A Dime"/"Gone Gone Gone"

Foghat	Bearsville Pro 579	1974	7 inch 33 1/3 EP; b/w "Honey Hush"/"Step Outside"
Foghat	Bearsville BSV 0019	1974	B/w "Wild Cherry"
Francoise Hardy	Reprise 5014 (Canada)	1968	B/w "Will You Love Me Tomorrow"; Hardy is a French pop icon
Bobby Hart	DCP 1113	1964	B/w "Turn On Your Love Light," a cover of Bobby Bland
Dick Holler and The Holidays	Vital 64 V-106	1964	B/w "All These Things"; only credited to "B. Holly"
Eddie James and The Ambers	Oakridge 2511	1960s?	B/w "Think It Over," another Buddy Holly/The Crickets cover
Rockwell T. James	Razzle K-6757 (Australia)	1977	B/w "12 Bar Superman"
Johnny Mac	W & G WG-S-2642 (Australia)	1966	B/w "You Give Me Heartaches"
Dave Miller and The Byrds	Zodiac EPZ/131 (New Zealand)	1966	EP with "Help Me"/"Ain't Got You"/"Tough Enough"/"Let The Four Winds Blow"
Jerry Naylor	MGM K14393	1972	B/w "Hands"; lead vocalist for The Crickets from 1961 to 1964
The Nowhere Boys	RCA 88697 630267 / BOY01 (UK)	2010	B/w "In Spite Of All Danger," a song penned by Paul McCartey and George Harrison; from the film *The Nowhere Boy* that is about John Lennon's younger days
Orangewood Morning	Gokat 1513 (matrix number)	1974?	B/w "Lady"; San Francisco, CA, label; made in Canada; no label number

Larry Page	Columbia DB 4012 (UK)	1957	B/w "Please Don't Blame Me"
Jerry Palmer	Chattahoochee 676	1965	B/w "Together With Love"; Canadian artist; also released in Canada on Gaiety G-110
Don Perry	Audiogenic A-25 (UK)	Late 1970s-1980s?	Medley with "Think It Over"; EP with "My Life"/"I Can't Help Believing"/"Midnight Over Athens"
Pure Prairie League	RCA PB-10679	1976	Cracked *Billboard's* country chart for two weeks, peaking at #96; "Bubbled Under" at #106; b/w "I Can Only Think Of You"
The Q-Tees with The Jazzmen	Viking V66-2 (New Zealand)	1957	B/w "Diana"
Tommy Roe	Ampar MX-10,966 (Australia)	1965	EP with "Party Girl"/"I Wanna Be Your Man"/"Oh, How I Could Love You"
Linda Ronstadt	Asylum 45340	1976	*Billboard* charted for 11 weeks, peaking at #11; b/w "Try Me Again"
Rosebud Band	Blackvinyl 414	???	B/w "Whoa Mule Whoa"
Shiver Showband	Redbelly RB 018 (UK)	1979	EP with "Apache"/"Save The Last Dance For Me"/"Crystal Chandeliers"
Tuesday's Children	King KG 1051 (UK)	1967	B/w "A Strange Light From The East"
Kenny Vernon	Capitol 3331	1972	Peaked at #56 on *Billboard's* country chart; b/w "I'd Go Right Back Again"

Frank Wilcox, Jr.	Pro-Gress 8825	1972	Titled "Good Times Medley" with "Josephine" and "Heartbreak Hotel," prefaced by "Where did all the good times go"; b/w "First Lonely Night"

The Everly Brothers on Warner Brothers (1963)

The Crossfires (pre-Turtles) on "Lucky" Token (1964)

SAME TITLE, DIFFERENT SONG

Several other 45s have been issued with the same title, but which are not the same song, including:

ARTIST	LABEL	YEAR	COMMENTS
Kay Adams with The Cliffie Stone Group	Tower 269	1966	B/w "Little Pink Mack"; produced by Cliffie Stone; also released in Canada on Sparton P 1531
Ken & Karol Craig	Bertram International 219	1961	B/w "I Dreamed You'd Gone"; country songs
Marvin Gaye & Kim Weston	Soulwax (UK)	???	Unreleased Motown from 1966; unofficial, one-sided record

Connie Russell	Era 1020	1956	B/w "You And Your Ways"; with Pete King and Orch.
Pamela Stanley	EMI America 8033	1979	B/w "What I Like Is You"
Statler Brothers	Columbia 4-43868	1966	B/w "Makin' Rounds"

"THAT'LL BE THE DAY" IN THE MOVIES

In addition to being the title of a 1973 UK film starring David Essex, Ringo Starr, Billy Fury, and Keith Moon, it can be heard in the following movies:

MOVIE TITLE	YEAR	COMMENTS
That'll Be The Day	1973	UK film, with the lead played by David Essex, of "Rock On" fame; "That'll Be The Day" is sung by Bobby Vee, who performed with The Crickets following Buddy Holly's tragic death
American Graffiti	1973	Performed by Buddy Holly/The Crickets; high grossing coming-of-age movie starring Ron Howard, among others; one of the teenagers portrayed in the movie famously comments, "Rock 'n' roll's been going downhill ever since Buddy Holly died"
The Buddy Holly Story	1978	Performed by Gary Busey who portrayed Buddy Holly in the movie, for which he was nominated for an Oscar as best actor

Mischief	1985	Performed by Buddy Holly & The Crickets; romantic comedy
Sweet Dreams	1985	Performed by Buddy Holly & The Crickets (Decca version); biopic of country star Patsy Cline, who was portrayed by Jessica Lange;
The Real Buddy Holly Story (title taken from the Sonny Curtis song of the same name) (UK)	1987	Performed by Buddy Holly and The Crickets (archival footage); documentary co-produced by Paul McCartney to tell the story of Buddy's life through interviews with members of The Crickets, Sonny Curtis, Vi Petty, etc., in contrast to the depiction of Buddy's life in *The Buddy Holly Story*, the 1978 film starring Gary Busey as Buddy
Action Jackson	1988	Performed by The Knudsen Bros; action/comedy cult favorite starring Carl Weathers
October Sky	1999	Performed by Buddy Holly & The Crickets; true story about Homer Hickum (played by Jake Gyllenhaal), who took up rocketry against his father's wishes after the 1957 Russian launch of Sputnik
Walking Across Egypt	1999	Performed by Tom Leonard; co-starring Ellen Burstyn and Mark Hamill; elderly widow befriends troubled teenager
Wildwood Days	2008	Performed by Buddy Holly & The Crickets; documentary about the famous New Jersey resort as told by DJ Jerry "The Geator" Blavat, Bruce Willis, Dick Clark, Chubby Checker, Bobby Rydell, and others
Nowhere Boy (UK)	2009	Performed by Aaron Taylor Johnson, who portrayed Lennon in the film; story of the childhood and teenage years of John Lennon (1944-1960)

The Roaring 20s: Mick Jagger's Golden Years (UK)	2011	Performed by Buddy Holly and The Crickets; documentary exploring the musical influences of Mick Jagger during the period 1963 to 1972

1973 UK movie *That'll Be The Day*

1983 U.S. movie *The Buddy Holly Story*

DOCUMENTED CONCERT PERFORMANCES OF "THAT'LL BE THE DAY"

As of May 1, 2024, *Setlist.fm* documented that "That'll Be The Day" has been performed in concert 197 times by 54 different artists. In addition to Buddy Holly/The Crickets (19), artists who have included it on their set lists on more than five occasions include Linda Ronstadt (62), Dave Edmunds (6), Denny Laine (6), and Pure Prairie League (6).

HONORS AND ACCOLADES FOR "THAT'LL BE THE DAY"

- Inducted into the Grammy Hall of Fame in 1998
- Added in 2005 to the National Recording Registry of the Library of Congress, to which songs that are "culturally, historically, or aesthetically significant" are added annually
- Listed on *Time* magazine's unranked list of the 100 "most extraordinary English-language popular recordings since the beginning of TIME magazine in 1923," which were described as "songs of enduring beauty, power and inventiveness"

- Ranked #52 on *Mojo* magazine's "Big Bangs: 100 Records That Changed the World" (June 2007); described as a list of "The most influential & inspirational recordings ever made, they changed music, the way it was played, bought or even imagined"
- Ranked #76 on Joel Whitburn's *Honor Roll of Hits*
- Chosen by the Rock & Roll Hall of Fame as one of the "500 Songs That Shaped Rock and Roll," an unranked list that includes songs from all eras
- Ranked #39 on the *Rolling Stone's* list of the "500 Greatest Songs of All Time"
- Ranked #45 on the VH1 2004 list of the "100 Greatest Songs of Rock and Roll"
- Ranked #33 in Dave Marsh's 1989 book, *The Heart of Rock & Soul: The 1001 Greatest Singles Ever Made*
- Ranked #52 on *Mojo* magazine's 2007 all-era list of "Big Bangs: 100 Songs That Changed the World"

ALSO WORTH NOTING . . .

- The original shellac 78 pressing of "That'll Be The Day" was kept by John Duff, the drummer for the Quarry Men at the session where it was recorded. Twenty-three years later in 1981 he sold it to Paul McCartney for a reported £5,000. Paul subsequently had 150 copies of the records pressed that he gave out to family and friends. According to *Popsike.com*, a copy of this repro fetched slightly over $2,000 in a 2017 *eBay* auction. In 2004 *Record Collector* magazine listed the original recording as the most valuable record in existence with an estimated value at the time of £100,000 pounds, or about $160,000 in 2004.
- "That'll Be The Day" has been quoted in other songs, including, most famously, by Don McLean in "American Pie," a record he dedicated to Buddy Holly, thereby removing any doubt about the impetus for the song.
- In 2011, an all-star ensemble that included Stevie Nicks, Peter Asher, Chris Isaak, Boz Scaggs, and Graham Nash performed the song for the PBS special *Listen to Me*.
- The Crickets (with Buddy Holly) performed "That'll Be The Day" on Dick Clark's *American Bandstand* on August 26, 1957.
- It has been suggested by some that the guitar intro to "That'll Be the Day" may have been taken from the intro to "Switchie Witchie Titchie," a record by The Midnighters released in April 1955, on King 12220. While a comparison of the two guitar intros does show some similarities, they are not identical.

ADDITIONAL SOURCES

Marv Goldberg's R&B Notebooks, "The Ravens, Part 3," which first appeared in *Goldmine* #93 (February 1996)

Goldrosen, John, *The Buddy Holly Story* (Bowling Green University Popular Press, 1979)

Goldrosen, John, and Beecher, John, *Remembering Buddy* (Penguin Books, 1986; Da Capo Press, 1996)

Gribbin, John, *Not Fade Away: The Life and Music of Buddy Holly* (Icon Books, UK, 2009)

Laing, Dave, *Buddy Holly* (Collier Books, 1972)

Lewisohn, Mark, *The Complete Beatles Recording Sessions* (Harmony Books, 1988; Hamlyn, 1988, UK)

Lewisohn, Mark, *Tune In: The Beatles: All Those Years, Vol. 1* (Crown Archetype, 2013)

Mann, Alan, *The A-Z of Buddy Holly* (Aurum Press Ltd., 1996)

Marcus, Greil, *The History of Rock 'N' Roll in Ten Songs* (Yale University Press, 2014)

Port, Ian, *The Birth of Loud* (Scribner, 2019)

CHAPTER 15

"NOT FADE AWAY"

BUDDY HOLLY AND THE CRICKETS (OCTOBER 1957)

Billboard full-page ad, 11/4/57

Original release of "Not Fade Away"

Original A-side release on Brunswick

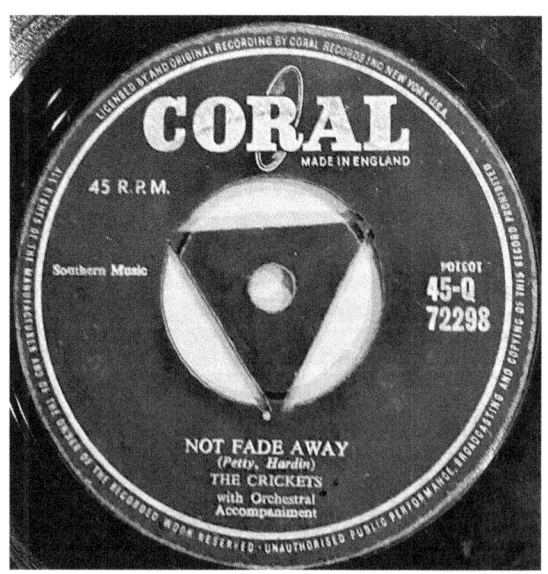

1957 UK release on Coral 45-Q.72298

"NOT FADE AWAY" — THE BASIC FACTS

Label: Brunswick 9-55035 (45) and Brunswick 55035 (78)

Writers: Buddy Holly (as Charles Hardin) and Norman Petty

Date recorded: May 27, 1957

Date released: October 27, 1957

B-Side: "Oh, Boy!" (although "Oh Boy!" was released as the A-side)

Producer: Norman Petty

Billboard charts: Somewhat surprisingly, "Not Fade Away" did not make any of *Billboard's* charts. However, "Oh Boy!" did chart.

THE SONG AND ITS IMPACT

Written by Buddy Holly and Norman Petty, "Not Fade Away," as shown in the *Billboard* ad above, was the designated B-side with "Oh, Boy!" being the A-side. It adopted the Bo Diddley beat, but as the editors of *Rolling Stone* observed in ranking it #107 on its list of "The 500 Greatest Songs of All Time," Buddy Holly and The Crickets "made the rhythm their own, thanks to drummer Jerry Allison, who pounded out the beat on a cardboard box." *Rolling Stone* also reported that Allison "claims to have written most of the lyrics, though his name never appeared in the songwriting credits."

Holly was familiar with the "Diddley Beat," having recorded a demo version that was released posthumously in 1963 on Coral 62356 (b/w "True Love Ways") and in England on Coral Q.72463 (b/w "It's Not My Fault"). The UK release spent 12 weeks on the UK charts, reaching #4 on July 17, 1963.

Knowing that Bo Diddley had influenced The Everly Brothers, Buddy offered "Not Fade Away" to them, but they turned it down. When they later recognized their mistake, Don said that they were concerned that it sounded too much like "Bo Diddley." Of course, as noted below, they would later record their own version of "Not Fade Away" for RCA in 1972.

With The Everly Brothers opting not to record "Not Fade Away," it became the B-Side to "Oh Boy!" that was released on October 27, 1957, as the follow up to their smash hit, "That'll Be The Day" (*See* Chapter 14). *Billboard's* November 4, 1957, review touted "Oh Boy!" as "a good bet" to follow in the footsteps of "That'll Be the Day," but noted that the flip was merely "an interesting interpretation of off-beat material." On the other hand, *Cash Box's* review, while raving that "Oh Boy!" is "an exciting rock and roll sequel to the boys' tremendous smash 'That'll Be The Day,'" favorably reviewed "Not Fade Away," noting: "It's 'a rockin' Bo Diddleyish jumper with guitar and tom toms supplying only the backdrop. And a pause-rhythm gimmick makes the side exciting." "Not Fade Away" did not chart, but "Oh Boy!" was on the *Billboard* pop chart for 20 weeks, rising to #10. In the UK, the record was released on December 22, 1957, on Coral Q72298; the A-side, "Oh Boy," made the UK charts for 15 weeks, topping out at #3.[85]

---

85 It is worth noting that the UK group Mud had a #1 hit with "Oh Boy!" in 1975 on RAK 201. It was not released in the United States.

After noting that it was "one of his best performances," Holly biographer Ellis Amburn described his take on "Not Fade Away":

> Cocky and brash, it explodes like a string of firecrackers. Jerry [Allison] performs his customary magic, again eschewing drums, this time in favor of a paste-board box. Syncopated background vocals, overdubbed by Buddy, Niki [Sullivan], and Jerry, turn Bo Diddley's jungle rhythm into a rockabilly riot…. [Buddy] orders his girl to make love to him, promising she'll get something bigger than a Cadillac…. For a pounding danceable rocker, the song packs a lot of meaning.

On the other hand, after commenting that "Not Fade Away" was "probably the oddest Buddy Holly record of all," Greil Marcus in his book *The History of Rock and Roll in Ten Songs*, gave this assessment:

> On paper it's nothing but an under-orchestrated Bo Diddley imitation. But as you hear it, no matter how many times you've heard it, it sounds nearly impossible. You can't date it by its sound, its style, the apparent recording technology…. With verbs evaporating out of the lyric, the song feels less like any kind of pop song than a folk song, and less like The Rolling Stones' 1964 wailing-down-the-highway version ….

"Not Fade Away" is the clear outlier among the songs selected for this book. Unlike many other releases by Buddy Holly, either under his own name on Coral or by The Crickets on Brunswick, it did not chart when it was released in October 1957, nor has it been placed on the National Registry of Recordings maintained by the Library of Congress or inducted into the Grammy Hall of Fame. So, why was it selected? The reasons are threefold. First, "Not Fade Away" was what most consider to be the first American 45 release by The Rolling Stones. Second, it was the first 45 release by Rush. Third, and ultimately what carried the day, it was the Grateful Dead's adoption of "Not Fade Away" as perhaps the band's signature concert song, with over 550 documented performances.

The Rolling Stones. In the UK, The Rolling Stones' version of "Not Fade Away," backed with "Little By Little," was released on February 21, 1964. It entered the UK charts on April 4, 1964, and peaked at #3, while spending 15 weeks on the UK charts. It is very likely The Rolling Stones learned the "Bo Diddley" beat the year before when they toured with Bo. Their version was released in the U.S. on March 6, 1964, on London 9657, and was backed with "I Wanna Be Your Man," a Lennon/McCartney-penned song. Greil Marcus observed that "The Rolling Stones heard the open spaces in 'Not Fade Away,' and what they did with it is a proof of how much room there is in Holly's songs."

Most people consider this release to be The Rolling Stones' first American release. Technically, however, London Records released "I Wanna Be Your Man" on London 9641 backed with "Stoned" in February 1964. Despite a decent review in *Cash Box* on February 22, 1964, it was quickly withdrawn due to the strong drug connotations of "Stoned."

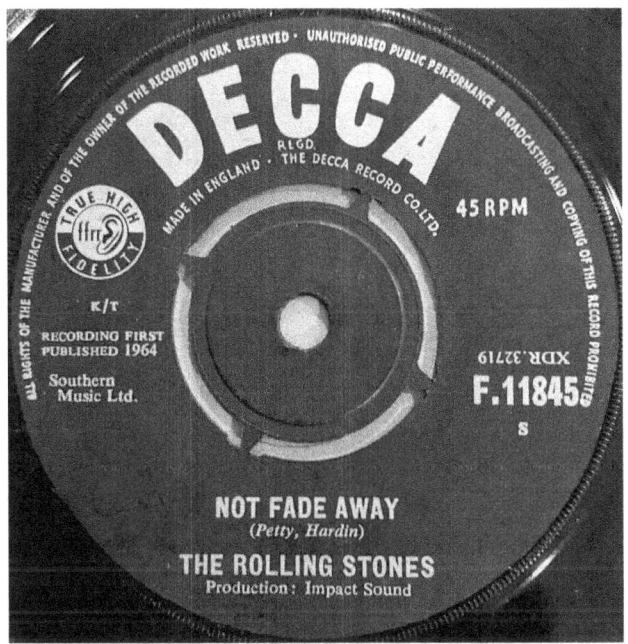

Original release in England on Decca

Original U.S. London picture sleeve

Two weeks later London replaced "Stoned" with "Not Fade Away," which became the first The Rolling Stones' record to chart in the U.S. It was on *Billboard's* "Hot 100" chart for 13 weeks, but it rose to only #48.[86]

London promo pressing

THE ROLLING STONES
(London 9641)

(B+) "I WANNA BE YOUR MAN" (1:44) [Gil-BMI — Lennon, McCartney] Here's a Beatle-fashioned opus by the Rolling Stones in the same vein as the "I Want To Hold Your Hand" offering by the hit group. It's a fast-moving while-back sounding rock tune that could see some action here and there.

(B) "STONED" (2:10) [Southern-ASCAP — Jagger, Phelps] A funky-guitar spiced instrumental aimed at those who like their dancing slow and easy.

Cash Box review, 2/22/64

---

86 "I Wanna Be Your Man" was the Rolling Stones' second record release in the UK and their first to chart in the top 15 of the UK charts.

Rush. After establishing their line up and honing their skills playing at various venues ranging from bars to high school dances, Rush released "Not Fade Away" as their first single in 1973 on Moon MN 001, a Canadian label that band had formed.

The B-side was an original composition, "You Can't Fight It," written by Geddy Lee and John Rutsey (the band's first drummer who was replaced by Neil Peart in 1974). The record was not a success, reaching only the very lower reaches of the Canadian charts. One *discogs.com* commentator, however, noted: "Energetic, well-produced, kick-ass version of Buddy Holly tune."

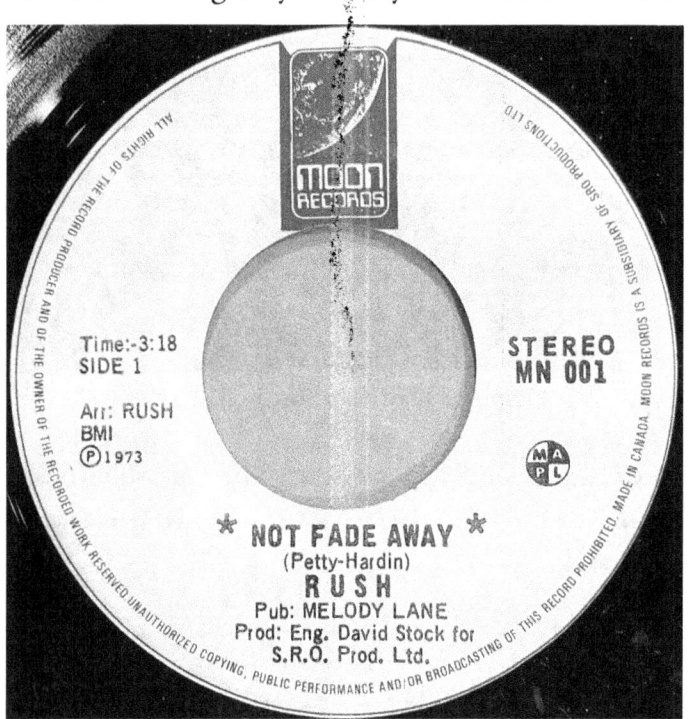

Rush next released an album on Moon MN100, sans "Not Fade Away," which was picked up by Mercury Records and re-issued on Mercury LP SRM-1-1011. Thereafter, there was no looking back for Rush, which was inducted into the Rock & Roll Hall of Fame in 2013. Both the Moon 45 and LP are rare, with many collectors suggesting that the Moon 45 is the rarest Rush vinyl release. [87] But buyer beware, there is a repro of the 45. The original can be identified by the catalogue number etched in the dead wax, something that the repro does not have.

Grateful Dead. "Not Fade Away" was first performed by the Grateful Dead on June 19, 1968, at San Francisco's Carousel Ballroom. Before disbanding in 1995, they had performed it over 550 more times. The Grateful Dead regrouped in 2015 (Phil Lesh, Bob Weir, Mickey Hart, Bill Kreutzmann, and Trey Anastascio from Phish taking the place of Jerry Garcia, who had died in 1995, for the "Fare Thee Well" tour to celebrate the band's 50th anniversary. The tour ended with three concerts in Chicago's Soldiers Field on July 3-5, 2015. In an article for the *Manchester Guardian* on July 6, 2015, titled "Grateful Dead: final concerts unite fans and band as legends fade away," Mark Guarino wrote:

---

87 *Popsike* documents that a copy of the Moon 45 sold for $2,333 on December 15, 2020.

The final hour was dedicated to the gravity of the Dead's exit, though without mawkishness. On the grandly autumnal "Days Between," one of the last collaborations between Garcia and Dead lyricist Robert Hunter, Weir gave one of his best vocal performances of all three days. Then came Buddy Holly's "Not Fade Away," a lightning strike of early Rock 'n' Roll set to Bo Diddley's primal beat. Weir, Lesh and Anastascio bundled their vocals, but the stadium owned the lyrics as tens of thousands of voices shouted the song's defiant title long after the music stopped, their hands clapping that insistent rhythm into the night.

As the article on "Not Fade Away" in *Wikipedia* summarized, "The song is closely associated with the Grateful Dead as one of their signature tunes, one which the band transformed from Holly's 1950s boy/girl romanticism to one reflecting the 1960s' more spiritual universal love."

Surprisingly, the Grateful Dead never released a 45 of "Not Fade Away." Its first appearance on vinyl was on their eponymous 1971 album, which was subsequently dubbed by Deadheads as the "Skull and Roses" LP based on Alton Kelley's cover art. This LP on Warner Brothers 2 WS 1935, which was their first to be certified gold by the RIAA, captures a nine minute and 14 second live version of "Not Fade Away" coupled with "Goin' Down The Road Feeling Bad."

Other Artists Who Covered "Not Fade Away." Ironically, while Buddy Holly and The Crickets did not achieve chart success with their original version of "Not Fade Away," more than a few other artists did, starting with The Rolling Stones as discussed above. The other artists whose cover versions hit the charts are Tanya Tucker (1979), Eric Hine (1981), and Trish Lynn (1989).

Additional artists who released 45s of "Not Fade Away" include Joe Ely, The Everly Brothers, and Bobby Fuller. Even Bo Diddley, whose beat Buddy Holly and The Crickets unmistakably wove into their original version, responded by issuing his own version for RCA in 1976, with Billy Joel on keyboards, Elvin Bishop and Albert Lee on guitars, and Joe Cocker assisting on the vocal. As they say, "Turnabout is fair play."

The continuing impact of "Not Fade Away" is evidenced by the issuance of two albums carrying the title of *Not Fade Away*, the first by the Nitty Gritty Dirt Band (CD/LP, 1992) and the second a Buddy Holly tribute CD (1996) of his songs (including "Not Fade Away") sung by a wide variety of artists, including Waylon Jennings with Mark Knopfler and Nanci Griffith with The Crickets.

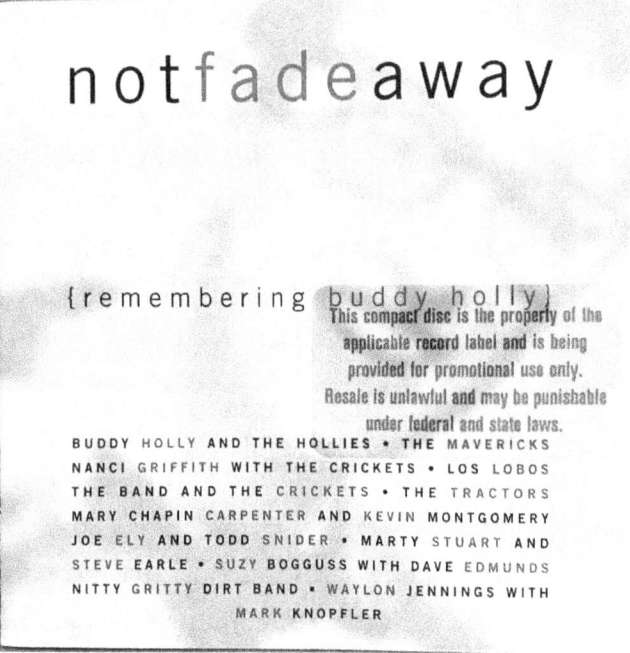

CONTEMPORANEOUS COVER VERSIONS OF "NOT FADE AWAY"

Presumably because it was not a hit, there were no contemporaneous cover versions.

CONTEMPORANEOUS BUDGET LABEL COVERS OF "NOT FADE AWAY"

Likewise, there were no budget label covers. There were, however, at least three budget label covers of the A-side, "Oh, Boy!" The first was on Gateway 1237 by Gootch Jackson with The Four Jacks, the second was on Gilmar G-216 by Steve Marks, and the third was on Promenade HIT 24 by The Grasshoppers.

LATER RELEASES OF "NOT FADE AWAY" BY BUDDY HOLLY/CRICKETS

ARTIST	LABEL	YEAR	COMMENTS
The Crickets	Brunswick EB71036	1957	EP titled "The 'Chirpin' The Crickets" with "That'll Be The Day"/"Oh Boy!"/ "I'm Lookin' For Someone To Love"
The Crickets	Coral FEP 2003 (UK)	1958	EP with "Oh, Boy"/"Maybe Baby"/ "Tell Me How"
The Crickets Featuring Buddy Holly	Coral 62407	1964	B/w "Maybe Baby"

Buddy Holly & The Crickets	Old Gold OG 9223 (UK)	1982	B/w "Oh, Boy!"
Buddy Holly & The Crickets	MCA BH 3 (UK)	1984	B/w "Oh, Boy!"; one of ten 45s in "The Buddy Holly Box Set"
The Crickets	American Pie 9099	1991	B/w "Oh, Boy!"; manufactured by MCA
The Crickets (Buddy Holly lead vocal)	Collectables 90098	1991	B/w "Oh, Boy!"; manufactured by MCA
The Crickets	Coral B0018025-21	2013	B/w "Oh, Boy!"; "Courtesy of Geffen Records"

1964 reissue on Coral

Circa 1990s reissue on Collectables

SUBSEQUENT COVER VERSIONS OF "NOT FADE AWAY"

ARTIST	LABEL	YEAR	COMMENTS
The Bees	Virgin VS 1926 (UK)	2007	B/w "Who Cares What The Answer Is?"

P.J. Belly And The Lone Star Blues Band	Nor-Va-Jak 1335	1987	B/w "Down Of Main"; P.J. Belly co-produced the 5 ½ hour 1986 R&R concert held in Lubbock, TX, to celebrate Buddy Holly's birthday; the lineup included The Crickets, Bo Diddley, Carl Perkins, Del Shannon, and Bobby Vee
Black Oak (also known as Black Oak Arkansas)	Capricorn CPS-0284	1977	B/w "Feel So Good"; the promo issue has mono and stereo versions of "Not Fade Away"
Gary Busey	Epic 8-50607	1978	Titled "Clear Lake Medley" with "Maybe Baby" and "Oh, Boy!"
Gary Busey	Moon Nest MMXVIII	2018	B/w "All The Way"; Malibu, CA, label
Barry Capp	Cannon 022 (UK)	1964	Budget label EP with covers of 5 other songs
The Chapman Forts	Damaged Goods 507 (UK)	2018	B/w "I Wanna Be Your Man," the Lennon/McCartney penned song that The Rolling Stones recorded as the B-side of "Not Fade Away"
Corporate Image	MGM K13614	1966	B/w "I'm Not The Same"
Crouch/Prosser/ Bouret Band	Robaley MG-4018	1981	B/w "Hold On"; scarce private pressing from Baltimore, MD
Sheryl Crow	A&M/Interscope (digital single)	2007	Hit #63 on the *Billboard's* "Pop 100" chart
Dick and DeeDee	WB 5426	1964	B/w "The Gift"
Bo Diddley	RCA PB-10618	1976	B/w "Drag On"

Division	Transaction T-710	1969	B/w "Please, Please Me," a cover of The Beatles; La Crosse, WI, label; garage
Joe Ely	South Coast EPS33-1736	1981	7-inch 33 1/3 EP b/w "Crazy Lemon"/"Treat Me Like A Saturday Night"/"Wishin' For You"; produced by Al Kooper
The End	Cha Cha C-746	1966	B/w "Memorandum"; Chicago garage band
The Everly Brothers	RCA 74-0901	1972	B/w "Ladies Love Outlaws"; produced by Chet Atkins
The Everly Brothers	RCA 228 (UK)	1972	B/w "Lay It Away"; produced by Chet Atkins
Florence + Machine	Decca CD single (UK)	2011	Promo only
Bobby Fuller	Eastwood NO8W-0345	1962	B/w "Nervous Breakdown" (NO8W-0344); RCA pressing
Fumble	RCA 2479 (England)	1974	B/w "After The Dance"; produced by Shel Talmy
Group Axis	Atco 6642	1969	B/w "Smokestack Lightning," a cover of Howlin' Wolf; produced by Norman Petty; "Not Fade Away" was the plug side
Steve Hillage	Virgin VS 197 (UK)	1977	Titled "Not Fade Away (Gild Forever)," credited to Hardin/Petty
Eric Hine	Montage P-A-1200	1981	B/w "After Dark"; Los Angeles, CA, label; synth-pop; recorded in England
Eric Hine	Radioactive RAD 505 (UK)	1982	B/w "Expectation (Brave New World)"

The Innocents and The LeRoys	Regal Zonophone RZ 502 (UK)	1964	EP with "Don't Throw Your Love Away"/"My Girl Lollipop"/"I Love You Because"/"I Believe"/"Tell Me When"; an early Robert Stigwood production
The Jaybirds	Embassy WB 621 (UK)	1964	B/w "Over You"
Jumpin' Beans and Moustashes	Ball BA-5953	2000s?	B/w "Gloria"; Gardiner, ME, label
Stanley Knox	CRM UR3143	1982	B/w "Loving Me"; Harlem, GA, label; produced by Buzz Clifford
Trisha Lynn	Oak 1062	1989	Spent five weeks on the *Billboard* country chart, peaking at #69
Vic Maile	Bronze BRO-129 (UK)	1981	B/w "It's The Same Old Thing"
Stevie Nicks	India CD single (UK and Europe)	2013	Promo only CD; produced by Peter Asher
Raw Holly	Youngblood YB 1007 (UK)	1972	B/w "Rock Me My Baby" and "Raining In My Heart"
Tim Rice	Chrysalis CHS.2059 (UK)	1974	B/w "Nothing Different (Nothing Altered, Nothing Changed)"
The Rolling Stones	London 9657	1964	First charted American release; peaked at #48; b/w "I Wanna Be Your Man"
The Rolling Stones	London L. 9657 (Canada)	1964	B/w "I Wanna Be Your Man"
The Rolling Stones	London 5N 9657	1974	B/w "I Wanna Be Your Man"; later reissue
The Rolling Stones	Decca STONE 4 (UK)	1980	B/w "Little Red Rooster," a Willie Dixon penned song; "Electronically Reprocessed for Stereo"

The Rolling Stones	London / ABKCO018771836117	2016	B/w "I Wanna Be Your Man"
The Rolling Stones	1960s REP 036 (UK)	2019	1964 NME Poll Winners concert; recorded live on 4/26/64; EP with "High Healed Sneakers"/"I Just Want To Make Love To You"/"I'm Alright"
Rubberband	American Pla-Boy AP-1973	c. 1970s	Erroneously credited to Jagger-Richards; b/w "Yellow Rose (Golden Hair)"; produced by Huey P. Meaux
Rush	Moon MN 001 (Canada)	1973	B/w "You Can't Fight It"; first release by Rush
Southerland Brothers and Quiver	Island WIP-6157 (UK)	1973	B/w "(I Don't Wanna Love You But) You Got Me Anyway"
Streetboy	Private Stock PVT 173 (UK)	1978	B/w "Rip It Up," a Little Richard cover
Tanya Tucker	MCA 40976	1978	B/w "Texas (When I Die)"
Tanya Tucker	MCA S45-1999	1978	Mono/stereo versions
Tanya Tucker	MCA 508 (UK)	1979	B/w "I'm The Singer, You're The Song," a song co-penned by Phil Everly
Frank White	Fantasy FTC 121 (UK)	1976	B/w "Move On"
The Why Four	Rampro R-118	1966	B/w "Hard Life"; garage band; record has been bootlegged; Janesville, WI, label
X-Boys	Sidewinder MUSA 887-1 (UK)	1988	B/w "Kim"; 12-inch 45 rpm single

Uncredited	Top Six No. 3 (UK)	1964	Budget label EP b/w "I Believe"/ "Just One Look"/"Can't Buy Me Love"/"Boys Cry"/"Tell Me When"

1964 Bobby Fuller release

1973 The Everly Brothers release

"NOT FADE AWAY" IN THE MOVIES

"Not Fade Away" is the name of a 2012 movie that has a soundtrack of 50 songs with archival footage of many major R&R artists (e.g., The Beatles, Bob Dylan, The Rolling Stones, Kinks, and Bo Diddley), but the song is not one of them! However, it can be heard in a few movies, including the following:

MOVIE TITLE	YEAR	COMMENTS
The Buddy Holly Story	1978	Performed by Gary Busey who portrayed Buddy Holly for which he was nominated for an Oscar as best actor
Grateful Dead: Dead Ahead	1981	Concert recorded at Radio City Music Hall in NYC on October 30-31, 1980; performed by the Grateful Dead
Christine	1983	Horror/thriller based on a Stephen King book; performed by Buddy Holly & The Crickets
Walking Across Egypt	1999	Performed by Ron Dante and Ted Perlman; an elderly widow (Ellyn Burstyn) befriends a teenage delinquent (Mark Hamill); described by *IMDbPro* as "comedy/crime/drama"
The Music Never Stopped	2011	Performed by the Grateful Dead; drama about a father and an estranged son who connect via music
Long Strange Trip: The Untold Story of the Grateful Dead	2017	Performed by the Grateful Dead; 6-part documentary that was nominated for a best musical Grammy
Tea with the Dames (UK)	2018	Performed by The Rolling Stones; Dames Judi Dench, Maggie Smith, and others discuss their careers over tea

DOCUMENTED CONCERT PERFORMANCES OF "NOT FADE AWAY"

As of May 1, 2024, *Setlist.fm* documented that "Not Fade Away" has been performed in concert 4,308 times by 330 different artists. In addition to Buddy Holly/The Crickets, artists who have included it on their set lists on fifteen or more occasions include the Grateful Dead (561), Los Lobos (519), The Rolling Stones (196), Bob Dylan (147), Patti Smith (115), James Taylor (50), and Jon Bon Jovi (15). In 2023, "Not Fade Away" was on concert play lists 211 times, the most of any year in *Setlist.fm's* database. Not too shabby for a song initially released more than six decades ago.

HONORS AND ACCOLADES FOR "NOT FADE AWAY"

- Ranked #107 on *Rolling Stone's* 2004 list of "The 500 Greatest Songs of All Time"

ALSO WORTH NOTING . . .

- Although the film *The Buddy Holly Story* (1978) depicts Buddy Holly singing "Not Fade Away" as the last song in his final concert on February 2, 1959, in Clear Lake, Iowa, both the master of ceremonies for the concert, Bob Hale, and one of The Crickets, Tommy Allsup, have both said that the final song was Chuck Berry's "Brown-Eyed Handsome Man" and that it was sung by all the concerts' acts.

- At The National Academy of Popular Music/Songwriters Hall of Fame's 2001 awards dinner, all the artists in attendance, including Willie Nelson, Dolly Parton, Dave Matthews, Eric Clapton, and Elvis Costello, sang "Not Fade Away" as the evening's grand finale.

- The *Austin City Limits* October 3, 2014, show celebrating four decades ended with an over six-minute rendition of "Not Fade Away" sung by an all-star cast that included Bonnie Raitt, Sheryl Crow, Kris Kristofferson, Jimmie Vaughn, and Joe Ely.

- Acclaimed rock critic Ben Fong-Torres's book of his articles written for *Rolling Stone* entitled *Not Fade Away: A Backstage Pass to 20 Years of Rock & Roll* published in 1999, contains nary a single mention of the song or the Grateful Dead's repeated performance of the song for encores. Go figure!

ADDITIONAL SOURCES

Amburn, Amos, *Buddy Holly: A Biography* (St. Martin's Griffin, 1995)

Gribben, John, *Not Fade Away: The Life and Music of Buddy Holly* (Icon Books, UK, 2009)

Himes, Geoffrey, "Not Fade Away: 10 Essential Buddy Covers" in *Texas Music*, 2009/Issue 37

White, George R., *Bo Diddley: Living Legend* (Castle Communications, 1995)

CHAPTER 16

"GREAT BALLS OF FIRE"

JERRY LEE LEWIS (NOVEMBER 1957)

Original 1957 Sun 78 release

Original 1957 London UK release

Original Sun 45 release

Full page *Cash Box* ad, 11/18/56

"GREAT BALLS OF FIRE" — THE BASIC FACTS

Label: Sun 281 (both 45 and 78)

Writers: Otis Blackwell and Jack Hammer

Date recorded: October 8, 1957

Date released: November 3, 1957

B-Side: "You Win Again"

Producer: Sam Phillips

Billboard charts:

<u>Pop Chart</u>
- Debut: 11/25/57
- Peak: #2
- Duration: 21 weeks

<u>R&B Chart</u>
- Debut: 12/09/57
- Peak: #3
- Duration: 12 weeks

<u>Country Chart</u>
- Debut: 12/02/57
- Peak: #1 (2 weeks)
- Duration: 19 weeks

THE SONG AND ITS IMPACT

While Jerry Lee Lewis was in New York to appear on several national TV shows in July and August 1957, his manager and Sun publicist, Jud Phillips, Sam's brother, inked a contract for Jerry Lee to appear in *Jamboree*, a low budget Rock 'n' Roll exploitation film with 23 different artists singing songs, including Carl Perkins, Charlie Gracie, Buddy Knox, and Jimmy Bowen. Also while in New York, Jud dropped by Hill and Range, Sam Phillips' music publishers, and requested that their staff writers produce a follow up to "Whole Lotta Shakin' Goin' On." That task fell to Otis Blackwell, the writer of such hits as "Don't Be Cruel" and "All Shook Up" for Elvis Presley.

During the recording session in early October 1957, after many false starts and takes, Lewis and Phillips got into a heated and somewhat lengthy argument about religion, with Lewis declaring that the song was the work of the devil, and Phillips trying to convince him otherwise.[88] A day or two later, Lewis returned to the studio to cut what would be the record that was ultimately released. Peter Guralnick, author of the definitive Sam Phillips biography, quotes Phillips as saying, "'Great Balls of Fire' was the toughest song to start that I ever tried to record. We worked our ass off because those breaks had to be exactly synched with his voice." Guralnick summed up the result thusly:

---

[88] This exchange was captured on tape, transcriptions of which can be found in both Peter Guralnick's book about Sam Phillips and Nick Touches' book about Jerry Lee.

In the end, his performance was a masterpiece, a song that in anyone else's hands would have been little more than an exuberant novelty number, but through the controlled application of energy and belief in the triumph of technique, an exquisitely etched miniature of proportions. Perhaps most surprising of all, through Sam's sure sculpting of the raw material, it became a drums and piano duet, with guitar and bass lost in the mix (the result of deft microphone placement), and voice and piano alone, augmented by lavish use of slapback, carrying all the excitement.

Sun released the record on November 3, 1957, complete with a picture sleeve of Jerry Lee with Mamie Van Doren, the blonde bombshell who starred in *Jamboree*. And, in an unusual marketing ploy, Sun also released an EP by Jerry Lee Lewis titled "The Great Ball of Fire."

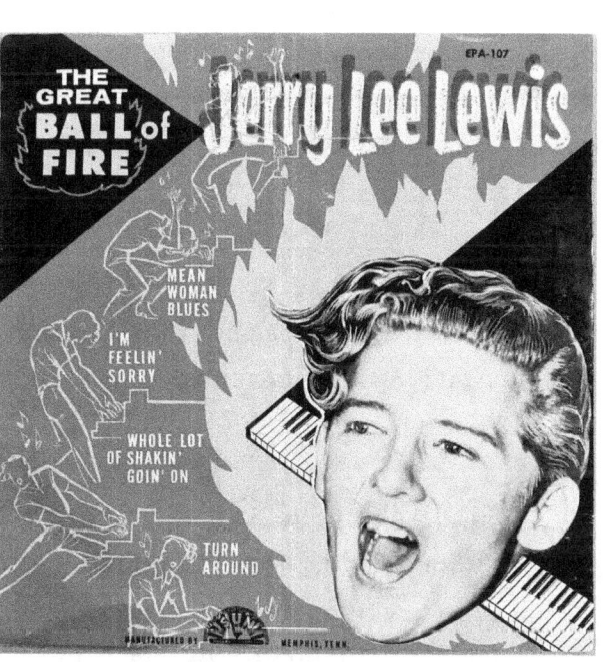

Picture sleeve for Sun 281   **EP cover for Sun EPA-107**

Interestingly, the EP's four songs did not include "Great Balls of Fire," but rather Jerry Lee's then-current hit, "Whole Lotta Shakin' Goin' On," plus "I'm Feeling Sorry," "Mean Woman Blues," and "Turn Around," the latter two being covers of Elvis Presley and Carl Perkins.

The release of the single and the EP on November 3 coincided with Lewis's third appearance on the Steve Allen Show where he debuted the song to a national TV audience. *Billboard* glowingly reviewed the record in all three musical genres for 45s that it covered at that the time, i.e., pop, C&W, and R&B. The song was further propelled by Jerry Lee's Thanksgiving Day appearance on *American Bandstand* and subsequently by his December 6 appearance on The Howard Miller Show, a CBS musical variety TV program. According to *IMDbPro*, *Jamboree*, the film that highlighted "Great Balls of Fire," premiered on December 7, 1957.

These promotional efforts paid off, with "*Great Balls of Fire*" entering the pop, country, and R&B charts on November 25, December 2, and December 9, 1957, respectively. Ultimately, the song peaked at #2 on the pop chart, #1 on the country chart, and #3 on the R&B chart. It spent 21 weeks on the pop chart. "Great Balls of Fire" was released in the UK in December 1957, and, according to *officialcharts.com*, it entered the UK charts later that month, rising to #1 for two weeks in mid-January 1958. In the history of the famed Sun label, "Great Balls of Fire" was its biggest seller.

There was only one contemporaneous major label cover, by Georgia Gibbs on RCA, but it offered no competition to Jerry Lee Lewis's frenetic original. Over the years "Great Balls of Fire" has been covered by a wide variety of artists, ranging from Black Oak Arkansas to Mae West. Two made the *Billboard* charts. The first was by Tiny Tim—yes, the same artist who previously had a novelty hit with "Tip-toe Thru' The Tulips with Me,"—on Reprise in 1969, which made the lower reaches of the "Hot 100" chart for three weeks. It is a surprisingly good rocking version. In the UK, *Record World* made it a "Four Star" pick on January 25, 1969, noting: "Low down, high up singing by that crazy Tiny Tim. He sounds like a kaleidoscope of singers here. Goodness gracious." The second was by Dolly Parton on RCA in 1979. Her cover of "Great Balls of Fire" spent 13 weeks on *Billboard's* country chart, peaking at #7. But, as rock critic Robert Palmer, observed:

> Listen to any later version of the song, by Lewis or anybody else, and the difference is immediately apparent. There's no guitar on the original, no backup vocals, no bass, nothing but the utter conviction of Lewis's singing and piano playing and the faultless accenting provided by [drummer] James Van Eaton.

"Great Balls of Fire" was the title of the 1989 Jerry Lee Lewis biopic starring Dennis Quaid as Jerry Lee, Winona Ryder as his youthful bride Myra, and Alec Baldwin as his cousin Jimmy Swaggart.

The following comment on *45cat.com* sums it up best: "Like the Golden Gate Bridge, hot dogs, Wrigley Field, Converse All-Stars, and Jack Daniel's, 'Great Balls of Fire' is of the uppermost echelon of cultural exports America has ever produced."

CONTEMPORANEOUS COVER VERSION OF "GREAT BALLS OF FIRE"

There was only one contemporaneous cover by Georgia Gibbs on RCA 47-7098.

Billboard ad, November 18, 1956

CONTEMPORANEOUS BUDGET LABEL COVERS OF "GREAT BALLS OF FIRE"

ARTIST	LABEL	COMMENTS
Billie Case	Promenade RR 20	B/w "Peggy Sue" and "Rock And Roll Music" by different artists
Billie Case	Promenade RR 21	B/w five other songs by different artists
Billie Case	Promenade RR 24	EP with "Why Don't They Understand"/"Only Because"/"Don't"/"Kisses Sweeter Than Wine"/"Whole Lot Of Shakin' Goin' On"

Billie Case	Promenade RR 25	EP with "Jo-Ann"/"April Love"/"The Stroll"/ "Don't"/"Kisses Sweeter Than Wine"
Billie Case	Promenade RR 27	EP with "Jo-Ann"/"Breathless"/"The Stroll"/ "Don't"/"Kisses Sweeter Than Wine"
Hambone Jackson	Gateway 1234	B/w "April Love" by Dale Hampton
Steve Marks	Gilmer G-215	B/w "Peggy Sue"/"Rock And Roll Music"/"All The Way"/"At The Hop"/"Kisses Sweeter Than Wine"
Steve Marks	Value 150	B/w "All The Way"/"At The Hop"/"Kisses Sweeter Than Wine"
Bob Miller	Bell 69	B/w "Why Don't They Understand"
Pat Thorne	Tops 45-R415-49	B/w "Jo-Ann"/"Peggy Sue"/"The Stroll"
Hal Willis	Country and Western CW-7	B/w "The Story Of My Life"/"Anna Marie"/"My Shoes Keep Walking Back To You"/"Waitin' In School"/"Don't"/"I Beg Of You"
Hal Willis	Waldorf CA-4	B/w "Treat Me Nice"/"Little Bitty Pretty One"/ "Raunchy"/"Buzz Buzz Buzz"/"I'll Come Running Back To You"/"Honeycomb"/"Dede Dinah"/"Don't"/"Stood Up"/"The Stroll"/"Kisses Sweeter Than Wine"
Hal Willis	Waldorf TH-17	B/w "Peggy Sue"/"Don't"/"Waitin' In School"/ "Get A Job"/"Dede Dinah"/"I Beg Of You"/"La Dee Dah"
Hal Willis	Waldorf Top Tune Hits TH-16-1	B/w "The Story Of My Life"/"Could This Be Magic"/"Melody D'Amour"/"I'll Come Running Back To You"/"The Joker"/"Peggy Sue"/ "Raunchy"
None Listed	Western HB-46	B/w "The Teen Queen"/"Love My Lady"/ "Jailhouse Rock"/"Walkin' To The Dance"/"I Found My Girl In The U.S.A."

None Listed	Variety EPV-6023	B/w "Raunchy"/"At The Hop"/"A Very Special Love"/ "Jailhouse Rock"/"Silhouettes"

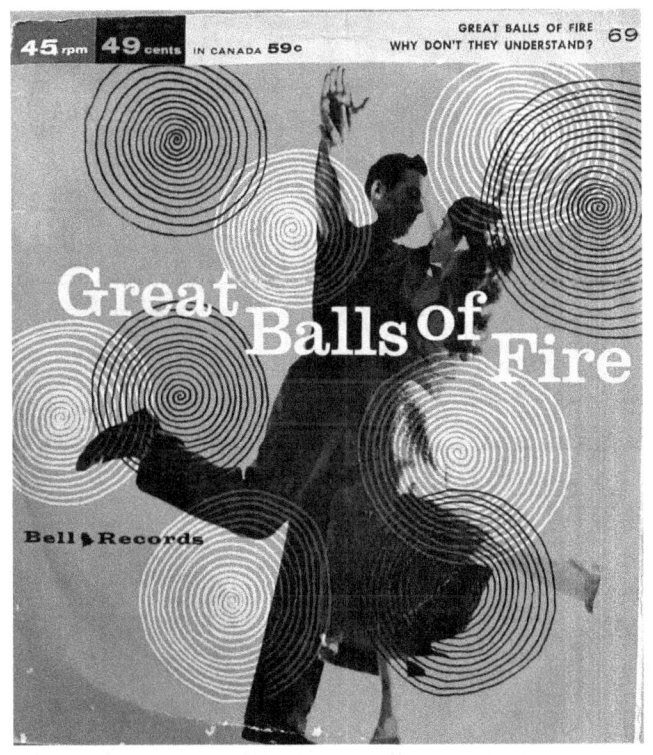

Bell Records picture sleeve   **Hambone Jackson budget label cover**

LATER RELEASES OF "GREAT BALLS OF FIRE" BY JERRY LEE LEWIS

LABEL	YEAR	COMMENTS
London RE.S 1040 (UK)	1958	EP with "It'll Be Me," "You Win Again," and "Whole Lotta Shakin' Goin' On"; original Sun recordings
Smash S-1413	1965	Re-recorded; "All Time Smash Hits"; b/w "High School Confidential"
Mercury MF 1024 (UK)	1968	B/w "Whole Lotta Shakin' Goin' On"; re-recordings; "Revived 45's" series
Mercury MF 1110 (UK)	1969	B/w "Whole Lotta Shakin' Goin' On"; re-recordings with females backing—ouch!
Sun 6094 004 (UK)	1970	B/w "Breathless"

Sun 6094 007 (UK)	1971	B/w "Whole Lotta Shakin' Goin On" and "High School Confidential"; "Maxi Single" with three songs per 45
UA ROCK 601 (UK)	1972	EP titled "Rock Samples," with "Ain't That A Shame" by Fats Domino, "Three Steps To Heaven" by Eddie Cochran, and "Let There Be Drums" by Sandy Nelson; "Maxi-Rock Single"
Charly CYS 1028 (UK)	1977	B/w "In The Mood"
Sun 21	c . 1979	Sun "Golden Treasure Series"; b/w "You Win Again"
Old Gold OG 9110 (UK)	1981	B/w "Whole Lotta Shakin' Goin' On"; licensed from Charly from the Sun original masters
Collectables 3089	1984	B/w "High School Confidential"
Sun Sampler 7-169	1984	B/w "Whole Lotta Shakin' Goin' On"
Memory Lane QSDJ-4	???	B/w "Walking After Midnight" (by Patsy Cline)/"Venus In Blue Jeans" (by Jimmy Clanton)/"Sea Cruise" (by Frankie Ford)
Sun JLL 002 (UK)	1985	B/w "Put Me Down," "I'll Sail My Own Ship Alone," and "Let's Talk About Us"; previously unreleased alternative takes
Original Sound OBG 4538	1985	B/w "Breathless"; "Oldies But Goodies" series
Atlantic 7-89361	1986	Medley of songs from the movie *Stand By Me*; b/w "Stand By Me" by Ben E. King
Polydor 889 312-7	1989	B/w "Breathless"; from the movie "Great Balls Of Fire!"; played by Dennis Quaid but with Jerry Lee's vocals
Polydor 889 798-7	1989	B/w "Crazy Arms"; produced by T-Bone Burnett
Polydor PO 57 (UK)	1989	B/w "Breathless"; produced by T-Bone Burnett
Ripete R45-125	1989	B/w "Whole Lotta Shakin' Goin' On"

Telstar HOH 1 (UK)	1993	B/w "Head Over Heels" by Nick Haverson, Theme from the British Carlton TV series
Sun 281 (TMR 226)	2013	Third Man Records reissue with redesigned Sun sleeve; b/w "You Win Again"
Demon 4500/5 (EU)	2016	B/w "Whole Lotta Shakin' Goin' On"; reissues from Sun originals

1984 Collectables reissue

2013 Third Man Records Reissue

SUBSEQUENT COVER VERSIONS OF "GREAT BALLS OF FIRE"

ARTIST	LABEL	YEAR	COMMENTS
5.6.7.8's	Third Man Records TMR 078	2011	B/w "Hanky Panky," a cover of Tommy James and The Shondells
Wild Bill Armstrong	Barrelhouse BH-700	???	B/w "Sweet Little Sixteen"
Black Oak Arkansas	MCA 40536	1976	B/w "Highway Pirate"
Black Oak Arkansas	MCA 242 (UK)	1976	B/w "Highway Pirate"

Donnie Bryan & The Raging Storms	Keldon 324	1964	B/w "Share Your Love With Me"; pressed by King Records
Brian Campbell	Kal 100267	???	B/w "Man That Sings In A Band"; an internet search turned up no info on this artist or label
Linda Cowans	Bejay BJ22582	1980s??	B/w "Crazy," a cover of Patsy Cline and Willie Nelson; Ft. Smith, AR, label
The Crickets	Coral EC 81192	1962	EP with "Baby My Heart"/"Don't You Know"/"It's Too Late"
Dr. Feelgood	UA FEEL 2 (U.K.)	1979	EP with "Lights Out"/"The Blues Had A Baby (And They Called It Rock 'n' Roll)"/Riot In Cellblock No. 9"; free with *As It Happens* LP
The Hassles	UA 50586	1969	Group included a then unknown Billy Joel; b/w "Travelin' Band," song penned by Billy Joel (as W. Joel) and not the CCR record
Bobby Hegner	Cartwheel 112	1978	Medley with "Whole Lotta Shakin'"; b/w "18 Wheels Of Hell"
Harry Hepcat & The Boogie Woogie Band	Resurrection 6380	1977	Rite press; b/w "Sea Cruise"
Sammy King and The Voltairs	MGM K13249	1964	B/w "What's The Secret"; released in the UK on HMV POP 1285
Wally Krider	K & R NR3252	1970	B/w "Whole Lotta Shakin"; Illinois label
Gary Lewis	Liberty 56158	1970	B/w "I'm On The Right Road Now"
New Grass Revival	Starday 965	1972	B/w "I Wish I Said (I Love You More Than One Time)"
The Newbeats	Hickory 1539	1969	B/w "Thou Shalt Not Steal"

Nightmare	PVK PV 30 (UK)	1979	Psycho punk; b/w "Witch Woman"
Outer Limits	Snow DEROY 1049 (UK)	1974	B/w "(I'm Not) Your Stepping Stone"
Dolly Parton	RCA PB-11705	1979	Spent 13 weeks on the *Billboard* country chart, peaking at #7; b/w "Sweet Summer Lovin'"
Dolly Parton	RCA PB 9434 (UK)	1979	B/w "Do You Think That Time Stands Still"
"Groovy" Joe Poovey & Friends	Misty Mountain EP-500	1981	Rockabilly; Joshua, TX, label; EP with "Lightning Across The Sky"/"You Are My Sunshine"/"Louisiana Fiddle Man"
Royale Monarchs	Dell Star DS-104	1964	B/w "Teen Scene"
Mike St. Shaw and Thee Neon	Atco 6648	1969	Medley with "Whole Lotta Shakin' Goin' On"; b/w "Joint Meeting"
Steve and The Emperors	Best 103	1963	B/w "Breeze And I" (instrumental); Long Beach, CA, label; band name later morphed to "Emperor"
Rindy Sumerlin	Earth ER0111580	1980	B/w "Sweet Music Man"; Houston, TX, label
The Thundermen	Thundermen 1199	1985	B/w "Little Darlin'"; WI, label
Tiny Tim	Reprise 0802	1969	It was BB "Spotlight Pick" on 1/18/69 and was described as a "wild revival" of JLL's hit; b/w "As Time Goes By"; produced by Richard Perry
Tiny Tim	Reprise RS 20802 (UK)	1969	B/w "As Time Goes By"

Tiny Tim	Reprise 0740	1972	B/w "Tip-Toe Thru' The Tulips With Me"; "Back to Back Hits" series
Dave Travis	Polydor 56280 (UK)	1968	B/w "Drivin' Down The Highway"
Joey Welz Bluze Revival	Palmer P-5032	1970	Medley with "Rip It Up," "Rumble," and "Rock Around The Clock"; co-produced by Ray Vernon, Link Wray's brother; b/w "A Rose And A Baby Ruth" by Joey Welz
Mae West	MGM 14491	1973	From an MGM album of the same name; b/w "The Naked Ape"
Mae West	MGM 2006-206 (UK)	1973	B/w "Men"
None Listed	Avant 2117	c. 1970's	B/w "Bye Bye Blackbird"; described on label as an "Educational Record"

1969 Tiny Tim cover on Reprise

1973 Mae West cover on MGM

"GREAT BALLS OF FIRE" IN THE MOVIES

In addition to being the name of the 1989 movie about Jerry Lee Lewis starring Dennis Quaid, "Great Balls of Fire" has been featured in more than a dozen other movies, including the following:

MOVIE TITLE	YEAR	COMMENTS
Jamboree! Also known as *Disc Jockey Jamboree* in the UK	1957	Performed by Jerry Lee Lewis; movies like *Jamboree!* are sometimes referred to as "jukebox musicals"; Otis Blackwell, the great song writer (e.g., "Don't Be Cruel," "Fever," and dozens of others) was the musical director for this flick; Dick Clark's first film appearance
The Sporting Club	1971	Performed by Jerry Lee Lewis; sports related comedy/drama
That'll Be the Day (UK)	1973	Performed by Jerry Lee Lewis; lead played by David Essex, of "Rock On" fame; cast also included Ringo Starr, Billy Fury, and Keith Moon; loosely based on John Lennon's early days
Slumber Party '57	1976	Performed by Jerry Lee Lewis; six girls recount their first sexual encounters; Debra Winger's film debut
American Hot Wax	1978	Performed by Jerry Lee Lewis; story of legendary DJ Alan Freed
Riding High	1981	Performed by Jerry Lee Lewis; UK movie about a young motorcycle messenger training for a major competition

Top Gun	1986	Performed by Anthony Edwards, Meg Ryan, Tom Cruise, and Kelly McGillis; action thriller starring Tom Cruise
Stand By Me	1986	Performed by Jerry Lee Lewis; based on a Stephen King novella about the search for the body of a missing boy by one of his friends
America 3000	1986	Performed by Jerry Lee Lewis; sci-fi action flick
Rock Odyssey	1987	Performed by Robert Jason; a jukebox narrated by Scatman Crothers documents a woman's search for true love based on four decades of rock music; animated by Hanna/Barbera
Stealing Home	1988	Performed by Jerry Lee Lewis; romantic drama starring Mark Harmon, which is about a washed-up baseball player who returns home
Lover Boy	1989	Performed by Jerry Lee Lewis; Australian movie about a teenager and an older woman as they discover the force of their sexuality
The Delinquents	1989	Uncredited; movie about parents trying to break up two teenager lovers; movie debut for Kylie Minogue
Funny About Love	1990	Performed by Jerry Lee Lewis; romantic comedy starring Billy Wilder and Christine Lahti
Jerry Lee Lewis: The Story of Rock 'n Roll	1991	Performed by Jerry Lee Lewis; biopic about the Killer's career
Ladybugs	1992	Performed by Jackee Harry and Rodney Dangerfield; comedy starring Rodney Dangerfield
Needful Things	1993	Performed by Jerry Lee Lewis; fantasy crime drama
Priest	1994	Performer not identified by *IMDbPro*; controversial BBC produced drama about a gay priest

Naked Gun 33 1/3: The Final Insult	1994	Performed by Jerry Lee Lewis; movie stars Leslie Nielsen and Priscilla Presley; crime comedy
Songwriter	1994	Performed by Lesley Ann Warren, who played Gilda in the movie; starring Willie Nelson and Kris Kristofferson
Rogue Trader	1999	Performed by Jerry Lee Lewis; historical crime drama about the bankrupting of Barings Bank
Some Kind of Heaven	2020	Performed by Blue Stone Circle; award nominated documentary about the ups and downs of living in The Villages, a large Florida retirement community
Top Gun: Maverick	2022	Performed by Miles Teller (who portrayed Rooster in the film) and other cast members; Tom Cruise drama/action pic

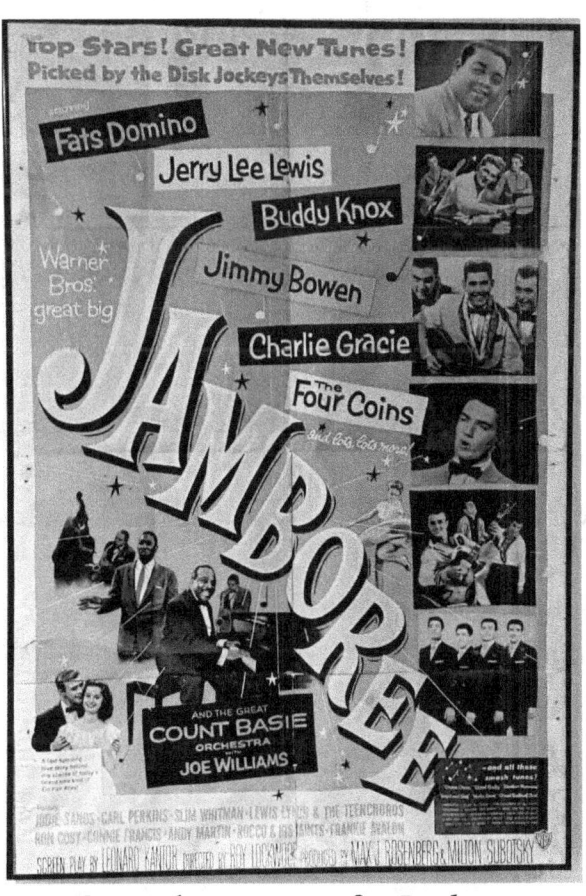

Original 1957 poster for *Jamboree*

1989 *Great Balls of Fire* movie

DOCUMENTED CONCERT PERFORMANCES OF "GREAT BALLS OF FIRE"

As of May 1, 2024, *Setlist.fm* documented that "Great Balls of Fire" has been performed in concert 1,823 times by 204 different artists. In addition to Jerry Lee Lewis (314), artists who have included it on their concert play lists more than five times include Elton John (includes Elton & Billy Joel) (208), Electric Light Orchestra (189), Chris Isaak (89), Brian Setzer (72), Styx (58), and Fleetwood Mac (15). Other artists who have played it five or more times include Dolly Parton (9), Bon Jovi (6), and Bruce Springsteen (6).

HONORS AND ACCOLADES FOR "GREAT BALLS OF FIRE"

- Inducted into the Grammy Hall of Fame in 1998
- Listed in the National Public Radio's 1999 *NPR 100*, an unranked list compiled by NPR's musical editors of the 20th century's 100 most important musical works
- Ranked #64 by the National Endowment for the Arts (NEA) and the Recording Industry Association of America (RIAA) on its list of the top 365 songs of the 20th century
- Ranked #17 on Joel Whitburn's *Honor Roll of Hits*
- Chosen by the Rock & Roll Hall of Fame as one of the "500 Songs That Shaped Rock and Roll," an unranked list of songs from all eras
- Ranked # 96 in *Rolling Stone's* 2004 list of "The 500 Greatest Songs of All Time"
- Ranked #53 on the VH1 2004 list of the "100 Greatest Rock Songs"
- Ranked #183 in Dave Marsh's 1989 book, *The Heart of Rock & Soul: The 1001 Greatest Singles Ever Made*

ALSO WORTH NOTING . . .

- The B-side, "You Win Again," a Hank Williams penned song, peaked at #4 on the *Billboard* country chart and at #95 on the *Billboard* pop chart.
- The Fireballs, an instrumental group produced by Norman Petty and who charted with such songs as "Torquay" and "Bull Dog" on the Top Rank label and who backed Jimmy Gilmer on the mega #1 hit "Sugar Shack" on Dot 16487, got their start after winning a talent show with their rendition of "Great Balls of Fire," hence the inspiration for their name.
- The Hassles (featuring a then unknown Billy Joel) released their version as a single in 1969.
- In 2017, WWE held a professional wrestling event titled *Great Balls of Fire* that included use of the song.

ADDITONAL SOURCES

Bragg, Rick, *Jerry Lee Lewis: His Own Story* (Harper/Collins, 2014)

Cain, Robert, *Whole Lotta Shakin' Goin' On*, (Dial Press, 1981)

Escott, Colin and Martin Hawkins, *Sun Records: The Brief History of the Legendary Record Label* (Quick Fox, 1980)

Escott, Colin, with Martin Hawkins, *Good Rockin' Tonight: Sun Records and the Birth of Rock 'N' Roll* (St. Martin's Press, 1991)

Guralnick, Peter, *Sam Phillips: The Man Who Invented Rock 'n' Roll* (Little, Brown, 2015)

Guralnick, Peter, and Colin Escott, *The Birth of Rock 'n' Roll: The Illustrated Story of Sun Records* (Weldon Owen, 2022)

Lewis, Myra, with Murray Silver, *Great Balls of Fire: The Uncensored Story of Jerry Lee Lewis* (Quill, 1982)

Palmer, Robert, *Jerry Lee Lewis Rocks!* (Delilah Books, 1981)

Tosches, Nick, *Hellfire* (Grove Press, 1982)

CHAPTER 17

"JOHNNY B. GOODE"

CHUCK BERRY (MARCH 1958)

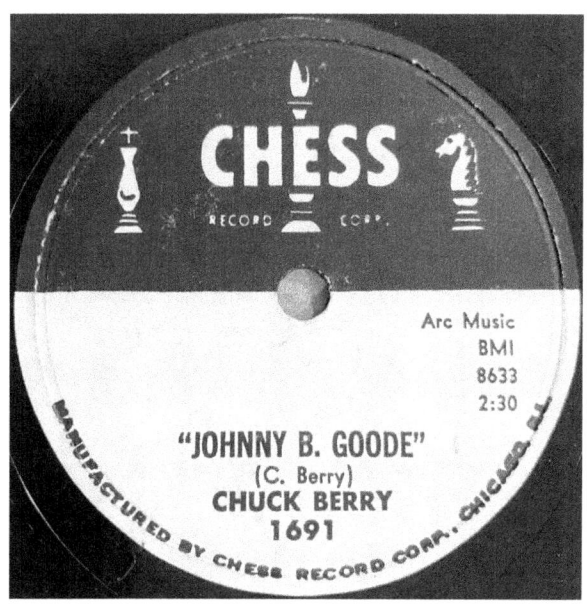

Original Chess 78

Original Chess 45

U.S. sheet music

Billboard ad, April 7, 1958

"JOHNNY B. GOODE" — THE BASIC FACTS

Label: Chess 1691 (both 45 and 78)

Writer: Chuck Berry

Date recorded: January 6, 1958

Date released: March 31, 1958

B-Side: "Around & Around"

Producers: Leonard and Phil Chess

Billboard charts:

Pop Chart

- Debut: 4/28/58
- Peak: #8
- Duration: 5 weeks

R&B Chart

- Debut: 5/05/58
- Peak: #2
- Duration: 12 weeks

THE SONG AND ITS IMPACT

"Johnny B. Goode" was penned by Chuck Berry over the course of just two weeks. In his autobiography he credited his mother as the source for the song "in that she was the one who repeatedly commented that I would be a millionaire someday." Although Berry said the "Johnny" in the song "was more or less myself," he said he "wrote it intending it to be a song about [his longtime pianist] Johnnie Johnson." Originally, he wanted to sing "Up in the woods there lived a colored boy named Johnny B. Goode," but said he changed "colored boy" to "country boy" so that it would appeal to a wider audience, something that he was very adept at doing. As a result, as Dave Marsh observed, "he created a character who also symbolized the likes of Elvis Presley, another kid whose momma promised that 'someday your name will be in lights.'"

It was recorded on January 6, 1958, and released on March 31, 1958. It debuted on the *Billboard* pop chart on April 28, 1958, eventually peaking at #8. It did even better on the *Billboard* R&B chart, reaching #2. And it hit #1 on the *Cash Box's* "R&B Top 20." In the UK "Johnny B. Goode" was released in April 1958 on London 45-HLM-8629, but surprisingly, given the subsequent impact it had on future UK musicians, it did not make the UK charts.[89]

Berry penned two more songs that played off the "Johnny B. Goode" theme to try to catch lightning in a bottle again. The first was "Bye Bye Johnny," which tells the story of his mother's "giv[ing] him a goodbye kiss" after buying him a ticket on a Greyhound bus to go to Hollywood to

---

89 For the year 1958, Berry had an incredible run of *Billboard* pop charted records, including "Rock and Roll Music," (which was released in late 1957 but spent most of its 19 weeks on the pop chart in 1958), "Sweet Little Sixteen," which peaked at #2, and "Carol," which peaked at #18.

make motion pictures, released on Chess 1757.[90] The second was "Go Go Go Johnny B. Goode," that was only released on Collectables 3475.[91] Like most attempted sequels, neither charted.

The impact of "Johnny B. Goode" on future artists was immense. As Dave Marsh observed, "Without the Chuck Berry Riff, we'd lose not just The Beach Boys, but essential elements of The Beatles, The Rolling Stones, Bob Dylan, Bob Seger, and Bruce Springsteen—to mention only the most obvious examples." In introducing Berry for his induction into the Rock & Roll Hall of Fame, Keith Richards of The Rolling Stones said, "It's hard for me to induct Chuck Berry, because I lifted every lick he ever played." And John Lennon remarked, "If you tried to give rock 'n' roll another name, you might call it 'Chuck Berry.'" As rock writer Paul Williams observed, "Berry's "performance [of Johnny B. Goode] established the *sound* of the rock and roll guitar (as taught by Chuck's apostles: Carl, George, Keith, Jimi, Jimmy, et al.)." According to *Rolling Stone*, "Johnny B. Goode" was "the first rock & roll hit about rock & roll stardom" and "the greatest rock & roll song about the democracy of fame in pop music."

"Johnny B. Goode" was one of just three songs chosen as cultural artifacts for inclusion on NASA's 1977 Voyager space probe. Who knows what the impact will be if intelligent life somewhere in outer space encounters "Johnny B. Goode"? It brings to mind Buchanan and Goodman's 1956 break-in novelty hit, "The Flying Saucer" (Luniverse 101), with an excerpt narrated by "your outer space disc jockey."

With John Lennon doing the vocals, The Beatles recorded a "live" version on January 7, 1964, which was later broadcast by the BBC on February 15, 1964. It can be found on the *Live at the BBC* double LP released by Apple Records in both the UK and the U.S. in 1994. According to *The Beatles Bible* (*www.beatlesbible.com*), "Between 1957 and 1966, The Beatles performed more songs written by Chuck Berry than by any other artist." As if to confirm this fact, The Beatles covered eight Chuck Berry songs on the *Live at the BBC* double LP.

As documented below, "Johnny B. Goode" has been covered on 45s by a wide variety of artists, both famous and not so famous. Both Dion and Johnny Winter made the *Billboard* charts with their cover versions. And, Buck Owens, a well-known country artist, hit #1 on *Billboard's* country chart in 1969 with his cover version; it also "Bubbled Under" at #114 on the pop chart. Reggae artist Peter Tosh, as well as both Jimi Hendrix and the Grateful Dead, released cover versions. Even Elton John and Judas Priest, a heavy metal band, covered "Johnny B. Goode" on 45s. It was also a staple of many 1960s' garage bands.

BMI in its comments following the announcement of Chuck Berry's death in 2017, noted: "'Johnny B. Goode'—among many others—remain timeless additions to the canon of American popular music, and sound as vibrant today as they did upon their release over a half-century ago."

---

90 In 1978, La Rue Cannon released a cover titled "Bye Bye Johnnie B. Goode" on King's Music City 5044, a Nashville, TN, label.

91 The flip side of this release on Collectables 3475 was "Time Was," a song also penned by Berry that was recorded in 1957 but not previously released. Berry "completists" take note.

CONTEMPORANEOUS COVER VERSIONS OF "JOHNNY B. GOODE"

Given Chuck Berry's guitar virtuosity, it is not too surprising that none of the major record companies chose to issue a cover of "Johnny B. Goode."

CONTEMPORANEOUS BUDGET LABEL COVERS OF "JOHNNY B. GOODE"

It did, however, attract a few budget label covers.

ARTIST	LABEL	COMMENTS
Sam Cee	Bell 82	Good guitar; b/w "Kewpie Doll";
Sugar Beat	Promenade A-41 6	Described on the web as a "boss guitar ripper," unlike most of the "crap on PROMENADE"; b/w "Kewpie Doll"/"For Your Love"/"Return To Me"/"Wear My Ring Around My Neck"/ "Chanson D'Amour"
Sugar Beat	Promenade A-41 8	See above; b/w "Kewpie Doll"/"For Your Love"/ "Return To Me"/"Jennie Lee"/"Chanson D'Amour"
Steve Todd	Tops 45-R419-49	B/w "Kewpie Doll"/"All I Have To Do Is Dream"/"Looking Back"

LATER RELEASES OF "JOHNNY B. GOODE" BY CHUCK BERRY

LABEL	YEAR	COMMENTS
Chess EP 5126	1959	EP with "Jo Jo Gun"/"Around And Around"/"Sweet Little Rock And Roller"
Pye Int'l NEP 44011 (UK)	1963	EP titled "Chuck Berry" with "School Day (Ring! Ring! Goes The Bell)," "Back In The U.S. A.," and "Oh, Baby Doll"
Chess CRS 8075 (UK)	1968	B/w "Sweet Little Sixteen"
Chess 2131	1972	B/w "My Ding-A-Ling," which ironically was his only #1 song
Chess 6145 007 (UK)	1972	EP b/w "Rock And Roll Music" and "School Days"

Chess 6145 012 (UK)	1972	EP titled "Big Daddies" b/w "Down The Road Apiece" and two songs by Bo Diddley, i.e., "You Can't Judge A Book By Its Cover" and "We're Gonna Get Married"
Chess CH 9021	1972	B/w "Sweet Little Sixteen"; Chess "Blue Chip Series"
Eric 224	1979	B/w "Carol"
Mercury C30146	???	B/w "Rock And Roll Music"; "Celebrity Series"; 1966 re-recordings, not the Chess originals
Chess CH-101	1982	B/w "Little Queenie"
Collectables COL 3400	1984?	B/w "Little Queenie"; "Back to Back Hit Series"
Chess CH-91000	1984	B/w "Little Queenie"
Chess CRES 4000 (UK)	1985	EP with "School Day"/"Roll Over Beethoven"/"Sweet Little Sixteen"; Chess "Mini Masters" series
Ripete R45-200	1989	B/w "Little Queenie"
Old Gold OG 9847 (UK)	1989	B/w "Roll Over Beethoven"
Crosley B0001383-21	2003	B/w "Maybellene"; "Crosley Collectors Series"
Sleazy SR138-2 (Spain)	2017	Alternate take; EP with "Sweet Little Sixteen," "Beautiful Delilah," and "21 Blues"; one of a six EP box set titled "Chuck Berry From The Chess Vaults"

SUBSEQUENT COVER VERSIONS OF "JOHNNY B. GOODE"

ARTIST	LABEL	YEAR	COMMENTS
Michelle Adams	Kin K 3183	c. mid 70's	B/w "Help Me Make It Through The Night"; Farmington, NH, label
David Anthony	Belmont 028	1981	B/w "Want You Back Again"; Belmont, MA, label
The Beach Boys	Capitol EAP4-2198 (UK)	1965	EP with "Let's Go Trippin'"/"The Little Old Lady From Pasadena"/"Papa-Oom-Mow-Mow"
Big Wheelie and The Hub Caps	Scepter 12375	1973	Medley with "Sweet Little Sixteen"; b/w Elvis Presley medley with "Hound Dog," "All Shook Up," and "Jailhouse Rock"
Ginny Biron and the G Notes	NCS 811122	1980's?	B/w "Don't Tell Me Goodbye"; "Recorded at North Country Sounds, Auburn, N.H."; an exhaustive internet search did not turn up anything on this artist or label

The Bo Street Runners	KR 0117	1966	B/w "Aladdin"
The Cannonballs	Bobby 222	1964	Garage version; b/w "Be-Bop-A-Lula"; Erie, PA, garage band
The Casuals	Toltec 12	1960's	B/w "Work With Me Annie"; Phoenix, AZ, label
The Contenders	Chattahoochee 656	1964	Garage; b/w "Rise 'N' Shine," a rockin' instrumental; LA-based band
The Coronados	Parliament 750	1967	B/w "Shook Me Down"; distributed by Amy/Mala/Bell Records
The Coronados	Stateside SS 2043 (UK)	1967	B/w "Shook Me Down"
The Curiosities	Seeburg Discotek 3015	1965	B/w "The Memphis Style"; "Discoteen Series"
Curly and The McClary Bros.	GoMack NR10243	1972	B/w "The Grass Grows High"; Chickasha, OK, label
Link Davis	Al's 1503; Western 1001	1961	Same song but titled "Johnny Be Good"; b/w "My Last Goodbye"
Harry Deal & The Galaxies	Eclipse 1014	1972	Titled "50's Medley," with "At The Hop," "Get A Job," "Little Darlin'," and "Blue Moon"; b/w "In Between The Lines"
Patty Dee	Graceland 107A	1960s?	B/w "I Know That I Will Be Happy"; NYC, label
Dion	Columbia 4-43096	1964	Reached #71 on *Billboard's* pop chart; b/w "Chicago Blues"
Dion Di Muci [sic]	CBS AAG 224 (UK)	1964	B/w "Chicago Blues"
Dr. Feelgood	UA FEEL 1 (U.K.)	1976	B/w "Riot in Cellblock No. 9"

Paul Dragon	Dragon 100	1974	B/w "Heartbreak Hotel"
Evergreen Blueshoes	Amos 115	1969	B/w "Walking Down The Line," a song penned by Bob Dylan; produced by Mike Post
Cova Elkins	Cova IRDA 502	1978	Produced by Harold Bradley; b/w "'Looking For A Rainbow"; Nashville, TN, label
The Facets	Terrible Tommy's 2672	1965	Great surf music sound; b/w "Jeannie"; Mt. Hood, OR, label
The Five Emprees	Freeport FR-1010	1966	Garage; b/w "Hey Lover"
Flaxton	Flaxton FLA 101 (UK)	1972	EP with "Cracklin' Rosie"/"Take Me Home Country Roads"/"One More Time"
Johnny Glass	Fox JCMM 20-36	1976	B/w "I Don't Mind"
Grateful Dead	Fillmore WB 7627	1972	45 promo mono and stereo versions; stock copy b/w "So Fine" by the Elvin Bishop Group
Grateful Dead	WB 7653	1972	B/w "Truckin'"; "Back To Back Hits" series
Guadalcanal Diary	Elektra EKR 23 (UK)	1985	7-inch small-hole 45; b/w "Watusi Rodeo" and "Sleepers Awake"; American band from Marietta, GA.
The Four Blazers	Columbia EP B-2147	c. 1957-58	B/w "Wishing For You Love"/"I Wonder Why"/"For Your Love"
Dale Hawkins	Lincoln 002	1972	Same song but titled "Johnny Be Good"; b/w "Baby We Had It"; Dallas, TX, label with address and phone number
Ronnie Hawkins	Quality 2426 (Canada)	1982	B/w "Wild Little Willie," which Hawkins penned
Jimi Hendrix	Polydor 2001-277 (UK)	1971	B/w "Little Wing"

Jimi Hendrix	Reprise 1082	1972	B/w "Lover Man," penned by Hendrix; promo has M/S versions of "Johnny B. Goode"
Jimi Hendrix	Barclay 61550 (France)	1972	B/w "Blue Suede Shoes"; extended distorted Hendrix guitar break
Jimi Hendrix	Experience Hendrix 886979362178	2011	Recorded "live" at the Berkeley Community Theatre, Berkeley, CA, on 5/30/70; limited and numbered edition of 5,000 45's; b/w "Purple Haze"
Colin Hicks and His Cabin Boys	Broadway Int'l 45 (Italy)	1960	Same song but titled "Johnny Be Good"; b/w "Sexy Rock"
Colin Hicks and His Cabin Boys	Blakey 4001 (Italy)	2019	B/w "Put Me Down"; British band; Colin Hicks is Tommy Steele's younger brother; reissues of recordings circa 1959-62
Jet	Seven Sun 10 (UK)	1974	"Johnny B. Goode" goes glam rock; b/w "Rocking Machine"
Jim & Jesse and The Virginia Boys	Epic 5-9890	1966	B/w "Dancing Molly"; produced by Billy Sherrill
Elton John	MCA 41159	1979	An 8:06 version is on his album *Victim of Love*, MCA-5104; also, the 8:06 version was issued as a promo on MCA L33-1854 as the only song on both sides of a 12-inch 33 1/3; b/w "Georgia"
Elton John	Rocket Record Co. XPRES 24 (UK)	1979	B/w "Thunder In The Night"
The Singing Jones Family	Sunnyland 1416	1970	EP with "Troubled Land"/"It's Too Late"/"Stepping Along"
Johnny Kline	Jet 114	c. late 1980s	B/w "I'm Walkin'" (Jet 113), "Recorded at Sun Studios in Memphis, TN"

Judas Priest	Atlantic 7-89114	1988	Rose to #47 on *Billboard* rock chart; b/w "Rock You All Around the World";
Judas Priest	Atlantic A9114 (UK)	1988	Rose to #64 on UK charts; b/w "Rock You All Around the World"
Tony Mac	Jewel 806J-0928	1966	B/w "Love's Hall Of Fame"; Mt. Healthy, OH, label owned by Rusty York
Madura	Columbia 4-45483	1971	Parts I and II; produced by James William Guercio
Marty McFly with The Starlighters	MCA 52650	1985	Sung by both Chuck Berry and Mark Campbell as Marty McFly, which was produced by Bones Howe; Michael J. Fox played Marty McFly; from the movie *Back to The Future,* which was the highest grossing film in 1985; b/w "Back To The Future (Overture)"
Marty McFly with The Starlighters	MCA 1019 (UK)	1985	See immediately above; b/w "Back To The Future (Overture)"
Dave Miller	Alvera 1140	Late 1970s?	B/w "I'll Remember You"; Tulsa, OK, label
Connie Moore	Spur 1004	1970	B/w "I Still Care A Lot About You"; Washington, DC, label; recorded in Nashville, TN
Mickie Most	Rave REP 37 (South Africa)	c. early 1960s	Incorrectly credited to "Chutberry" [*sic*]; EP with "Mean Mean Woman"/ "I Need Money"/"Make Love to Me"; although born in England, he lived in South Africa for several years in the early 1960s during which time he recorded many #1 hits there, usually covers of U.S. rock and roll songs; upon returning to England he produced such acts as The Animals, Herman's Hermits, and Donovan

The Mudd Family	Scepter 12151X	1966	B/w "Stand Back And Look At Yourself"
Night Beats	Cuca C-1001	1962	B/w "Night Rider"; Sauk City, WI, label
Buck Owens	Capitol 2485	1969	Spent 2 weeks at #1 on *Billboard's* country chart, 15 weeks overall; b/w "Maybe If I Close My Eyes (It'll Go Away)"
Buck Owens	Capitol CL 15593 (UK)	1969	B/w "Maybe If I Close My Eyes (It'll Go Away)"
Buck Owens	Capitol 6147	1970	B/w "Whose Gonna Mow Your Grass"; "Starline Series"
Billy Peek and His Fabulous Guitar	Marlo 1521	1961	Essentially the same song with some added twist lyrics; credited to Chuck Berry; b/w "7-Come-11"
The Penny Rockets	Festival FX-5055 (Australia)	1958	EP with "The Storm Is Over"/"What Am I Living For"/"Loving Woman"
The Pirates	Warner Bros. K 17179 (UK)	1978	B/w "Johnny B. Goode's Goode," not a Chuck Berry penned song
The Reflections	Sonic 207	Early 70s	Garage; b/w "Whole Lotta Shakin'"; Iowa/Wisconsin label
The Rockets	Wide AF 935	Mid 60s	Titled "Jonny B. Goode," same song; vocal by Johnny Vesdos; b/w "What'd I Say" (Wide AF 936); Reading, PA, label; Capitol custom pressing
The Sanchers	Essar 718	1964	B/w "He Is The Boy"; web described as a "killer chick frat band"
Norman Seldin & The Joyful Noyze	Pandora's Box PB1A	c. 1970s	B/w medley of "Blue Suede Shoes" and "Chantilly Lace"

Smiley and Co.	Jet 759 (UK)	1975	Medley with "Long Tall Sally" and "Bony Maronie"; b/w "You Got Me Runnin'"
Snow	Castle 108	1972	B/w "Sunflower"; Camden, NJ, label
Sonics Inc.	Sonic SP 0002	1966	B/w "Louie Louie"
Space Truck and The Freight Yard Marshalls	United Artists UP 35460 (UK)	1972	B/w "Mommy Won't Be Home For Christmas" by Help Yourself
Starship	Lion 132	1972	B/w "It's Amazing To Me," penned by Micky Dolenz; the group included Dolenz, a former member of The Monkees
Wendell "Duane" Stewart and The Shadows	Carib 1026 (Bahamas)	1964	B/w "Lonesome Town"
T.J. and The Drifters	Alvera 1090	c. early 70s	B/w "Twelve Rooms Of Loneliness"; Tulsa, OK, label
Stormy Tempest	Everbimes EVB 0071 (UK)	1989	B/w "Since You've Been Gone"; Tempest is a male UK artist
Jim Thaxter and The Travelers	Sundazed SEP-150	2000	EP with "Cyclon" [sic]/"Sally Jo"/"Shorten' Bread"; pre-Trashmen
Terry Thompson	Ven-Jence 7	1973	B/w "Shadow In The Window"; Carlisle, IA, label
Peter Tosh	EMI B-8159	1983	Reggae version; rose to #83 on *Billboard's* "Hot 100" chart; b/w "Peace Treaty"
Peter Tosh	EMI RIC 115 (UK)	1983	B/w "Peace Treaty"
Triangles	Kare 108	1972	Titled "The Chuck Berry Collection," a medley with "Johnny B. Goode" and other Berry songs; b/w "The Platters Collection"

Caryl Walker	Damon (acetate)	c. Pre-1975???	Acetate recorded at Damon Recording Studios, Kansas City, MO; b/w "I Could Have Loved You So Well"
Wayne and His Mustangs	Kingston (no label nos.)	1966	Titled "Johnny Be Good," same song; b/w "I'm Comin' Home"; matrix nos. ZTSP-94666 & ZTSP 94667; N. Kingston, RI, garage band
Al White and The Hi-Liters	Satin 2-101	1963	B/w "Let The Guitar Roll"; New Orleans, LA, label
Johnnie White	M-S 242	1973	Medley titled "Memories Of Rock N' Roll" with "Blue Suede Shoes"/"Party Doll"/"Long Tall Sally"/"Whole Lotta Shakin' Goin' On"; b/w "Auctioneer"
Johnny Winter	Columbia 4-45058	1970	Reached #92 on *Billboard's* "Hot 100" chart; b/w "I'm Not Sure"
Johnny Winter	CBS 4794 (UK)	1970	B/w "I'm Not Sure"
George Young and The Youngsters	Pacesetter 4002	1967	B/w "Mechanic From Hamtramck," an instrumental
The Wisco Kid with Linda and The Blaze	NR 15301	1982	Titled "Brewers Be Good" and credited to Chuck Berry; same song with changed lyrics including "Go Brewers Go," etc.; b/w "Brewers Champ Polka," based on "The Beer Barrel Polka"
None Listed	Seeburg Discoteen DN-301	c. mid 60s	7" 33 1/3; b/w "Heat Wave"/"Mojo Workout"/"Hound Dog"/"I Feel Fine"/"Chicken Back"; "Stereo Discoteen Series"

Grateful Dead on Fillmore (1972)

Jimi Hendrix on Reprise (1972)

"JOHNNY B. GOODE" IN THE MOVIES

"Johnny B. Goode" has not only lent its name to a full-length movie, but it can also be heard in other movies released over the years, including the following:

MOVIE TITLE	YEAR	COMMENTS
Go, Johnny, Go!	1959	Performed by Chuck Berry; a so-called "music jukebox" with a thin plot line and lots of music; Alan Freed takes center stage
The T.A.M.I. Show	1964	Performed by Chuck Berry; musical documentary hosted by Jan and Dean
American Graffiti	1973	Performed by Chuck Berry

Birth of The Beatles (UK)	1979	Performed by Rain; musical biodrama of The Beatles during their Hamburg, Germany, years, their signing by Brian Epstein, and their rise to fame; The Beatles opposed the film
Things Are Tough All Over	1982	Performed by Chuck Berry; action thriller starring Cheech and Chong
Back to The Future	1985	The lead character, Marty McFly played by Michael J. Fox, who sings "Johnny B. Goode," but in actuality it was Mark Campbell who sang Fox's vocals; when Marty came on stage to perform the song, he uttered this memorable line to the band: "It's a blues riff in B, watch me for the changes, and try to keep up"; movie was the highest grossing film in 1985
Johnny Be Good [sic]	1988	Performed by both Chuck Berry and Judas Priest; cast includes Robert Downey, Jr., and Uma Thurman
Back to The Future II	1989	Performed by Mark Campbell
Long Strange Trip: The Untold Story of the Grateful Dead	2017	Six-part documentary that was nominated for a musical Grammy; performed by the Grateful Dead
Troop Zero	2019	Performed by Chuck Berry; family comedy about a makeshift troop of Birdie Scouts
Some Kind of Heaven	2020	Performed by Music by Mike and Terrie; award nominated documentary about the ups and downs of living in The Villages, a Florida retirement community

From the 1985 movie *Back to The Future*   From the 1988 movie *Johnny Be Good*

DOCUMENTED CONCERT PERFORMANCES OF "JOHNNY B. GOODE"

As of May 1, 2024, the website *Setlist.fm* reported that "Johnny B. Goode" had been played in concert 5,184 times by 702 different artists. In addition to the 293 times by Chuck Berry, the artists who sang it the most in concert were Elvis Presley (404), Johnny Winter (386), Grateful Dead (283), Blues Traveler (239), and Brian Wilson (144). As recently as 2017 "Johnny B. Goode" was played in concert 349 times, more than any other year. In 2023 the number was 200.

HONORS AND ACCOLADES FOR "JOHNNY B. GOODE"

- Inducted into the Grammy Hall of Fame in 1999
- Listed #27 on the RIAA/NEA list of the "Top 365 Songs of the 20th Century"
- Included by National Public Radio on its 1999 *NPR 100*, a list compiled by NPR's musical editors of the 20th century's 100 most important musical works
- Listed on *Time* magazine's unranked list of the 100 "most extraordinary English-language popular recordings since the beginning of TIME magazine in 1923," which were described as "songs of enduring beauty, power and inventiveness"
- Ranked #86 on Joel Whitburn's *Honor Roll of Hits*
- Chosen by the Rock & Roll Hall of Fame as one of the "500 Songs That Shaped Rock"
- Ranked #7 on *The Rolling Stones'* 2004 list of "The 500 Greatest Songs of All Time"
- Ranked #1 of the 100 greatest guitar songs by *Rolling Stone* in 2008
- Ranked #2 on Dave Marsh's 1989 book, *The Heart of Rock & Soul: The 1001 Greatest Singles Ever Made*
- Ranked #15 on the VH1 2004 list of the "100 Greatest Rock Songs"

- Ranked #12 *Mojo* magazine's "Big Bangs: 100 Records That Changed the World" (June 2007); described as a list of "The most influential & inspirational recordings ever made, they changed music, the way it was played, bought or even imagined"

ALSO WORTH NOTING . . .

- In 1969 an LP titled *Concerto in "B Goode"* was released on Mercury SR 61223, which Lester Bang in his *Rolling Stone* review said:

> The entirety of side two is given over to "Concerto in B Goode," an eighteen-minute flood of instrumental interpolations on Johnny B. Goode and all of his relatives. For all thematic and improvisatory repetition, you can't help but dig it, because it's so happy, driving, and exuberant, ever flowing with the spirit of life joyously lived—the essential spirit of our music.

- According to an August 12, 2009, *Billboard* article, "Johnny B. Goode" was the most downloaded song from the decade of 1950s.
- When Chuck Berry was inducted into the Rock & Roll Hall of Fame's inaugural class in 1986, he played "Johnny B. Goode" and "Rock and Roll Music" with the backing of Bruce Springsteen and The E Street Band.
- Perhaps a mere coincidence, but Chuck Berry was born at 2520 Goode Avenue in St. Louis, Missouri.
- Chuck Berry played "Johnny B. Goode" on July 5, 1958, at The Newport Jazz Festival.
- Johnny Winter played "Johnny B. Goode" at Woodstock in 1969.
- At the Summer Jam in Watkins Glen, NY, in 1973, the Grateful Dead, The Allman Brothers, and The Band played "Johnny B. Goode" as an encore to what has been called the largest ever rock concert with an estimated 600,000 rock enthusiasts in attendance.
- Although the song was partially inspired by Johnnie Johnson, Berry's long-time pianist, it was Lafayette Leake on piano for the original Chess recording.
- As a follow-up to "Itchy Twitchy Feeling" (Sue 706), Bobby Hendericks released "Molly B. Good" on Sue 708; although the title is seemingly based on "Johnny B. Goode," the song is really an answer to Little Richard's "Good Golly Miss Molly."
- In the song "All American Boy" on Fraternity 835, which peaked at #2 on the *Billboard* pop chart in 1959, Bill Parsons (AKA Bobby Bare) sang the lines:

> And all around town it was well understood
> that I was knocking 'em out like Johnny B. Goode

- There are any number of records that play off "Johnny B. Goode", but which are not strictly covers such as "Johnny B. Goode Is In Hollywood" by Eddie Bell and the Bel-Airs on Lucky 45-1005, which nevertheless borrow some of the lyrics and Berry guitar riffs.
- "Johnny B. Goode" was one of the songs performed by Laine Hardy, the 2019 American Idol winner, which has been viewed on *YouTube* nearly 8 million times.
- A song titled "(I said) Johnny Be Good" by Cathy Saunders was released in 1962 on Edit 45-00-2002.
- Hank Williams, Jr., recorded a song titled "Tired of Being Johnny B. Good" on Electra E-46593.

ADDITIONAL SOURCES

Bang, Lester, "Concerto In B. Goode," *Rolling Stone* (album review, August 9, 1969)

Chuck Berry, *The Autobiography,* with Foreword by Bruce Springsteen (Harmony Books, New York, NY, 1987)

Williams, Paul, *Rock and Roll: The 100 Best Singles*, Ch. 11 ("Johnny B. Goode") (Carroll & Graf 1993)

CHAPTER 18

"SUMMERTIME BLUES"

EDDIE COCHRAN (JULY 1958)

Original 45 promo release on Liberty

Original 78 release on Liberty [Image: *Discogs*]

Original UK release on London

1966 Sunset *Summertime Blues* LP

"SUMMERTIME BLUES" — THE BASIC FACTS

Label: Liberty F-54503 (45) and Liberty 54503 (78)

Writers: Eddie Cochran and Jerry Capehart

Date recorded: March 23, 1958

Date released: July 21, 1958

B-Side: "Love Again"

Produced by Eddie Cochran (per *Genius.com*)

Billboard charts:

> Pop Chart
> - Debut: 8/04/58
> - Peak: #8
> - Duration: 16 weeks

> R&B Chart
> - Debut: 9/22/58
> - Peak: #11
> - Duration: 7 weeks

THE SONG AND ITS IMPACT

The inspiration for the song, according to Eddie Cochran's manager, Jerry Capehart, who along with Eddie penned the song, was that "there had been a lot of songs about summer, but none about the hardships of summer." Based on that idea and with Cochran providing a guitar lick, the song was laid on tape in less than an hour at the Gold Star studio in Hollywood, California. As Dave Marsh summarized, "Summertime Blues" has "a great acoustic guitar riff, a nice bass voice gimmick (Eddie overdubbed in a voice he derived from Kingfish on 'Amos 'n' Andy') and terrific lyrics, probably written by his chief collaborator, Jerry Capehart."

The record was released on July 21, 1958, with "Love Again" initially designated as the A-Side,[92] which was penned by Sharon Sheeley, who had previously provided Ricky Nelson with the mega hit, "Poor Little Fool."[93] The music trade magazines, however, rated "Summertime Blues" more highly than "Love Again," the putative A-side. In its July 21, 1958, review, *Billboard* noted that Cochran "sings infectious tune brightly" and that "he might have another hit here with this driving effort." But *Billboard* only gave "Summertime Blues" a numerical rating of 78, which in *Billboard's* rating terminology was "Good," but not "Tops" (90-100), or even "Excellent" (80-89). *Cash Box's* July 26, 1958, review observed that "[s]trong gimmick combo-vocal support is the big attraction in the Cochran sung opus about a fella trying to quit summer work so he can pay more attention to his gal."

---

92 As Rik Flynn commented in the *Vintage Rock* 2020 UK publication tribute to Cochran, "Unbelievably it was originally lined up to play second fiddle to Sharon Sheeley's far less offensive 'Love Again,' but when DJs favoured the former it took its place as the main event."

93 Sheeley, who reportedly once said after seeing a movie photo of Cochran that she was going to marry him, did in fact become his girlfriend.

But it only received a B on *Cash Box's* rating scale of A (disk of the week or sleeper of the week), B+ (excellent), B (very good), C+ (good), C (fair), and D (mediocre).

"Summertime Blues" entered the *Billboard* pop chart on August 4, 1958. It eventually reached #8 and spent 19 weeks on the *Billboard* pop chart. It also crossed over to the *Billboard* R&B chart for seven weeks, peaking at #11. In the UK, "Summertime Blues" was released in October 1958 on London HLU-8702, but only made it to #18 when initially released. However, it was reissued as a 45 single three more times in the UK and each time it made the UK charts, the first in 1966 on Liberty LIB 10233 (peaked at #55), the second in 1968 on Liberty LBF 15071 (peaked at #34), and the third in 1975 on UA UP 35796 (peaked at #53). Mention should also be made to the Eddie Cochran UK EP, titled "C'mon Everybody," on London R-EU 1214 that, in addition to "Summertime Blues," included "20 Rock Flight," "C'mon Everybody," and "Sittin' in the Balcony." It made the UK EP charts for an amazing 27 weeks between mid-1960 and early February 1961, rising as high as #2.

To say that Eddie Cochran and Gene Vincent were much bigger stars in England than in the United States would be an understatement of the first magnitude. Although both Eddie and Gene had made multiple live appearances in England prior to 1960, it was the nearly four-month tour that they co-headlined in 1960 that took these two American rock and roll stars to literally every corner of the UK (England, Scotland, and Wales) that etched their place in the conscience of an entire generation of UK fans. This tour is meticulously documented in John Collis' book, *Gene Vincent and Eddie Cochran: Rock 'n' Roll Revolutionaries.* It began in Ipswich on January 24, 1960, and ended in Bristol on April 16, 1960. In addition to Ipswich and Bristol, they appeared on shows in Coventry, Worcester, Bradford, Southampton, Glascow, Sheffield, Woolwich (London neighborhood), Taunton, Leicester, Dundee, Wembley Area in London, Stockton, Cardiff, Leeds, Birmingham, Liverpool, Newcastle, and Finsbury Park (London neighborhood), several of which were weeklong engagements. Following the last show in Bristol, Eddie, Eddie's girlfriend Sharon Sheeley, and Gene took a taxi to head to Heathrow for a plane trip back to the United States, but the trip ended tragically when the taxi crashed in Chippenham, killing Eddie, and injuring both Gene and Sharon. This heartbreaking accident, which was widely reported in the UK press, indelibly punctuated their status as Rock 'n' Roll icons in the UK.

Although Cochran had considerable chart success on this side of the pond (8 charted songs), on the other side it was enormous (15 charted UK songs, several more than once). Proof positive of Cochran's enduring fame in England is that his song "C'mon Everybody," was reissued on Liberty EDDIE 501 and rose to #14 in 1988! To underscore the point, *45cat.com* lists 74 different Cochran UK releases versus only 38 different Cochran U.S. releases.

There were more than a few notable subsequent covers of "Summertime Blues," at least three of which deserve special mention. First, in 1968 the American psychedelic blues-rock band Blue Cheer issued its cover version on Philips 40516. In his review in *AllMusic.com*, Joe Viglione observed:

> "This song is actually the ultimate in garage rock gone metal. Pure anger and frustration, Leigh Stephens' guitar encapsulated inside Dickie Peterson's bass and Paul Whaley's drums. The three minutes and forty-seven seconds probably inspired The Amboy Dukes, The Litter and Grand Funk Railroad as well. This was the sledgehammer Blue Cheer used to tell the world it was here, the prototype of attitude fused fury."

Blue Cheer's "Summertime Blues" reached #16 on the *Billboard* "Hot 100" chart, making it the first heavy metal record to chart. It was also ranked #73 on Rolling Stone's list of "The 100 Greatest Guitar Songs of All Time."

Second, The Who's version was released in 1970 on Decca 32708 and it became their first charted record in the U.S. It was a song that they had previously played at the Monterey Pop Festival in 1967 and at Woodstock in 1969. It featured John Entwistle voicing the words of the boss ("No dice son, you gotta work late"), the father ("Son, you gotta earn some money"), and the congressman ("Sorry son, you're too young to vote"). In addition to Entwistle, this track features the other three original members of The Who—Peter Townshend, Roger Daltrey, and Keith Moon. In its July 4, 1970 review, *Billboard* said that The Who give it a "wild updating" and that it was "certain to put them right up there at the top." In a 1971 interview with England's *Record Mirror*, Townshend said:

You listen to Eddie Cochran's "Summertime Blues" and there it is. The whole baggy trousered American dream is contained on the one disc, the production, the sound, the lyrics, the voice, and the music——that's the fucking art. It's a piece of history!

It turned out to be one of the very few of The Who's charted hits that was not penned by Pete Townshend.

Third, in 1994 Alan Jackson's country version of "Summertime Blues" topped *Billboard's* country chart for three weeks during its 20-week stay. *Billboard's* Deborah Evans Price gave the song a strong thumbs up, noting that Jackson "gives the oft-covered Eddie Cochran oldie the full, twangy 'Chattahoochee' treatment" and she goes on to say that "until the vocal starts, you may not know which song you're listening to. But who cares?" Continuing, she said that Jackson with his "signature laid-back vocal style, the long, tall Georgian turns this '50s teen anthem into a '90s country classic." On the other hand, *Country Universe* critic Kevin John Coyne was not impressed, observing that "charm of the Eddie Cochran original is lost by forcing those country line-dance beats into the backing track."

The long-lasting impact of "Summertime Blues" can be seen by its inclusion on one or more of *Billboard's* charts in four different decades, starting with in the 1950s with Eddie Cochran's original version, and continuing to the 1960s with the Blue Cheer's version, to the 1970s with the cover versions by The Who and Jim Mundy, and to the 1990s with Alan Jackson's mega country version.

In 2004 Rush released its *Feedback* vinyl LP and CD of eight covers of songs that influenced the band in its formative days. As Neil Peart explained in the liner notes: "We thought it would be a fitting symbol to commemorate our thirty years together if we returned to our roots

and paid tribute to those we had learned from and were inspired by. We thought we might record some of the songs we used to listen to, the ones we painstakingly learned the chords, notes, and drum parts, and even played in our earliest bands."

The CD leads off with "Summertime Blues," which Peart explained was a song that his first band—Mumblin' Somethin'—played, albeit covering the Blue Cheer's heavy metal version. Interestingly, in advance of the release of the *Feedback* CD, Atlantic issued promo CDs of "Summertime Blues" in both the U.S. (Atlantic PRCD301512, *see* above) and the UK (Atlantic PRO4967).

Like Bill Haley, Buddy Holly, Little Richard, and Gene Vincent, Eddie Cochran helped to introduce Rock 'n' Roll to The Beatles. In fact, Paul McCartney has said that it was his ability to play Eddie's "Twenty Flight Rock" that first impressed John Lennon and led to the eventual formation of The Beatles. Both Lennon and George Harrison attended Eddie Cochran's concerts. While neither The Beatles nor any of the individual Beatles recorded "Summertime Blues," Paul McCartney recorded "Twenty Rock Flight" on his so-called "Russian Album," *Choba B CCCP*. He also recorded "Cut Across Shorty," the B-side of Cochran's 1960 UK posthumous #1 hit, "Three Steps to Heaven," but it was not released with the album. Paul also rehearsed the song for his 1991 "*Unplugged*" concert, and it was later broadcast as part of the 1995 *Oobu Joobu* Westwood One radio show, which was created by McCartney. McCartney later commented, *"They're little relics from my teenage years, really."*

In a 2004 internet post, Eric Olsen commented:

"Summertime Blues" sounds like it was recorded yesterday and rocks like there is no tomorrow. Rock has never been harder. Cochran's rhythm is built like a boa constrictor: dangerous incompressible shiny muscle. Maybe that's the difference between rock 'n' roll and metal. Rock 'n' roll—no matter how hard—is made of muscle and bone and skin. Metal is metal: inorganic alloys mined and smelted, not birthed and nurtured.

"Summertime Blues," as Cochran and Vincent chronicler John Collis correctly observed, "has become a rock anthem as titanic as 'Blue Suede Shoes' and 'Johnny B. Goode,' and it has spoken to every succeeding generation." And Steve O'Brien, the editor of an excellent collection of articles documenting Eddie Cochran's life and career that was published in 2020, commented that "Eddie's music still feels as vital, as exhilarating and as downright dangerous as it did when he was alive." Amen!

CONTEMPORANEOUS COVER VERSIONS OF "SUMMERTIME BLUES"

Continuing a trend that began before, there were no contemporaneous cover versions of "Summertime Blues." The major labels had learned that trying to cover iconic singers like Eddie Cochran was futile. Although *Billboard* listed the Rene Hall Trio's song "Summertime Blues" on Decca 48217 (1951) as an available copy, it is not the same record. Parenthetically, Rene Hall was a guitarist from Louisiana who after moving to Los Angeles in the mid-1950s' was a studio musician and/or arranger on numerous R&B records in the late '50s' and beyond, including many by Sam Cooke. He also recorded any number of records in his own name, including three on Specialty.

CONTEMPORANEOUS BUDGET LABEL COVERS OF "SUMMERTIME BLUES"

Even though many budget labels were cutting back their releases by 1958, it was still surprising that an exhaustive search of all the budget label releases listed by *45cat* did not turn up a single cover version of "Summertime Blues."

LATER RELEASES OF "SUMMERTIME BLUES" BY EDDIE COCHRAN

LABEL	YEAR	COMMENTS
London R-EU 1214 (UK)	1959	EP with "C'mon Everybody"/"20 Rock Flight"/"Sittin' In The Balcony"; rose as high as #2 on the UK EP charts
Liberty 54503	1962	B/w "Teenage Heaven"; "All Time Hits Series"
Liberty LEP 2111 (UK)	1963	EP with "C'mon Everybody"/"20 Rock Flight"/"Sittin' In The Balcony"; reissue of London R-EU 1214; spent 11 weeks on the UK *Record Mirror* EP chart, peaking at #9
Liberty G45 19 (UK)	1964	B/w "Twenty Rock Flight"; EMI "Golden 45's"
Liberty LIB 10233 (UK)	1966	B/w "C'mon Everybody"; made *Record Mirror's* "Bubbling Under" chart for two weeks
Liberty LBF 15071 (UK)	1968	B/w "Let's Go Together"; NME (4/6/68): "Liberty has coupled two of [Cochran's] very best numbers on one re-issue and this is one item no self-respecting collector should be without"
United Artist XW014	1972	B/w "Cut Across Shorty"; "Silver Spotlight Series"
UA UP 35408 (UK)	1972	B/w "Cotton Picker"
UA UP 35796 (UK)	1975	B/w "C'mon Everybody"; reissued to mark the 15th anniversary of Cochran's 1960 tragic death in England

UA FREE 16 (UK)	1980	Promotional EP "20th Anniversary Album Sampler" with "Weekend"/"Latch On"/"Three Steps to Heaven"/"Peg Leg Pants"/"Don't Wake Up The Kids"
Liberty G45 19 (UK)	1984	B/w "Twenty Rock Flight"; EMI "Golden 45's" series
Maybelline 6	1987	B/w "Three Steps to Heaven"; picture disc "Made in E.E.C." (i.e., the European Economic Community); bootleg
American Pie 9060	c. 1990	B/w "Run To Him," by Bobby Vee; "Courtesy EMI, Under License from CEMA Special Markets"
Collectables COL 6009	1992	B/w "Sittin' In The Balcony"; "CEMA Special Markets"
Demon 45001/4 (UK)	2016	B/w "C'mon Everybody"; "Classic 45s" series

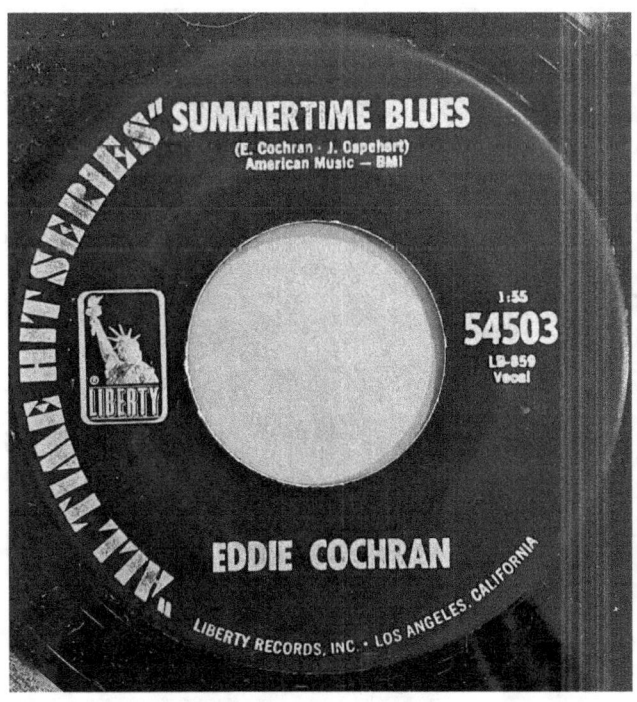

1962 Liberty reissue

1980s Capitol reissue

SUBSEQUENT COVER VERSIONS OF "SUMMERTIME BLUES"

ARTIST	LABEL	YEAR	COMMENTS
The All-Niters	GMA 1	1964	Garage band from Michigan's Upper Peninsula; b/w "You Talk Too Much"; first release on this Chicago, IL, label
Johnny Angel	Liberty 55895	1966	B/w "The Biggest Part Of Me"
The Apolloes	Soupa SR-001	1966	Garage version; the subsequent versions on Look and by the Swinging The Apolloes as they later were known on White Cliffs are better; b/w "Gone"; Atlanta, GA, label
The Apolloes	Look 101	1967	Garage version; b/w "Slow Down," a cover of Larry Williams; Atlanta, GA, label
The Aztecs	GNP Crescendo 346X	1965	B/w "Whatcha Gonna Do 'Bout It"; with Billy Thorpe; Australian rock band
The Aztecs	Apex 76961 (Canada)	1965	B/w "Whatcha Gonna Do 'Bout It"
BB Express	Mic NR 13799-I (matrix no.)	1982	B/w "Blues Stay Away From Me"; Lambertville, MI, label
The Beach Boys	Capitol EAP-1-20548 (Australia)	1964	EP with "Little Deuce Coupe"/"409"/"Little Surfer Girl"
Fred Bergin	Rinx 45-467	???	B/w "Lonesome Road"

Jules Blattner	Tee Pee 45-20	1967	B/w "Pledging My Love," a cover of Johnny Ace; Appleton, WI, label; Blattner was from St. Louis and recorded for the local Bobbin and Norman labels
Blue Cheer	Philips 40516	1968	On the *Billboard* pop chart for 13 weeks, peaking at #14; the first heavy metal record to make a *Billboard* chart; b/w "Out Of Focus"
Blue Cheer	Philips DJP-18	1968	Promo mono/stereo versions
Blue Cheer	Phillips BF 1646 (UK)	1968	B/w "Out Of Focus"
Blue Cheer	Philips TOP 018 (Canada)	1970s???	B/w "Na Na Hey Hey Goodbye" by Steam
Blue Cheer	Mercury C-30173	1976	B/w "(We Ain't Got) Nothin' Yet" by The Blues Magoos
Blue Cheer	Collectables COL 4239	1986	B/w "Signs" by the Five Man Electrical Band
Blue Cheer	Philips 872 804-7	1989	B/w "Just A Little Bit Longer"; "Double Hit Series"
Boston Rockabilly Conspiracy	Black Rose BR 2001	1981	EP with "It'll Be Me"/"Tryin' To Get To You"/"Matchbox"/"Twenty Rock Flight"; Saugus, MA, label
Ray Brown and The Whispers	Leedon LX-11,109 (Australia)	1966	EP with "In The Midnight Hour"/"Rockin' Pneumonia"/"High School Confidential"
Ray Burch	Yellowstone 1744	1972	B/w "Diggy Liggy Lo": Miles City, MT, label; also released in Canada on Boot 050
Boomer Castleman	BNA 006	1981	Same track on both sides

Boomer Castleman	Cream CRE 8145	1981	Same matrix number as BNA 006; promo only 45
Boomer Castleman	SRO 218	1986	Apparently only issued as a promo
Johnny Chester and His Chessmen	W&G WG-S-1537 (Australia)	1963	B/w "I Love Mary"
Alex Chilton (former lead singer of The Box Tops)	Ork 81978	1978	EP with "Free Again"/"Singer Not The Song"/"Take Me Home And Make Me Like It"/"All Time"
The Crickets	Liberty LEP-2094 (UK)	1963	EP with "Willie And The Hand Jive"/ "Searchin'"/"What'd I Say"
Cruis-o-matic	No Big Deal A-8100	1980s???	B/w "Time Won't Let Me"; Atlanta, GA, label
Dave Curtiss and The Tremors	Philips BF 1330 (UK)	1964	B/w "I'm A Hog For You Baby," a Leiber/Stoller penned song
Steve Davis	Epic 14-02190	1981	B/w "Road Song," with Janie Fricke; from the movie "Take This Job and Shove It"
The Flying Lizards	Virgin VS 230 (UK)	1978	B/w "All Guitars"; described on the back of the pic sleeve as "petulant minimalism"
The Go Go's	RCA WLP-7-100	1965	7" stereo EP with "At The Beach" and "Peek-A-Boo Swimsuit"; b/w three songs by the Isley Brothers; titled "Wurlitzer Discotheque Music Selected by Arthur Murray Studios"
Johnny Goodison	Epic S EPC 4382 (UK)	1976	B/w "Wanting You"

The Greatest Memories Band	Jiwo ER/HH 1 (UK)	1988	Medley with "I Saw Her Standing There" and "Caroline"; b/w "Rock 'N' Roll Radio"; charity record to support Helping Hands
Alan Gregory	Arny's Shack AS 046 (UK)	1980	EP with "I Believe"/"Crying In My Heart"/ "It's Now Or Never"
Heinz	Roller Coaster RCEP-114 (UK)	1993	Tribute EP with "I Remember"/"Just Like Eddie"/"Tribute To Eddie"; all songs originally released on a Decca UK LP in 1964; Heinz is a former member of the Tornadoes, the British group famous for their 1962 hit "Telstar"
Levon Helm	Capitol 1A 006-86505 (Europe)	1982	B/w "Money"
Joan Jett & The Blackhearts	Boardwalk E4-8499 (Canada)	1982	7" small hole 33 1/3; one-sided single; PS says "New! Bonus Song"
Alan Jackson	Arista 12697-7	1994	B/w "Hole In The Wall"; on *Billboard's* country chart for 20 weeks, peaking at #1 for three weeks
Myron Lee	Garrett 4009	1964	B/w "Fat Man"; Minnesota label; reissued on Sleazy SR-189, see below
Myron Lee	Sleazy SR-189 (Spain)	2019	Reissue of Garrett 4009; b/w "Fat Man," likewise a reissue of Garrett 4009, and "Peter Rabbit," a reissue of M&L 1004 demo

The Legends	Capitol 5014	1963	B/w "Run To The Movies"; Milwaukee, WI, group; CB review: "It's an exciting session that the group pounds out with solid sales authority"; produced by Jim Economides
Larry Moore	Original Sound 30	1963	Same melody but different lyrics; titled "Hooray For Weekends"; credited to Cochran/Capehart; b/w "Two Young Lovers"
Jim Mundy	Hill Country HC-778	1977	On the *Billboard* country chart for eight weeks; b/w "Gilpen County Sidewalks"
Olivia Newton-John	EMI 2304 (UK)	1975	B/w "Follow Me"
The Nite People	Fontana TF 885 (UK)	1967	Instrumental version with one chant, "The boss said, no dice son, you gotta work late"; b/w "In The Springtime"
Outsiders	Knight K-104	1966	B/w "Set You Free This Time"; Tampa, FL, label
Phantoms	IRC 6937	1965	B/w "My Generation"
Pitmen	Earth 45-101	c. mid-60s	B/w "Susie Q," a cover of Dale Hawkins; Dallas, TX, label
Popcorn	A.D.R. P.R. 10383 (UK)	1983	Medley titled "Popcorn 1960's" with "Beautiful Sunday" and "Boney Maronie"; b/w "Alloah"/"Help Me Make It Through The Night"/"Unchained Melody"
The Princeton Five	Princeton 711	1964	B/w "Sure Know Alot About Love"; Michigan garage band

The Regents	Peoria 008	1966	B/w "You Don't Love Me"; garage band from California; Hollywood, CA, label
Dick Rivers	Pathe 77.810 (Canada)	1969	B/w "I Was Made To Love Her"
The Shandells	Studio City SC 1037	1965	B/w "Here Comes The Pain"; Minneapolis, MN, label; group from Eau Claire, WI
Johnny Shane	B.B.J. 100	1964	B/w "And Then You"; same artist as Johnny Angel who recorded on Liberty per *45cat*; see above for the Johnny Angel entry
Bruce Springsteen	XY 42	1985	August 1978 Cleveland concert; b/w "Sweet Little Sixteen"; unofficial
Spic and Span	Len 1013	1961	B/w "End Up With The Blues"; Philadelphia, PA, label; later became The Chartbusters who had the 1964 hit, "She's the One," on Mutual 502
Sweet Daddy Siki	Siki ST 103 (Canada)	1969	B/w "Bad, Bad Whiskey"
Swingin' Apolloes	White Cliffs 262	1967	One of four *Cash Box* "Newcomer Picks" on 7/15/64; b/w "Slow Down," a cover of Larry Williams; Atlanta, GA, garage band; formerly known as The Apolloes (see entries above)
Tino and The Revlons	Etc… [*sic*] ER-229	1963	B/w "Maybe Baby," a Buddy Holly cover

Tyrannosaurus Rex	Blue Thumb 7121	1970	B/w "Ride A White Swan"; lead singer is Marc Bolan; with the original release in the UK the group had shortened its name to T. Rex, but the US record label assumed it was just an abbreviation for their real name
T. Tex	Fly BUG 1 (UK)	1970	B/w "Ride A White Swan" and "Is It Love"
T. Rex	Stardust URC 1256 (Canada)	c. 1980s	B/w "Get It On (Bang A Gong)"
T. Rex	Fly Universal 1744372 (UK)	2007	A-side is "Ride A White Swan," with "Summertime Blues" and "Is It Love" as the B-side, which plays at 33 1/3 rpm as opposed to the A-side at 45 rpm
T. Rex	Easy Action EARS 129 (UK)	2017	RSD EP with two versions of "Summertime Blues" and two versions of Carl Perkins' "Honey Don't"
Tom and The Cats	Paula 242	1966	Garage version with great guitar break; b/w "Walkin' Man"; from Shreveport, LA
A Touch of Velvet	Velvet 1 (UK)	1980	B/w "Cry ('Cause Your Dreams Won't Come True)"
The Tropics	Columbia 4-44248	1967	Medley with "Land Of A Thousand Dances"; b/w "This Must Be The Place"; Florida group
The Velaires	Palms 730	1962	B/w "I Will"; Arizona label

The Vipers	Parlophone R 4484 (UK)	1958	B/w "Liverpool Blues"; British skiffle group that influenced The Beatles; released in October 1958; as one *45cat* commentator said, "… it's too darn slow … needs to have teenage energy"
The Young Chicagoans	Destination 636	1967	B/w "(Such A) Bad Boy"; Chicago garage band; Chicago label
Bobby Warren	Trucking 7461	1975	B/w "Motorcycle Mania"; Oklahoma label
Wellington Five	Quest QS-302	1966	B/w "Please Have Mercy"; Lynwood, WA, label
Joey Welz	Bold B1-304	c. 1990s	B/w "Shake, Rattle And Roll"; Welz was one of Bill Haley's Comets in the mid-60s
The Who	Decca 32708	1970	Peaked at #27 on *Billboard* pop chart; b/w "Heaven And Hell"
The Who	Tracker 2094 002 (UK)	1970	B/w "Heaven And Hell"
The Who	UK Polydor 0602527492803	2010	Bonus 45 included with the re-release of their *Live At Leeds* LP
The Who	Tracker 2094 002 (UK)	2015	B/w "Heaven And Hell"; disc 8 of box set of 15, titled "The Track Singles 1967-1973"

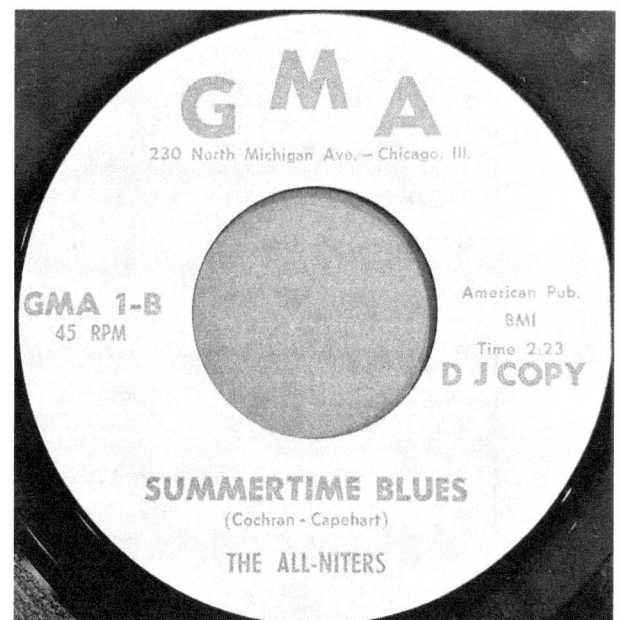 

Covers by The All-Niters (1964) and Tyrannosaurus Rex (AKA T. Rex) (1970)

"SUMMERTIME BLUES" IN THE MOVIES

Over the years, "Summertime Blues," as performed by Eddie Cochran, The Who, Blue Cheer, and others, can be heard in 21 movies, including:

MOVIE TITLE	YEAR	COMMENTS
Woodstock	1970	Performed by The Who
American Hot Wax	1978	Performed by Eddie Cochran; the film is the about Alan Freed, the DJ credited with coining the phrase "Rock 'n' Roll"; first film credit for Jay Leno who played Mookie

Caddyshack	1980	Performed by Eddie Cochran; golf comedy starring Chevy Chase and Rodney Dangerfield
Take This Job and Shove It	1981	Performed by Steve Davis; comedy
Running Brave	1983	IMDbPro does not list who performed the song; film is about a native American, Billy Mills, who won the 10,000 meter race in the 1964 Tokyo Olympics
Losin' It	1983	Performed by Eddie Cochran; teen sex comedy, starring Tom Cruise
Rockin' Road Trip	1985	Performed by The Cheryl Wilson Band
Meatballs III: Summer Job	1986	Performed by Eddie Cochran; romantic fantasy comedy
Troll	1986	Performed by Blue Cheer; horror movie
Born in East L.A.	1987	Performed by Cheech Marin, of Cheech & Chong fame; comedy about an American citizen mistaken as an illegal Mexican alien
La Bamba	1987	Performed by Brian Seltzer of the Stray Cats who portrayed Eddie Cochran in the movie; biopic about Ritchie Valens
Summertime Blues (Germany)	1988	Performed by Eddie Cochran; a German comedy
Night on Earth	1991	Starring Winona Ryder; performed by Blue Cheer; comedy, drama
This Boy's Life	1993	Starring Robert Di Nero, Leonard DiCaprio, and Ellen Barkin; performed by Eddie Cochran; movie about relationship between a rebelling teenager and his alcoholic father
Camp Nowhere	1994	Performed by Nathan Cavaleri; comedy adventure

The War	1994	Performed by Eddie Cochran; drama about an emotionally changed returning Vietnam veteran who tries to counsel his kids
Shake, Rattle and Roll: An American Love Story	1999	Performed by Gary Allan; TV mini-series, which won the Golden Reel Award for best sound editing for TV movies
Summer of Sam	1999	Performed by The Who; directed by Spike Lee and it is his take on the 1977 "Son of Sam" murders in NYC
Amazing Journey: The Story of The Who	2007	Performed by The Who; documentary about The Who
The Who Live in Texas '75	2012	Performed by The Who; Houston, TX, concert held on November 20, 1975, to promote their new LP, "The Who By The Numbers"
Summer Days, Summer Nights	2018	Performed by Eddie Cochran; drama about reconnecting with an old flame

DOCUMENTED CONCERT PERFORMANCES OF "SUMMERTIME BLUES"

As of May 1, 2024, *Setlist.fm* documented that "Summertime Blues" has been performed in concert 2,168 times by 195 different artists. In addition to Eddie Cochran, artists who have included it on their set lists on more than 30 occasions include The Who (381), The Beach Boys (294), Alan Jackson (127), Rush (87), John Entwistle (86), Bruce Springsteen (39), Patti Smith (36), and Blue Cheer (32). As recently as 2023 it was performed in concert 141 times.

HONORS AND ACCOLADES FOR "SUMMERTIME BLUES"

- Inducted into the Grammy Hall of Fame in 1999
- Chosen by the Rock & Roll Hall of Fame as one of the "500 Songs That Shaped Rock and Roll," an unranked list included songs from all eras
- Ranked #73 on the Rolling Stone's list of the "500 Greatest Songs of All Time"
- Ranked #118 on Joel Whitburn's *Honor Roll of Hits*
- Ranked #77 on the VH1 2004 list of the "100 Greatest Songs of Rock and Roll"
- Listed at #16 of *Billboard's* list of the top 100 Summer songs, noting that "[t]he most enduring legacy of 'Summertime Blues' is the number of artists who have covered it"

- Ranked #826 in Dave Marsh's 1989 book, *The Heart of Rock & Soul: The 1001 Greatest Singles Ever Made*
- Ranked #77 on *Q Magazine's* 2005 list of the "100 Greatest Guitar Tracks"

ALSO WORTH NOTING . . .

- The Who performed the song at the June 1967 Monterey Pop Festival. For the next 10 years it was a staple of their concerts.
- Marc Bolan of T. Rex has reverently spoken about carrying Cochran's guitar case after a 1960 English concert. As noted above, he recorded a cover of "Summertime Blues."
- "Draft Times Blues" on KG 100 by The Midnight Sons, a garage band from Vancouver, WA, is a reworking of "Summertime Blues" to focus on the Vietnam War draft, but it is not credited to Cochran/Capehart.
- The song was covered in French by Johnny Hallyday. His version, titled "La Fille De L'Eté Dernier," was released in 1975 and spent one week at #1 on the French singles chart.
- In 1948, blues singer Big Bill (AKA Big Bill Broonzy) recorded a 78 titled "Summertime Blues" b/w "Ramblin' Bill" on Columbia 38180; it's definitely not the same song, but its shufflin' beat, however, is reminiscent of Wilbert Harrison's "Kansas City."
- In a 2021 auction, a rather dirty 10-inch Gold Star Recording Studios acetate of "Summertime Blues" drew 45 bids and fetched $4,777.77.

ADDITIONAL SOURCES

Cochran, Bobby, with Susan Van Hecke, *Three Steps to Heaven: The Eddie Cochran Story* (Hal Leonard Corporation, 2003)

Collis, John, *Gene Vincent and Eddie Cochran: Rock 'N' Roll Revolutionaries* (Virgin Books Ltd., UK, 2004)

Kelly, Michael (AKA "Doc Rock"), *Liberty Records: A History of the Recording Company and Its Stars, 1955-71* (McFarland & Company Inc., 2014)

Mundy, Julie & Darrell Higham, *Don't Forget Me: The Eddie Cochran Story* (Mainstream Publishing, Great Britain, 2000), (*Billboard* Books, U.S., 2001)

Vintage Rock, *Eddie Cochran 1938-1960: A Celebration of an Icon* (Steve O'Brien, editor, Anthem Publishing, UK, 2020)

CHAPTER 19

"KANSAS CITY"

WILBERT HARRISON (MARCH 1959)

Original 1953 release by Little Willie Littlefield

4/25/53 *Cash Box* ad

Original 1959 releases by Wilbert Harrison on 45 and 78 without writer credits

"KANSAS CITY" — THE BASIC FACTS

Label: Fury 1023 (both 45 and 78)

Writers: Jerry Leiber and Mike Stoller

Date recorded: Early March 1959

Date released: Late March 1959

B-Side: "Listen, My Darling"

Producer: Bobby Robinson

Billboard charts:

Pop Chart
- Debut: 4/13/59
- Peak: #1 (2 weeks)
- Duration: 16 weeks

R&B Chart
- Debut: 4/20/59
- Peak: #1 (7 weeks)
- Duration: 15 weeks

THE SONG AND ITS IMPACT
Little Willie Littlefield's Original 1952 Version

"Kansas City" was among the first songs penned by Jerry Leiber and Mike Stoller when they were still teens living in Los Angeles. It was specifically written for Little Willie Littlefield, a West Coast R&B singer. It was recorded on August 18, 1952, with Little Willie on piano and Maxwell

Davis on tenor sax. As Mike Stoller commented, "Max's boogie woogie arrangement had a great groove, like a train heading for Kansas City."

Although "Kansas City" was the name given to the song by Leiber and Stoller, Ralph Bass, the head of Federal Records in Los Angeles, changed it to "K.C. Loving" based on his belief that it would relate better with African American record buyers as opposed to being a song named after a city. Since Federal had the publishing rights, Leiber/Stoller had no legal right to object. It was released in late December 1952 on Federal 12110, backed with "Pleading at Midnight," a Fats Domino-like blues song. *Billboard* in its January 3, 1953, review stated:'

> A real rocker is handled in good style by the warbler, while the ork comes thru with a
> solid beat. It's a good side and should grab some loot.

On January 17, 1953, *Cash Box* noted that Little Willie "sings a moderate rhythmic jump item with feeling," and gave it a "B" rating ("Very Good"). Despite these encouraging reviews, "K.C. Loving" failed to make any of the *Billboard* or *Cash Box* charts. It wasn't heard from again until 1959.

Author Larry Birnbaum in his book, *Before Elvis: The Prehistory of Rock 'N' Roll*, noted that although Wilbert Harrison's version was "plainly superior," "Littlefield's halfheartedly sung original, with its oddly popping backbeat and greasily suave Maxwell Davis tenor saxophone solo, has its own shuffling charm." And rock critic Dave Marsh observed: "It's a good journey jump blues, nothing more."

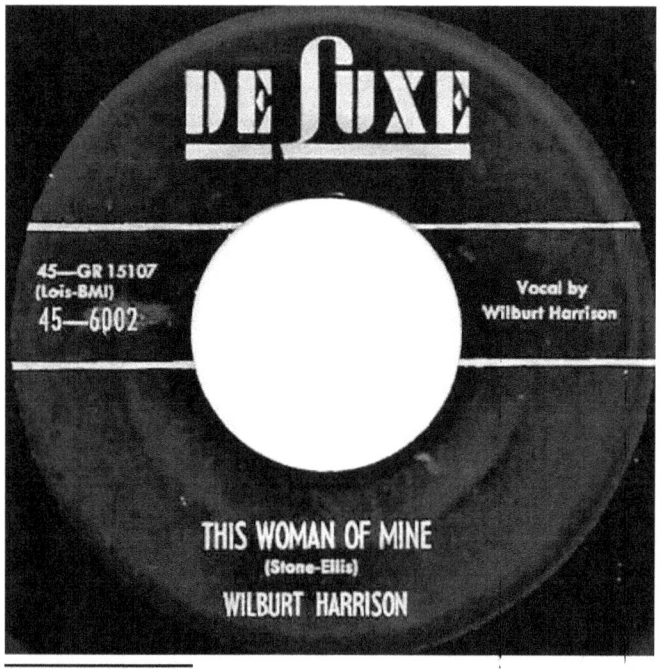

Wilbert Harrison's 1959 Mega Hit Version

But then along came Wilbert Harrison, to borrow a phrase from another Leiber/Stoller composition, "Along Came Jones." Harrison was a journeyman R&B artist who recorded at least nine different records released between 1953 and 1959 on the Rockin', DeLuxe, Savoy, Chart, and Glades labels, but none charted. But of particular interest considering subsequent events is Harrison's first release, "This Woman of Mine," which was released in 1953, first in July on Rockin' 526 and shortly thereafter on DeLuxe 6002 [Image: Barry Soltz],[94] albeit with Wilbert's first name misspelled. This song

---

94 In 1951 Syd Nathan, head honcho of King Records in Cincinnati, purchased the rights to the DeLuxe label and subsequently asked Miami record man Henry Stone to help him resuscitate the label. Thus, he reissued "This Woman of Mine," backed with "The Letter" on DeLuxe 6002. To appreciate the important relationship between Harrison's "This Woman of Mine" and his later recording of "Kansas City," listen to Harrison's "This Little Woman of Mine" on *YouTube*.

has essentially the same arrangement, melody, and shuffling beat of his 1959 version of "Kansas City." Although the melody, beat, and arrangement of this song bears a resemblance to Little Willie Littlefield's "K.C. Loving," it is credited to Stone and Ellis, with Stone presumably being Henry Stone, the Miami record man who first recorded and released "This Woman of Mine" on Rockin' 526.

Fast forward to 1959. After Herman Lubinsky, the head of Savoy Records turned down Harrison's request to record "Kansas City" because it was "too risqué," Harrison turned to Bobby Robinson, another noted record man who owned the Fury and Fire labels, among others. The record, which Harrison had performed to appreciative audiences for years, was recorded in just two takes in March 1959. While the first take used the same lyrics as Little Willie Littlefield's original version, the second take used somewhat altered lyrics that Robinson liked better. This latter take followed the arrangement and distinctive shuffling beat of "This Woman of Mine." In addition, there was one noteworthy change in the lyrics:

Original Leiber & Stoller lyrics	"They got a crazy way of lovin' there, and I'm gonna get me some"
Revised Harrison Lyrics	"They've got some crazy little women there and I'm gonna get me one"

Thus, Harrison's version went from getting some "lovin" to getting "me one," i.e., a woman. The session musicians included Wild Jimmy Spruill, who provided an inspired guitar break.

Harrison recorded "Kansas City" in March 1959, and it was released later that month. It was a *Billboard* "Spotlight Pick" on March 30, 1959. In its review of Harrison's version, as well as those by Rocky Olson on Chess 1723, Little Willie Littlefield on Federal 12351,[95] Rockin' Ronald and the Rebels on End 1043, and Hank Ballard & the Midnighters on King 5195, *Billboard* noted that the song "is a finger-snappin' blues with a highly contagious sound." Harrison's version debuted on *Billboard's* "Hot 100" chart on April 13, 1959, and hit #1 on May 18, 1959. It debuted on *Billboard's* R&B chart on April 20, 1959, and hit #1 on May 11, 1959. Altogether it was on the *Billboard's* Hot 100 and R&B charts for 16 weeks and 15 weeks, respectively. In addition to Harrison, the covers by Little Richard, Hank Ballard, and Rocky Olson made the lower reaches of *Billboard's* "Hot 100" chart, which is documented below in the chart of contemporaneous major label covers.

The initial release on both 45 and 78, as shown on the above label photos, did not have a writer credit. When King Curtis, who was present, but did not participate in the session when "Kansas City" was recorded, told Jerry Leiber and Mike Stoller that they had a hit, they were dumbfounded. They quickly made sure that all subsequent pressings carried their names as the writers of the song.

---

95 This was a reissue of the same track as his original version but with the name changed from "K.C. Loving" to "Kansas City," but backed with a new B-side, "The Midnight Hour Was Shining."

Although Harrison changed some of their original lyrics, Mike Stoller said that "in the history of the blues, messing around with the lyrics was common, so we let it go."

Harrison's version was released in the UK on Top Rank JAR 132 in May 1959, but it did not make the UK charts. Of the other contemporaneous cover versions released in the U.S., only the covers by Hank Ballard & the Midnighters and Little Richard were released in the UK, on Parlophone 45-R 4558 and London HLU-8868, respectively. Little Richard's version of "Kansas City" was the only UK release to make the UK charts, where it remained for five weeks in late 1959, peaking at #26.[96] As discussed in detail below, it was Little Richard's version that The Beatles later covered.

As soon as "Kansas City" began to get traction in New York, Savoy Records sued the Fury label claiming that Wilbert Harrison was still under contract with Savoy. The lawsuit sought to enjoin Fury from using Harrison's services and issuing records recorded by him while he was still under contract with Savoy. Although it was ultimately settled in Fury's favor, Fury opted to not release any further records by Harrison until his alleged contract with Savoy expired in August 1959. Thereafter, playing off the success of "Kansas City," and perhaps trying to catch lightning in a bottle once again, Harrison recorded two other KC-themed songs. The first was "Good Bye Kansas City" on Fury 1028 that was released in January 1960. Although it mimicked many of the elements of "Kansas City," including very good guitar work by Wild Jimmy Spruill, it only reached #102 on *Billboard's* "Bubbling Under" chart. The second was "Kansas City Twist" on Fury 1059 that was released in December 1961, but it failed to chart.

Wild Jimmy Spruill, whose superb guitar work contributed so much to "Kansas City," likewise tried to cash in on its success by issuing "Kansas City March" in late 1959 on Fire 1006, a Fury sister label. *Cash Box* issued a strong review, noting it was an "instrumental version" of Harrison's hit "carved out with hard rock, big beat march authority by Spruill's pro combo." It is more accurate to describe it as an instrumental variation in the manner of "Kansas City." It did not chart, however.

Over the years, three subsequent versions of "Kansas City" made the *Billboard* charts. Two were released in 1964. The first was by Fats Domino on ABC-Paramount 10596, which barely dented the *Billboard* "Hot 100" at #99. Trini Lopez's cover on Reprise 20,236 was the second and it did much better, rising to #23 during its 10-week stint on the *Billboard* "Hot 100" chart. Three years later James Brown's cover on King 6086 reached #21 on the *Billboard* R&B chart and #55 on its "Hot 100" chart.

In his take on "Kansas City," author Dave Marsh concluded: "In the critical history of rock and roll, Wilbert Harrison's place of honor is permanent and assured, as (it should go without saying) is Leiber and Stoller's."

Although it never charted in either the U.S. or the UK, the story behind the version by The Beatles is interesting. According to author Mark Lewisohn, it was Paul McCartney who first heard Little Richard's version of "Kansas City," which Paul revered. At that time Paul was unaware of Wilbert Harrison's version. Given this background, it is not surprising that the version of "Kansas City" sung

---

96 Little Richard's "Kansas City" was released in Germany on London DL 20 195 in April 1958, backed with "By the Light of the Silvery Moon." Harrison's version was released in Germany in 1959 on Top Rank 75 009A.

by The Beatles was based on Little Richard's version. As author Barry Miles recounts in his book, *Paul McCartney: Many Years From Now*:

The Beatles saw Little Richard perform the medley in concert and adopted it for their own set in 1962. They performed twice with him in England in October that year and became friends with him during a two-week stint at Hamburg's Star Club in November.

In addition to performing "Kansas City" during their days at the Star Club, they also played it during their first TV appearance in England on August 22, 1962, at Liverpool's Cavern Club. And, in the period 1963-1964, the BBC recorded "Kansas City" by The Beatles for later radio broadcast on three different dates. Then, they sang "Kansas City" at their September 17, 1964, Kansas City, Missouri, concert to a wildly appreciative audience. A month later when they were back in England, with George Martin producing, they laid down the track, with Paul doing the lead vocals.[97] As author Barry Miles quotes McCartney:

I could do Little Richard's voice, which is a wild, hoarse, screaming thing; it's like an out-of-body experience. You have to leave your current sensibilities and go about a foot above your head to sing it. You have to actually go outside yourself. It's a funny little trick and when you find it, it's very interesting.

"Kansas City" made its initial appearance on their UK LP, *Beatles for Sale,* in December 1964 and six months later in June 1965, on their U.S. LP, *Beatles VI.* On October 11, 1965, it was released as a 45 on Capitol Star Line 6066, as the B-side to "Boys." *Billboard,* in its October 23, 1965 "Top 20 Pop Spotlight" review, noted that it was "[f]inally released [as a single] by popular demand from an early LP." Although the Capitol Star Line label was customarily used for reissues, this was the first U.S. release of the single. It was not until its release on Collectables 1507 that the title was changed to "Kansas City/Hey-Hey-Hey," but the writer credits were only given to Leiber and Stoller on these releases, The Beatles were covering Little Richard's version, not Wilbert Harrison's version.

---

97 "Kansas City" was the first song on McCartney's so-called 1987 "Russian Album," *Choba B CCCP,* which was released in Canada in 1991 as a vinyl LP on Capitol C2 97615.

Since The Beatles' version was directly based on Little Richard's cover, it is worth reviewing Little Richard's version in greater detail. After he left Specialty for the ministry, the label cobbled together an LP of tracks that Little Richard had recorded earlier, including his 1955 version of "Kansas City." This LP, titled *The Fabulous Little Richard*, was released in the UK in 1958 on London HA-U 2193 and in the U.S. in March 1959, on Specialty 2104. Shortly thereafter, the single was released in the U.S. on Specialty 664 in April 1959, and in the UK on London HLU 8868 in May 1959, to compete with Harrison's version on Fury. As the following comparison demonstrates, however, Little Richard's version is vastly different than Wilbert Harrison's version, although Leiber and Stoller were still assigned writers' credit:

Harrison's version	Little Richard's version
I'm going to Kansas City / Kansas City, here I come / I'm going to Kansas City / Kansas City, here I come / They got some crazy / Little women there / And I'm gonna get me one /	Goin' to Kansas City / Gonna get my baby one time, hey, hey / Yes, Kansas City, gonna get my baby one time, hey, hey / It's just a 1, 2, 3, 4, 5, 6, 7, 8, 9 / Yes, Kansas City / Gonna bring my baby back home, yea, hey / Kansas City, gonna bring my baby back home, hey, hey / A long, long time since my baby been gone

In his version, following the above quoted opening verses, Little Richard launched into the chorus of "Hey-Hey-Hey-Hey," a song he penned that had been released on Specialty 624 as the B-side to his hit "Good Golly Miss Molly." Harrison's version and Little Richard's version are as different as night and day. Yes, they both mention going to Kansas City, but the reason for going is entirely different. As initially issued on Specialty 664, the title was listed as "Kansas City" and only credited to Leiber-Stoller. Although this version of "Kansas City" included a major portion of "Hey, Hey, Hey, Hey," it is not referenced on the label. Subsequently, Specialty 664 was reissued with the title changed to "Kansas City/Hey-Hey-Hey-Hey (A Medley)" and with writers' credit being given to both Leiber-Stoller and R. Penniman, Little Richard's real name. As shown below, the label also referenced that it was "From the Specialty LP 'The Fabulous Little Richard.'"

In addition to The Beatles, other well-known artists who have released 45s of "Kansas City" include The Everly Brothers, Fabian, Bill Haley, George Jones and Johnny Paycheck (duet), Brenda Lee, Peggy Lee, and Clyde McPhatter. In their 2009 autobiography, *Hound Dog*, Mike Stoller commented that "'Kansas City' became one of our most recorded tunes, with more than 300 versions out there."

Among the honors accorded to Harrison's "Kansas City" are its induction into the Grammy Hall of Fame and its inclusion on the RIAA/NEA list of the top 365 songs of the 20th century.

Specialty 664 as originally released

Specialty 664 as later reissued

CONTEMPORANEOUS COVER VERSIONS OF "KANSAS CITY"

By 1959, contemporaneous covers were becoming uncommon, but "Kansas City" is clearly an exception. As mentioned above, three of these covers charted, perhaps the last time this has happened.

ARTIST	LABEL	COMMENTS
Hank Ballard	King 5195	Peaked at #70 on *Billboard's* pop chart and at #16 on its R&B chart; b/w "I'll Keep You Happy"
Hank Ballard	Regency R-789X (Canada)	B/w "I'll Keep You Happy"
Hank Ballard	Parlophone 45-R 4558 (UK)	B/w "The Twist," the original version before Chubby Checker's cover version became a mega hit
Little Richard	Specialty 664	On *Billboard's* pop chart for 7 weeks, peaking at #95; b/w "Lonesome And Blue"
Little Richard	London 45-HL-U-8868 (UK)	B/w "She Knows How To Rock"
Rocky Olson	Chess 1723	On *Billboard's* pop chart for 4 weeks, peaking at #60; b/w "Jet Tone Boogie" by the Jet Tones

Rockin' Ronald and the Rebels	Orchid 5005	B/w "Cuttin' Out"; the Orchid the master was purchased by End released on End 1043
Rockin' Ronald and The Rebels	End 1043 Quality K1876 (Canada)	B/w "Cuttin' Out"; although many have believed that Rockin' Ronald was Ronnie Hawkins, he has adamantly denied it was him
Little Willie Littlefield	Federal 12351	A re-release of his original 1953 version, but with the title changed from "K.C. Loving" to "Kansas City"; b/w the same B-side, "The Midnight Hour Was Shining"
Johnny Duncan and The Blue Grass Boys	Columbia 45-DB 4311 (UK)	B-side listed as "That's All Right Honey" on some releases and as "That's All Right Darling" on others

'Kansas City' Newest Trade Hit Threat

NEW YORK — The singles record business, always a hot box of excitement, created some new frenzy this week for the second week in a row, with another hot record, and many new hot covers. Last week the industry was simmering over "Tell Him No"; this week the noise is over "Kansas City," an old-fashioned rhythm and blues rocker which looks like it has a chance for hit status.

The original record was cut by Bobby Robinson, vet New York record and music man, on the (Continued on page 45)

'Kansas City'
● Continued from page 3

Fury label with warbler Wilbert Harrison. After the record started to get action Robinson was and still is being approached by a number of record firms anxious to buy the master. Meanwhile, the covers started to come in. Deejay Joe Finan of KYW, Cleveland, cut a record of the tune with Rocky Olson and sold it to Chess Records. Bill Buchanan cut the tune with Rockin' Ronald and the Rebels and sold it to End Records. Meanwhile, King Records cut two versions of the tune, one on the King label with Hank Ballard and the Midnighters, and another on the Federal label with Little Willie Littleford. The battle and the noise is on!

Billboard, **March 30, 1959**

Hank Ballard cover

Rocky Olson cover

Rockin' Ronald cover

CONTEMPORANEOUS BUDGET LABEL COVERS OF "KANSAS CITY"

ARTIST	LABEL	COMMENTS
Al Christi and The Coasters	A Coast to Coast Parade of Hit Records 1280	B/w "Since I Don't Have You"
Al Christi	Big Buy 250	EP with , "Kookie, Kookie (Lend Me Your Comb)"/"A Teenager In Love"/"Since I Don't Have You"
Buddy Durham	Emperor EM-H-4-59	EP with "Pink Shoe Laces"/"Battle Of New Orleans"/"A Fool Such As I"/"Guitar Boogie Shuffle"/"White Lightning"
John Garrison	Prom 113	B/w "Endlessly" by Dick Stetson
John Garrison	Promenade A-55-8	Double EP titled "Hits A' Poppin" with 11 other hits of the day by various artists
Johnny Newton & The Tags	Bell 113	B/w "Kookie, Kookie (Lend Me Your Comb)"
Johnny Newton & The Tags	Gala 45XP 1054 (UK)	EP titled "America's Top Pops" with "Tallahassee Lassie"/"Sorry (I Ran All The Way Home)"/"A Teenager In Love"

Tommy Paris	Tops 45-S24	EP with "Pink Shoe Laces"/"Tell Him No"/"Tiajuana Jail"/"Come Softly To Me"/"Sorry, I Ran All The Way Home"
Tommy Paris	Tops 45-S26	EP with "The Happy Organ"/"Goodbye, Jimmy, Goodbye"/"Tallahassee Lassie"/"Sorry, I Ran All The Way Home"/"A Teenager In Love"
Jerry Rood	Top Hit Tunes TH-31-3	Six song EP with "With My Eyes Wide Open I'm Dreaming"/"I'll Never Smile Again"/"A Teenager In Love"/"I Cried For You"/"Kookie, Kookie (Lend Me Your Comb)"; Waldorf Record Corp.

Budget label cover by Johnny Newton

Budget label cover by John Garrison

LATER RELEASES OF "KANSAS CITY" BY WILBERT HARRISON

The sheer number of later releases by Wilbert Harrison of "Kansas City" on multiple labels probably takes top honors in this category, if there were such a record collecting category.

LABEL	YEAR	COMMENTS
Barrel 604 (Canada)	1959	B/w "Listen, My Darling"; "By Arrangement Fury Records"

Barry BAGT-566X (Canada)	1960s???	"By Arr. With Vee Jay International U.S. A."; b/w "Ya Ya" by Lee Dorsey
Oldies 45 OL 11	1963	B/w "Ya Ya" by Lee Dorsey
Roulette GG-48	1960s ???	B/w "Red's Dream" by Louisiana Red; "Golden Goodies Hit Series"
Lost-Nite 365	Late 1960s???	B/w "Listen, My Darling"
Eric 161	1969	B/w "Listen, My Darling"
Trip 21	1969 or 1970	Incorrectly listed as by Wilbur Harrison; b/w "Ya Ya" by Lee Dorsey
Goldies 45 D-2424	1973	B/w "Listen, My Darling"; distributed by ABC/Dunhill Records
Barry 566	???	B/w "Listen, My Darling"; manufactured by Quality Records "By Arr. With Vee Jay International, U. S. A."
Pop Classics 1076 (Canada)	1974	B/w "I'm Sticking With You" by Jimmy Bowen; distributed by Polydor; licensed by Roulette Records
MCA D-2524	1978	MCA release on brown and white label; later MCA releases were on the blue rainbow label; b/w "Listen, My Darling"
Quality GC 343X (Canada)	1982	B/w "Let's Work Together"; "Quality Gold Collection"
Collectables COL 1625	1980s???	B/w "Listen, My Darling"
Original Oldies, Volume 4 (UK)	1984	33 1/3 EP with "Desiree"/"La Bamba"/"Cherry Pie"/ "Stagger Lee"/"Twilight Time"
Ripete R45-141	1984	B/w "Leader Of The Pack" by the Shangrilas

| Ripete R45-256 | 1990 | B/w "Ain't Got No Home" by Clarence "Frogman" Henry |
| House of Sounds 101 | ??? | B/w "Ya Ya" by Lee Dorsey; bootleg??? |

Reissue on Oldies 45 OL 11

Reissue on Eric 161

SUBSEQUENT COVER VERSIONS OF "KANSAS CITY"

ARTIST	LABEL	YEAR	COMMENTS
92 Blues	Rinx 45-514	???	Played by Johnny Neill; incorrectly credited to Harrison; b/w "Nightmare" played by Fred Bergin; label noted for releasing organ music for skating rinks
A-Jaes	Oak RGJ 132 (UK)	1964	B/w "I'm Leaving You"
Ray Anthony	Ranwood RLP-8033	1968	7-inch stereo EP with "Tuff" / "Are You Sincere" / "Creole Love Call" / "Soul Serenade" / "Rainin' In My Heart"; produced by Randy Woods and arranged by Bill Justis

Lynn August	Maison de Soul	1988	B/w "Whatever Boils Your Crawfish"
Hank Ballard	King EP-451	1959	EP with "I'll Keep You Happy" / "Tore Up Over You" / "In The Doorway Crying"
Hank Ballard	King KG 522	1977	B/w "Sexy Ways"; reissues
Hank Ballard	King 45-15025	???	B/w "Sexy Ways"; "Old Gold Series"
Hank Ballard	Gusto GT4-2103	1979	B/w "Sexy Ways"
Hank Ballard	Collectables COL 3607	1988	B/w "Sexy Ways"; "Back to Back Hit Series"
Bandit	Alibi YJ-100	???	B/w "If You Can Stand It"; Memphis, TN, label
The Beatles	Capitol 6066	1965	B/w "Boys"; "Star Line" series; George Martin plays piano on this track
The Beatles	Collectables 1507	1982	Titled "Kansas City / Hey Hey Hey"; B/w "Ain't Nothin' Shakin' (But The Leaves On The Tree)"
The Beatles	Baktobak 1001, Stab 2015 (UK)	1988	Titled "Kansas City / Hey Hey Hey Hey"; live recording from December 31, 1962, Hamburg, Germany's Star Club; B/w "Till There Was You"; boxset of 15 45s labeled Stab 2001 through Stab 2015
The Beatles	1960's REP 044 (UK)	2021	Two versions, one by Paul with John and George and one by Paul alone; EP with "I'm Loser" / "Boys" / "Old Folks At Home"; "Shindig October 1964"; unofficial
The Beatles	1960's REP 053 (UK)	2023	EP with seven other songs; 1964 recordings; unofficial

The Beatles	1960's REP 054 (UK)	2024	EP with seven other songs; 1964 recordings; unofficial
Peter Best	Cameo 391	1965	Drummer for The Beatles before Ringo Starr; B/w "Boys"; the same pairing as The Beatles 1965 release on Capitol 6066; Beatle lyrics with "Hey Hey Hey Hey"
Bi-Du's	Bi-Du's at Caberfae Lodge ZTEC-125720	Late 60s	B/w "That Sunday"; ZTEC-125719; probably a lounge act that performed at the Caberfae Lodge, a ski resort in Cadillac, MI
Big Mama Jo	M.C.I. 1010	1976	Natchitoches, LA, label; B/w "Who's [*sic*] Lips Do You Want To Kiss"
Black Hollow Ramblers and Sharon	Bonny 201	1971	B/w "(Don't Ever Become A) Truck Driver's Wife"; Tonica, IL, label
Sterling Blythe	Door Knob DK 84-21	1984	B/w "You're Not Going To Hurt Me Again"
David Bromberg	Play Back AS 64 [Columbia]	1973	7-inch stereo 33 1 / 3 record; B/w "Watch Yourself" by Michael Fennelly, "Love Has No Pride" by Florence Warner, and "Who Ever Told You" by Chi Coltrane
James Brown	King 6086	1967	Peaked at #55 on the *Billboard* "Hot 100" chart; B/w "Stone Fox"
James Brown	Delta D-3232 (Canada)	1967	B/w "Stone Fox"
Butts Band	Blue Thumb 252	1974	B/w "I Won't Be Alone Anymore"
Freddy Cannon	Top Rank JKP 2058 (UK)	1960	EP with "Indiana" / "California, Here I Come" / "Carolina In The Morning"

Bennie Carew	Fenton 2022	1966	B/w "Bye Bye Blackbird"; Michigan label
Eldon Carl (West's Fastest Gun)	Ring 73062	1973	B/w "Couldn't Hurt Any Worse"; El Cajon, CA, label
Cash & Mommie Cotton	Summit 153	c. early 70's	B/w "God Gave Me A Heart"; Concord, AK, label; lounge act duo
Chisolm Gang	Harlem 118	1961	Incorrectly credited to Harrison rather than Leiber-Stoller; B/w "Anita"; San Antonio, TX, label
Riff Corio	Twin Hits 5043	1963	B/w "Forget Him"
Danny and The Zeltones	Bigtop 45-3074	1961	B/w "Steel Guitar Rag"
Fats Domino	ABC-Para. 10596	1964	Hit #99 on *Billboard's* "Hot 100" chart; B/w "Heartbreak Hill"
Fats Domino	ABCS 510	1965	7-inch 33 1 / 3 stereo EP with "Heartbreak Hill" / "Wigs" / "When My Dream Boat Comes Home" / "Ballin' The Jack" / "The Girl I Gonna Marry"
Jim Easter & The Artistics	Cha Cha C-721	1962	Same song but erroneously titled "Kansas City 'Oklahoma'" and incorrectly credited to Hammerstein / Rodgers; Chicago garage version; B/w "Stroll And Boogie"
The Everly Brothers	Warner Brothers WEP-609 (UK)	1964	B/w "Hound Dog" / "I'm Gonna Move To The Outskirts Of Town" / "Lonely Weekends"
Fabian	Chancellor 1086	1961	B/w "Tongue-Tied"

Curley Fields and The Kentuckians	Top Gun 6811	1968	B/w "Trouble, Sweet Trouble"
Freddie and The Dreamers	Columbia SEG 8323 (UK)	1964	EP with "I'm A Hog For You" / "Over You" / "Come Back When You're Ready"
Georgia Gibbs	Epic 70659	1073	B/w "I Will Follow You"; special edition 7-inch 33 1 / 3 release
Bill Haley and The Comets	Warner Brothers WEP 6001 (UK)	1960	B/w "Crazy Man Crazy" / "Stagger Lee" / "I'm In Love Again"
Bill Haley and The Comets	Warner Brothers WEP 6136 (UK)	1964	B/w "Rock Around The Clock" / "Shake, Rattle And Roll" / "Love Letters In The Sand"
Bill Haley and The Comets	Scoop 33 (UK)	1983	EP with "Shake, Rattle And Roll" / "Rip It Up" / "Rock Around The Clock" / "Whole Lotta Shakin' Goin' On" / "Me And Bobby McGee"
Wayne Hancock	Corduroy 109 (Australia)	2002	B/w "Nearly Lose Your Mind"; from Wayne's 2002 Australia Tour; recorded live on March 25, 2002
Rikki Henderson	Embassy 45-WB 339 (UK)	1959	B/w "The Heart Of A Man"
Herman's Hermits	Columbia DO-4736 (Australia)	1966	B/w "Dandy"; produced by Mickie Most
Adolph Hofner	Sarg 249	1975	Vocal by Dave Mazoch, with Cecil Moore on guitar; B/w "Fast Women, Slow Horses And Wine" with vocal by Jimmy Tutt; Texas label
Hothouse Flowers	London 269 (UK)	1990	B/w "I Can See Clearly Now," a cover of Johnny Nash

Eddy Howard Orchestra with Norman Lee	Marian U-51079 / 80	c. 1960s	B/w "Hot Pants Polka"; Wichita, KA, label; Eddy Howard was a big band leader who was popular in the post WWII era
Eddie Howell with The Bob Paris Combo	Zodiac Z45-1014 (New Zealand)	1959	B/w "Big Girl"
Peter Jay and The Jaywalkers	Decca F 11757 (UK)	1963	Original Leiber / Stoller lyrics with "Hey, Hey, Hey" added; B/w "The Parade Of Tin Soldiers"
Jack Jolly	Music Town Records MTR 209	c. late '60s???	B/w "Amnesia" (MTR 210)
George Jones and Johnny Paycheck	Epic 9-50891	1980	B/w "When You're Ugly Like Us (You Just Naturally Got To Be Cool)"; produced by Billy Sherrill
Bob Kames	King 6186	1962	Instrumental version; B/w "It's A Small World," likewise an instrumental
Jim King and His Cosden Cowboys	Starlite 1010-71-05	1971	Country version; B/w "Don't Let Me Cross Over"
King, Mel, with The Elites	MK 743	1970s???	Country version; B/w "Today I Started Loving You Again"; King was one of Buck Owens' many drummers
Carl "Little Rev" Lattimore	Capitol 4715	1962	B/w "Carl's Dance Party"; produced by Nick Venet
Brenda Lee	Decca 32330	1968	B/w "Each Day Is A Rainbow"
Brenda Lee	Decca ED 2704	1961	EP with "Lover Come Back To Me" / "All The Way" / "On The Sunny Side Of The Street"

Peggy Lee	Capitol XE-1671	Early 1960s	B/w "Basin Street Blues"; 7-inch 33 1 / 3 stereo record; "Capitol 33 Compact"
Little Jesse Jr. and His Teardrops	Metra-Dome 1002	1971	B/w "Giving Up On Love"
Trini Lopez	Reprise R20,236 (UK)	1963	B/w "Lonesome Traveler"
Trini Lopez	Reprise 20,236	1964	B/w "Lonesome Traveler"; peaked at #23 on the *Billboard* pop chart
Trini Lopez	Warner Brothers ZTEP 124178	1967	EP with "A-ME-RI-C-A" / "If I Had A Hammer" / "The Blizzard Song"; Coca Cola Fresca promotional record
Trini Lopez	Reprise 0725	1968	B/w "La Bamba"; "Back to Back Hits"
Dale Magee	K-Ark 1067	1971	Erroneously credited to Wilbert Harrison, not Leiber-Stoller; B/w "Green Back Dollar"
Johnny Mastrio	Frankie FR-18	1963	B/w "Roman Guitar"; Hartford, CN, lounge singer
Leon McAuliff	ABCS 394-3	1961	One of a set of five 7-inch 33 1 / 3 stereo records made for jukeboxes; B/w "Hoodle Addle"; McAuliff was a long-time member of Bob Wills' Texas Playboys
Ron McFarlin	Slim-Slo-Slider 3S-1	1980s	B/w "Big Money Blues"; Delta Nos. 94147 & 94147-X
Claude McLin Combo	Allegro 1462	1961	B/w "The Growler"; incorrectly credited to Wilbert Harrison and not Leiber-Stoller
Barbara McNair	Signature 12049	1970	B/w "Love Talk"

Clyde McPhatter	Mercury MEP-80	1960	EP with "C.C. Rider," "The Clock," and "Fever"
Memphis Slim	Collector Records Jen 5 (UK)	1960	EP titled "Memphis Slim Goes To Kansas City"; B/w " Slow And Easy" and "Sad And Lonesome"
Marilyn Michaels	ABC 11043	1968	Decent bluesy version; B/w "Show Me (From 'My Fair Lady')"; produced by Bob Thiele
Mixed Company	Catamount 121	c. 1979-early 80s	Acapella version; B/w "Yes, I'm Ready"; Jersey City, NJ, label
The Nashville All Stars	Royal American 63	1972	B/w "Big Boss Man"; instrumentals
Bobby Paris	Capitol 5929	1967	B/w "I Walked Away," which is a rare northern soul song that regularly fetches + / - $500 per *Popsike.com*
Graham Parker and Rumor	Phonogram GPS 1 (UK)	1976	Produced by Nick Lowe; free single "From the Bootleg Album"; B/w "Silly Thing"
Jack Parnell	HMV POP 630 (UK)	1959	Original Leiber / Stoller lyrics; good version; small-hole 45; B/w "The Golden Striker"
Gary Paxton	Felsted 8691	1963	Instrumental version; B/w "Sweet Senorita From Santa Fe"
Johnny "Blueboy" Perry & The Soul Rockers	Adell 610	1969	B/w "Corn Bread"
Cheryl Poole	Paula 1282	1970	B/w "With You"

Lou Rawls	Capitol SU-1824 and Capitol SXA-1824	1963	7-inch stereo jukebox EP with "Roll'em Pete" / "Everyday I Have The Blues" / "Strange Fruit" / "(What Did I Do To Be So) Black And Blue" / "How Long, How Long Blues"
Billy Lee Riley	Mercury SR-645-C	1964	7-inch Compact 6 Stereo EP with "Cottonfields" / "Memphis" / "High-Heel Sneakers" / "You Got Me Runnin'" / "You Can't Judge A Book By The Cover"
Johnny Robinson	Epic 5-10578	1969	B/w "God Is Love"; produced by Willie Mitchell
Glenn Russell	Rolling Recording Studio 12248	1980	EP with "Endless Sleep" / "My Way" / "Ghost Riders In The Sky"; Carpentersville, IL, label; "Recorded live at Gerardo's"
The Sanshers	Kweek ZTSC 96832 / 3	1964	B/w "Gonna Git That Man"; garage version with female lead
Tiger Joanne Scott	Light In The Attic 45-036	2016	B/w "Baby I Need Your Lovin'"; both songs recorded in 1964 when she was 14, but previously unreleased; RSD record; AKA Joan Kaplan, the cult star of AMC's *Small Town Security*
Ron Shaw	Pacific Challenger 1634	1979	B/w "I'll Cry Instead," a Beatles cover, which made the lower reaches of the *Billboard* country chart; Cerritos, CA, label
Shewry Stamper and the Virginians	Page 507	1962	Raw female RAB with wild guitar break; Johnstown, PA, label; B/w "I'm Leaving"
Warren Storm	Zynn 1019	1962	B/w "Blues Stop Knocking (At My Door)"

Hayden Thompson	Spade EP-105 (UK)	1971	B/w "I'm Left You're Right She's Gone" / "Mystery Train" / "That's Alright Mama"
Tommy Wills	Juke 2025	1973	soul / funk; B/w "K.C. Drive"
Bill Woodly	Nashville Imitators 1971-2	1971	Country version; B/w "Help Me Make It Through The Night" by John Stiver; Orwigsburg, PA, label
None Listed	Statler 517	???	B/w "Mobile"; instrumental educational dance record
None listed	Seeburg DN-310-B	1965	Six song juke box EP with "Susie Q" / "Shake Him Loose Baby" / "The Twist" / "I'm Walkin'" / "Wait Till My Bobby Gets Home"

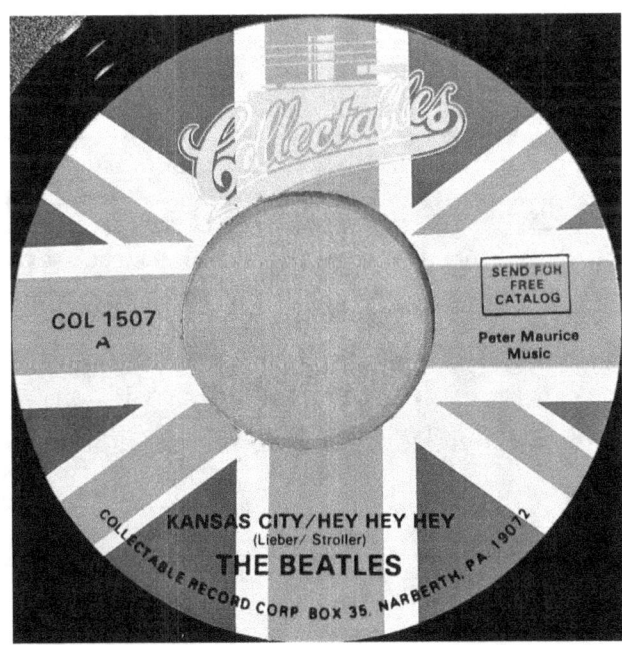

"KANSAS CITY" IN THE MOVIES

Despite its tremendous popularity, Wilbert Harrison's hit version of "Kansas City," as best as can be determined, has never appeared on a motion picture soundtrack. However, a Wilbert Harrison song that he penned, "Let's Work Together," can be heard in at least three movies, including *Forrest Gump* (1994), *Big Fish* (2003), and *Invincible* (2006). However, in each instance the song was performed by Canned Heat, not Wilbert Harrison. Harrison's original single was released on Sue 11 (1969), his only other top 40 charted record.

"Kansas City" has appeared on the soundtracks of a few movies, albeit not sung by Wilbert Harrison:

MOVIE TITLE	YEAR	COMMENTS
DysFunktional Family	2003	Performed by James Brown; documentary about comedian Eddie Griffin
The Wrecking Crew!	2008	Performed by Conrad Janis; movie is about the famous studio musicians (i.e., Hal Blaine, Earl Palmer, *et al*) who provided the instrumental tracks for literally dozens and dozens of hits
The Music Never Stopped	2011	Performed by Count Basie; drama about a father and an estranged son who eventually connect via music
Mr. Dynamite: The Rise of James Brown	2014	Performed by James Brown; HBO movie about Brown's career

DOCUMENTED CONCERT PERFORMANCES OF "KANSAS CITY"

As of May 1, 2024, *Setlist.fm* documents that "Kansas City" has been performed in concert 357 times by 118 different artists. In addition to Wilbert Harrison and The Beatles (12), artists that have included "Kansas City" on their set lists more than five times include Muddy Waters (37), Albert King (26), Leon Russell (19), Van Morrison (12), James Brown (11), and Willie Nelson (6).

HONORS AND ACCOLADES FOR "KANSAS CITY"

- Inducted into the Grammy Hall of Fame in 2001
- Ranked #236 on the RIAA/NEA list of the top 365 songs of the 20th century
- Included on *Rolling Stone*'s 2004 list of "The 500 Greatest Songs of All Time"
- Chosen by the Rock & Roll Hall of Fame as one of the "500 Songs That Shaped Rock and Roll," an unranked list
- Ranked #181 in Dave Marsh's 1989 book, *The Heart of Rock & Soul: The 1001 Greatest Singles Ever Made*

ALSO WORTH NOTING …

- "Kansas City" was among the last #1 records to be released as a 78.
- Little Willie Littlefield answered his original version with "Miss K.C. Is Fine" on Federal 12148, a song that Little Willie penned about a chick who "had a crazy way of loving." who he met "while standing on the corner of 12th and Vine." Like his original, it failed to chart.
- "Kansas City" is the official song of Kansas City, Missouri.
- Both the versions by Wilbert Harrison and The Beatles are frequently played at Kansas City Royals baseball games.
- Marva Whitney performed "Kansas City" at the conclusion of James Brown's funeral, something that he had requested shortly before he died in 2006.

ADDITIONAL SOURCES

The Beatle Bible, at www.beatlebible.com/songs/kansas-city-hey-hey-hey-hey/

Holzer, Steven; Black, Jack Jr.; and Settlemier, Tyrone, *ROCKIN' 78 rpm numerical listing discography*, The Online Discographical Project, 27 Nov. 2007, accessed April 15. 2021

Leiber, Jerry and Mike Stoller with David Ritz, *Hound Dog: The Leiber and Stoller Autobiography* (Simon & Schuster Paperbacks, 2009)

Miles, Barry, *Paul McCartney: Many Years From Now* (Random House of Canada Ltd., 1997)

Myers, Marc, *Anatomy of a Song*, Chapter 4 ("K.C. Loving") (Grove Press, 2016)

CHAPTER 20

"WHAT'D I SAY"

RAY CHARLES (JUNE 1959)

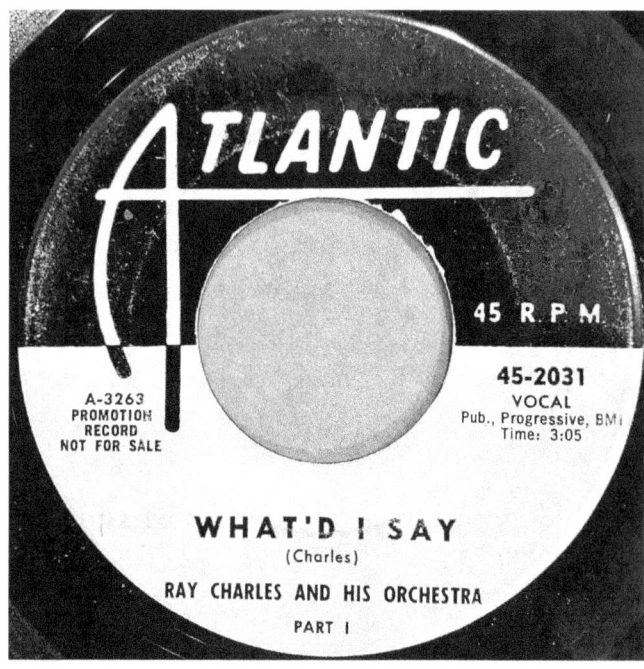

Atlantic standard black/white promo label

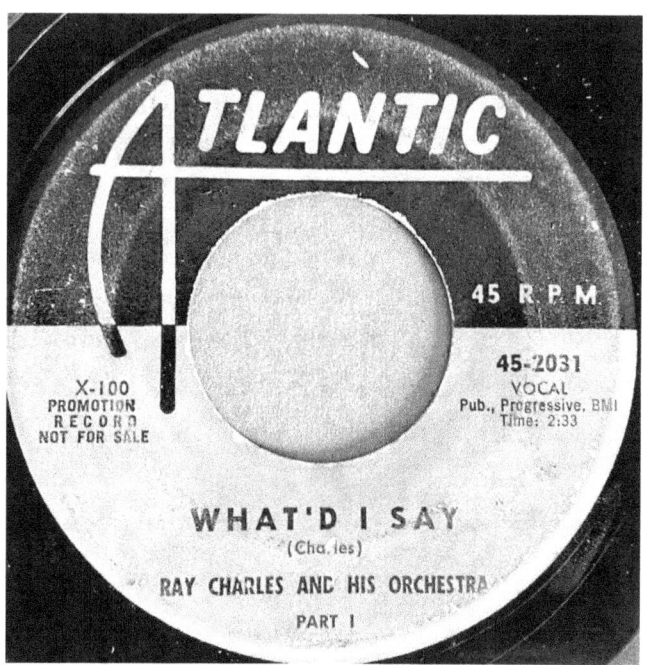

Atlantic retro yellow promo label

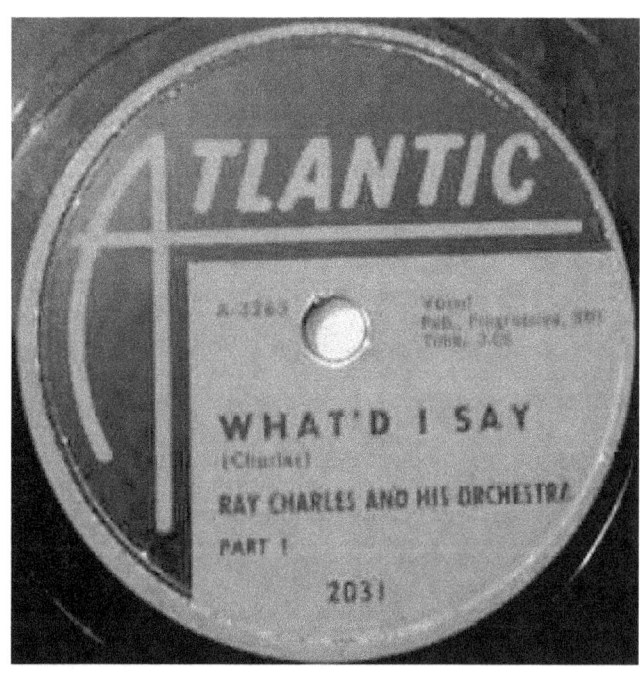

Atlantic stock 78 release (Discogs)

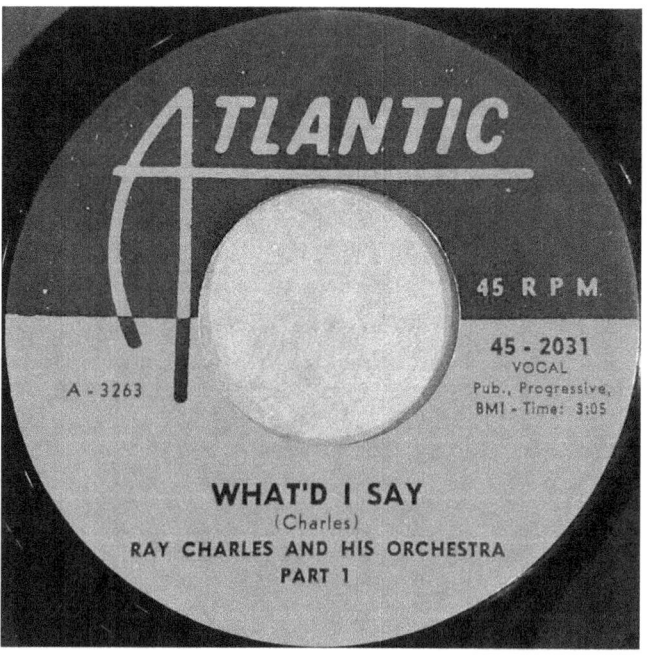

Atlantic stock 45 release

"WHAT'D I SAY" — THE BASIC FACTS

Label: Atlantic 45-2031 (45); Atlantic 2031 (78)

Writer: Ray Charles

Date recorded: February 18, 1959

Date released: June 8, 1959

B-Side: "What'd I Say, Part 2"

Producers: Ahmet Ertegun and Jerry Wexler

Billboard charts:

  Pop Chart

- Debut: 7/06/59
- Peak: #6
- Duration: 15 weeks

  R&B Chart

- Debut: 7/13/59
- Peak: #1 (1 week)
- Duration: 17 weeks

THE SONG AND ITS IMPACT

"What'd I Say" is a song that Ray Charles literally worked out while performing at a concert in December 1958. The liner notes to the Rhino CD, *Ray Charles' Ultimate Hits Collection* (2000), quotes Ray as follows:

> On this one particular night we'd run out of arrangements. Man, we'd run out of tunes. It was 1 a.m. and the owner said we needed to play another ten minutes, so I just started jamming and told everyone, including The Raeletts, to follow me. That jam became 'What'd I Say.' By the crowd reaction I knew we had something. The crowd went wild. We stormed into New York a few weeks later and cut it.

It was recorded on February 18, 1959, at Atlantic's New York City studio, with Atlantic head honcho, Ahmet Ertegun, and Atlantic A&R head, Jerry Wexler, producing. The Raeletts (sometimes referred to as the Raelets, Raylettes, or Raelettes) provided the essential backup vocals. Because Charles and the Raeletts had perfected the song while touring, it took only a few takes to get "What'd I Say" on tape. It was cut on an Ampex eight track recorder, which Tom Dowd, the engineer for the session, had purchased a year earlier, one of only two in existence at the time; Les Paul had the other. Nesuli Ertegun, Ahmet's brother, observed "that's why the quality's so good—the sound today is still unbelievable."

Tom Dowd recommended that the song be divided into two parts because of its length. As edited, Part I timed in at 3:05 and Part II at 1:59. The full-length 6:25 version was released in 1961 on Ray's *Do the Twist!* album on Atlantic 8054.

Although the record was recorded in February 1959, Atlantic opted to delay the release until early June when dance records tended to find favor with teenagers and young adults. And find favor it did. "What I'd I Say" was a *Billboard* "Spotlight Pick" on June 15, 1959, with the notation that "Charles shouts it out in persuasive style, and he backs his vocal with some great piano work and good ork support." On June 20, 1959, it was a *Cash Box* "Pick of the Week," with the notation: "It's a sure-fire two-sided winner, with the big edge to Part II, r&b and pop-wise. It's a smash." A week later *Cash Box* listed "What'd I Say" as one of the "R&B Sure Shots."

It debuted on *Billboard's* pop chart on July 6, 1959, and was listed as a "Best Buy" on July 13, 1959. It topped out at #6. On *Billboard's* R&B chart it debuted a week later and rose to #1 during its 17-week stay. It made its first appearance on *Cash Box's* "Top 100" chart on July 4, 1959, and rose to #6 during its 16 weeks on that chart. On the *Cash Box* "Top 50" R&B chart, it was #1 for three weeks amidst it 16-week chart run.

The lyrics, and especially the moaning and groaning between Charles and The Raeletts, caused a fair amount of criticism, with some radio stations refusing to play it. As one critic, Tony Russell, observed, "… the dialogue between himself and his backing singers that started in church and ended up in the bedroom." Charles took the criticism in stride, wryly commenting in his biography, "I'm not one to interpret my own songs, but if you can't figure out 'What I Say', then something's wrong. Either that, or you're not accustomed to the sweet sounds of love."

As can be seen in the above label scans, Atlantic issued two different promo releases, both of which bear the same label number, Atlantic 2031. One is on the standard white and black promo label with the same matrix numbers (A-3263 and A-3264) and with same times (3:05 for Part 1 and 1:59 for Part II) as the stock release. But of particular interest to collectors of Atlantic Records is the retro yellow label promo release on which the matrix numbers and times are very different, i.e., the matrix numbers are X-100 and X-200 and the times for Part I and Part II are significantly different at 2:33 and 1:43, respectively.[98]

Most likely, the issuance of the retro yellow label promo was Atlantic's response to the many radio stations that banned the playing of "What'd I Say" because of its overtly sexual lyrics. Thus, the yellow label promo was edited to remove objectionable content, thereby shortening the length timewise of both Part I and Part II. The following are among the verses that were edited out:

Hey, mama, don't you treat me wrong
Come and love your daddy all night long
All right now, hey hey all right
See the girl with the diamond ring
She knows how to shake that thing
******

---

98 Atlantic started using a red label for stock 45s with The Clovers' release on Atlantic 1083. Initially, it was issued with the usual yellow label, but shortly thereafter, Atlantic switched over to a red label, which Atlantic used for all subsequent stock releases.

Baby shake that thing now now (baby shake that thing)
Baby shake that thing (baby shake that thing)
Baby shake that thing right now (baby shake that thing)
Baby shake that thing (baby shake that thing)

Moreover, the use of the retro yellow label served to differentiate for DJs the sanitized promo version from the original white and black label promo version. As Pete Grendysa, the reigning expert on Atlantic Records, told me in an email, "They [Atlantic Records] hoped the yellow label would keep the radio stations from quickly throwing it out." Interestingly, no changes were made to the stock release; Atlantic continued to press it with the original lyrics.

Despite the initial rejection by some because of its perceived overt sexuality, "What'd I Say" yielded Charles his first gold record and it was Atlantic's best-selling record up to that time.

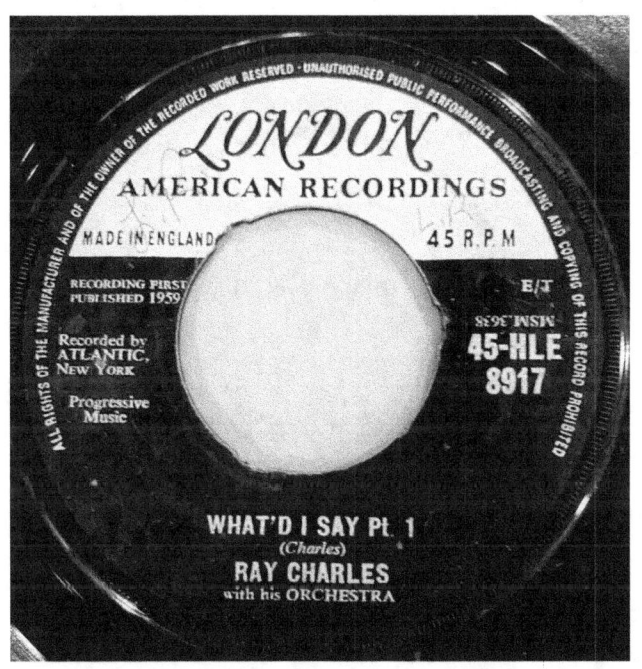

In the UK, the two-part "What'd I Say" was released on London HLE 8917 in July 1959. Although it did not chart in the UK, it had a significant impact on many British artists, including The Beatles, Eric Burdon, Mick Jagger, and Steve Winwood. For example, it was a staple of the future Beatles during the time they were honing their skills playing various clubs in Hamburg, Germany. They particularly liked the shout and response nature of the song since they were able to extend the length of the song in live performances with the help of audience participation.

A recorded version of the song was captured by German producer Bert Kaempfert (who had a 1960 #1 pop hit with "Wonderland by Night" on Decca 31141) on a 12-song album that was released on Polydor in Germany, the UK, and the U.S. in 1964, 1967, and 1969, respectively. The U.S. release on Polydor 24-4504 was titled *In the Beginning (Circa 1960)* by The Beatles featuring Tony Sheridan. While eight of the songs on this LP include the participation of John, Paul, and George, the backing on "What'd I Say" was by the Beat Brothers, which did not include any of the future Beatles. The Beatles did record a short but unreleased version of "What'd I Say" as part of the "Get Back" sessions on January 7, 1967.[99]

More importantly in terms of The Beatles, "What'd I Say" played a role in the decision by John Lennon, Paul McCartney, and George Harrison to make Ringo Starr their drummer, thereby replacing Peter Best. It came about when Ringo backed up John, Paul, and George on "What'd I Say" at a 1962 gig at Liverpool's Cavern Club. As Paul recounted, "What'd I Say" was a song they played

99 What'd I Say (song) (the-paulmccartney-project.com)

"but none of the drummers could get it. It's quite a hard drum part." Referring to that gig with Ringo subbing on drums, Paul later said:

> I have this very vivid recollection of kind of looking at John and him looking at George and him looking at me, and the three of us going, "What the fuck, this is fucking amazing."

"What'd I Say" has been covered by five different artists whose releases have charted. The first was by Jerry Lee Lewis in 1961 on Sun 356. It was produced by Sam Phillips at the first recording session in his new Nashville studio on February 9, 1961. Peter Guralnick observed that Lewis "offered a masterly lesson in controlled, con brio pianistics,… marred only by a cooing chorus,… a poor substitute for the writhing, orgiastic exchange between Charles and his Raelettes on the original." It debuted on the *Billboard* pop chart on April 3, 1961, where it spent eight weeks, peaking at #30. It also made both the *Billboard* R&B and country charts, peaking at #26 and at #27, respectively. In the UK, it did even better, peaking at #10 during its 14-week chart run.

The other four artists who subsequently released covers of "What'd I Say" that charted in either the U.S. and/or the UK are:

- Bobby Darin's 1962 cover that was released on Atco 45-6221 reached #24 on the *Billboard* "Hot 100" chart
- The Big Three's 1963 UK EP, titled "At The Cavern," on Decca DFE.8552, which included "What'd I Say," peaked at #6 on the UK EP chart in late 1963 and early 1964 during its 17-week stay
- Elvis Presley's 1964 cover topped out at #21 on the *Billboard* pop chart and #10 on the UK chart; Glen Campbell played guitar on this recording
- Rare Earth's 1972 cover rose to #62 on the *Billboard* "Hot 100" chart

Other well-known artists who have recorded 45 rpm versions of "What'd I Say," include Soloman Burke, Eddie Cochran, Etta James, Brenda Lee, Trini Lopez, Roy Orbison, Cliff Richards, and Dionne Warwick. Parenthetically, Charles always referred to the song as "What I Say," not "What'd I Say," the title Atlantic used. This may be the reason why some of the cover versions are titled "What I Say," as noted below in the chart of subsequent covers.

Interestingly, four years earlier, Atlantic had released a different song with the same title— "What'd I Say"—by Ruth Brown on Atlantic 1072 that Ahmet Ertegun had penned under the *non de plume* "Nugetre," which is his last name spelled backward.[100] Stylewise, it is reminiscent of her early hit, "(Mama) He Treats Your Daughter Mean" on Atlantic 986. Likewise under the heading of *caveat*

---

100 The A-side, "Its Love Baby (24 Hours of the Day)," rose to #4 on the *Billboard* R&B chart.

emptor, Earle Thomas Conley released a slightly different titled song, "What I'd Say," a 1988-89 #1 *Billboard* country hit on RCA 8717-7- R. It, too, is a totally different song.

In terms of honors and accolades, as set forth in more detail below, "What'd I Say" is pure gold. It gained a Grammy, was listed by NPR as one of the 100 most influential records of the 20th century, was added to the Library of Congress National Recording Registry, a list of recordings that are "culturally, historically, or aesthetically significant," and was listed by *Time* magazine as one of the 100 "most extraordinary English-language popular recordings since the beginning of TIME magazine in 1923." In ranking "What'd I Say" tenth on its list of "The 500 Greatest Songs of All Time," *Rolling Stone* said, "Charles' grunt 'n' groan exchanges with the Raeletts were the closest you could get to the sound of organism on Top Forty radio during the Eisenhower era."

Ray Charles, in merging gospel with blues in such songs as "I Got A Woman" and, especially, "What'd I Say," led to the birth of Soul. Referring to "What'd I Say," musician and writer Lenny Kaye said, "In an instant, the music called Soul comes into being. Hallelujah!" In an article in *The Wall Street Journal* (9/21/2020) entitled "Ray Charles, Genius With Grit," John Edward Hasse, curator emeritus of American Music at the Smithsonian Institute, commented:

> His explosive 1959 Atlantic recording "What'd I Say" innovated by combining boogie-woogie figures, a 12-bar blues structure, a gospel feel, sizzling syncopations, Latin percussion rhythms, and electric piano, while doubling the usual running time of singles. The erotic back-and-forth between Charles and his female backup quartet, the Raelettes, helped the song attract a wide pop audience

What Charles was so successful in doing, as author Arnold Shaw noted in his book *Honkers and Shouters,* was to combine "the excitement of gospel... to the sensuality of the blues," which reached its peak in "What'd I Say." Although there are other claimants, a strong case can be made that this was the first Soul record.

CONTEMPORANEOUS COVER VERSIONS OF "WHAT'D I SAY"

As far as can be determined, there were no contemporaneous major label covers of "What'd I Say."

BUDGET LABEL COVERS OF "WHAT'D I SAY"

Only two budget label covers of "What'd I Say" were found, both on the Hit label, which were issued in the 1960s, i.e., not contemporaneously:

ARTIST	LABEL	COMMENTS
Ray Fowler	Hit 9	B/w "Soul Twist" by Hit Combo
Jerry Poncher	Hit 124	B/w "Every Little Bit Hurts" by Peggy Gaines

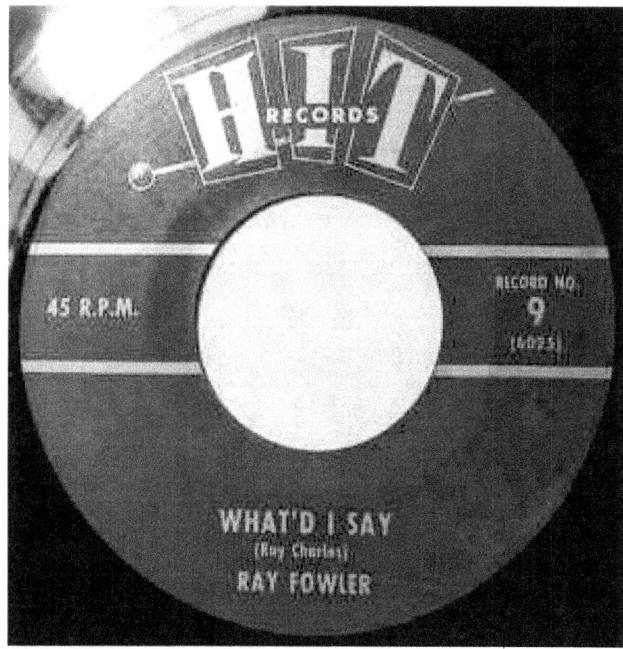 

LATER RELEASES OF "WHAT'D I SAY" BY RAY CHARLES

LABEL	YEAR	COMMENTS
Atlantic 2031	Early 1960s	Later pressing with "fan" label; b/w "What'd I Say, Part II"; "Atlantic Golden Oldies" series
London Atlantic 45-RE-K 1306 (UK)	1961	A-side all one track, not split between Part I and Part II as the original 45 was; b/w "Rockhouse" and "Tell All The World About You"

Atlantic SD 8029	1964	7" 33 1/3 jukebox EP with "What'd I Say, Parts I-II"/"My Bonnie"/"You Be My Baby"/"Tell All The World About You"
Atlantic 584093 (UK)	1967	Live version from the 1964 Los Angeles Shine Auditorium concert; b/w "I Got A Woman"; "Fan" label
Atlantic GS 45717 (Canada)	???	B/w "What'd I Say, Part 2"; "Gold Standard" series
Atlantic K 10239X (UK)	1972	EP with "Yes, Indeed"/"I Got A Woman"/"Don't Let The Sun Catch You Crying"
Atlantic AT 2031 (Canada)	1972	B/w "What'd I Say, Part 2"; "Gold Standard" series
Atlantic OS 13033	c. 1973	B/w "What'd I Say, Part 2"; "Oldies Series"
Atlantic 45-RB-108 (UK)	2015	B/w "What'd I Say, Part 2"; Atlantic "RB Series"

SUBSEQUENT COVER VERSIONS OF "WHAT'D I SAY"

ARTIST	LABEL	YEAR	COMMENTS
Chet Atkins	RCA 47-9116	1967	Very good guitar version; b/w "Charlie Brown," likewise an instrumental
Atlantic Boys	EMI 2807 (UK)	1978	B/w "Loving You Seemed To Be So Magic"
The Big Three	Decca DFE.8552 (UK)	1963	B/w "Zip-A-Dee-Doo-Dah"/"Don't Start Running Away"/"Rockin' And Reelin'"; charted in the UK in late 1963 and early 1964, peaking at #6; recorded live at the Cavern Club, the Liverpool club made famous by The Beatles

Bill Black Combo	Hi HSP-2	1961	Special 7" 33 1/3 promotion disk with five other songs
Blue Echoes	Raynard RS10019	1963	Same song but titled "What I Say"; garage version; b/w "Moonride," a good surf instrumental; Milwaukee, WI, label
Solomon Burke	Atlantic 45-2566	1968	B/w "Get Out Of My Life Woman"; produced by Tom Dowd
Calvin Carter	Vee Jay 419	1961	Good instrumental version; b/w "The Roach"
Calvin Carter	Oldies 45 OL 50	1963	Listed as by Cal Carter; b/w "Pricilla" [sic] by Eddie Cooley
Clarence Carter	Ichiban 87-131	1987	B/w "Grandpa Can't Fly His Kite"
Eddie Cochran	Rockstar RSR-SP 3001 (UK)	1979	B/w "Milk Cow Blues"; "Issued by arr. with the B.B.C. and U.A. Records"
The Cousins	Chancellor C-1074	1961	Garage version; b/w "Boston Hop" by The Playboys
The Crickets	Liberty LEP 2094 (UK)	1963	EP with "Summertime Blues"/"Searchin'"/ "Willie and The Hand Jive"
Bobby Darin	Atco 45-6221	1962	Reached #24 on *Billboard's* "Hot 100" chart; b/w "What'd I Say (Part II)"
Bobby Darin	London 45-HLK 9540 (UK)	1962	B/w "Ain't That Love"
Defiants	Defiant Records of Espanola 7Q315	1966	Garage; b/w "End Of The Highway"; Fairview, NM, group

The Diamond Boys	RCA 1351 (UK)	1963	B/w "Hey Little Girl"
Ronnie Dio and The Red Caps	Seneca S 178-102	1960	B/w "An Angel Is Missing"; Syracuse, NY, label
Jack Eubanks	Monument MSP-010 No. 1	1961	Special 7" 33 1/3 promotion disk with five other songs
Jack Eubanks	Monument 434	1961	B/w "Chiricahua," an instrumental
Jack Eubanks' Orchestra	London 45-HL-U 9312 (UK)	1961	B/w "Chiricahua," an instrumental
Tommy Fuller	Giant 1005	1962	B/w "Soul Twist"
Gerry and The Pacemakers	Columbia SEG 8388 (UK)	1965	EP with "My Babe"/"Skinny Lizzy"/ "Away From You"
The Halos	7 Arts S-720	1961	B/w "Come On"
Dick Hyman	Command RS 45-4041	1964	B/w "S'Posin'"; organ instrumentals
Etta James	Argo 5459	1963	Same song but titled "What I Say"; b/w "Baby What You Want Me To Do," a cover of Jimmy Reed; both sides recorded live
Eddy Jansen & The Van Dells	Jansen 6345	c. 60's?	Same song but titled "What I Say"; garage version; b/w "Janie"
The Jesters	Candy Cane cc-201	c. 60s?	Garage version; b/w "The Big T"; Buffalo, NY, label; "Recorded live at the Candy Cane Lounge, Buffalo, N.Y."
Johnny and The Shy Guys	Regal Records West RR 200	1964	B/w "What'd I Say—Part II"; "Featuring Rudy Von Rudin"; garage; La Crosse, WI, group; live recording

Joye, Col	Sunday Telegraph TEL 001 (Australia)	1964	7" EP with three other songs by different artists; "Under 21 Special Record"
Louis Jordan	Tangerine 45- TRC-937	1964	Same song, but titled "What I Say"; b/w "Old Age"
Key Largo Band (with "Big Al & Helen Lucille")	Largo 100	1983	B/w "Know I'll Keep You (Satisfied)"; Roanoke, VA, label
The Killer Joe Orchestra	Atlantic SLD 201	1965	7" small-hole 33 1/3 EP with five other songs
Brenda Lee	Brunswick 05915 (UK)	1964	B/w "Is It True"; produced by Mickie Most; Brenda Lee's "What'd I Say" was not released in the U.S.
Jerry Lee Lewis	Sun 356	1961	B/w "Livin' Lovin' Wreck"
Jerry Lee Lewis	Sun 48		B/w "Livin' Lovin' Wreck"; Sun "Golden Treasure Series"
Jerry Lee Lewis	London HLS 9335 (UK)	1961	B/w "Livin' Lovin' Wreck"; on the UK charts for 14 weeks, rising to #10
Jerry Lee Lewis	London M. 17165 (Canada)	1961	B/w "Livin' Lovin' Wreck"
Jerry Lee Lewis	London American RE-S 1296 (UK)	1961	EP with "Livin' Lovin' Wreck"/"John Henry"/"Hang Up My Rock And Roll Shoes"
Jerry Lee Lewis	London HLS 10193 (UK)	1968	B/w "I've Been Twistin'"
Jerry Lee Lewis	Charly CYS 1048 (UK)	1979	B/w "Hello Josephine," a cover of Fats Domino

Jerry Lee Lewis	Scoop 33 7SR 5014 (UK)	1983	7" small hole 33 1/3 EP with "Great Balls Of Fire"/"Whole Lotta Shakin' Goin' On"/"Breathless"/"High School Confidential"/"Good Golly Miss Molly"
Little Bones	Prann 5001	1963	B/w "Ya Ya," a cover of Lee Dorsey; produced by Ike & Tina Turner
Trini Lopez	Reprise R 30013 (UK)	1963	EP with "If I Had A Hammer" and a medley of five songs
Trini Lopez	Reprise SR 6093	1963	7" small-hole 33 1/3 EP with five other songs; apparently promo only
Brother Jack McDuff	Atlantic SD 71463	1966	7" small-hole 33 1/3 EP with four other songs
Gene McKay & The Ebb Tides	Clark CR-238	1965	B/w "Little Women"; Goodlettsville, TN, label
Sandy Nelson	Liberty LEP-4033 (UK)	1965	Instrumental; EP with "Rock House"/ "Walkin' To New Orleans"/"I'm Gonna Be A Wheel Someday"
Johnny O'Keefe	Leedon LX-10,135 (Australia)	1959	B/w "Shout, Parts I and II"/"I'm Moving On"/"That's My Desire"
Johnny O'Keefe with The Dee Jays & The Delltones	Leedon LS-575 (Australia)	1961	EP with b/w "Shout, Parts I and II"; also on Lee Gordon LS-575
Olympics	Arvee EP A-423	1960	EP "Boo-Dee Green" and "(Baby) Hully Gully"
Olympics	Arvee A-5073	1963	B/w "What'd I Say—Part II"

Roy Orbison	London HLU 9845 (UK)	1964	B/w "Borne On The Wind"
Roy Orbison	London Monument RE-U.1439 (UK)	1965	EP with "Cryin'"/"Running Scared"/"I'm Hurtin'"
Paul	Vampire 7001	1964	"Recorded Live"; b/w "Barbara"; Atlantic City, NJ, label
Elvis Presley	RCA 47-8360	1964	Reached #21 on the *Billboard* pop chart and #10 on the UK charts; Glen Campbell on guitar; b/w "Viva Las Vegas," which also charted, peaking at #29
Elvis Presley	RCA 1390 (UK)	1964	B/w "Viva Las Vegas"
Elvis Presley	RCA 447-0646	1965	B/w "Viva Las Vegas"; "Gold Standard" series
Prodigies	Rofran ER-1013	1965	B/w "I Want To Do It"; Urbana, IL, label; garage band
Rare Earth	Rare Earth 5043F	1972	Reached #62 on *Billboard's* "Hot 100" chart; b/w "Nice To Be With You"; Rare Earth is a Motown subsidiary; there is also a mono/stereo promo version
Cliff Richards and The Shadows	Columbia ESG 8105 (UK)	1961	EP with "True Love Will Come To You"/ "Lover"/"Blue Moon"
Cliff Richard and The Shadows	Columbia DC 758 (Export issue, UK)	1962	B/w "Blue Moon"; quite rare
Righteous Brothers	Festival FX-11,041 (Australia)	1965	EP with "My Prayer"/"Love Or Magic"/"In That Great Getting' Up Morning"
The Rockets	Wide AF 936	Mid 60s	Instrumental version; b/w "Jonny B. Goode" [*sic*] (Wide AF 935); Reading, PA, label

Ronettes	Raven RVS-03 (Australia)	1982	"Live At Cow Palace, San Francisco" b/w "Be My Baby"; produced by Phil Spector
Roger Rudy and The Pyramid	Pyramid PY 102	1970s???	B/w "Travelin' Band," a cover of Creedence Clearwater Revival; Wisconsin label and band
Savage Young Beatles with Tony Sheridan	Gecko 7 (UK)	1996	B/w "If You Love Me Baby"; no verification that The Beatles backed up Sheridan on "What'd I Say"; unofficial
The Searchers	Philips BF 1274 (UK)	1963	B/w "Sweet Nothin's"
Tony Sheridan and The Beat Brothers	Polydor 52 025 (Germany)	1963	B/w "Ruby Baby"; the Beat Brothers included any of the eventual Beatles on either side
Tony Sheridan	Collectables 1522	???	B/w "Sweet Georgia Brown" by The Beatles with Tony Sheridan
Jimmy Smith and Kenny Burrell	Verve VK 10299	1963	Instrumental "Bubbled Under" but stalled at #113; b/w "Theme from 'Any Number Can Win'," by Jimmy Smith alone
Jimmy Smith and Kenny Burrell	Verve VS 516 (UK)	1963	Instrumental version; b/w "Theme from 'Any Number Can Win'" by Jimmy Smith alone
Kenny Springs and The Scat Cats	DeWitt 5911	1960	B/w "Please"; group hailed from Kingsport, TN
Sound Studio One	Custom ER-1013	1965	Label notes that "Lyrics added by Sound Studio One"; b/w "I Want To Do It"; Urbana, IL, label

Taffy Thomas	Newport NP 130	1965	Good female garage version; b/w "I'm Coming Back"; Detroit, MI, label
Billy Thorpe and The Aztecs	Parlophone CEP0-70022 (Australia)	1965	EP with "Zip-A-Doo-Dah"/"Jenny Jenny"/"I'm A Hog For You Baby"
The Three Blonde Mice	Atco 45-6353	1965	B/w "Alley Cat"; group consisted of three blonde teenage girls
Unbeatables	Dawn 552	c. 1964	Garage version; b/w "I Love Paris"; Newburgh, NY, label
Unbeatables	Dawn 553	c. 1964	Reissued with a different B-side, i.e., "Peanuts"
Raymond Vasquez, Jr., Orchestra	Valmon VN-1-027	c. 1963	B/w "Moving, Going, Gone"; Austin, TX, label
Dionne Warwick	Scepter SGS-534	1966	7" small hole 33 1/3 mini-album with "I Love Paris"/"C'est Si Bon"/ "Message To Michael"/"The Good Life"/"La Vie En Rose"
Dionne Warwick	Pye International NEP 44054 (UK)	1966	EP with "Hold It Over" by Chuck Jackson, "Dedicated To The One I Love" by The Shirelles, and "Since I Found You" by Maxine Brown
Dionne Warwick	Scepter/Wand Forever SWF-21032	1969	B/w "This Little Light"
Bert Weedon	Polydor 2058 832 (UK)	1977	Medley titled "Rocking Guitar," which also includes "Guitar Boogie Shuffle"/"Shake, Rattle And Roll"/ "See You Later, Alligator"/"Blue Suede Shoes"/"Rock Around The Clock"; b/w "Bella Ciao"

Don Lee Wilson	Imperial 66038	1964	Titled "(Gul Durn It) What'd I Say (Part I)" and credited to Ray Charles; b/w "T'ain't Funny"; Wilson, with Bob Bogle, founded The Ventures
Rusty York	Gusto GO-127	1974	B/w "Horney," an instrumental; Nashville, TN, label
None Listed	Dixie DEP-307	c. early 60s	EP titled "Twist Hit Parade," with five other twist songs
None Listed	Hoctor H-1608	1964	B/w "Limbo Rock"; dance record
None Listed	Seeburg DN-302-B	1965	7" small-hole 33 1/3 EP with five other songs; "Discoteen" series
None Listed	Seeburg DN-305	1965	7" small-hole 33 1/3 EP with five other songs; "Discoteen" series

The Searchers on Philips (1964, UK)

Rare Earth red wax promo (1973)

"WHAT'D I SAY" IN THE MOVIES

In addition to *Ray*, the 2004 award winning movie about Ray Charles' life, "What'd I Say" can be heard in more than a dozen movies, including the following:

MOVIE TITLE	YEAR	COMMENTS
Viva Las Vegas	1964	Performed by Elvis Presley; starring Elvis and Ann-Margret
Ballad in Blue (UK)	1965	Performed by Ray Charles with backing by the Raeletts; movie is about Ray Charles who played himself trying to help a blind youngster; movie released in the U.S. in 1966 under the name *Blues for Lovers*
That'll Be The Day (UK)	1973	Sung by Billy Fury; lead played by David Essex, of "Rock On" fame, and the cast included Ringo Starr, Billy Fury, and Keith Moon; loosely based on John Lennon's early life musically
Hollywood Knights	1980	Performed by Ray Charles; comedy about a car club's Halloween antics
Black Rain	1989	Performed by Ray Charles; crime thriller starring Michael Douglas
Night and The City	1992	Performed by Ray Charles; dramatic comedy starring Robert De Niro and Jessica Lange
Calendar Girl	1993	Performed by Ray Charles; dramatic comedy about three men's quest to meet Marilyn Monroe

Heart and Souls	1993	Performed by Ray Charles; romantic fantasy comedy; Robert Downey, Jr., stars
Tommy Boy	1995	Performed by Chris Farley and Brian Dennehy; comedy adventure starring Chris Farley
Where the Heart Is	2000	Performed by Lyle Lovett; romantic comedy starring Natalie Portman
Behind Enemy Lines	2001	Performed by Ray Charles; action drama starring Owen Wilson and Gene Hackman
Showtime	2002	Performed by Ray Charles; action comedy starring Eddie Murphy and Robert De Niro
Ray	2004	Performed by Ray Charles; story of Ray Charles' life; Jamie Foxx won an Oscar for his portrayal of Charles
The Express	2008	Performed by Ray Charles; story about Syracuse University football player, Ernie Davis, the first Black Heisman Trophy winner; awarded an ESPY as the best sport movie in 2009
Inglorious Bastards	2009	Performed by Rare Earth; war drama starring Brad Pitt and directed by Quentin Tarantino
20 Feet from Stardom	2013	Performed by Ray Charles; story about backup singers
Wild Card	2015	Performed by Ray Charles; crime action drama starring Jason Statham

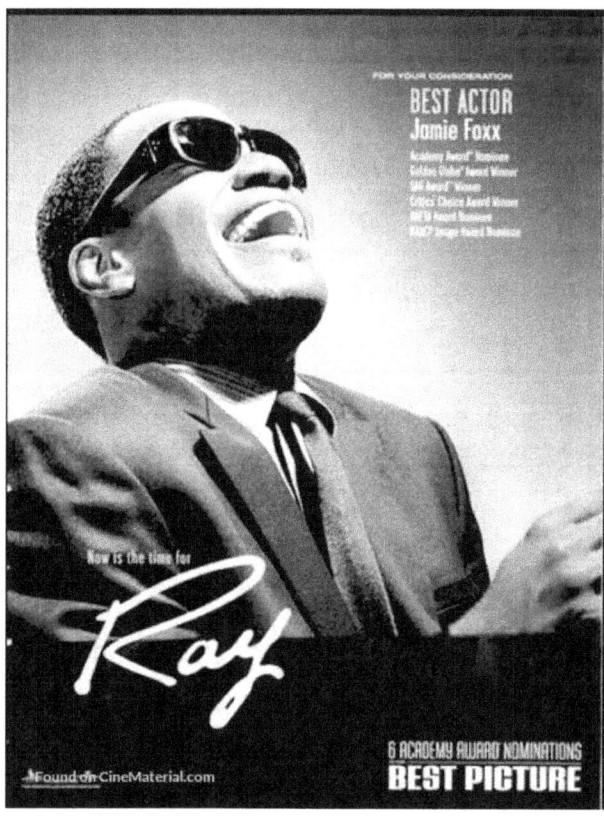

DOCUMENTED CONCERT PERFORMANCES OF "WHAT'D I SAY"

As of May 1, 2024, *Setlist.fm* documented that "What'd I Say " has been performed in concert 1005 times by 138 different artists. In addition to Ray Charles (132), artists who have included "What'd I Say" on their set lists more than five times include Elvis Presley (220), Jerry Lee Lewis (111), Van Morrison (71), Cliff Richard/Shadows (29), Dick Dale (20), Styx (11), and Prince (7).

HONORS AND ACCOLADES FOR "WHAT'D I SAY"

- Inducted into the Grammy Hall of Fame in 2000
- Included in the National Recording Registry of the Library of Congress by National Recording Preservation Board in 2002; the Board annually selects songs that are "culturally, historically, or aesthetically significant"
- Listed at #251 on the RIAA/NEA list of the "Top 365 Songs of the 20th Century"
- Listed on Time *magazine's* unranked list of the 100 "most extraordinary English-language popular recordings since the beginning of TIME magazine in 1923," which were described as "songs of enduring beauty, power and inventiveness"
- Chosen by the Rock & Roll Hall of Fame as one of the "500 Songs That Shaped Rock and Roll""
- Ranked #15 on Joel Whitburn's *Honor Roll of Hits*
- Ranked #10 on the *Rolling Stone*'s 2004 list of "The 500 Greatest Songs of All Time"
- Rank #43 on VH1's *100 Greatest Songs in Rock and Roll*

- Ranked #9 on *Mojo* magazine's "Big Bangs: 100 Records That Changed the World" (June 2007), i.e., a list of "[t]he most influential & inspirational recordings ever made, they changed music—the way it was played, bought or even imagined"

ALSO WORTH NOTING . . .

- For the rest of his career Charles closed every show with "What'd I Say," and was quoted as saying "When I do 'What'd I Say', you don't have to worry about it—that's the end of me; there ain't no encore, no nothin.' I'm finished!"
- "What'd I Say," along with "Be-Bop-A-Lula" by Gene Vincent, are referred to in the first line of "Walk of Life" by the Dire Straits:

  > Here comes Johnny singing oldies goldies,
  > Be-Bop-A-Lula baby What'd I Say

- Timothy White in his chapter on Ray Charles in *Rock Lives* (1990) stated that "What'd I Say" was "an unhinged ode to saturnalia that became a million-seller."
- Per Paul McCartney, the drums on "I Feel Fine" were inspired by "What'd I Say."

ADDITIONAL SOURCES

Charles, Ray & David Ritz, *Brother Ray: Ray Charles' Own Story* (Da Capo, 1992)

Evans, Mike. *Ray Charles: The Birth of Soul* (Omnibus Press, 2005)

Greenfield, Robert, *The Last Sultan: The Life and Time of Ahmet Ertegun (Simon & Schuster*, 2011)

Guralnick, Peter, *Sam Phillips: The Man Who Invented Rock 'n' Roll* (Little, Brown, 2015)

Guralnick, Peter, *Sweet Soul Music: Rhythm and Blues and the Southern Dream of Freedom* (Harper & Row, 1986)

CHAPTER 21

"MONEY (THAT'S WHAT I WANT)"

BARRETT STRONG (AUGUST 1959)

Original release on Tamla 54027

Original release on Anna 1111

UK release on London 45-HLU 9088
[Image: *45cat*]

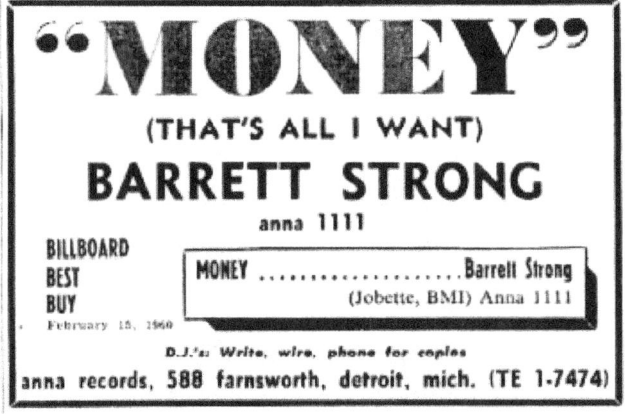

Billboard ad, February 22, 1960

"MONEY (THAT'S WHAT I WANT)" — THE BASIC FACTS

Label: Tamla 54027 (both 45 and 78) and Anna 1111 (both 45 and 78)

Writers: Berry Gordy, Jr., and Janie Bradford

Date recorded: August 1959

Date released: August 1959

B-Side: "Oh I Apologize"

Producer: Berry Gordy, Jr.

Billboard charts

   <u>Pop Chart</u>

- Debut: 2/1/1960
- Peak: #23
- Duration: 17 weeks

   <u>R&B Chart</u>

- Debut: 1/25/1960
- Peak: #2
- Duration: 21 weeks

THE SONG AND ITS IMPACT

As the calendar was closing in on a new decade, Berry Gordy, Jr., was just beginning to establish his Motown stable of labels, the first of which was Tamla.[101] Among the first ten songs released by the fledgling new label in 1959 was "Money (That's What I Want)," a song he wrote with Janie Bradford. In his autobiography Gordy said that he wanted to write about something other than love:

Everybody writes about love. I wanted to write about something different. But what? Then it popped into my head, the most obvious thing of all, the thing I needed the most—money.

After telling his receptionist and assistant, Janie Bradford, that he needed one more verse, Bradford matter-of-factly threw out the line, "Your love gives me such a thrill but your love don't pay my bills, gimme some money baby." Gordy liked the line so much that he gave her a songwriter's contract for a 50% interest in the song.

It was recorded by Barrett Strong in August 1959. Gordy described the circumstances surrounding the session:

"Money (That's What I Want)" was one of the first records cut at our little studio. It was less like any record session I can remember. More like an in-house rehearsal—a

---

101 Ironically, Tamla, a label noted for its R&B and soul records, was named after pop recording star Debby Reynolds' song "Tammy." Gordy settled on "Tamla" since "Tammy" had already been taken as the name for a Youngstown, OH, record label a year or two before.

party. One long party. It was a few days. We took take after take. Fun. I no longer had to worry about the cost of the studio. I owned it.

Being one of the earlier sessions, we recorded everything together, the band and the background voices. That gave it a raw, earthy feel.

The record was released later in August 1959, on Tamla 54027, backed with "Oh I Apologize." Gordy explained that he "purposely used a large number so people would not know how young my label was." When this release did not gain any traction, Gordy licensed the record to Anna, a label owned by Roquel Davis and two of his sisters, Anna and Gwen Gordy. In late December 1959, it was re-released on Anna 1111, using the Tamla masters. [102]

With Anna's better distribution via Chess Records and its ability to promote the record with ads in both *Billboard* and *Cash Box*, the record entered the *Billboard* and *Cash Box* R&B chart in late January 1960, some five months after it was initially released on Tamla. It debuted on the *Cash Box* R&B chart at #42 on January 23, 1960. A week later it was named the *Cash Box* "Pick of the Week," with the notation, "Looks like a sure-fire success." It entered the *Billboard* R&B chart on January 24, 1960. On February 15, 1960, it was listed by *Billboard* as a "Best Buy." It remained on the *Billboard* R&B chart for 21 weeks, peaking at #2.

As a precursor of things to come, "Money (That's What I Want)" crossed over to the *Billboard* pop chart for 17 weeks, rising to #23. This was a feat that Berry Gordy, Jr., soon would be doing with regularity with a long list of artists headed by The Supremes and Smokey Robinson and The Miracles. But importantly, "Money (That's What I Want)" was the first hit for Gordy and his budding Motown empire. It would turn out, however, to be Barrett Strong's only appearance near the top of the charts, but as Greil Marcus commented, "… that one time has kept him on the radio all his life."

Strong tried to follow up with another "Money" themed record, "Money and Me" co-penned by Berry Gordy, Jr., Janie Bradford, and two others on Tamla 54035, but like most follow ups, it failed to catch on. Parenthetically, the B-side is a good cover version of Marv Johnson's hit "You Got What It Takes," a song penned by B. Gordy, R. Davis, and G. Gordy. When Strong's recording career waned, he became a major Motown song writer, co-writing such songs as "Papa Was A Rolling Stone," "Just My Imagination (Running Away With Me)," and "Psychedelic Shack" for the Temptations, "I Heard It Through the Grapevine" for Marvin Gaye, and "War" for Edwin Starr.

Although Strong earned writer's credits and royalties for those subsequent songwriting efforts,[103] he was not given any credit for assisting in the writing of his signature song, something he later hotly disputed. In an August 31, 2013, article in the *New York Times* titled "For a Classic Motown Song About Money, Credit Is All He Wants," Strong said that "Money (That's What I Want)" was a

---

102 As shown above, label on the original release on Anna 1111 was gold and black, i.e., the same colors used for several stock releases both before and after Anna 1111 was released. A black and silver label was used on some later pressings, and it is rarer than the gold and black label pressings.

103 According to *New York Times* reporter Larry Rohter, Strong sold his right to royalties from those songs for $2 million. Unfortunately, Strong used that money to purchase a recording studio that subsequently failed.

collaborative effort between himself, Berry Gordy, Jr., and Janie Bradford. In Strong's telling, the song evolved from him playing a riff from Ray Charles' "What'd I Say" and that once the instrumental track had been recorded, words were added, some of which he said he helped to compose. Although Strong was listed along with Gordy and Bradford on the initial 1960 copyright entry filed with the Library of Congress, in 1962, Motown amended the copyright to remove his name, something that Strong said he was unaware of. Gordy's lawyers told the *New York Times* reporter that the listing of Strong's name on the original copyright form was a clerical error and that, in any event, Strong had not acted in a timely fashion to contest Motown's removal of his name as one of the song's writers.[104]

As the co-author of "Money," and as the sole owner of the publishing company—Jobete—and a whole stable of labels (Tamla, Motown, Gordy, Soul, etc.), it was in Berry Gordy, Jr.'s financial interest to go back to the well by releasing new versions of "Money" by other Motown artists, something that he did on at least five different occasions, which must set a record for the most subsequent cover records issued by different artists on labels affiliated with the original label. *Guinness World Records* take note. The first was in 1961 by Richard Wylie on Motown 1009. The next was in 1966 by Jr. Walker & The All-Stars on Soul 35026, which reached #35 on *Billboard's* R&B chart and #52 on its pop chart. That same year Motown released a six-song jukebox EP by the Supremes that included "Money." Then, in 1972 Blinky's bluesy cover version was released on Mowest 5019F. The fifth and last was Mandré's 1977 disco version on Motown 1429F.

In addition to the covers on Motown-affiliated labels, subsequent covers of "Money (That's What I Want)" on other labels have made the charts in the U.S. and/or the UK. In 1962 Jennell Hawkins' version hit #17 on the *Billboard* R&B chart. The next year Bern Elliott & the Fenmen's cover version hit #14 on the UK charts. In 1964 The Kingsmen's version spent 11 weeks on the *Billboard's* pop chart, reaching #16. Then, in 1979 The Flying Lizards' new wave version rose to #50 on the *Billboard* "Hot 100" chart and to #5 on the UK charts. Surprisingly, Dave Marsh ranked this version #506 in his 1989 book *The Heart of Rock & Soul: The 1001 Greatest Singles Ever Made,* noting that it "may have been the first record built around syndrums to hit the charts." Finally, in 1994, The BackBeat Band's version of "Money (That's What I Want)" spent six weeks on the UK charts, peaking at #48.

---

104 Ironically, Strong's name reappeared on the copyright filing for "Money" in 1987, only to be removed a year later.

With Brian Epstein at the helm, on January 1, 1962, The Beatles, with Pete Best on drums, went to the Decca studios in London for an audition. The first song they recorded was "Money (That's What I Want)," with George Harrison as the lead vocalist. It was unofficially released on Deccagone 1104 in 1977. Coincidentally, it was George Harrison who had discovered Barrett Strong's original version on London HLU 9088 in Epstein's London record store.

When Decca passed on signing The Beatles, Epstein signed them to England's Parlophone record label. With Ringo Starr now on drums, The Beatles recorded "Money (That's What I Want)" on July 18, 1963, and it was released on November 22, 1963, as the final track on their second UK album, *With The Beatles*. It was later included on *The Beatles Second Album*, which was released in the U.S. on April 10, 1964.

On this officially released version John Lennon rather than George Harrison does the lead vocal, backed by a piano intro added by George Martin and emphatic guitar work by John and Paul. Lennon's vocal is loud, insistent, and demanding; one could almost say crazed. Towards the end of the song, he altered the lyrics. Thus, Barrett Strong' reference to "all those lean greens, yeah (that's what I want)" was replaced with Lennon shouting, "I want to be free." As critically acclaimed rock critic Greil Marcus opined, "It is an argument about life." He further observed that The Beatles' version of "Money" was "the only recording they ever made that captured the chaos of Hamburg, what happened in the fourth set of the night, maybe the fifth, when John put the toilet seat over his head and all bets were off."

The fact that "Money (That's What I Want)" was one of The Beatles' favorite songs is best indicated by their more than 135 concert performances of the song. They also sang it six times for BBC radio.

Several months after The Beatles recorded their version, The Rolling Stones recorded their version of "Money (That's What I Want)." It was released in the UK on Decca DFE 8560, a four song EP. But "compared to The Beatles," in the opinion of Greil Marcus, "they were a skiffle band." Ouch!

In his summary interpretation of "Money (That's What I Want)," Greil Marcus stated:

> From its first line, as Berry Gordy and Janie Bradford wrote it, to its last line as John Lennon rewrote it, this song is about nothing but freedom, and the acceptance, the insistence, that money is the only freedom there is or ever will be, the only form freedom can take or should.

POSTSCRIPT

Prior to co-penning Barrett Strong's big hit, a year earlier, Berry Gordy, Jr., teamed with W. Robinson (AKA Smokey Robinson) to write "Money," a song recorded by Miracles and released on End 1029.[105] In its August 2, 1958, review, *Cash Box* said that it was a "delightful novelty item set to

---

105 The Miracles were led by Smokey Robinson, whose first release was "Got A Job" on End 1016, an answer record co-penned by Berry Gordy, Jr. to the mega hit "Get A Job" by the Silhouettes on Ember 1029. Subsequently, Gordy signed the Miracles to his Tamla label, for whom they had a long string of hits, both as The Miracles or as Smokey Robinson

a rock-a-cha-cha beat. Lyrics tell about a gal who keeps buggin' her hubby for those greenbacks." This Miracles song with the same flip ("I Cry") was re-released in January 1960 on End 1084, presumably to try to capture some sales in the wake of the success of Barrett Strong's record, even though it was not the same song.

Collectors of "Money" covers beware; there are more than a few records titled "Money" by well-known artists that are not covers of Barrett Strong's original, including 45s by Pink Floyd (Harvest 3609), Badfinger (Apple 1841), The Lovin' Spoonful (Kama Sutra 241), and Gladys Knight and The Pips (Buddah 487), the latter of which hit #4 on *Billboard's* R&B chart and #48 on its pop chart in 1975.

CONTEMPORANEOUS COVER VERSIONS OF "MONEY (THAT'S WHAT I WANT)"

There were no contemporaneous cover versions of "Money (That's What I Want)."

CONTEMPORANEOUS BUDGET LABEL COVERS OF "MONEY (THAT'S WHAT I WANT)"

With most of the budget labels having closed shop by late 1959, it is not surprising that an exhaustive internet search did not turn up even one budget label cover.

LATER RELEASES OF "MONEY (THAT'S WHAT I WANT)" BY BARRETT STRONG

LABEL	YEAR	COMMENTS
London HLU 9088 (UK)	1960	B/w "Oh I Apologize"; released in April 1960
Motown Y 504F	1973	B/w "Oh I Apologize"; "Motown Yesteryear Series"
Collectables COL-504	1980s?	B/w "Oh I Apologize"; "Back-to-Back Hit Series"
Tamla Motown ZB 41903 (UK)	1988	B/w "Do You Love Me" by the Contours
Tamla 54027 (B0003631-21)	2005	Bonus record that came with Hip-O Select's *The Complete Motown Singles Vol.1: 1959-1961* CD box

and the Miracles.

Tamla 53154	2009	B/w "Do You Love Me" by the Contours; back-to-back reissue series to commemorate Motown's 50th anniversary, complete with retro "lines" label with address and black/orange Tamla sleeve
Harkit HKRS 8471 (UK)	2013	B/w "Money (That's What I Want)" by Jackie Shane
Tamla Motown TMG 402 (UK)	2014	B/w "Oh I Apologize"
Tamla 54027	2015	B/w "Oh I Apologize"; Third Man Records reissue and marked discretely on label as TMR-354 with label logo
Outta Sight RSV-071 (UK)	2016	B/w "Misery"; reissues of the original Tamla sides; "Not For Sale In The U.S. A."

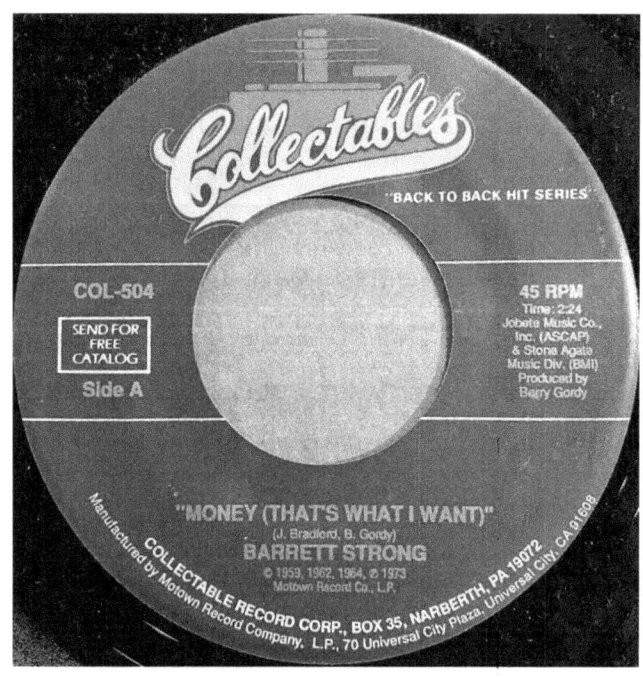

1980s reissue on Collectables

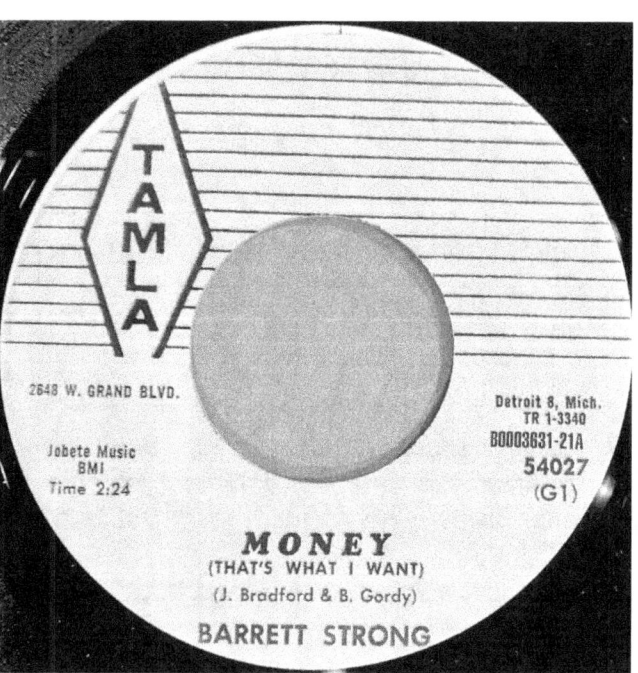

2004 box set reissue

SUBSEQUENT COVER VERSIONS OF "MONEY (THAT'S WHAT I WANT)"

ARTIST	LABEL	YEAR	COMMENTS
Bill Allan Trio	Vee Jay 542	1963	B/w "Pan Handle"
The Allisons	Tip 1011	1963	B/w "Surfer Street"
Steve Anthony	Crossbow XB 012	1964	EP with five other songs by different artists
The BackBeat Band	Dry Hump DH010	1994	7" small hole 45; b/w "Dizzy Miss Lizzy," a cover of Larry Williams; produced by Don Was
The BackBeat Band	Virgin VS 1489 (UK)	1994	B/w "He's Wearing My Bathrobe (End Title)"; produced by Don Was; from soundtrack of the movie "BackBeat"; hit #48 on the UK charts
The BackBeat Band	Virgin S7-17912	1994	B/w "Dizzy Miss Lizzie" and "He's Wearing My Bathrobe (End Title)"; "For Jukeboxes Only!"
The Beatles	Capitol SXA-2080	1964	7-inch 33 1/3 jukebox stereo EP with "Long Tall Sally"/"Thank You Girl"/"Devil In Your Heart"/"I Call Your Name"/ "Please Mister Postman"; very rare
The Beatles	Deccagone Pro-1104	1977	Lead vocal by George Harrison; recorded 1/1/62; b/w "Sure To Fall," a cover of Carl Perkins; multiple colors used for the vinyl; bootleg/repro

The Beatles	AFE AFS 1 (UK)	1982	B/w "Searchin" and "Till There Was You"; all three tracks are taken from the Decca audition on January 1, 1962
The Beatles	Rocks Lane KITTY27EP005 (UK)	2020	Unofficial EP with "Sure To Fall"/"Love Of The Loved"/"Till There Was You"/"To Know Her Is To Love Her"; taken from the 1/1/1962 Decca audition
John Belushi	MCA 40950	1978	B/w "Louie, Louie"
Hal Blaine	Dunhill #D-2	1965	Sampler; medley with "California Sun"/ "Oo Poo Pah Doo"/"La Bamba"/"Drums A' Go"; b/w "Rumble"/"Cannonball"/ "Wooly Bully"
Blinky	Mowest 5019F	1972	A very bluesy version; the promo issue is mono/stereo; b/w "For Your Precious Love," a cover of Jerry Butler & The Impressions
Larry Bright	Dot 16923	1966	B/w "Parchman Farm"
Buddy Britton and The Regents	Oriole 45-CB 1827 (UK)	1963	Same song, but simply titled "Money"; b/w "If You Got Make A Fool Out Of Somebody"; vocals by Geoff Groverwright, a Buddy Holly fanatic from Liverpool
Buddy Britton and The Regents	Oriole 45-CB 1889 (UK)	1963	Same song, but simply titled "Money"; b/w "Sorrow Tomorrow"; vocals by Geoff Groverwright
The Casuals	Minaret 109	1963	B/w "Big Hammer (John's Other Henry)"; Nashville, TN, label

The Casuals	Sparton S-1161-R (Canada)	1963	B/w "Big Hammer (John's Other Henry)"
Clifton Chenier	Arhoolie 539	1981	B/w "Jambalaya"
Don Covay	Mercury 73385	1973	B/w "I Was Checkin' Out She Was Checkin' In"
The Crickets	Liberty LEP 2173 (UK)	1964	EP with "Slippin' & Slidin'"/"A Fool Never Learns"/"Come On"
Skip Cunningham	Kapp K-455	1962	B/w "The Best Man Cried"
The Curiosities	Seeburg Discotek 3013	1965	B/w "Sunset Strip"
Jimmy Dutch	Bell 45,250	1972	B/w "This Place"; produced by Mike Post
Bern Elliott and the Fenmen	Decca F 11770 (UK)	1963	Reached #14 on the UK charts in late 1963; b/w "Nobody But Me," a cover of The Isley Brothers
The Fabulettes	Sound Stage SS45-2558	1966	B/w "Try The Worryin' Way"
The Fabulous Counts	Kim 811	Early 1960s	Great rocking wild guitar version, almost punk; b/w "I Can't Stop Loving You," a cover of Don Gibson; Philadelphia, PA, label
The Flying Lizards	Virgin VS-276 (UK)	1979	Rose to #5 on the UK charts; new wave version; b/w "Money B," an instrumental;
The Flying Lizards	Virgin VA 67003	1979	Ranked #506 in Dave Marsh's 1989 book *The Heart of Rock & Soul: The 1001 Greatest Singles Ever Made*; new wave version; b/w "Money B," an instrumental;

The Flying Lizards	Old Gold OG 9828 (UK)	1988	B/w "T.V."
Freddie and The Dreamers	Columbia DB 7214 (UK)	1964	EP with "Zip-A-Dee-Doo-Da"/"Send A Letter To Me"/"You Were Made For Me"
Levon Helm	Capitol 1A 006-86505 (Netherlands)	1982	Titled "Money," same song but incorrectly credited to Melvyn Gordon; b/w "Summertime Blues"
Jim Holt	Gulfstream 1062	1962	Credited to only Barry Cordy [sic]; b/w "Melody D' Amour"; Hollywood, FL, label
Jennell Hawkins	Amazon 708	1962	Spent five weeks on *Billboard's* R&B chart; b/w "More Money (That's What I Want)," credited to J. Bradford—B. Gordy, Jr., essentially the same song
Jennell Hawkins	Oldies 45 OL 78	Mid 60s	B/w "More Money (That's What I Want)," credited to J. Bradford—B. Gordy, Jr., essentially the same song
John Lee Hooker	Impulse 242	1966	Titled "Money," but same song; only credited to Berry Gordy, Jr.; b/w "Bottle Up And Go"; produced by Bob Thiele
Iggy and The Stooges	Cleopatra 1548	2014	B/w "Open Up and Bleed (single edit)"; part of a 7-record box set
The Jades	Valerie 228	1964	B/w "Summertime"; distributed by London Records
The Kingsmen	Wand 150	1964	Spent 11 weeks on the *Billboard* pop chart, reaching #16; b/w "Bent Scepter"

The Kingsmen	Scepter/Wand 21012	c. early 1970s	B/w "Little Latin Lupe Lu"; "Forever" series
The Kingsmen	Forever Oldies SWF-21-012	Mid-70s	B/w "Little Latin Lupe Lu"
Kon-Taks	Rondack RO7-9789	1966	Garage version; b/w "One Of These Days"; Plattsburgh, NY, label
Danny Lenn	Cinema Int'l 6902	1966	B/w "No One Will Ever Know"; San Diego, CA, label
Jerry Lee Lewis and The Nashville Teens	Philips 6837 398 (France)	1977	B/w "Great Balls Of Fire"; recorded live in 1964 at Hamburg, Germany's Star Club
Little Richard	Okeh 4-7286	1967	B/w "A Little Bit Of Something (Beats A Whole Lot Of Nothing)"
Little Richard	Columbia DB 8240 (UK)	1967	B/w "A Little Bit Of Something (Beats A Whole Lot Of Nothing)"
Little Harvey and His Kings of Soul	Jeroam Productions—FV 22896	1965	B/w "These Arms Of Mine," a cover of Otis Redding; Richmond, VA, label
Barbara Lynn	Jamie 1269	1964	B/w "Jealous Love"; produced by Huey P. Meaux
Majestics	Matrix # 291-034	1965	B/w "Walkin' The Dog"; Columbus, OH, group
The Main Line	Reo 8982X (Canada)	1967	Psychedelic version; made the Winnipeg radio station CKRC top 5 chart for two weeks; b/w "Don't Wait Around"
Mandre	Motown 1429F	1977	Disco version; b/w "Solar Flight (Opus 1)"

The Mob	Colossus CS 145	1971	B/w "Once A Man, Twice A Child"
The Mob	Polydor 2001 201 (UK)	1971	B/w "Once A Man, Twice A Child"
Ole and the Dairy-Aires	Thundermen 1206	1988	B/w "Osseo"; Eau Claire, WI, label
Jay Randall	Bad Weather 104	1977	B/w "When It Rains (It Really Pours)"; New Orleans, LA, label
Rocking Capris	Conco 145; Confederate 145	1962	Instrumental version; b/w "Lights Out"; Macon, GA, labels
The Rolling Stones	Decca DFE 8960 (UK)	1964	EP with "Bye Bye Johnny"/"You Better Move On"/"Poison Ivy"
The Rolling Stones	Decca/ABKCO 8909-1	2012	EP with "Bye Bye Johnny"/"You Better Move On"/"Poison Ivy"; 2012 RSD release
Roscoe & His Little Green Men	RGM 6101	1961	Same song but not credited to Gordy & Bradford; spirited version with very good sax break; b/w "Sabre Rock"; Philadelphia, PA, label
The Sonics	Norton 175	1997	B/w "Do You Love Me"
The Supremes	Motown MT-60649	1966	Small hole 7" 33/ 1/3 made for jukeboxes; 6-song EP with "You Can't Hurry Love"/"Come and Get Those Memories"/"I Can't Help Myself"/"This Old Heart of Mine (Is Weak For You)"/ "Love Is Like An Aching In My Heart"

The Thundermen	Soma 1194	1962	Same song but credited to Z. Turner; b/w "Flying High," a very good guitar and drum instrumental penned by Robert Velline (AKA Bobby Vee)
The Thundermen	Thundermen 207025	1982	Same song but titled "Money 1982," a reprise of their 1962 version on Soma; b/w "Aw She-Say She"; Eau Claire, WI, label
The Tikies	Tee Kee 100	1965	B/w "Moon Beams"; Madisonville, KY, label
Tom Troy	Huncar 3007	1963	B/w "Sea Of Love"
Dwight Twilley	Arista AS 0478	1979	B/w "Somebody To Love"
The Undertakers	Pye 7N 15562 (UK)	1963	B/w "What About Us"
Vibratones	Cuca J 1073	1962	B/w "Side-Winder"; Sauk City, WI, label
Cherry Wainer	Columbia 45-DB 4528 (UK)	1960	Hammond organ instrumental version; b/w "Happy Like A Bell (Ding Dong)"
Jr. Walker & The All Stars	Soul 35026	1966	B/w "Money (That's What I Want), Part 2"; produced by B. Gordy, Jr. & L. Horn
Jr. Walker & The All Stars	Tamla Motown TMG 586 (UK)	1966	B/w "Money (That's What I Want), Part 2"; made Radio London's Fab 40 chart for two weeks in December 1966, peaking at #27

Richard Wylie	Motown 1009	1961	B/w "I'll Still Be Around"; listed by "Popcorn Wylie & the Mohawks" on the West Coast Monarch pressings; be careful, as a 2014 bootleg exists
None listed	Seeburg DN-309-B	1965	Small-hole 7" 33 ½ EP with "Mashed Potatoes"/"Lariat"/"Do The Dog"/"Round And Round"/"Take Me Back"; "Discoteen" series

Bern Elliott (1963)   **The Fabulettes (1963)**   **The Kingsmen (1964)**

"MONEY (THAT'S WHAT I WANT)" IN THE MOVIES

Money is a constant driver of human affairs and, as the saying goes, "Money is the root of all evil." It is, therefore, perhaps not too surprising that "Money (That's All I Want)" has made an appearance in more than two dozen movies, the most of any song selected for this book. Those movies are:

MOVIE TITLE	YEAR	COMMENTS
Cooley High	1975	Performed by Barrett Strong; this film is sometimes referred to as the "Black American Graffiti"
National Lampoon's Animal House	1978	Played and performed by John Belushi; high grossing comedy
The Flamingo Kid	1984	Performed by Barrett Strong; a romantic comedy starring Matt Dillon
Caddy Shack II	1988	Performed by Cheap Trick; comedy starring Dan Aykroyd, Chevy Chase, and Jackie Mason
Night and the City	1992	Performed by Jr. Walker and the All-Stars; movie about an incompetent and crooked lawyer who wants to become a boxing promoter starring Robert Di Niro and Jessica Lange
Blank Check	1994	Performed by Zendetta; a 12-year old boy fills out a blank check for $1 million and starts spending it, but the gangsters from whom the money was taken are in hot pursuit
BackBeat (UK)	1994	Dramatization of The Beatles' German days prior to their rise to fame worldwide; performed by Greg Dulli, who portrayed John Lennon's voice in the movie; Don Was produced the movie's soundtrack
Milk Money	1994	Performed by Barrett Strong; movie is about young boys befriending a prostitute played by Melanie Griffith
Blue Chips	1994	Performed by John Lee Hooker; a college basketball coach breaks the rules to try to stay competitive, starring Nick Nolte

Empire Records	1995	Performed by The Flying Lizards; a musical comedy about 24 hours in the life of an independent record store; the movie's writer, Carol Heikkinen, was a former employee of Tower Records, a large chain of record stores that no longer exists
Happy Gilmore	1996	*IMDbPro* does not list who performed the song; sports comedy starring Adam Sandler
Just the Ticket	1998	Performed by Dr. John; romantic comedy
Mafia!	1998	Performed by Barrett Strong; a *Godfather* take off
The Wedding Singer	1998	Performed by The Flying Lizards; a musical romantic comedy starring Adam Sandler and Drew Barrymore
Free Money	1998	Performed by Dr. John; a crime comedy starring Marlin Brando and Charlie Sheen
Rogue Trader	1999	Performed by Barrett Strong; story about Nick Leeson whose fraudulent trading led to the downfall of a large British bank
Charlie's Angels	2000	Performed by The Flying Lizards; action-adventure comedy starring Lucy Liu, Cameron Diaz, Drew Barrymore, and Bill Murray
Josie and the Pussycats	2001	Performed by Josie and the Pussycats; musical comedy about putting subliminal messages in music
Startup.com	2001	Performed by John Waite (as the Babys); documentary about the startup of a new media. com company
Lord of War	2005	Performed by The Flying Lizards; an arms dealer played by Nicholas Cage comes to grips with the immorality of his job

The Bank Job	2008	Performed by The Storys; a crime thriller starring Saffron Burrows
Mad Money	2008	Performed by Barrett Strong; a crime comedy thriller starring Diane Keaton and Ted Danson
Lottery Ticket	2010	Performed by Barrett Strong; a comedy about a young man living in the projects who has a winning lotto ticket
George Harrison: Living in the Material World	2011	Performed by The Beatles; film about George Harrison's life directed by Martin Scorsese
Killing Them Softly	2012	Performed by Barrett Strong; crime thriller starring Brad Pitt
Wild	2014	*IMDbPro* does not list who performed the song; bio drama adventure with Reese Witherspoon and Laura Dern
Wild Card	2015	Performed by Bennett Strong; crime action drama starring Jason Statham
The Boss	2016	Performed by Charli XCX; movie is about a female exec who is sent to jail for insider trading and how she is treated after being released
Crazy Rich Asians	2018	Performed twice, first by Cheryl K and second by Cheryl K featuring Awkwafina; romantic drama/comedy
Ford v. Ferrari	2019	Performed by The Kingsmen; movie documents Ford's eventual successful effort to top Ferrari at "The 24 Hours of Le Mans" in 1956, with Matt Damon and Christian Bale in starring roles
Greed	2019	Performed by The Flying Lizards; comedy drama satire about the super-rich

DOCUMENTED CONCERT PERFORMANCES OF "MONEY (THAT'S WHAT I WANT)"

As of May 1, 2024, *Setlist.fm* documented that "Money (That's What I Want)" has been performed in concert 996 times by 179 different artists. In addition to The Beatles (139), artists who have included it on their set lists 10 or more times include Golden Earring (117), Bruno Mars (75), Charli XCX (21), Bryan Adams (15), Jerry Lee Lewis (14), The Doors (11), and Robert Plant (10).

HONORS AND ACCOLADES FOR "MONEY (THAT'S WHAT I WANT)"

- Chosen by the Rock & Roll Hall of Fame as one of the "500 Songs That Shaped Rock and Roll"
- Ranked #294 on the *Rolling Stone*'s 2004 list of "The 500 Greatest Songs of All Time"
- Ranked #232 in Dave Marsh's 1989 book, *The Heart of Rock & Soul: The 1001 Greatest Singles Ever Made*
- Selected by Greil Marcus for his 2014 book, *The History of Rock 'N' Roll In Ten Songs*

ALSO WORTH NOTING . . .

- John Lennon with the Plastic Ono Band sang "Money (That's What I Want)" at the *Live Peace in Toronto, 1969* concert; it is one of the songs on the concert's LP released on Apple SW-3362.
- Barrett Strong's original version of "Money (That's What I Want)" was on John Lennon's jukebox.
- "Money" was the first Gordy hit to be recorded in what was soon to be called Studio A, part of a two-story house purchased by Gordy at 2648 West Grand Avenue in Detroit, Michigan. Subsequently dubbed "Hitsville, U. S. A.," the house served as Motown's studio and headquarters until 1972. Today, it is the focal point of the Motown Museum, a major Detroit tourist attraction.
- In 2004, Barrett Strong was inducted into the Songwriters Hall of Fame.

ADDITIONAL SOURCES

Gordy, Jr., Berry, *To Be Loved: The Music, the Magic, the Memories of Motown* (Warner Books, 1994)

Lewisohn, Mark, *The Complete Beatles Chronicle* (Pyramid, 1992; paperback edition published by Hamlyn, 2003)

Marcus, Greil, *The History of Rock 'N' Roll in Ten Songs* (Yale University Press, 2014)

Rohter, Larry, "For a Classic Motown Song About Money, Credit Is All He Wants," *New York Times*, September 1, 2013

Singleton, Raymona Gordy, *Berry, Me, and Motown: The Untold Story* (Contemporary, 1990)

REVERBERATIONS IN RETROSPECT

The 1950s witnessed the emergence of Rock 'n' Roll as a major force in American music. It didn't start in the 1950s, but rather resulted from the convergence of various musical currents, including western swing, by such artists as Bob Wills & His Texas Playboys, country by such artists as Hank Williams, gospel by such artists as the Soul Stirrers and Sister Rosetta Sharpe, and the blues by such artists as Arthur "Big Boy" Crudup, Roy Brown, and John Lee Hooker.

The 21 songs selected for this book span the seven years between 1953 and 1959. Collectively, they capture the essence of 1950s Rock 'n' Roll. The impact that these songs had on future artists is beyond question and is still a work in progress. These songs continue to reverberate.

The impact of these songs and the artists who sang them was especially pronounced in England. Take The Beatles as the prime example. The first song they put on a record was "That'll Be The Day." The first song they recorded at their Decca Records audition on January 1, 1962, was "Money (That's What I Want)." And the last song they played before a paying audience at San Francisco's Candlestick Park was "Long Tall Sally."[106]

In doing the research for this book I was overwhelmed by the reverence that music fans in the UK heaped on such artists as Eddie Cochran, Gene Vincent, Bill Haley and His Comets, and Buddy Holly. In fact, these artists were and continue to be more revered on the other side of the pond. The facts are indisputable. Consider, for example, the number of 45s released by three of these artists in the U.S. versus in the UK:

ARTIST	U.S. RELEASES	UK RELEASES
Eddie Cochran	38	82
Buddy Holly and The Crickets	68	93
Gene Vincent	60	94

Moreover, these three artists had more charted records in the UK than they did in the U.S. , as the chart below documents:

---

106 Also consider that the first U.S. releases by The Rolling Stones and The Kinks were "Not Fade Away" and "Long Tall Sally," respectively.

ARTIST	# OF U.S. CHARTED RECORDS	# OF UK CHARTED RECORDS
Eddie Cochran	8	15
Buddy Holly and The Crickets	11	32
Gene Vincent	4	8

The fourth artist, Bill Haley and His Comets, had and still has a huge following in the UK. "Rock Around The Clock" was the first UK record to sell a million copies. While Haley had more releases and charted records in the U.S. , the impact of his records in the UK was much greater. For example, he had nine top ten hits in the UK, but just four top 10 hits in the U.S. Haley also had a big impact in other countries as well. Consider France. *Billboard* in an April 20, 1957, article titled "American Popular Music Booming in Overseas Markets," noted: "Even in France, Bill Haley's records have outsold Edith Piaf's for six months in a row."

Dion DiMucci, who had such hits as "When or Where" and "A Teenager in Love" with the Belmonts, and "Runaround Sue" and "The Wonderer" as a single artist, perceptively observed[107]:

Buddy Holly was the first self-contained rock 'n' roll group—two guitars, bass, and drums. Two guitars, bass, and drums were popular 50 years ago and they will be popular 50 years from now. This guy influenced every British group you can think of. And Americans don't get it sometimes, but Europeans get it. This guy influenced so many artists.

There is a vast difference between the music environment today and that of the 1950s. In the 1950s there were three basic music genres: pop, R&B, and country. Today, there are literally hundreds, which are cataloged by the internet site www.musicgenreslist.com. For example, under the heading "alternative," 21 subgenres are listed, including goth, grunge, and punk. And on and on. The point is that today's music categories are fragmented beyond belief.

In sharp contrast, in the 1950s all but two of this book's 21 songs that were initially targeted to the R&B, pop or country markets "crossed over" to another category. Amazingly, in retrospect, the following six songs made *all* three of the *Billboard* charts:

---

107 Dion DiMucci, "The True Buddy Holly Story," Rock & Hall of Fame History, February 3, 2015, which can be accessed on *YouTube*. It was produced by Terry Stewart, a past President of the Rock & Roll Hall of Fame.

- "Be-Bop-A-Lula" — Pop #7; R&B #8; Country #5
- "Blue Suede Shoes" — Pop #2; R&B #2; Country #1
- "Great Balls of Fire" — Pop #2; R&B #3; Country #1
- "Heartbreak Hotel" — Pop #1; R&B #3; Country #1
- "Hound Dog" — Pop #1; R&B #1; Country #1
- "Whole Lotta Shakin' Goin' On" — Pop #3; R&B #1; Country #1

Not only did all six of these songs make all three of the major *Billboard* charts, but all but "Be-Bop-A-Lula" made the top three or higher of *Billboard's* pop, R&B, and country charts.

Another 13 songs made both the *Billboard* pop and R&B charts:

- "Ain't That A Shame" — Pop #10; R&B #1
- "Johnny B. Goode" — Pop #8; R&B #2
- "Kansas City" — Pop #1; R&B #1
- "Long Tall Sally" — Pop #6; R&B #1
- "Money (That's What I Want)" — Pop #23; R&B #2
- "Rock Around The Clock" — Pop #1; R&B #3
- "Roll Over Beethoven" — Pop #29; R&B #2
- "Shake, Rattle and Roll" — Pop #22; R&B #1 (Big Joe Turner version)
- "Summertime Blues" — Pop #8; R&B #11
- "That'll Be The Day" — Pop #1; R&B #2
- "Tutti Frutti" — Pop #2; R&B #2
- "What'd I Say" — Pop #6; R&B #1
- "Why Do Fools Fall In Love" — Pop #6; R&B #1

Of the two remaining songs, "Bo Diddley" only made the R&B chart (#1), and "Not Fade Away" did not make any of *Billboard's* three charts, although the A-side, "Oh, Boy!", did reach #10 on *Billboard's* pop chart.

To put the broad popularity of this book's 21 songs in perspective, by the 1960s—just a decade later—The Beatles, who dominated *Billboard's* pop chart, did not have one song that crossed over and made either *Billboard's* R&B chart or its country chart!

That the 21 songs selected for this book continue to reverberate can be evidenced by the number of subsequent covers that have charted, their appearance on movie soundtracks, the number of times they have been performed in concert, and the honors and accolades they have received.

CONTEMPORANEOUS AND BUDGET LABEL COVER VERSIONS

But before moving on to discuss these topics, it is important to comment on the contemporaneous and budget label cover versions that are documented in each chapter. In the 1950s it was standard operating practice for the major labels, as well as some independent labels, to issue cover versions of songs that were showing signs of becoming hits. This practice diminished in the last half of the 1950s. Thus, of the five songs released in 1958 and 1959, only one attracted contemporaneous covers, i.e., "Kansas City." The practice of major labels issuing contemporaneous covers virtually disappeared in the 1960s and is, for intents and purposes, nonexistent today.

The same can be said for budget labels that were prominent in the first part of the 1950s, but their existence started to wane in the latter half of the 1950s and rather completely disappeared by 1961. The only major exception being the Hit label that issued over 350 cover records between 1962 and 1969 that were marketed to convenience stores with a selling price as low as 39 cents.[108]

SUBSEQUENT COVERS

Subsequent artists who have covered one or more of the 21 songs that have charted reads like a Who's Who of Rock 'n' Roll: The Beatles, The Beach Boys, Dion, Electric Light Orchestra, The Everly Brothers, Grateful Dead, Kinks, Jerry Lee Lewis, Little Richard, Elvis Presley, The Rolling Stones, Linda Ronstadt, Diana Ross, among many others. Overall, an amazing 71 subsequent 45 rpm covers of the 21 songs made one or more of *Billboard's* charts, led by subsequent covers of three songs that made the *Billboard* charts on four or more occasions: Buddy Holly and The Crickets' "Not Fade Away," Ray Charles' "What'd I Say," and Frankie Lymon and the Teenagers' "Why Do Fools Fall In Love." Three other subsequent covers, "Heartbreak Hotel" by Willie Nelson and Leon Russell, "Johnny B. Goode" by Buck Owens, and "Summertime Blues" by Alan Jackson, topped *Billboard's* country chart. The most recent cover to chart was Sheryl Crow's 2008 version of "Not Fade Away."

IN THE MOVIES

Collectively, this book's 21 songs can be heard in nearly 300 movies as documented in the "In the Movies" section of each chapter. Leading the way are "Money (That's What I Want)," "Great Balls of Fire," and "Summertime Blues" with 31, 23, and 21 appearances, respectively.

Two big budget 2022 movies also demonstrate the continuing power of this book's 21 songs. *Elvis*, the biography of Elvis Presley played by Austin Butler, as seen through the eyes of Colonel Thomas Parker played by Tom Hanks, features four of the songs: "Hound Dog," sung by both Butler portraying Elvis and Shonka Dukureh portraying Big Mama Thornton, "Tutti Frutti," sung by Les Greene portraying Little Richard, as well as "Heartbreak Hotel" and "Blue Suede Shoes," sung by Elvis and taken from footage of his *1969 Comeback Special.* The other 2022 movie is *Top Gun: Maverick*, the high grossing blockbuster starring Tom Cruise, which features the cast singing Jerry Lee Lewis's "Great Balls of Fire." Not too shabby for songs that were initially released in the 1950s!!!

Moreover, the use of this book's 21 songs in TV ads continues unabated. For example, two songs—"What'd I Say" and "Long Tall Sally"—were prominently featured in TV commercials that aired during the 2022 Super Bowl. *AdAge* noted, "What'd I Say" was a "chipper and bouncy number"

---

108 The Hit label was based in Nashville, Tennessee, and it had a large roster of artists who recorded the covers. Some of those artists, including Sandy Posey, Ray Stevens, and Sam Moore of Sam and Dave, later became popular recording artists for major labels.

that was "just the vibe to start Eugene Levy's joyride in a vibrant yellow Nissan," noting that Ray Charles kicked "off the ad with charm." Little Richard's "Long Tall Sally" was the background music for the NFL's "Bring the House Down" ad that featured in immersive 3D video game format with a cast of 25 NFL stars, past and present, referees, and coaches, which ended with Walter Payton scoring a TD on Super Bowl Sunday, something that he never did in real life.

IN CONCERTS

As writer Paul Williams has noted, "... great songs are made to be sung again and again by succeeding generations of singers even though the 'perfect' recording of said song may already have been accomplished. Songs live in performance." Based on the statistics compiled by *Setlist.fm,* as of May 1, 2024, and as set forth in each chapter, the continuing popularity of the 21 songs is further enhanced by the number of times that they have been performed in concert. Leading the way is "Johnny B. Goode," which has been performed in concert 5,184 times by an amazing 702 different artists. Twelve other songs have been performed in concert over 1,000 times: "Not Fade Away" (4,308 times by 330 different artists), "Roll Over Beethoven" (2,452 times by 230 different artists), "Summertime Blues" (2,168 times by 195 different artists), "Great Balls of Fire" (1,823 times by 204 different artists), "Blue Suede Shoes" (1,641 times by 237 different artists); "Whole Lotta Shakin' Goin' On" (1,609 times by 173 different artists), "Heartbreak Hotel" (1,527 times by 169 different artists), "Why Do Fools Fall In Love" (1,484 times by 27 different artists); "Ain't That A Shame" (1,479 times by 43 different artists, "Hound Dog" (1,432 by 220 different artists); "Long Tall Sally" (1,142 times by 152 different artists); and "What'd I Say" (1,005 times by 138 different artists).

HONORS AND ACCOLADES

The number of major honors and accolades for the 21 songs provides proof of their impact and continuing importance. Nineteen of the songs have been inducted into the Grammy Hall of Fame. Only "Money (That's What I Want)" and "Not Fade Away" have to date not received this prestigious honor. But each has been recognized in other significant ways:

- "Money (That's What I Want)" is one of the songs highlighted by music critic Marcus Greil his book *The History of Rock 'N' Roll in Ten Songs,* and, as noted above, it has appeared in more movies than any of the other 20 songs
- "Not Fade Away," as noted above, has been covered by four artists whose versions have made the *Billboard* charts

The Library of Congress's National Preservation Board has to date selected 10 of the songs for inclusion on the National Recording Registry of recordings that "are culturally, historically, or aesthetically important, and/or inform or reflect life in the United States":

"Be-Bop-A-Lula"

"Blue Suede Shoes"

"Bo Diddley"

"Hound Dog" (Willie Mae "Big Mama" Thornton's version)

"Rock Around The Clock"

"That'll Be The Day"

"Tutti Frutti"

"Whole Lotta Shakin' Goin' On"

"Roll Over Beethoven"

"What'd I Say"

Finally, five of the songs were among the songs of all genres on National Public Radio's list of the "Top 100 Songs of the 20ᵗʰ Century": "Ain't That A Shame," "Blues Suede Shoes," "Great Balls of Fire," "Hound Dog," and "Rock Around The Clock."

ALSO WORTH NOTING . . .

Despite the best opinions of record company executives, four of the 21 songs started out life as the designated B-side:

- "Be-Bop-A-Lula"
- "Bo Diddley"
- "Rock Around The Clock"
- "Summertime Blues"

Each of these songs, however, has been inducted into the Grammy Hall of Fame, as well as being the recipient of other major honors and accolades. And "Rock Around The Clock" is generally credited with being the largest selling Rock 'n' Roll song of all-time! It just goes to prove that the record buying public sometimes has a far better ear for what makes a hit record than the record company that issued the record.

Conversely, "Not Fade Away" definitely was the B-side when it was released in 1957. Yet it made the cut as one of the 21 songs selected for this book, all of which is discussed in detail in the "Not Fade Away" chapter.

It is also noteworthy that several of the B-sides of the 21 songs have gained wide popularity and have attracted multiple covers in their own right. First and foremost is "Don't Be Cruel," the B-side of Elvis Presley's "Hound Dog." As discussed in the "Hound Dog" chapter, "Don't Be Cruel" was Presley's largest selling record. Like "Hound Dog," it topped all three of *Billboard's* charts. In addition, it was inducted into the Grammy Hall of Fame, listed as one of NPR's top 100 songs of the 20ᵗʰ century, and ranked #68 on the NEA/RIAA's list of the top 365 songs of the 20ᵗʰ century.

Two other notable B-sides are "Honey Don't," the B-side of "Blue Suede Shoes," and "Slippin' and Slidin'," the B-side of "Long Tall Sally."

HISTORY'S VERDICT

There is perhaps no better way to conclude than to quote one stanza of Danny and the Juniors' "Rock and Roll Is Here To Stay":

Rock 'n roll will always be
Our ticket to the end
It'll go down in history,
Just you watch, my friend
Rock 'n roll will always be,
It'll go down in history

The 21 songs selected for this book have not only gone "down in history," but they are still being played today. What are the odds that any of today's songs will obtain such universal appeal and continue to be played 65 years from now?

ACKNOWLEDGEMENTS

I am very much indebted to Dan Kochakian for his willingness to read every chapter and offer his helpful editing suggestions. Some readers may know of Dan as the publisher and co-editor of *Whiskey, Women, and...*, an excellent research journal that focused on Rhythm and Blues artists and songs, which was published between 1971 and 1989. He is also a music researcher extraordinaire, who regularly contributes the fruits of his research to *Blues & Rhythm*, an excellent British blues magazine. I was indeed fortunate to have Dan review each chapter. As a result, this book is much better because of his careful eye for missing words, spelling errors, omissions, punctuation mistakes, etc. However, I take full responsibility for anything that escaped both his and my review.

The building of my record collection, including the voluminous covers of the 21 songs selected for this book, has been and continues to be an ongoing journey. In adding records to my collection over the years, I have purchased 45s from dozens of stores and hundreds of individual sellers. The stores, many of which no longer exist, include Beverly Records (Beverly, IL), Full Cyrkle Records (Crystal Lake, IL), Mean Mountain Records (Milwaukee, WI), Oak Park Records (Oak Park, IL), R & B Records (Upper Darby, PA), Shooting Stars Records (Algonquin and E. Dundee, IL), Siren Records (McHenry, IL), Toad Hall (Rockford, IL), Valhalla Records (Oak Park, IL), Vintage Vinyl (Evanston, IL), Wax Trax (Chicago, IL), and many others long since forgotten. The semi-annual Austin Record Show in Austin, Texas, hosted by Doug Hanners, also enabled me to shop for cover records from dozens of dealers at the same location.

Among the many record dealers and collectors who have helped me amass my collection are J. Barry Barslow, Ralph Barton, L. Stanley Baumruk, Ken Benedict, Jesse Birdsall, Dick Blackburn, Rod Branham, Bob Charboneau, Paul Daigle, Mike Demirdjian, L.R. Docks, Vernon Edwards, Dallas Ellis, John Gallagher, John Govi, Steve Gronda, Bill Hale, Doug Hanners, Jeff Hannusch, Todd Hutchinson, Lee Jackson, Bjorn Jantoft, Don Kirsch, Marshall "Skip" Kloepfer, Dennis Klopp, Dan Kochakian, Rocky Kruegel, Nick Lamia, Rip Lay, Tom Lincoln, Scot MacDonald, Jerry MacNeish, Henry Mariano, Frank Merrill, Bob Miner, Craig Moerer, Jay Monroe, Henry Nowak, Jr., Terry Pattison, Al Pavlow, George Paulos, Victor Pearlin, Pascal Perrault, Peter Salamone, Guy Savage, Dale Schubert, Ralph Shirley, Val Shively, Lou Silvani, Jim Small, Paul Solarski, John Stainze, Robert Stallworth, Darryl Stolper, Jeff Stolper, Greg Surek, John Tefteller, Chris Varelas, Ned Walters, Barry Weinstein, Dennis West, Mark Womble, and many others. I also need to give a "shout out" to my oldest son, David, to whom I passed along the record collecting bug many years ago, who kept an eye out for cover records that I may have missed and let me know about their existence.

At various times while writing this book I shared draft versions of chapters or portions of chapters with any number of knowledgeable record people, including Jesse Birdsall, David Clark, Joe Gagliardo, Peter Grendysa, Victor Pearlin, Barry Soltz, Robert Stallworth, Terry Stewart, John Tefteller, Jeff Tolle, Billy Vera, and Mark Womble . Thank you for your feedback and encouragement to complete the book!

I'd like to give a special "shout out" to Mark Goldstrom. In addition to his past experience as the Director of Marketing for a large corporation where it was his responsibility to proofread and approve all of the company's marketing and sales materials, Mark is a music enthusiast, both a big fan of such artists as The Kinks and Neil Young, and as the leader of his own rock band. With this background, I was fortunate that Mark was willing to proofread a pre-publication copy of my book. Mark's careful and thoughtful eye for detail caught any number of typos, misspelled words, and punctuations errors. Thank you, Mark!

I would also be remiss if I didn't mention *YouTube*. The vast majority of the records mentioned in this book can be found and heard on *YouTube*.

Finally, I especially want to thank my wife, Sandy, and our three children, David, Sarah, and Steven, for their enthusiastic support and encouragement. Over the years, they have had to endure many stops at record stores, flea markets, and antique malls so that I can look for records, including seeing parts of some towns that they would never have otherwise seen. Thank you!!!